The Social Dimension
of the European
Union

Ruth Nielsen and Erika Szyszczak

# The Social Dimension of the European Union

HANDELSHØJSKOLENS FORLAG

© Handelshøjskolens Forlag 1991
3. edition 1997

Printed by Reproset, Copenhagen
Cover designed by Kontrapunkt
Printed in Denmark 1997
ISBN 87-16-13357-9 ✓

Copenhagen Business School, Law Department
*Series G. Business Law Series, No. 19*

*Published by* Handelshøjskolens Forlag


Distribution

*Scandinavia:*
Munksgaard/DBK, Siljangade 2-8, P.O. Box 1731,
DK-2300 Copenhagen S, Denmark,
phone: +45 3269 7788, fax: +45 3269 7789

*North America:*
Global Management, LLC, Book Service, 2564 Branch Street, B2,
Middleton, WI 53562, USA
phone: +1 608 836 0088, fax: +1 608 836 0087
E-mail: 102135.2151 @compuserve.com

*Rest of the World:*
Marston Book Services, P.O. Box 269,
Abingdon, Oxfordshire, OX14 4YN, UK
phone: +44 (0) 1235 465500, fax: +44 (0) 1235 465555
E-mail Direct Customers: direct.order@marston.co.uk
E-mail Booksellers: trade.order@marston.co.uk

# CONTENT

# PREFACE

We have finished writing this book on the traditional Labour Day. For us, it also marks a day of excitement, since it has brought with it a change in the political administration of the United Kingdom and *perhaps* a more flexible attitude towards EU Social Policy Law. Whether this will prove to be a new hope or a false dawn adds to the anticipation that the challenge of creating a social dimension to the economic base of the EU has posed since the inception of the original Common Market in 1957.

We are once again indebted to colleagues and students throughout the EU and beyond who have given support and encouragement to continue working in the area of social policy and stimulated the debate over the scope and content of EU social policy law.

Collaboration on this book has been easy. Technological change in the form of "e-mail" and the "Internet" has made the production process even more enjoyable. Thanks are due for the secretarial help provided by Inge Nielsen, Law Department, Copenhagen Business School and Geraldine Gorham at the Law Department, London School of Economics. Richard Disney continues to iron out those word processing glitches with good humour (and even greater Euro-sceptism).

Copenhagen and London, 1 May 1997

Ruth Nielsen and Erika Szyszczak

# CHAPTER ONE

# THE HISTORICAL AND LEGAL BASE OF EUROPEAN UNION SOCIAL POLICY LAW

## 1.1. INTRODUCTION

Attempts to develop a coherent social policy for the Community have traditionally met with political opposition from the Member States who have disguised their hostility towards intervention by questioning whether there is an adequate legal base on which Community competence could be developed. Despite this opposition to Community intervention in the social policy field, the *range* of issues addressed by the Community has been varied, covering, *inter alia*, worker mobility, youth training, industrial and vocational training, education, equal treatment, health and safety at work and employment rights. To date, the focus of social policy law has been concentrated largely upon employment law issues because of the legal, political and economic constraints imposed by the Treaty of Rome 1957. More recent projects such as the "Normative Development Within The Social Dimension" at Lund University, Sweden,[1] take a very different view looking at the development of normative patterns in the legal regulation of employment, housing, family and social security from a European Integration perspective but looking at the needs of the citizen rather than the market. Streeck[2] has argued that social policy in an integrated Europe can only be understood if we disassociate ourselves from looking upon social policy as part of a steadily evolving European welfare state to analysing the function played by social policy in the political process of European integration. Streeck argues that EU social policy will always, for practical purposes, be made simultaneously at two levels: a supranational level and a national level. Spicker, however makes the point that social policy has come to occupy an increasingly prominent role in the policy agenda of the EU. In the Commission's Green Paper, *European Policy Options For The Future,*[3] social policy is no longer confined to looking at the implications of Internal

---

[1]   Details can be found at http://www.jur.lu.se/norma/norma960.html.

[2]   Streeck (1995) 31.

[3]   COM(93)551.

Market but is widened to include issues normally dealt with at the national level such as health care, employment and training, family structure, education, youth policy, racism, welfare of the elderly and rural development. Some commentators[4] see the subsequent White Paper, *European Social Policy - A Way Forward For the Union*[5] as a step backwards since it recognised, realistically perhaps, that the development of social policy might conflict with economic priorities. Spicker points out that the Green and White Papers do not question the legitimacy of EU intervention in these areas and within the White Paper we see reference to a "European model of the welfare state" and the idea of a "social Europe" which will ensure the "economic and social integration of all citizens". Majone argues that while many policy makers and scholars speak of the "social dimension" of European integration as if the expression were sufficiently precise to be operationally or analytically useful it is, in fact, an ambiguous expression encompassing a number of distinct and partly conflicting dimensions.[6] We are conscious of these difficulties of defining what is meant by "The Social Dimension of the EU" as well as the fact that many issues relating to social policy are dealt with in broad macro-economic terms rather than precise legal rules and case law. This book is intended primarily for a legal audience and, as we have discovered, is used mainly by lawyers interested in employment law/labour market issues. We have concentrated upon the main areas of legislation, case law and legal literature focussing primarily on social and labour law embracing the free movement of persons - including the attempts to regulate third country nationals - while trying to bring in wider debates on Citizenship rights and human rights where appropriate.

## 1.2. THE DIFFERENT PHASES OF COMMUNITY SOCIAL POLICY

The challenges facing the EU today are very different from those on which the premises of the original EEC were founded. Changes in demographic trends, family structure, environmental concerns, persistently high levels of unemployment, different labour market structures - and attitudes towards work, the heightened severity of economic cycles, the polarisation of wealth, social

---

[4]   Kuper (1994).

[5]   COM(94)333.

[6]   Majone (1993) 153; (1995) 227.

exclusion and poverty and the need to compete in a globalised economy[7] are but some of the radically different socio-economic factors which have brought pressure to bear on the EU which inherited a social dimension which has proved to be fragmentary, confused, inadequate and entrenched in post-war neo-liberalism.

It has become customary to divide the development of EU social policy into various phases where there are discernible trends in Community thinking on the nature and scope of social policy. These phases are:

- a period of neo-liberalism 1957 - 1972
- a period of social action 1972- 1980
- a period of stagnation or crisis 1980-1986
- a period of optimism 1986-1993

It is now argued that there is a fifth phase emerging after the publication of the Commission's White Paper, *European Social Policy - A Way Forward For The Union*.[8] There is now greater emphasis of involving the social partners in the decision-making process as well as a demonstrable shift away from efforts to *harmonise* social rights to a greater reliance upon subsidiarity, technocratic support, addressing macro-economic policy issues and the use of soft law.[9] The Commission has chosen new priorities in the social policy field - unemployment and social exclusion which need to be dealt with at a macro-economic level rather than a harmonisation of individual rights perspective.

## 1.3. THE HISTORICAL DEVELOPMENT OF SOCIAL POLICY LAW

Social policy issues received scant attention in the Treaty of Rome 1957. In the 1950s it was an issue of economic and political debate as to whether the functioning of the Common Market necessitated intervention in the social sphere. A Committee of Experts established by the ECSC, in conjunction with the ILO, examined the issue of whether unfair or distorted competition would impede the operation of the Common Market as a result of the different labour law standards in the Member States. The Committee of Experts concluded that intervention in social policy law was not necessary to achieve European

---

[7] As Barnard (1996) points out the external dimension of EU social policy is under-explored.

[8] COM(94) 333. See Cullen and Campbell (1996).

[9] For a discussion of the role of soft law see Wellens and Borchardt (1999) Snyder (1993); Klabbers (1994); Kenner (1995).

integration.[10] This conclusion was reached by distinguishing between the *general* level of labour costs and the differences between the *inter-industrial* pattern of labour costs. In relation to the *general* level of labour costs, it was argued that differences in wages and social costs broadly reflected differences in productivity. There was, therefore, no need for intervention to create European standards for such labour costs. But a different argument was made for the *inter-industrial* pattern of labour costs. Here, it was argued, there was justification for intervention where particular industries were subject to exceptionally low wages or social costs thus placing them at a competitive advantage. The Committee of Experts instanced some areas where there might be the necessity for harmonisation in order for a Common Market to function effectively. These areas included wages, methods of financing social security, working time, overtime premium rates. But the Committee recommended that any intervention should be minimalist in nature. It was suggested that international labour law conventions could be applied to the European forms of political co-operation as well as to individual states. It was specifically recommended that a special fund should be established to assist disadvantaged Member States in order to equalise aspects of labour costs such as training and welfare benefits.

These views underpinned the reason why the framers of the Treaty of Rome 1957 adopted a minimalist approach to social policy law. Collins[11] argues that the Treaty was negotiated and drafted quickly. It was a highly non-interventionist, market orientated legal document. There are only two references to social policy outlined in the principles of the EEC,[12] because the Treaty was regarded as a preliminary document addressing the first stages of creating a customs union and a Common Market and therefore only addressed those social issues deemed relevant to the immediate tasks. Collins argues:

> "In any case, to have gone further would not have been politically acceptable at that time for each member prided itself on its advanced welfare system, its union traditions,

---

[10] *Social Aspects of European Economic Co-operation: Report of a Group of Experts,* ILO Studies and Reports (New Series) No 46, Social Aspects of European Collaboration, Geneva, 1956, summarised (1956) 74 *International Labour Review* 99.

[11] Collins (1983).

[12] Article 3(c) advocates the abolition of obstacles leading towards the free movement of persons and Article 3(i) commits the Common Market towards the establishment of a Social Fund which will lead towards the general improvement of living standards of workers.

its dedication to social progress, and to have asked them to dismantle their cherished edifices would have met with no response."[13]

The legacy of this view is that until the Social Policy Agreement (SPA) annexed to the EC Treaty in 1992 there were no clear parameters of the scope of social policy for the Community - and no firm legal base - on which to anchor and push forward proposals for social policy law at times when the political mood was favourable to such ideas.

Article 2 EEC confirms the view that the rasing of living standards and social progress were perceived of as a *by-product* of economic integration. This belief is reinforced by the fact that only *two* activities of the Common Market address social policy issues: the abolition of obstacles to the freedom of movement for persons (Article 3c) and the establishment of the Social Fund (Article 3(i)). Article 7(2) EEC allowed the Council of Ministers, acting on a proposal from the Commission and after consulting the European Parliament, to adopt by qualified majority vote measures designed to prohibit discrimination on the grounds of nationality. Specific measures were contained in Part Two, Title III of the EEC Treaty to bring about, by progressive stages the free movement of persons.[14]

The Treaty of Rome 1957 contained a Title on Social Policy (Title III), but with the exception of the equal pay provision of Article 119 EC, the provisions were, for the most part, exhortatory. Article 117 EC merely repeats the aims of the Preamble. By itself it does not provide a basis for enacting social policy measures. Reference is made to the "approximation of provisions laid down by law, regulation or administrative action" and this is generally interpreted to be a reference to Article 100 EC. Subsequent case law has shown that while Article 117 EC is programmatic it may be used in conjunction with the Preamble to the Treaty as an aid to the *interpretation* of social policy law within the Community's competence. This role for Article 117 EC is applied in *Defrenne v Sabena (No 2)*[15] in order to raise the lower pay of women to the higher male wage. The interpretative role is seen also in *Zaera v Instituto Nacionale de la Seguridad Social*[16] where, although Community competence was denied in the issue under scrutiny, the ECJ states:

---

[13]  *Ibid,* at p 98.

[14]  See Article 49 EC; 51 EC, Article 54(1) EC, 57(1) and (2) EC.

[15]  Case 43/75 [1976] ECR 455, para 15.

[16]  Case 126/86 [1987] ECR 3697, para 14.

"The fact that the objectives of social policy laid down in Article 117 are in the nature of a programme does not mean that they are deprived of legal effect. They constitute an important aid, in particular for the interpretation of other provisions of the Treaty and of secondary legislation in the social field."

In *Firma Sloman Neptun Schiffahrts AG v Seebetriebsrat Bodo Ziesmer, der Sloman Neptun Schiffahrts Ag*[17] the ECJ went further in denying direct effect to Article 117 EC.

Article 117 EC is immediately circumscribed by Article 118 EC which delimits the extent of Community competence in the social policy sphere. Article 118 EC charges the Commission with the task of promoting "close co-operation" between the Member States in the social field in matters relating to employment, labour law and working conditions, basic and advanced vocational training, social security, the prevention of occupational accidents and diseases, occupational hygiene, the right of association and collective bargaining between employers and workers. The role of Article 118 EC was enhanced in *Germany and others v Commission*[18] in an action brought under Article 173 EC against a *Decision* of the Commission initiating a procedure for prior notification and consultation on migration policy in respect of non-Community states.[19] The Decision was based upon Article 118 EC and a number of soft law measures were mentioned in the Preamble. It was argued by five of the Member States that the Commission lacked the competence to enact such a Decision. The ECJ adopted two perspectives in its analysis of the competence issue. Asking first, did migration policies with regard to TCNs fall within the scope of collaboration envisaged by Article 118 EC, the ECJ roundly rejected the view that such policies fell entirely *outside* the scope of Article 118 EC. The second question addressed the issue of whether the Commission had competence to adopt *binding measures* under Article 118(2) EC. Here the ECJ stipulated that where an Article of the Treaty conferred a specific task on the Commission

"it must be accepted, if that provision is not to be rendered wholly ineffective, that it confers on the Commission necessarily and *per se* the powers which are indispensable in order to carry out that task."[20]

---

[17] Joined Cases C-72/91 and C-73/91 (1993) ECR 887; Nielsen and Szyszczak (1994).

[18] Joined Cases 281/85, 283-85/85 and 287/85 [1987] ECR 3203.

[19] Decision 85/381/EEC OJ L 1985 217/25.

[20] Para 28.

The power given to the Commission was a procedural power to establish the notification and consultation machinery leading towards the adoption of a common position on the part of the Member States. However the ECJ accepted the Member States' contention that the Commission had, in this case, exceeded its powers: the Commission had no power to determine the result to be achieved in the consultation process and it could not prevent the Member States from implementing measures which the Commission might consider to be contrary to Community policies and action. Furthermore, in extending consultation to cover issues relating to the cultural integration of TCNs the Commission had gone beyond its competence.[21]

It was - and still is - possible to utilise Articles 100 EC and 235 EC as a means of promoting social policy measures. Article 100 EC provides for the approximation of laws if the Council of Ministers agrees on the matter by a *unanimous* vote. Only Directives may be issued and they must "directly effect the establishment or functioning of the Common Market". Thus, any social policy measures passed under Article 100 EC must further the economic aims of the Common Market. Article 235 EC is the provision adopted in the Treaty of Rome 1957 to fill lacunae. Three conditions must be met in order to trigger this area of legislative competence. There must be:

(i)    the need for Community action
(ii)   to obtain one of the objectives of the Treaty in the course of the Common Market
(iii)  the Treaty has not provided the necessary powers.

Article 235 EC is subject to unanimous voting. Until recently, however, the ECJ has taken a broad approach to Article 235 EC - arguably taking the Member States political will to enact measures as sufficient basis to find Community competence. The first case to pull in the reins on Article 235 EC was an Opinion delivered by the ECJ on the competence of the Community to accede to the ECHR 1950.[22]

The reasons for the failure of the Community to develop a coherent social policy law have, therefore, both a political and a legal dimension, summarised by Vogel-Polsky:

"The question assumed a dialectical nature: on the one hand the Treaties do not give the Community bodies the power to create a new social order at supranational level which would be independent of the national legal orders. But on the other hand, Article

---

[21]   See Simmonds (1988); Szyszczak (1992a).

[22]   Opinion 2/94 [1996] ECR I-1759.

117 EEC leads to suppose that the Member States are committed *to promote social progress* by means of a Community social policy."[23]

We can now turn to consider the development of the five distinct periods of Community social policy.

## 1.4. ECONOMIC NEO-LIBERALISM 1957-72

### 1.4.1. *Free Movement of Labour*

The period 1957-72 was period of economic boom and most Member States introduced legal and welfare rights for workers as well as moving towards industrial democracy. At the Community level the principle of the free movement of persons was regarded as a check on any distortion of competition within the labour market.

The first Community legislation enacted under Article 49 EC was Regulation 15/61. This *authorised* (as opposed to *granting* a specific right) nationals of one of the Member States to take up employment in another Member State if there were no available workers in the national labour market. One problem which emerged was the question of whether Community preference should be given to nationals of one of the Member States or whether Member States such as the GDR and France could continue to utilise migrant labour from non-Community states to maintain an economic advantage. The Regulation did not tackle this issue and the legacy of this failure to address labour flows of TCNs at a Community level remains with us today.

### 1.4.2. *Social Security*

A number of bilateral social security agreements had been signed prior to 1957. The transferability of social security benefits and entitlement was seen as an important aspect of realising the free movement of persons in the Community. Article 51 EC established the obligation to adopt such measures as was necessary to provide for the realisation of this principle.

Regulations 3/58 and 4/58 were passed in 1958. The former established an Administrative Committee to settle questions of administration and interpretation of social security matters. It was composed of members of the Commission, the Member States and the ILO. It provided a forum for discussing issues of further co-ordination of the Member States' social security systems. These Regulations established the fundamental principles upon which the co-ordination of social security was built. These were the equal treatment of all

---

[23] Vogel-Polsky (1989).

workers, the aggregation of benefits within the Community and the transferability of social security benefits between Member States. Regulations were passed in 1963 and 1968 which enabled migrant workers to obtain a wide range of social security benefits for themselves and their families if they went to work in another Member State.[24]

The Community initiatives in the field of social security have remained at the level of co-*ordination* rather than harmonisation. There have been a number of factors mitigating against the full achievement of the principles laid down in Regulations 3/58 and 4/58, *inter alia,* social security levels have differed between the Member States, in some Member States the tax and social security systems are integrated, Member States use their social security systems to achieve different demographic, fiscal and economic policies.

### 1.4.3. Youth Exchange Schemes

A youth exchange scheme was envisaged by Article 50 EC in order to foster a European awareness and establish a European basis for the training of young workers. The Member States established national advisory committees and the Commission co-ordinated the various exchange schemes.

### 1.4.4. Wages

Although wage policies of the Member States were outside Community competence the Council of Ministers enacted Regulation 10/60 which gave the Commission power to collect statistics and other information on wages and labour costs within the Member States. The aim was to standardise information and definition of such costs. This information formed the basis of labour force surveys of the Community.

The only specific measure relating to a Community standard in the area of wages was Article 119 EC, introduced as a competition measure at the insistence of France.[25] In fact the concept of "equal pay for equal work" contained in Article 119 EC was a narrower formula than the principle of equal pay for work of equal value established in ILO Convention 100 and Recommendation No 90.[26] Four of the original six Member States had ratified ILO Convention 100 but it was felt that the "equal value" standard was too vague

---

[24] For a fuller discussion see Watson (1980).

[25] See Hoskyns (1996); Forman (1982); Szyszczak (1985) McCrudden (1986) and Curtin (1989).

[26] UN Treaty Series, vol 165, 303.

a concept to implement at the Community level. Warner questions the commitment to implement the even weaker concept of "equal pay for equal work" arguing that it was included merely to pay lip service to French economic demands.[27] Equal pay was to be achieved within four years (*ie* by 1 January 1962, the end of the first phase of the transitional period). In 1960 the Commission issued a Recommendation reminding the Member States of the obligation to implement Article 119 EC.[28] The Member States were unable to fulfil this requirement and in 1961 a Resolution was issued affirming the commitment to equal pay by introducing measures in various stages.[29] But even this revised schedule was not adhered to. Moreover the Commission identified certain Member States where job classification structures were revised deleting references to sex but women were nevertheless crowded into the lower end of such classification schemes.[30] The Member States were unaware that Article 119 EC was directly enforceable and it was not until the efforts of a Belgian lawyer, Eliane Vogel-Polsky, breathed life into Article 119 EC through a series of test cases in the Belgian courts that the significance of Article 119 EC was realised.[31] These cases are discussed in Chapter Four.

### 1.4.5. Health and Safety Issues

The Commission established an Industrial Health and Safety Division in 1962. Between 1964-65 three Directives were proposed but only one was accepted by the Council of Ministers. This was a harmonisation measure dealing with the classification, labelling and packaging of certain dangerous substances.[32] The Council also approved a series of Recommendations during this period which established minimum standards in the areas of industrial disease compensation, protective legislation for young persons, industrial medicine facilities.

---

[27]  Warner (1984).

[28]  *Bulletin of the EC* 1960 Nos 6/7, 45-6.

[29]  *Bulletin of the EC* 1962 No 1, 7-9.

[30]  *Bulletin of the EC* 1962, para 37; *Bulletin of the EC* 1964, para 30.

[31]  Hoskyns (1996).

[32]  Council Directive 67/548/EEC, OJ 1967 L 196/1.

## 1.4.6. The European Social Fund

The ESF did not become operational until 1962. In the early years of the operation of the ESF there was a significant cross-subsidisation of contributions made by the large industrial states (France and Germany) to Italy. Allocations from the ESF were used for skills training and resettlement of migrant workers with the focus upon facilitating the free movement of workers principle but in later years it was expanded to embrace wider social policy action.

## 1.5. SOCIAL ACTION: 1972-80

The turning point in the direction of social policy is traced back to the Declaration of the Heads of State or Government in Paris 1972, the eve of the expansion, of the Community when it was deemed that they:

> "... attached as much importance to vigorous action in the social field as to the achievement of economic union ... it is essential to ensure the increased involvement of labour and management in the economic and social decisions of the Community".

There is some academic debate as to the motivation for the changes in social policy in the 1970s. Lodge[33] argues that economic and fiscal crises, unemployment and persistent imbalances between the Member States were contributing factors to the commitment to greater social intervention at the Community level. In contrast Shanks[34] argues that the political upheavals of the 1960s led to a greater questioning of the underlying political and economic policy of the Treaty of Rome 1957. In particular politicians such as the West German Chancellor Brandt were conscious of the need to paint a "human face" on the economic policy of the Community. The ECJ also began to emphasise the social dimension of the Community. In *Defrenne v Sabena (No 2)*[35] it was expressed that:

> "...[Article 119 EC] forms part of the social objectives of the Community, which is not merely an economic union, but at the same time intended, by common action, to ensure social progress and seek the constant improvement of the living and working conditions [of the people of Europe]."

---

[33] Lodge (1978).

[34] Shanks (1977).

[35] Case 43/75 [1976] ECR 455, para 10.

A Social Action Programme (SAP) 1974-76 followed on from the Declaration of Paris 1972.[36] The programme was ambitious but was introduced at a time when the oil crisis was beginning to bite and recession and technological change were being felt across Europe. Attention was paid to the problems of TCNs in the Community but few concrete measures emerged, largely because the Member States wanted to keep their treasured sovereignty in this field. The SAP 1974-76 concentrated upon achieving full and better employment, the improvement of living and working conditions and movement towards greater industrial democracy. A series of proposals were put forward by the Commission but only three concrete legislative measures materialised:

- a Directive protecting the Acquired Rights of Workers on the transfer of an undertaking
- a Directive on Redundancies
- a Directive protecting workers' rights on Insolvency

Proposals relating to the protection of workers involving an amalgamation of undertakings and proposals relating to worker participation and consultation in industry did not achieve acceptance from the Council of Ministers.

The equal treatment principle received a boost from the ruling in *Defrenne v Sabena (No 2)*[37] that Article 119 EC could be applied directly in the national courts. The French sociologist, Sullerot, presented a report to the Commission which showed that widespread sex discrimination existed within the Member States. Thus the impetus for Community action was there and the Commission produced a rather tentative proposal for a Directive on equal pay. This was amended after strong Opinions from the European Parliament and the Economic and Social Committee. The final version of the Equal Pay Directive, 75/117/EEC[38] clarified Article 119 EC and in Article 1 embraced the concept of equal pay for work of equal value.[39] This was followed by Directives on equal treatment generally in employment, state and occupational social security. (Discussed in Chapter Four)

An Action Programme was adopted in the field of health and safety at work and, within this framework, a number of Directives were adopted dealing with the classification, packaging and labelling of dangerous substances, electrical equipment, vinyl chloride monomer and safety signs at the workplace.

---

[36]  *Bulletin of the EC,* Supp 2/74 p 8.

[37]  Case 43/75 [1976] ECR 455.

[38]  OJ 1975 L 45/19.

[39]  See Szyszczak (1985).

But the initial impetus for a social dimension to the Community was lost. Even in the areas where intervention was achieved the measures were piecemeal and limited in scope. Hepple[40] notes that even in the Commission's proposals the emphasis was not upon "harmonisation upwards" as envisaged in the Preamble to the Treaty. By the end of the 1970s a number of economic and social factors were mitigating against intervention in the social field and it was evident that the underlying principles of the Treaty of Rome 1957 had not succeeded in fulfilling the economic imperatives of a Common Market. The recession had led to high unemployment throughout Europe and there were pressures arising from the need to adapt to new technology and competition from the United States and Japan where it was perceived that labour market flexibility gave a competitive edge. Thus restructuring of industry and labour markets began to take place throughout Europe bringing about a change in direction and thinking of the role of Community intervention.

During the late 1960s and into the 1970s a number of inter-sectoral advisory committees were established composed of representatives of national trade unions and employers' organisations and governments. Their role is to advise the Commission on drawing up and implementing specific policies.[41] These committees mirror the Consultative Committee which was established for the ECSC and in turn have provided the precedent for newer committees in the EU consultative structure such as the committee for the LEONARDO training action programme and the consultation procedure over the Structural Funds. The Commission is now critical of these kinds of Committees arguing that systematic and timely consultation does not always take place and that the social partners do not have an effective input into policy making in this kind of form.[42] The Standing Committee on Employment (SCE) was set up in

---

[40]  Hepple (1987)

[41]  There are currently 6 interprofessional advisory committees still in existence: the Advisory Committee on Social Security for Migrant Workers (established 1971); the Advisory Committee on Freedom of Movement for Workers (established 1968); the Advisory Committee on Vocational Training (established 1968); the Advisory Committee on Safety, Hygiene and Health Protection at Work (1974); the Advisory Committee on Equal Opportunities for Women and Men (established 1981, reconstituted in 1996) and the European Social Fund Committee (established 1957). With the exception of the Advisory Committee on Equal Opportunities the committees are made up of national rather than European level-social partners. It is envisaged that in the future these committees will be streamlined.

[42]  *Communication on the Development of the Social Dialogue at Community Level*, COM(96) 448 final.

1970.[43] It is composed of representatives of workers and employers through European-level organisations and representatives of the Commission and the Council. The Commission's assessment of the SCE is also poor, pointing out that while it has managed to discuss a wide range of employment-related issues as a forum it has only rarely led to real consultation resulting in "... a ritual with no obligation to achieve a result, the Committee no longer attracts the attention of the leading players."[44]

## 1.6. STAGNATION OR CRISIS: 1980-86[45]

Few legislative measures were enacted in the social policy sphere in the 1980s. The change in approach to social policy is seen in the resort to a number of soft law options to restructure the Community labour market, for example, Resolutions by the Council and the European Parliament on the re-organisation of working time. The Commission issued proposals for Directives on part-time work, temporary work and flexible retirement. The aim of these proposals was regulatory: to make forms of "atypical work" attractive by affording it legal protection in order to encourage workers to move from full-time jobs and over-time working. The measures were greeted enthusiastically by women's groups who saw them as a way on enhancing the protection of vulnerable workers engaged in work which was traditionally viewed as marginal. Much of the blame for the failure of social policy law to develop in the 1980s has been directed at the Thatcher-led Conservative governments of the UK. But many of the other Member States pursued orthodox and conservative attitudes towards social policy law in the 1980s. Many of the Commission's proposals merely reflected the changes towards "flexibility" in legislation and collective agreements throughout Europe but the UK government was insistent that the moves towards Community regulation of such issues was a form of "interfer-ence", contrary to the philosophy of de-regulation which the government was pursuing at an ideological level.

As a result of this conflict in ideology few legislative measures were enacted in the social policy sphere in the 1980s. Two Directives enhanced the equal treatment programme - one on occupational social security and one on equal treatment for the self-employed. These were supplemented by soft law initiatives in the form of Action Programmes and a Recommendation on

---

[43]   Council Decision 1970, amended 1975.

[44]   *Communication on the Development of the Social Dialogue at Community level,* COM (96) 448 final.

[45]   See Hepple (1987).

28

Positive Action. Soft law options were also utilised to deal with vocational training and the employment of disabled people. During this period, however, some initiatives were not even translated into soft law, for example, the proposal for a Directive on parental leave and the reversal of the burden of proof in sex discrimination cases - both proposals - along with the Directive on atypical work - have emerged in the 1990s under the new Social Policy Agreement introduced by the Protocol on Social Policy to the Treaty on European Union 1992. The Directive on parental leave being the first measure to be introduced by an agreement drawn by the employer's and employee's representatives. However, as subsequent chapters will show, the ECJ delivered some bold and imaginative rulings during the 1980s which strengthened and extended the existing social policy law provisions.

As in the 1970s there was most success in the health and safety field. In 1984 a second Action Programme was adopted and this provided the framework for the adoption of Directives on particular hazards - accidents, lead asbestos, harmful agents, noise and ionising radiations. Proposals were initiated dealing with carcinogens, benzene and microwaves. A third Action Programme in 1987 dealt with safety and ergonomics at work.

During the 1980s some progress was made in incorporating education policies into the community sphere. In 1987 the ERASMUS programme (dealing with mobility and exchanges in higher education) was agreed upon, as was the COMMETT programme (dealing with education and training for technology).

## 1.7. PERIOD OF OPTIMISM: THE INTERNAL MARKET: 1986 - 1993

### 1.7.1. The Delors Initiative: A European Social Space?

Delors, the then President of the Commission, resolved to break the legislative deadlock by linking social policy to the objective of realising an Internal Market by 1992. The equivalence of social laws was seen as necessary in order to prevent "social dumping" whereby Member States with low levels of social protection could gain a competitive edge and disrupt the workings of the Internal Market. He envisaged that:

> "The creation of a vast economic area, based on the market and business co-operation, is inconceivable - I would say unattainable-without some harmonisation of social legislation. Our ultimate aim must be the creation of a European social area."[46]

---

[46] *Bulletin of the EC* 1986, 12.

Delors' idea was to initiate a dialogue on social policy thinking leading to a shift away from social policy harmonisation and instead a focus upon a convergence of objectives and policies which could be implemented within the Member States' existing industrial relations framework. Two working parties were established, christened the *Val Duchesse* talks. One working party dealt with the implications of new technology and work and the other dealt with employment and macro-economic policies. The *Val Duchesse* talks established a better relationship between the social partners but few initiatives emerged from the talks, one reason being that the UK persuaded the Irish and Italian governments to back an alternative approach to social policy in the Action Programme for Employment Growth which was adopted by the Council of Ministers during the British Presidency on December 11 1986. The Action Programme called for attention to be focussed upon the removal of rigidities in Member States' labour markets focussing upon the promotion of flexible employment patterns and conditions of work, the recognition of the needs, particularly in the field of training of the long-term unemployed, the promotion of training in management and entrepreneurship and a re-alignment of the priorities of the Social Fund to promote small and medium-sized businesses. This initiative reflected economic policies that were being pursued at a national level and although the Commission had begun to address issues of "flexibility and "de-regulation" the UK initiative represented a clear departure from the previous direction of Community policy. The Commission was keen to maintain the balance of social policy law towards social protection and thus a tension developed within the Community over the future direction of social policy law.

The development of a social dimension to the Internal Market began during the Belgian Presidency of the Council in 1987. The Community's Structural Funds were reformed in 1988 following the insertion of Article 130d by the SEA 1986. These reforms gave rise to structural operations centred on 5 objectives[47] and three funds:

- the European Regional Development Fund
- the European Social Fund
- the European Agricultural Guidance and Guarantee Fund

---

[47] See Frazer (1995) .Council Regulation 2052/88 OJ L 1988 L 185/9 lays down the 5 objectives (i) promoting the development and structural adjustment of the regions whose development is lagging behind (ii) converting the regions, frontier regions or parts of regions(including employment areas and urban communities) seriously affected by industrial decline (iii) combatting long-term unemployment (iv) facilitating occupational integration of young people (v) speeding up the adjustment of agricultural structures and promoting the development of rural areas.

## 1.7.2. The Single European Act 1986

The changes which emerged from the Single European Act 1986 (SEA) in relation to social policy were minimal. A new Article 8A was added to the Treaty of Rome 1957 referring to the free movement of persons as one of the fundamental principles of the Internal Market. Article 7(2) EEC was amended to permit qualified majority voting in the Council and the greater involvement of the European Parliament by the use of the cooperation procedure. In *Parliament v Council*[48] the Parliament challenged the legal base of Council Directive 90/366/EEC which granted rights of residence to students studying in another Member State. Although at this time the European Parliament did not have *locus standi* to use Article 173 EC the ECJ granted standing to the Parliament to challenge measures taken where a fundamental prerogative - in this instance the use of the cooperation procedure - was infringed. The European Parliament successfully argued that the Directive could be based upon Article 7(2) EEC - the Commission's initial choice of legal base which had been altered by the Council to Article 235 EC. The Court ruled that although the right to free movement went beyond the right to non-discrimination on the grounds of nationality, Article 7(2) EEC could be used to create rights necessary to achieve rights flowing from Article 7(1) EEC.

More concrete adjustments to the social policy provisions are to be found in the addition of Articles 118A and B EC. Article 118A EC grants express power to the Community to enact legislation concerned with the *health and safety of workers* provided that the legislation does not impose administrative, financial and legal constraints in a way which will hold back the creation of small and medium-sized undertakings. Qualified majority voting may be used, involving the cooperation procedure with the European Parliament. The Commission took a cautious approach to Article 118A EC - limiting its proposals to measures with a clear health and safety content.[49] Nevertheless some innovative measures were taken, for example, a Council Directive protecting pregnant workers and workers who have recently given birth[50] (discussed in Chapter Eight). A boost to the scope of Article 118A EC was given in the ruling of the ECJ in *UK v Council*[51] when the Court was asked to rule on the scope of Article 118A EC in an action brought by the UK asking

---

[48]  Case C-295/90 [1992] ECR I-4193.

[49]  See Kessler and Meyer (1992); Banks (1993).

[50]  Council Directive 92/85/EEC OJ 1992 L 348/1.

[51]  Case C-84/94 [1996] nyr.

for the annulment of Council Directive 93/104/EC of 23 November 1993 concerning certain aspects of the organisation of working time.[52] Until this case the ECJ had only dealt with the scope of Article 118A EC indirectly. For example, in *Opinion 2/91 on Convention No 170 of the ILO Concerning Safety in the Use of Chemicals At Work*[53] the ECJ stated:

> "... in order to help achieve this objective [that is, harmonisation, referred to in Article 118a(1) EC] the Council has the power to adopt minimum requirements by means of directives"

The Court then proceeded to infer that the Community thus enjoyed legislative competence in the area of social policy concluding that Convention No 170 fell within the purview of Community competence.[54] In *Kirsammer-Hack*[55] the ECJ simply noted:

> "... by providing that directives adopted in the fields of health and safety of workers are to avoid imposing administrative, financial and legal constraints in a way which would hold back the creation and development of small and medium-sized undertakings, Article 118A of the EEC Treaty, which was introduced by the Single European Act into the chapter concerning social provisions indicates that such undertakings may be the subject of special economic measures."[56]

A request for a preliminary ruling in *ASTI*[57] proved to be irrelevant on the interpretation of Article 118 A EC. In *UK v Council* Advocate General Léger relied heavily upon the Danish interpretation of the concept of the working environment, arguing that the concept was a very broad one, covering the performance of work and conditions at the workplace as well as technical equipment and the substances and material used. Danish legislation was not, therefore, limited to classic health and safety measures but covered measures concerning working hours, psychological factors, the way work is performed, training in hygiene and safety and the protection of young workers and worker representation in relation to security against dismissal or any other attempt to undermine working conditions. He argued that "The concept of 'working

---

[52]  OJ 1993 L 307/18.

[53]  [1993] ECR I-1061.

[54]  See Nielsen and Szyszczak (1994).

[55]  Case C-189/91 [1993] ECR I-6185, paras 16 and 17.

[56]  Para 34.

[57]  Case C-213/90 [1991] ECR I-3507.

environment' is not immutable, but reflects the social and technological evolution of society." Interestingly, in a passing footnote[58] Advocate General Léger points out that Article 118A EC may be applicable to *self-employed* persons where such measures are necessary for the protection of the health and safety of (employed) persons. For example, Council Directive 92/57/EEC of 24 June 1992 on the implementation of minimum safety and health require-ments at temporary or mobile construction sites includes within its scope the activities of self-employed persons, in so far as they may affect the safety or health of employed persons.[59] He also points out that in the eighth recital to the Framework Directive 89/391/EEC[60] there is also reference to the possibility of taking health and safety measures which "... preserve the health and safety of persons residing [with workers]."

The Court looked at the principal aim of the Working Time Directive to see if its aim was to protect the safety and health of workers. If this was the case Article 118 A EC could be used even though the Directive may have ancillary effects on the functioning of the Internal Market. The Court followed the Advocate General's approach arguing that the recitals to the Directive gave a clear indication that the regulation of working time had an impact upon workers' overall physical and pyschological health. No evidence was shown that Article 5 of the Directive, which provided for Sunday as the normal day of weekly rest should have an impact on health and safety matters and therefore the Court was willing to annull this particular provision.

In contrast to Article 118A EC Article 118B EC is a rather vague measure - the residue of attempts to develop a more ambitious base to social policy law. Article 118B EC attempts to institutionalise the role of collective bargaining by developing a "social dialogue" The *Val Duchesse*[61] intersectoral social dialogue was launched in 1985 bringing together the European Trade Union Confederation (ETUC), the Union of Industrial and Employers' Confederation of Europe (UNICE) and the European Centre of Enterprises with Public Participation (CEEP). Since the introduction of Article 118B EC the *Val Duchesse* talks have become formalised with the use of a "social dialogue committee" but the process is still informal and voluntary. The *Val Duchesse* dialogue has resulted in a series of joint opinions and declarations and two agreements - an agreement on the role of the social partners in the reform of

---

[58]   Footnote 17 of the Opinion of 12 March 1996.

[59]   OJ 1992 L 245/6.

[60]   Council Directive 89/391/EEC OJ 1989 L 183/1.

[61]   Hepple (1993), Davies (1992), Hall (1994).

the Treaties (October 1991) and a framework agreement on parental leave (December 1995) and seven "summits" with the President of the Commission.

A new Article 100A EC was introduced by the SEA 1986. This circumscribes the powers of the Member States by allowing for measures to be taken by a *qualified majority* vote in the Council involving the European Parliament in the *cooperation* procedure where the measure affects the functioning and establishment of the Internal Market. While Article 100A(3) EC provides that the Commission in its proposals concerning health and safety will take as a base a high level of protection. Article 100A(2) provides that *unanimity* voting is still required for measures relating to fiscal provisions, *the free movement of persons* and *the rights and interests of employed persons.* Thus there is some ambiguity and legal uncertainty created between the relationship of Article 100A(1) and Article 100A(2) EC.[62]

The Court has had the opportunity to rule upon the scope of Article 100A EC in a number of "legal base" disputes. Every Community act must be based upon a specific legal base. Within the EC Treaty there are a number of different kinds of legal base. Firstly, there are legal bases which govern vertically integrated sectors such as the free movement of persons. Secondly, there are Articles 100 and 100a EC which regulate the establishment and the functioning of the Common and Internal Markets. Thirdly, there are legal bases which regulate horizontal activities (for example, environment, consumer health issues) which cut across a number of sectors of the economy. Fourthly there are legal bases establishing flanking policies (culture, education, industry, development co-operation) which do not regulate particular sectors. Finally, as we have seen there is the residual legal base of Article 235 EC. [63] This number of legal bases exist uncomfortably with each other. One of the aims of the current IGC is to simplify the EC Treaty and the legislative structure of the EU. Because different voting procedures are required under the different bases and different methods of involvement of the European Parliament a number of legal disputes have arisen over the delimitation of the legal bases, particularly the role of Article 100A EC.

Initially the Court in *Commission v Council (Titanium Dioxide)*[64] established a hierarchy of legal bases with Article 100A EC enjoying precedence over horizontal policies such as the environment but not over vertically integrated sectors such as the free movement provisions. It was felt, however, that this approach was too wide ranging and obscured the legal base for

---

[62] See Bercusson (1989); Vogel-Polsky (1990).

[63] Case C-295/90 *Parliament v Council* [1992] ECR I-2867.

[64] Case 300/89 [1991] ECR I-2867.

horizontal policies. In *Commission v Council (Belgium Waste)*[65] the Council adopted a Framework Directive on Waste using Article 130S(1) EC. The Commission challenged the use of this legal base, arguing that Article 100A EC would have been more appropriate. The ECJ ruled that Article 130(s)(1) EC was the correct legal base arguing that the approach to be adopted in such matters was to look at the Community instrument's predominant aim and content. In particular whether horizontal policy principles are chosen or whether the purpose of the instrument is market liberalisation in which case Article 100A EC can be used.

Article 100A(4) EC provides that where harmonising legislation has been passed by a qualified majority vote, Member States seeking to apply national provisions on the grounds of major needs relating, *inter alia,* to the working environment, must notify the Commission. The Commission may then confirm that the provisions are necessary and compatible with Community law in that they do not constitute a means of arbitrary discrimination or disguised restriction on trade between Member States. Where it is though that a Member State is making improper use of its powers the Commission or another Member State may bring a case before the ECJ. Although Article 100A(4) EC expressly refers to the situation where harmonising legislation has been enacted by a qualified majority vote. It has been suggested that it could be applied to legislation passed by a unanimous vote to meet unforseen emergency situations.[66] To date Article 100A(4) EC has not been utilised in the area of the working environment.

### 1.7.3. The Charter of Fundamental Social Rights of Workers 1989

In May 1988 Delors promised the Congress of the European Trade Union Federation that work would begin on a draft Charter guaranteeing minimum social rights. The social dimension was double-edged. On the one hand, it appeared to resurrect the idea of a social protection base to Community law. On the other hand, it served to meet economic needs of avoiding "social dumping". In 1988 the Commission established a working group which proposed a set of social rights. Both the European Parliament and the Economic and Social Committee passed Resolutions and Opinions stressing the need for a binding legal framework of social rights to form the basis of a system of legal remedies. In particular the European Parliament called upon the Commission to utilise the new measures in the SEA 1986 and extend the use

---

[65]  Case C-155/91 [1993] ECR I-939.

[66]  Flynn (1987).

of qualified majority voting and cooperation procedures to all areas dealing with the social dimension of the Internal Market.[67]

The final document agreed at the Strasbourg Summit of December 1989 was greeted with disappointment, particularly since it addressed only labour market issues and not social rights in general. Vogel-Polsky questioned whether it would bring about any innovations in social policy.[68] Its main weakness was that it was not a legally binding document - it is called a "Solemn Declaration" and did not create a new legal base for the development of a social policy. The content of the Charter was neither radical or innovative - and contained a number of omissions - most notably by not addressing the issue of race discrimination. The Social Charter 1989 outlines 12 fundamental social rights:

- freedom of movement
- freedom to choose and engage in an occupation and to be fairly remunerated
- improvement of living and working conditions
- social protection
- freedom of association and collective bargaining
- vocational training
- equal treatment
- information, consultation and participation
- protection of health and safety at the workplace
- protection of children and young persons
- protection of the elderly
- protection of the disabled

The European Council asked the Commission to propose initiatives within the Community's competence and anticipating that agreement would be reached on the Charter, the Commission produced an Action Programme in November 1989 outlining its proposals to implement the Charter.[69] But implementation of the Action Programme was slow. In the *First Report on the Application of the Community Charter of the Fundamental Social Rights of Workers*[70] the Commission argued that it attempted to provide a sound base for the minimum provisions of a social policy by applying three cardinal principles: subsidiarity, diversity, competitiveness. By the end of 1991 the Commission had presented all of the 47 initiatives laid out in the Action Programme but very few had been approved by the Council of Ministers. The disappointing progress is attributed

---

[67] Bercusson (1990).

[68] Vogel Polsky (1990).

[69] COM(89) 568 final.

[70] COM(91) 511 final. See Szyszczak (1992b).

to the inadequacies of the legal base for a social policy programme in the Treaty and the lack of political will on the part of the Member States creating the legislative log jam in the Council of Ministers. The Action Programme resulted in only six major social policy Directives outside the area of health and safety matters:

- A Directive on an employer's obligation to inform employees of the conditions applicable to the contract or employment relationship (October 1991)
- a revision of the 1975 Directive on the approximation of the laws of the Member States relating to collective redundancies (June 1992)
- a Directive relating to measures to encourage improvements in the safety and health of pregnant workers and women workers who have recently given birth and women who are breastfeeding (October 1992)
- certain aspects of the organisation of working time (November 1993)
- the protection of young people at work (June 1994)
- posting of workers in the framework of the provision of services (December 1996).

With the adoption of the Directive on the posting of workers[71] in 1996 it is now felt that the era of the Social Charter 1989 has elapsed. There are some notable areas where there has been no progress in the social field, for example, the draft Council Regulation on the Statute for a European Company and the draft Council Directive complementing the Statute with regard to the involvement of employees in the European Company (and other related forms of European business organisation).[72] Three draft health and safety Directives on chemical agents, physical agents and transport have been dormant since 1993.

## 1.8. THE TREATY ON EUROPEAN UNION 1992

At the Maastricht Summit December 1991 the Member States agreed upon a revision of the Treaty of Rome 1957 and signed a new Treaty on European Union on February 7 1992. The Treaty was eventually ratified by the Member States and came into force on 1 November 1993.

A number of concessions were made to Denmark at the Edinburgh Summit of December 1992 allowing for special treatment in the areas of defence, citizenship, monetary union, ownership of property and immigration. The TEU

---

[71] 96/71/EC, OJ 1997 L 18/1.

[72] Proposed Council Regulation on the Statute for a European Company and accompanying Directive on the involvement of employees in the European Company, OJ 1989 C 263/41 and 69, amended OJ 1991 C 176/1 and COM(91) 174 final, OJ 1991 C 138/8. Proposed Council Regulations on Statutes for European Associations, cooperative societies and mutual societies and accompanying Directives on employee involvement, OJ 1992 C 99/17 and 37, amended OJ 1993 C 236/2 and 36.

created a new legal entity entitled the European Union (EU) comprising three pillars: the European Community and two inter-governmental pillars addressing matters relating to Justice and Home Affairs and a Common Foreign and Security Policy. The Treaty of Rome 1957 was re-organised and re-named the EC Treaty. There are five important developments for social policy as a result of the TEU:

### 1.8.1. Subsidiarity

A new Article 3B EC defines the concept of subsidiarity. Although there is still much academic discussion as to whether subsidiarity is justiciable and how it should be defined. The Commission acted quickly, undertaking to justify all its future proposals with regard to the principle of subsidiarity and in October 1992 issued a Communication to the Council of Ministers seeking to *explain* the application of subsidiarity rather than provide a definitive statement of the principle.[73] The Communication states that national powers are the rule and Community powers the exception and that the functions handed over to the Community are those which the Member States, at the various levels of decision-making, can no longer discharge satisfactorily. But the Commission also warns that "...subsidiarity cannot be used to bring the Commission to heel by challenging its right of initiative and in this way altering the balance of power established by the Treaties."[74]

At the Edinburgh Summit December 1992- as part of the package of concessions to ease through the second referendum in Denmark on ratification of the TEU[75] - the European Council issued a further Communication on the definition and application of the principle of subsidiarity. A three stage test was to be applied for new and existing legislation: first, it will be questioned whether the Community has the competence to act; second, if the Community does have competence is it impossible to achieve the desired result at the national level? third, if measures are not attainable at the national level, what is the minimum Community intervention necessary? The Edinburgh Summit also agreed to more openness and transparency in Community decision-making.

There are questions as to whether Article 3B EC is justiciable. The Edinburgh Council 1992 took the view that it was, although the Council did

---

[73] *The Principle of Subsidiarity*, SEC(92) final, Brussels 27 October 1992. See Spicker (1996); Neunreither (1993).

[74] *Ibid* 2.

[75] Worre (1995).

not think that Article 3B EC gave rise to direct effect. The Council considered that the ECJ was responsible for interpreting the principle and for reviewng compliance with it by other Community Insitutions. The ECJ has had few opportunities to consider the application of the subsidiarity principle. In *Bosman*[76] the German government intervened to argue, referring to the freedom of association and autonomy enjoyed by *private* sporting federations, that by virtue of the principle of subsidiarity, taken as a general principle, intervention by public, and particularly Community, authorities in the rules laid down by sporting associations must be confined to what is strictly necessary. The ECJ rejected such arguments stating that fundamental rights such as those contained in the free movement provisions were *not* to be interpreted in the light of the subsidiarity principle. In the challenge to the Working Time Directive,[77] one of the arguments put forward by the UK government was that the Directive breached the subsidiarity principle. The ECJ considered that Article 118A EC imposed a duty upon the Council to impose *minimum* health and safety requirements. These requirements presupposed Community-wide action leaving detailed implementation to the member states. The ECJ did not address the UK government's argument that the Directive *exceeded* the minimum requirements allowed by Article 118 A EC.

Dehousse[78] argues that looking at the ECJ's case law in the past it would be most unlikely for the Court to strike down measures for having failed to comply with the subsidiarity principle since the Court is reluctant to intervene to substitute its own view as to the extent of the powers of the Community Institutions. Emilou[79] has suggested that the ECJ should restrict itself to a marginal review of subsidiarity, intervening only where there is a patent error or misuse of power. Scharpf[80] , in contrast, argues that substantive review of the subsidiarity principle is possible.

### 1.8.2. Citizenship of the Union

A new Part Two of the EC Treaty creates the concept of Citizenship of the Union in Article 8 EC. This new legal concept is applicable only to people holding the nationality of one of the Member States and is defined by reference

---

[76]  Case C-415/93 [1995] ECR I-4921.

[77]  Case C-84/94 nyr.

[78]  Dehousse (1994).

[79]  Emilou (1992).

[80]  Scharpf (1994).

to a set of positive rights: the right to free movement (Article 8a EC); the right to stand and vote in municipal elections and elections to the European Parliament (Article 8b);[81] the right to diplomatic or consular protection by any of the Member States in a third state; the right to petition the European Parliament and the right to apply to the Ombudsman. Article 8e EC provides some dynamic to the concept of Citizenship of the Union by allowing the Council, acting unanimously on a proposal from the Commission and after consulting the European Parliament to adopt provisions to strengthen or add to the Citizenship provisions. The concept has been criticised for not including a human rights dimension and for failing to grant Citizenship rights to TCNs lawfully resident within the EU.[82]

### 1.8.3. Amendments To the Social Policy Title to the Treaty of Rome

Title III of Part Three of the Treaty of Rome becomes Title VIII of Part Three and is re-named "Social Policy, Education, Vocational Training and Youth". Articles 117 - 122 EC remain the same but Article 123 EC now extends the scope of the Social Fund to facilitate the adaption of workers to industrial changes and to changes in production systems, in particular through vocational training and retraining.[83] The detailed rules of the administration of the Social Fund are simplified in Article 125 EC by allowing the Council to act by a qualified majority vote using the co-operation procedure of the European Parliament and after consulting the Economic and Social Committee.

In a separate chapter entitled "Education, Vocational Training and Youth" new Articles 126-127 EC distinguish between education in general and vocational training as a specialised form of education having particular significance for the Internal Market. The Member States continue to have competence for the content and organisation of general education and vocational training.[84] This is discussed in Chapter Three. Of significance since the TEU is the use of the European Social Fund to support vocational training, pre-training, temporary employment aids and the development of appropriate training, employment and support structures, including the training of support

---

[81]  Oliver (1996).

[82]  See: Habermas (1992); O'Leary (1992); O'Keeffe (1993); Twomey (1993); Ward (1996).

[83]  See Vandamme (1990).

[84]  See Lonbay (1989); Shaw (1992).

staff and the provision of care services for dependants.[85] These provisions have built upon the "right" contained in Article 15 of the 1989 Social Charter which provides that "Every worker ... must be able to have access to vocational training and to benefit therefrom throughout his working life."

In the White Papers on Social Policy and on *Growth, Competitiveness and Employment*[86] the Commission gave notice that its intention was to build within the framework of Article 127 EC an EU guarantee that no young person under the age of 18 years should be unemployed since they would be guaranteed a place in education and training. A new training programme, called *Leonard da Vinci*[87] laid down a framework of objectives for *national* measures concerning vocational training policies. The EU has also organised a number of specific projects:

- COMETT and COMMETT II[88] : to provide support for partnership and mobility between university and industry in the field of training and technology.
- EUROTECNET:[89] provides for vocational training for technological change for workers in industry;
- ERASMUS/SOCRATES[90] provide for the mobility of students and inter-university cooperation in higher education;
- TEMPUS and TEMPUS II[91] apply the principles of ERASMUS to central and Eastern European states.
- LINGUA[92] aims to improve the teaching of foreign languages

---

[85] Regulation 2084/93 OJ 1993 L193/39.

[86] COM(94) 333.

[87] Council Decision 94/819/EC establishing an action programme for the implementation of a European Community vocational training policy OJ 1994 L340/8.

[88] Council Decision 86/365/EEC OJ 1986 L 222/17 and Council Decision 89/27 OJ 1989 L 13/28. See Joined Cases C-90/89 and C-94/89 *UK v Council* [1991] ECR I-2757.

[89] Council Decision 89/657/EEC OJ 1989 L 393/29.

[90] Council decision 87/327/EEC OJ 1987 L 166/20 amended by Council decision 89/663/EEC OJ 1989 L395/23. See Case 242/87 *Commission v Council* [1989] ECR 1425.

[91] Council Decision 90/233/EEC OJ 1990 L131/21; Council Decision 93/246/EEC OJ 1993 L112/34

[92] Council Decision 89/489/EEC OJ 1989 L239/24.

- PETRA[93] gives the Member States financial backing to ensure that all young people have the opportunity to follow a course of vocational training for at least one year after their compulsory education;
- IRIS is to increase women's awareness by making known to them what training is available
- MATTHAEUS[94] provides for the vocational training of customs officers
- HELIOS II[95] provides for vocational training for disabled people
- FORCE [96] provides for a three year action programme for the development of continuing vocational training
- SOCRATES[97] is designed to simplify and rationalise Community activity and take account of the increased competence of the new Article 126 EC.

Article 128 EC becomes a separate Title on "Culture" where new competence is conferred upon the Community to contribute to the "flowering of the cultures of the Member States" through intergovernmental activities.[98]

### 1.8.4. Economic and Social Cohesion

Articles 130 a-e were introduced by the SEA 1986, with economic and social cohesion identified as one of the six priority areas in the completion of the Internal Market.[99] The Structural Funds as well as the European Investment Bank have been used to support economic and social cohesion. In the TEU cohesion is seen as necessary to fulfil the principal objective of economic and monetary union. Thus the TEU strengthened the importance of such cohesion in Article 3(j) and Article 2 and provided a new Chapter XIV, Articles 130a-e EC. The essential policy and its implementation remained the same: to promote overall harmonious development and to reduce disparities amongst the regions of the EU through the Structural Funds and the application of the principal of additionality in the conduct and coordination of national economic policies.

---

[93] Council Decision 87/569/EEC OJ 1987 L346/31 amended by Council Decision 91/387/EEC OJ 1991 L214/69.

[94] Council Decision 91/341/EEC OJ 1991 L 187/41; Commission decision 92/39/EEC OJ 1992 L16/14; Commission Decision 93/136/EEC OJ 1993 L56/30;

[95] Council Decision 93/136/EEC OJ 1993 L56/30.

[96] Council Decision 90/267/EEC OJ 1990 L156/1.

[97] COM(94) 80 final.

[98] See McMahon (1995).

[99] *The Single Act: A New Frontier for Europe* COM(87) 100.

The Structural Funds were subject to a thorough review in anticipation of the TEU.[100] Although the *scheme* of the structural fund operation remains the same in that the objectives are divided into a hierarchy of tasks the objectives have been refined:

**Objective 1** - the promotion of the development and structural adjustment of the regions whose development is lagging behind - now has the additional task of investment in education and health charged to the European Regional Development Fund.

**Objective 2** - converting the regions, frontier regions or parts of regions (including employment areas and urban communities) seriously affected by industrial decline has been adjusted to cover geographical areas which may be regarded as declining industrial areas.

**Objectives 3 and 4** were combined into Objective 3 anticipating the amendment to Article 123 EEC

**Objective 4** is now new - of combatting long-term unemployment and facilitating the integration into working life of young people and of persons exposed to exclusion from the labour market and facilitating the adaptation of workers of either sex to industrial changes and to changes in production systems. The new Objective 4 is seen as a reflection of the effects of the completion of the Internal Market - of industrial restructuring brought about by changes in technology.

**Objective 5** has been amended to take into account the structural changes to the Common Agricultural policy[101]

**Objective 6** was added on the accession of Finland and Sweden - the development of the Arctic regions.

The amended Article 130d EC required the Council of Ministers to establish a Cohesion Fund by 1994[102] which would contribute to projects in the fields of environment and trans-European networks on transport infrastructure Article 130b also stipulates that the formulation and implementation of policies and activities of the Internal Market must take into account and contribute to the achievement of the policy objectives of economic and social cohesion. It has been questioned whether these new policy objectives will provide nothing more than "Band Aid" to cover the yawning economic disparities within the

---

[100] Commission, *From the Single Act to Maastricht and Beyond: The Means To Match Our Ambitions(the "Delors II Package")*, COM (92) 2000; Commission, *The Community's Finances Between Now and 1997*, COM (92) 2001; Commission, *Community Structural Policies - Assessment and Outlook*, COM (92) 84.

[101] The so-called MacSharry Reforms, see [1991] 5 *EC Bull Supp.*

[102] A Cohesion Financial Instrument was adopted by the Council under Article 235 EC: Council Regulation 792/93 OJ L 1993 79/84.

EU.[103] Although expenditure under the Structural Funds has doubled the Commission[104] estimated that support for economic and social cohesion would require commitment appropriations of ECU 11 thousand million by 1997 which would require significant reforms of the compulsory component of the Community budget. At the Edinburgh Council Meeting 1991 the Member States agreed upon an average increase in resources for the Structural Funds of ECU 1.5 thousand million per year and a commitment to the Cohesion Fund of just over 15 thousand million to the end of 1999.

The Structural Funds and the Cohesion Fund are likely to play important roles after the completion of economic and monetary union. What will transpire to be the instruments of economic adjustment in the EU after EMU which will take the place of the exchange rate mechanism has yet to materialise. MacDougall[105] has argued for the necessity of automatic regional redistribution in federal and unitary states, but at present the EU has not adopted any tools to deal with crises in member States or regions which fall into recession, although Article 103a EC allows for financial assistance for member states hit by adverse exceptional circumstances or natural disasters. Emerson[106] has argued that it would be a natural evolution for the Regional and Cohesion Funds to acquire a quicker shock-absorbing capacity, held in reserve for justified crises.

The Structural Funds are programmed to reach 0.46% of the EU's GDP by 1999.[107] The Commission reports that there has been a trend towards greater convergence,[108] leading to a reconsideration of the priority regions. The most notable example is the growth of the "Euro-Tiger" economy of Ireland. Although some regional problems continue to persist and it is not altogether clear whether EU grants do stimulate economic reform policies for such regions. Also on the agenda will be the possible accession to the EU of some

---

[103] See Lane (1993) 962; Shaw (1994) 305; Kenner (1994).

[104] *From the Single Act to Maastricht and Beyond: The Means To Match Our Ambitions (the Delors II Package")* COM(92) 2000.

[105] MacDougall(1977).

[106] Emerson(1996).

[107] Wulf-Mathies (1996).

[108] Over the period 1983-1995 the average income per head of the 4 poorest national economies of the EU (Spain, Portugal, Greece and Ireland) increased from 66% to 74% see Commission, *First Cohesion Report 1996 OOPEC, Luxembourg.*

of the Central and Eastern European states and the needs of smoothing their entry.[109]

### 1.8.5. The Social Policy Protocol and Agreement

The main bulk of the Chapter on Social Policy was taken out of the draft Treaty at the eleventh hour of the Maastricht Summit and annexed as a Protocol and Agreement to the EC Treaty. This was because the then UK Prime Minister Major made it clear that the UK would not adhere to a new Chapter on Social Policy and it seemed to be the only way of salvaging the draft Treaty - and perhaps create a new dynamic to social policy.[110] The Social Policy Protocol authorised the then 11 Member States

"... to have recourse to the institutions, procedures and mechanisms of the Treaty for the purposes of taking among themselves and applying as far as they are concerned the acts and decisions required for giving effect to the [Social Policy Agreement]."

However, such action is to be without prejudice to the provisions of the Treaty, particularly those which relate to social policy which constitutes an integral part of the *acquis communautaire*. Initially the legality of the Social Policy Protocol - or "opt-out" as it is more generally referred to was questioned.[111] The Protocol is considered to be legally binding, from its wording which, as a matter of international law and Article 239 EC, is an integral part of the Treaty of Rome 1957. Article 1 of the SPA affirms Community competence in the area of social policy law, continuing to subordinate social policy to the economic objectives of the Treaty. The innovation is found in Article 2(2) which allows the Council to adopt Directives by a *qualified majority* vote[112]

---

[109] Commission, *Preparation of the Associated Countries of Central and Eastern Europe for the Integration of the Internal Market of the Union* COM(95) 163 final.

[110] Falkner (1996) On how far the UK has managed an "opt-out" see Barnard (1992); Hargreaves (1997). On taking office on 1 May 1997 the new Labour government opened negotiations to secure the UK's adherence to the SPA and gave support for a new Employment Chapter to be included in the proposed Treaty of Amsterdam 1997.

[111] Curtin (1993); Szyszczak (1993).

[112] Article 2 of the SPP states that the UK "shall not take part in the deliberations and the adoption by the Council of Commission proposals made on the basis of the Social Policy Protocol and the Social Chapter Agreement." The voting procedure in the Council is adapted to allow for a qualified majority vote of 52 votes (instead of the usual 62 votes) and unanimity on the basis of UK non-participation.

using the cooperation procedure with the European Parliament or by a *unanimous* vote involving only consultation of the European Parliament in the following areas:

- improvement of the working environment to protect workers' health and safety;
- the information and consultation of workers;
- equality between men and women in labour market matters;
- integration of persons excluded from the labour market.

Article 2(3) requires unanimity voting in the following areas:

- social security and social protection of workers;
- redundancy
- representation and collective defence of the interests of workers and employers, including co-determination;
- conditions of employment for third country nationals legally resident in the Community;
- financial contributions for the promotion of employment and job creation.

Articles 3 and 4 are significant in bolstering Article 118B EC. Article 3 charges the Commission with offering "balanced support" for the consultation of management and labour ("the social partners") and must consult management and labour on the possible direction of Community action before submitting any proposals. If, after this process of consultation, the Commission considers that Community action is advisable the Commission must then consult the social partners on the *content* of the envisaged proposal. The social partners will then forward an opinion or a recommendation to the Commission. The social partners may inform the Commission that they wish to invoke the procedure of Article 4 of the SPA whereby they may reach an agreement on the Commission's initiative. The social partners have nine months in which to act - although with the agreement of the social partners and the Commission the period may be extended.

Article 4 states that "1.Should management and labour so desire, the dialogue between them at Community level may lead to contractual relations, including agreements." Such agreements concluded at the Community level shall be implemented either in accordance with the procedures and practices specific to the social partners and the Member States or, in matters covered by Article 2 of the SPA at the joint request of the social partners by a Council decision on a proposal by the Commission. The Council will vote by either a qualified majority or by unanimity according to the subject matter of the agreement.

Article 2(6) states that the SPA does not apply to pay, the right of association, the right to strike or the right to impose lock-outs.

The new role for the social partners under the SPA has two dimensions- one consultative and one of negotiation. This is a dramatic up-grading of the role of collective bargaining as a means of implementing social policy. In the past Member States such as Italy and Denmark have fallen foul of Community law when they implemented Community social policy law through collective agreements. The ECJ entertained some doubts about the use of collective agreements in this way arguing, *inter alia,* that collective bargaining lacks a normative quality, it does not benefit non-trade union members, it does not apply to undertakings outside of the employers' association, it does not exist in all economic/industrial sectors and it may not always cover the exact scope of Community obligations.[113] The role of collective bargaining was up-graded in the final version of the Social Charter 1989 which states that agreement on social rights might be attained "through action by the Member States, the two sides of industry and the Community".[114] But the Community has no power to compel collective bargaining and neither the Social Charter or the SPA facilitate the development of collective bargaining. There is controversy about how far the "social dialogue" will contribute to the development of a Community social policy. Blanpain, for example, has argued that trade unions do not have enough power at the European level to force the employers' associations or multinational groups to meet around the bargaining table.[115] In contrast Bercusson is more enthusiastic arguing that the social dialogue offers a unique opportunity to be utilised as an instrument for developing the substantive content of, as well as applying fundamental social rights.[116] Arguing that principle and experience support the use of the social dialogue at the Community level Bercusson argues that the social dialogue provides flexibility and consensus by the maximum democratic involvement of workers and employers. But some of this flexibility is lost in the SPA - a process of bargaining under the threat of legislation if the social partners cannot agree - which Bercusson describes as "bargaining in the shadow of the law".

One problem has been the question of which organisations representing the social partners should be involved in the SPA processes. As we have seen the involvement of the social partners in formulating policy is not new but the fragmented nature of trade unionism in the EU has made it particularly difficult to draw up appropriate and fair criteria for the inclusion of worker representa-

---

[113] For comment see Lyon-Caen (1989); Adinolfi (1988).

[114] Bercusson (1990).

[115] Blanpain (1990).

[116] Bercusson (1990) 641.

tives in the consultation process. In 1993 the Commission commissioned a study into the representatives of various European-level organisations and as a result drew up a set of criteria to be satisfied in order for organizations to be consulted under Article 3 of the SPA.[117] The organisations must be:

- cross-industry
- must consist of organisations which are themselves "an integral and recognised part of Member State social partner structures" and have the capacity to negotiate agreements and are representative of all Member States as far as possible
- must have adequate structures to ensure their effective participation in the consultation process.

In a *Communication on the Development of the Social Dialogue at Community Level*[118] the Commission expresses the view that to date the consultations have worked very well but some procedural problems have arisen. It suggests that it may be necessary to re-evaluate the criteria on which the original list was based. The European Parliament has suggested adding two further criteria:

- that the organisations should be composed of organisations of which membership is voluntary at both national level and European level and
- have a mandate for their members to represent them in the Community social dialogue and can demonstrate this representative interest.

The Commission keeps the list of organisations to be consulted under review and plans to promote linking structures between the social partners paying special attention to the due representation of small and medium-sized undertakings.

As it turns out the SPA, has proved to have had a number of teething problems and it is arguable that it has not proved to have been particularly dynamic. A delicate balancing act is in place - between the desire to retain uniformity and keep the UK at the bargaining table without giving away too many concessions and the temptation to resort to the SPA automatically if the UK starts being difficult. The first measure to be passed to the SPA was the Proposed Council Directive on the Establishment of a European Works Council in Community-Scale Undertakings for the Purposes of Informing and Consulting Employees.[119] The proposal was submitted to the Council of

---

[117] *Social Partners Study*, V/614/93, EC Commission, Brussels. See Streeck (1994).

[118] COM(96) 448 final.

[119] For a discussion of the history and strategy employed in this initiative see Hall (1992).

Ministers on 12 December 1990.[120] Despite the existence of a broad consensus among the majority of the Member States the Council meeting of 12 October 1993 was unable to reach a unanimous agreement on the proposal and so it became the first measure to be transferred to the SPA. The negotiations between the social partners broke down rather quickly after two exploratory meetings and a formal social dialogue meeting between ETUC, UNICE and CEEP. It became apparent that there was not enough common ground between the two sides to negotiate with UNICE and CEEP claiming that the ETUC preferred the legislative route through the SPA.

At the Council Meeting of 22 June 1994 the Council arrived at a common position on a Directive on the proposal and this was accepted by a majority vote at the Council meeting of July 1994 with Portugal abstaining. The formal text was then forwarded to the European Parliament for a second reading as part of the cooperation procedure in Article 189C EC.[121] The measure was finally adopted as Council Directive 94/45/EEC.[122]

The second measure to be considered under the SPA was a proposal for a Directive on parental leave. As with the Works Council proposal the idea for such a Directive had been kicking around the Community for a number of years and had met with a hostile response from the UK government.[123] In the Commission's *Communication on the Development of the Social Dialogue at Community Level*[124] observations are made on the negotiations that took place over the parental leave agreement. It is pointed out that there was only a very short time (7 months) between the conclusion of the framework agreement and the Council's adoption of the Directive. The European Parliament reacted critically to the fact that it has no role to play in the decision-making procedure. While the Council accepted that it could not modify the agreement it expressed concern that it created problems for some Member States on the procedural and insitutional implications for implementing the content of the Directive in the Member States. Certain sections of the social partners criticised their being left out of the negotiations, questioning the validity of the agreement and one such organisation - UEAPME has instigated an action

---

[120] OJ C 1991 39/10, amended OJ C 1991 336/11.

[121] See McGlynn (1995).

[122] OJ L 1995 254/64.

[123] OJ 1983 C 33/6; OJ 1984 C 316/7.

[124] COM(96) 448 final.

before the ECJ.[125] The Commission responded to these criticisms claiming that UNICE, ETUC and CEEP fufilled the criteria necessary to make the agreement valid. It also held an information meeting of organisations consulted on the proposal but which were not party to the negotiations.

In the *Communication* the Commission has sought the views of interested parties over the way the parental leave Directive was negotiated. The issue of participation is addressed by the Commission arguing that only the social partners themselves can develop their own dialogue and negotiating structures and that it cannot impose participants on a freely undertaken negotiation. But in the case of agreements which might replace planned legislation the SPA imposes on the Commission an obligation to assess the validity of an agreement which requires an assessment of whether those affected by the agreeemnt have been represented. This, it argues, can only be assessed on a case-by-case basis, since participation will vary with the subject matter. The Commission's criteria are whether the negotiating parties have a genuine interest in the matter and can demonstrate significant representation in the domain concerned.

Finally Articles 6(1) and (2) of the SPA reproduce the equal pay provisions of Article 119 EC with an additional provision in Article 6(3) allowing the Member States to adopt positive action measures. This complements the tolerance of positive action found in Article 2(4) of the Equal Treatment Directive 76/207/EEC but after the rulings in *Commission v France*[126] and *Kalanke*[127] it is likely that Article 6(3) will be interpreted restrictively. These issues are discussed in Chapter Four.

### 1.8.6. Summary of the Legislative Routes For Social Policy Law After the TEU

Post the TEU there are four possible legislative routes for social policy measures:

### 1.8.6.(i). Consultation

The consultation procedure applies to proposals based upon Article 100 and 235 EC. The Commission submits a proposal to the Council of Ministers. The European Parliament - and often the Economic and Social Committee - are

---

[125] T-135/96, OJ 1996 C 318/21.

[126] Case 312/86 [1988] ECR 6315.

[127] Case C-450/93 [1995] ECR I-3051.

consulted and give an Opinion. The Commission may amend its proposals on receipt of these Opinions and the Council may also amend the proposal. Voting in the Council takes place by a unanimous vote.

### 1.8.6.(ii). Cooperation

Where proposals are based upon Article 118a EC and 127 EC the cooperation procedure applies. Here, when the Council receives the revised Commission proposal it does not take a final decision but adopts "a common position" by qualified majority vote. The common position is then sent to the European Parliament for a second reading. The European Parliament may:
- approve the common position or make no decision within three months. The proposal is then automatically adopted by the Council; automatically adopted by the Council;
- reject the common position. The Council can then only adopt the proposal on a *unanimous* vote;
- propose amendments to the common position. The Commission must then re-examine the proposal and submit a new proposal to the Council within one month (which may take into account all or some of the proposed amendments). The Council may then adopt the amended proposal by a qualified majority vote. If it wishes to pursue amendments proposed by the European Parliament but ignored by the Commission or introduce amendments of its own it must do so by a *unanimous* vote.

The Council must act within three months otherwise the proposal lapses.

### 1.8.6.(iii). Co-Decision

The new codecision procedure (or "negative assent procedure") was introduced by the TEU. It applies to proposals based upon Articles 49, 54 and 56, 57. The co-decision procedure amends the cooperation procedure by allowing the European Parliament a *right of veto* over proposals at the second reading stage. Where the European Parliament decides to amend a proposal and the Council will not accept the amendments a new conciliation procedure has been introduced to attempt a compromise position.

### 1.8.6.(iv). Social Policy Agreement

The SPA is used as a residual legislative route where unanimity cannot be reached in the ouncil of Ministers because of the UK's opposition to a proposal. Here the Social Partners play a prominent role. When formulating proposals the Commission must consult European level representatives of management and labour

*firstly:* on the possible direction of Community action, prior to submitting any proposal;

*secondly:* on the content of the envisage d proposal, if the Commission still considers action advisable after the first round of consultation.

At the second stage of the consultation process, the social partners should send opinions or recommendations on the envisage d proposal. They may also decide that they wish to reach a European-level agrteement on the issue. The social partners then have nine months to reach such an agreement (but the Commission may agree to a request from the social partners to extned this period). Any agreement reached may be implenmented by a Council decision (taken by unanimous or qualified majority voting depending upon the subject matter) or "in accordance with the procedures and practices specific to management and labour and the Member States".

Where the social partners do not reach an agreement the Commission may issue a proposal for legislation which will then proceedd under the cooperation or co-decision procedure with qualified or unanimity voting depending upon the subject matter.

### 1.8.7. Other Special Protocols

In addition to the Social Policy Protocol there are a number of other Protocols which represent "special pleadings"[128] on the part of the Member States and which impinge upon social policy issues.

### 1.8.7.(i). The Irish Abortion Protocol

Protocol No. 17 creates a special case for the Irish constitutional right to life of the unborn which was considered to come under threat after the ruling of the ECJ in *SPUC v Grogan.*[129] This is discussed in Chapter Two.

### 1.8.7.(ii). The "Barber" Protocol

Protocol No 2 on Article 119 EC seeks to explain the application of the principle of equality in relation to occupational pension schemes after the

---

[128] See Curtin (1993).

[129] Case C-159/90 [1991] ECR I-4685.

ruling of the ECJ in *Barber v GRE*[130] This Protocol is discussed in greater detail in Chapter Four.

### 1.8.8. Immigration

Immigration policy *vis a vis* third country nationals is now brought within the sphere of Community competence as a result of Article 100 EC . This is discussed in greater detail in Chapter Two. The TEU created a new legal structure for the EU based upon a three pillar approach. The first pillar constitutes the activities of the Community and is supported by two other pillars relating to Justice and Home Affairs and Foreign Security Policy. These latter two pillars constitute areas for inter-governmental action and involve a number issues which concern TCNs. There is a *passerelle* provision in Article 100C(6) EC which envisages the transfer of competence of some of areas within the Justice and Home Affairs pillar into the decision-making framework of the Community.

## 1.9. A FIFTH PHASE TO SOCIAL POLICY?

In looking at the future of social policy that the EU is standing at the cross-roads. On the one hand, if the new Labour administration in the UK agrees to incorporate the SPA into the main body of Community processes we will have, for the first time a clear and uniform basis for the development of social policy law. This does not necessarily mean that there will be any greater output of legislation at the Community level or indeed any greater consensus as to how the EU labour market can and should be regulated and how social policy issues should be addressed. On the other hand, in recent years we have seen a dramatic shift in Commission policy. [131] Although the White Paper, *European Social Policy - A Way Forward For The Union*[132] affirms the Commission's support for basic minimum standards in recent initiatives, for example the Directive on Working Time[133] and the Directive on the Protection of Young People at Work[134] contain a wide variety of derogations to accomodate the Member States. Equally, we have seen resort to an increasing number of soft

---

[130] Case C-262/88 [1990] ECR I-1889.

[131] See Whiteford (1995); More (1995); Cullen and Campbell (1996)

[132] COM(94)333, 5.

[133] Council Directive 93/104/EC, OJ 1993 L 307/18.

[134] Council Directive 94/33 OJ 1994 L216/12.

law measures, which, despite the ruling in *Grimaldi* [135] are often ignored by the Member States and under-utilised by lawyers and other activitists in pursuing social policy law rights.

An important development in the formulation of future social policy initiatives is the use of a consultative document in the form of a Green Paper[136] followed by a White Paper looking at more specific proposals following the consultative process. These Papers need to be read in conjunction with the White Paper, *Growth, Competitiveness and Employment*[137] We see the Commission linking social policy issues with other economic issues, particularly the capacity of EU business to competein the globalized economy. The White Paper identifies as the cause of structural unemployment the functioning of the labour market: lack of flexibility, wages and mobility. Compulsory social security contributions are cited as barriers to employment creation and seen as barriers for job seekers. The Commission argues that the social security systems of the Member States have had negative effects upon employment since many systems protect those in paid work at the expense of those not in paid work. Thus the Commission seems to favour a solution involving fundamental reform of the labour market to encourage more flexible organisation of work: flexible organisation, flexible working time, lower wage costs, more vocational training and a more active emplyment policy. But from the White Paper it is clear that there is no consensus amongst the Member States and it is apparent that the underlying tension of how to regulate the EU labour market continues to restrict the Commission to an uneasy compromise between those who argue that excessively high labour standards result in costs which blunt the competitive edge of firms and those who believe that productivity is the key to competitiveness and that high labour standards form an integral part of a competitive labour market.[138] The White Paper was followed up in the Medium Term Social Action Programme (1995-1997)[139] In this the Commission proposes few binding measures - and many of these are a "mopping up exercise" of proposals which have been hanging around the Community legislative process from the 1980s.

---

[135] Case C-322/88 [1989] ECR 4407.

[136] COM(93) 551, Brussels 17 November 1993. See the European Parliament Resolution, *Social Europe* 2/94, 156. Kuper (1994).

[137] COM(93) 700.

[138] See Grahl and Teague (1992); Henley and Tsakalotus (1992); Deakin and Wilkinson (1994).

[139] COM (95) 134.

## 1.10. RIGHTS, REMEDIES AND THE EFFECTIVENESS OF EU LAW: THE ROLE OF THE ECJ

Throughout the periods under discussion the ECJ has established itself as a key actor in the legislative process. The case law will be discussed in subsequent chapters but here we need to pause for a moment to comment upon the Court's remarkable role. In addition to the tools of direct and indirect effect the ECJ has frequently laid the ground for legislative change, most notably in the area of protection for pregnant workers, the reversal of the burden of proof in sex-discrimination claims and part-time work. The Court has even cut across existing legislation, seen for example, in the litigation surrounding the interaction of Article 119 EC and the state/occupational social security Directives. It has also taken the lead in ensuring the effectiveness of Community law in the Member States.

### 1.10.1. Use of the General Principles of Community Law/Human Rights Standards

The ECJ has played a pivotal role in elevating certain social rights - notably in the area of the free movement of persons and equal treatment between men and women into fundamental rights of EU law, protected by the ECJ and binding upon the Member States.[140] The development of the general principles of EU law, for example, proportionality, equality, non-discrimination have played an important role in firming up the skeletal social policy provisions.[141] The Court has taken cognisance of international social law conventions and standards in providing the inspiration for a set of Community based- social rights in cases *Defrenne v Sabena (No.3),*[142] *Blaizot v University of Liege,*[143] *Johnston v RUC,*[144] *Rutili v Minister For the Interior*[145].

---

[140] See Arnull (1990); Docksey(1991); Temple-Lang (1991).

[141] It is arguable that the general principles of Community law are capable of *horizontal* direct effect. See Oliver (1993); Curtin (1994).

[142] Case 149/77 [1978] ECR 1365.

[143] Case 24/86 [1988] ECR 379.

[144] Case 222/84 [1986] ECR 1651.

[145] Case 36/75 [1975] ECR 1219.

Some commentators[146] have suggested that the Community should accede to international social law conventions in order to enhance the global uniformity of social law but looking at the two Opinions delivered by the ECJ in this area such forms accession may be difficult to achieve from a legal and political perspective because the Member States are reluctant to give up sovereignty in this field.[147]

### 1.10.2. Enforcement of Community Law: Direct and Indirect Effect and State Liability

As well as the limitations in the *substantive* content and scope of EU social policy law a further limitation is that the majority of social policy legislation is enacted in the form of Directives or soft law measures. The ECJ responded to these limitations by affirming the binding nature of soft law in *Grimaldi*[148] and ruling that provisions of the Treaty, such as Article 119 EC, are capable of both vertical and horizontal direct effect and that Directives may create vertical direct effect. It has broadened the parameters of direct effect to allow individuals to rely upon the provisions of a Directive in the national courts even where a Member State may choose between several different options when implementing a directly effective provision.[149]

A second weakness in using Directives to implement social policy law is that the ECJ has drawn a distinction between horizontal and vertical direct effect, denying horizontal direct effect to Directives.[150] To close the loophole in the uniformity of application of Community law and legal remedies the ECJ created the concept of indirect effect. [151] This is described as a duty upon the

---

[146] Vogel-Polsky (1990); Hepple (1990c).

[147] Opinion 2/91 *Re Convention No.170 of the ILO Concerning Safety in the use of Chemicals at Work* [1993] ECR I-1061; Opinion 2/94 of 28 March 1996.

[148] Case C-322/88 [1989] ECR 4407.

[149] Case 286/85 *McDermott and Cotter v The Minister For Social Welfare and the Attorney General* [1987] ECR 1453; Joined Cases C-6 & 9/90 *Francovich and Bonifaci v Italy* [1991] ECR 5357.

[150] Case 152/84 *Marshall v Southampton and South West Hampshire Area Health Authority (Teaching)* [1986] ECR 723. See Wyatt (1983).

[151] Case 14/83 *Von Colson and Kamman* [1984] ECR 1891.

national courts arising from Article 5 EC. In *Marleasing SA v La Commercial Internacional de Alimentacion SA[152]* the Court states the duty as:

"... in applying national law, whether the provisions in question were adopted before or after the directive, the national court called upon to interpret it is required to do so, as far as possible, in the light of the wording and the purpose of the directive in order to achieve the result pursued by the latter and thereby comply with the third paragraph of Article 189 of the Treaty."

Even when encouraged to re-think the position of horizontal direct effect of Directives by its Advocates General the ECJ declined to do so.[153] Instead the Court has attempted to seal the interface between direct and indirect effect by creating the right to damages against a Member State which fails to implement Community law in *Francovich and Bonifaci v Italy*.[154] Here the applicants brought an action against the Italian state for failing to implement the Insolvency Directive 80/987/EEC. They were unable to claim for lost wages from their insolvent employer and claimed instead against the Member State, either by way of having the guarantees in the Directive enforced against the state or by way of action in damages against the state. The Court ruled that there were three conditions in order to satisfy state liability: the Community law concerned should grant rights to individuals, it should be possible to identify those rights on the basis of the Community law and that there must be a causal link between the breach of the state's obligations and the loss suffered by the individual.

The principles of state liability have been refined in further rulings by the ECJ[155] in *Brasserie du Pecheur SA v Federal Republic of Germany and R v Secretary of State For Transport ex parte Factortame,*[156] *R v Ministry of Agriculture, Fisheries and Food, ex parte Hedley Lomas (Ireland) Ltd.*[157] and

---

[152] Case C-106/89 [1990] ECR I-4135.

[153] See Advocate General van Gerven in Case C-271/91 *Marshall (No.2)* [1993] ECRI-4367; Advocate General Jacobs in Case C-316/93 *Vaneetveld v SA Le Foyer* [1994] ECR I-763; Advocate General Lenz in Case C-91/92 *Faccini Dori* v *Recreb* [1994] ECR 3325.

[154] Joined Cases C-6/90 & 9/90 [1991] ECR I-5357.

[155] See Hervey and Rostant (1996).

[156] Joined Cases C-46/93 and C-48/93 [1996] ECR I-1029

[157] Case C-5/94 [1996] ECR I-2553.

*R v HM Treasury ex parte British Telecommunications plc.*[158] In the latter case we see the ECJ finding the UK had not manifestly or gravely disregarded the limits of the exercise of discretionary powers in implementing Community law and therfeore no liability was found. From the case law the ECJ has built up a list of factors which must be taken into account by the national court in deciding whether there has been a sufficiently serious breach of Community law

- the clarity and precision of the rule breached
- the measure of the discretion left to national authorities
- whether the infringement and damage caused were intentional or voluntary
- whether any error of law was excusable
- whether the position taken by the Community Institutions may have contributed to the Member State's breach of Community law
- whether the breach persisted after an infringement was established or a preliminary ruling clarified the issue.

### 1.10.3. Other Community-based Procedural Rights and Remedies

The Court has played a pivotal - but not consistent - role in developing Community-based procedural rights and remedies.[159] The Court's initial stance was that where there were no Community rules relating to procedures and remedies it would not intervene in the procedural/arena but to leave it to the Member States to apply their own procedural rules and remedies in applying Community law at the national level with the caveat that the national rules must not make it impossible to exercise directly effective rights of Community law and that the conditions attached to the national rules enforcing Community-based rights must not be less favourable than those attached to similar national actions.[160] Recently the Court has refined these principles.[161]The Community has enacted some secondary legislation in the social policy field which addresses procedural and remedial rights, the most litigated being Article 6 of the Equal Treatment Directive 76/207/EEC which is

---

[158] Case C-392/93 [1996] ECR I-1631.

[159] Cf Ward (1995); Curtin (1994),

[160] Case 33/76 *Rewe -Centralfinanze eG and Rewe Zentral Ag v Landwirtschaftskammer fur das saarland* [1976] ECR 1989 and Joined Cases C-430/93 and C-431/93 *Jeroen Van Schijndel and Johannes Nicolaas Cornelis Van Veen v Stichting Pensioenfonds Voor Fysiotherapeuten* [1995] ECR I-4705.

[161] See Hoskins (1996); Szyszczak (1996), Szyszczak and Delicostopolous (1997).

discussed in Chapter Four, the ECJ has also played a significant role in this area. The Court has also allowed the suspension of time limits where a Member state has failed to implement Community law correctly in *Emmott v Minister For Social Welfare and the Attorney General*[162] although in later cases the ECJ has not regarded this as a general rule.[163] In *Steenhorst-Neerings*[164] the Court allowed a Member State to impose a limit upon the amount of back-dating of compensation allowed. In Dekker,[165] *Marshall (No. 2)*[166] and in *Draempaehl*[167] the ECJ was willing to overrule national rules which did not provide for effective remedies. In *Danfoss*[168] the ECJ allowed for the partial reversal of the burden of proof in equal pay claims where there was no transparency in the wage determination process.[169]

---

[162] Case C-208/90 [1991] ECR I-4269.

[163] In Case C-2/94 *Denkavit International BV v Kramer van Koophandel en Fabrieken voor Midden-Gelderland and others* nyr, Advocate General Jacobs distinguished *Emmott* on the following grounds: unlike Ireland in *Denkavit* the Netherlands had implemented the Directive in question in good faith; whereas Emmott was denied any effective opportunity to rely on the Directive for the period in question in *Denkavit* the appellants had had a number of opportunities to challenge the levy imposed upon them; in *Denkavit* the litigants were large commercial undertakings whereas Emmott was in the particularly unprotected position of an individual dependent on social welfare.

[164] Case C-338/91 [1993] ECR I-5475. See also Case C-410/92 *Johnson v Chief Adjudication Officer* [1994] ECR I-5483; Case C-66/95 *Sutton* judgment of 22 April 1997, nyr.

[165] Case C-177/88 [1990] ECR I-3941.

[166] Case C-271/91 [1993] ECR I-4367. See also Case C-127/92 *Enderby v Frenchay Health Authority and the Secretary of State For Health* [1993] ECR I-5535; Case C-400/93 *Royal Copenhagen* [1995] ECR I-1275.

[167] Case C-180/95 *Nils Draempaehl v Urania Immobilienservice OHG* judgment of 22.4.1997, nyr.

[168] See Szyszczak (1997).

[169] The Commission had attempted to introduce a Directive relating to the burden of proof (OJ 1988 C 176/5) but the proposal was not taken up by the Council of Ministers The discussion of the draft was re-opened in 1993 but no progress made and so the proposal was transferred to the SPA.

## 1.11. FUTURE PROSPECTS

From the Green and White Papers we see the Commission shifting the focus of the social dimension of the EU to focus upon goals rather than harmonisation of individual rights: the two dominant goals being the reduction of unemployment and the elimination of social exclusion. In relation to (un)employment five areas were identified at the European Council meeting in Essen 1994:

(I)   Improving employment opportunities for the labour force by promoting investment in vocational training;
(II)  Increasing the employment intensiveness of growth
(III) Reducing non-wage labour costs extensively
(IV)  Improving the effectiveness of labour market policy
(V)   Improving measures to help groups which are particularly affected by unemployment.

The European Council asked the Commission to monitor employment trends and national policies and to report back to the European Council The Commission has encoraged the Member States to take acount of the Essen objectives in their convergence programmes and has made a number of proposals for Decisions in the employment field and approved projects relating to the Essen employment strategy.[170]

Social exclusion is given a wide definition in Community policy[171] and has included poverty, racism, disability. Three Poverty Programmes have been initiated enabling the Community to fund research and pilot projects which the Commission argues has helped to disseminate information about poverty and stipulate debate as to how to tackle it. But there is opposition from some of the Member States. For example, the UK has questioned whether the concept of "social exclusion" has any utility[172] Germany has joined with the UK in blocking the Poverty 4 proposal.[173] But what is perhaps important is that Community competence in the area has been established. Social exclusion is being integrated into other Community policies, for example, the SOCRATES

---

[170] Commission, *Follow-up to the Essen Council on Employment* COM (95) 74.

[171] See Tiemann, "Opinion on Social Exclusion" OJ 1993 C 352/13; Commission, *Towards A Europe of Solidarity - Intensifying the Fight Against Social Exclusion. Fostering Integration* COM (92) 542.

[172] COM (94) 333 final, II, 268.

[173] COM (93) 435. See Joined Cases C-239/96R and C-240/96R *United Kingdom v Commission* 24 September 1996.

Decision on education policy of 1995 laid emphasis upon the elimination of social exclusion and the reduction of racism and xenophobia in the EU. Equally attempts to extend Community competence to intagrate TCNs and deal with racism and xenophobia are seen as part of the social exclusion goal. The Council has adopted two Recommendations on social exclusion[174] and the Commission has issued Reports[175] on the Member States' policies and kept alive the debate on social exclusion.[176]

The prospect of further legislation in the social policy field seems seems remote. There are very few proposals in the legislative process at present and these are a mixed bag of issues - relating to atypical work, transfers of undertakings, information and consultation of workers and sexual harassment. In the Commission's Work Programme for 1996[177] action was promised on individual dismissals, workers' privacy and aspects of working time (excluded from the 1993 Directive) but to date little progress has been made on any of these issues. In the 1996 work programme of 102 initiatives only 19 were legislative proposals. The remainder were 35 initiatives to stimulate public discussion and 48 action plans or other such initiatives. The 1997 work programme[178] is even more minimalist with attention focussed upon action in the area the composition of the crew of ships, rest time and sailing time and a European voluntary service for young people. The rest of the programme is devoted to tackling the macro-economic problems of unemployment.

In June 1997 we have the promise of a new Treaty of Amsterdam - and with a new administration in the UK - the chance to incorporate the SPA into the main body of the EC Treaty. The IGC Meetings have taken place in an atmosphere of perceived crisis in the legitimacy of the EU and its uncertain journey into even closer economic and political integration. This has mobilised the forces of political realism to attach importance to creating a constitutional order which recognises, *inter alia*, certain basic individual social and political rights to citizenship, democratic participation and human rights. A memoran-

---

[174] Recommendation 92/441 on commmon criteria concerning sufficient resources and social action in social protection schemes, OJ 1992 L 245/46 and Recommendation 92/442 on the convergence of social policy objectives and policies, OJ 1992 C 245/49.

[175] See Commission, *Medium Term Action Programme to Control Exclusion and Promote Solidarity,* COM (95) 457.

[176] COM(95) 435.

[177] COM (95) 512 final.

[178] COM(96)507.

dum and text prepared by Professors Blanpain, Hepple, Sciarra and Weiss suggests the amendment to Article 117 EC to set out a framework of fundamental social rights.[179] This would be a statement of common social and political values of democratic European societies drawn into a "fidelity clause" similar to Article 5 EC. These values would be gleaned from the Member States' Constitutions and international human social rights documents. In addition a list of ten specific rights are identified, including a general equality standard. These rights are not seen as static but it is proposed that there content would change in the light of economic and social developments. The Commission established a Comité des Sages which produced a Report, *For A Europe of Civic and Social Rights.* This Report proposed, *inter alia,* that the current IGC should consider incorporating fundamental social and civic rights into the EC Treaty. These calls for a broader, fundamental/human rights perspective to social policy may be reflected in the final draft of the Treaty of Amsterdam. In December 1996 the Irish Presidency of the Council produced a *General Outline For A Draft Revision of the Treaties, The European Union Today and Tomorrow, Adapting The European Union For The Benefit of Its Peoples and Preparing It For The Future.*[180] In Section II entitled "The Union and The Citizen" there are proposals for an Employment Chapter and a Chapter on Social Provisions. There are also proposals to strengthen the protection of fundamental human rights in Community law ( a new Article Fa TEU) and increase judicial control of repect for human rights (a new Article 3c EC). The proposal for a new Article 6a EC creating a general non-discrimination clause covering sex, racial, ethnic or social origin, religious belief, disability, age and sexual orientation is discussed in Chapter Four.

## 1.12. THE FUTURE OF THE SOCIAL DIALOGUE

The TEU and the priority given to employment - and attacking unemployment[181] - has given unprecedented attention to the future development of the social dialogue. The Commission sees social partners as key actors in the future development of social policy and has been eager to involve the social partners in the current plans for the European Confidence Pact For Employment. In the *Communication on the Development of the Social*

---

[179] *Fundamental Social Rights: Proposals For the European Union* (1995). See also Hepple (1995).

[180] CONF 2500/96, Brussels 5 December 1996.

[181] See Commission, *White Paper on Growth, Competiveness and Employment*, COM (93) 700.

*Dialogue at Community Level*[182] the Commission evaluated the progress of the social dialogue, raising a series of questions for the social partners, the Member States and the EU Insitutions to address by the end of 1996. It is envisaged that a second Communication will be issued in 1997 based on these responses. A number of general issues for the overall development of the dialogue are raised, for example, it is suggested that the social dialogue should focus upon the employment/unemployment issue at a sectoral and intersectoral level since the social partners have a key role to play in determining working conditions, particularly issues such as flexibility but also issues such as training and the intergration of young people into the labour market. The Commission also sees itself as a facilitative tool to develop links and practical co-operation with the social partners in Central and Eastern Europe. Other joint initiatives are planned such as the European Centre For Industrial Relations and the need to assist the development of new levels of social dialogue in transnational industries and at a regional level, particularly in the cross- border regions. The Commission's evaluation of the *Val Duchesse* dialogue is such that it believes the dialogue has made positive contribution and helped stimulate and orientate Community developments in the areas of employment, macro-economic policy and training as well as drafting parts of the SPA. However it is acknowledged that the results of the social dialogue are not made sufficiently clear to the social partners at grassroots level and that greater transparency and awareness are required.

## 1.13. CRYSTAL BALL GAZING

EU social policy has a number of economic and political factors to adjust to. Although crystal ball gazing is not our speciality there are two particular certaintities which need addressing. First, the effects of meeting the convergence criteria for the second stage of EMU are now being felt - quite harshly in some Member States: Germany, France and Spain are experiencing dramatic unemployment levels. There is, therefore, the need for labour market adjustments to tackle structural problems which perhaps cannot be solved durably by exchange rate adjustments anyway. Does this mean a policy of further de-regulation, liberalisation of non-trade goods and service sectors and further "reform" of labour market institutions? Intervention at the EU level can both ease adjustment by assuming minimal social policy standards or it can act as a constraint.[183]

---

[182] COM(96) 448 final.

[183] See Addison and Siebert(1997).

The second factor is the re-drawing of the economic and political map of Europe. We have already touched upon the impact the countries of Central and Eastern Europe will have upon the Structural Funds. But other scenarios need consideration Krugman and Venables[184] argue that integration may lead to changes in the *location* of industries in the EU. Who would have believed, say five years ago, that Ireland would now be described as the "Euro-Tiger" economy? Krugman and Venables argue that it is likely that European industries will become much more concentrated rather like the industrial geography of the United States. This will result in major adjustment costs making the peripheral regions of Europe vulnerable to de-industrialisation and focussing concern on redistributive social policy issues. But they may be a different scenario. We are already witnessing German capital moving to the Czech Republic and Poland in an effort to dilute the high labour costs in Germany and recapture global competivity. New patterns of investment are also occurring from Finland and Sweden into the Baltic states of Estonia, Latvia and Lithuania and German, United States and Japanese investment in the Czech Republic, Poland and Hungary, (particularly in the motor vehicle industry) similar to the pattern witnessed with Japanese capital into the Tiger economies of Asia. This again will compel the EU to analyse the role of social policy in the wider Europe in any new Accession agreements - and maybe re-think its attitude towards the existing Europe Agreements.

---

[184] Krugman and Venables (1996).

# CHAPTER TWO

## FREE MOVEMENT OF PERSONS

### 2.1. THE PARAMETERS OF THE PRINCIPLE OF FREE MOVEMENT OF PERSONS

The free movement of persons within the EU is one of the fundamental tenets of the Internal Market. Articles 3(c), 7a, 8a and 48-66 EC guarantee this freedom as a basic principle of EC law in the areas of citizenship rights, workers, provision and receipt of services and establishment. In addition, the right to free movement of persons has been elevated into one of the fundamental rights of EC law by the ECJ[1] and extensive immigration and social rights have been granted to members of a migrant's family. Rights of residence have been granted specifically to students, retired persons and to people who have sufficient funds and social security insurance to remain independent in another Member State.[2] While the EU has taken an approach towards market liberalisation similar to that adopted in relation to the free movement of goods the parallels between the economic freedoms have diverged since Member States have been reluctant to dismantle all immigration control over the internal borders within the EU and give competence to the EC/EU to maintain an external frontier for Third Country Nationals (TCNs) wishing to enter the EU. Nationals of the European Economic Area states also have a right to free movement in the EU and the EU has implemented a number of international agreements which grant limited rights to enter the EU to engage in economic activities for non-EU nationals from the signatory states.[3]

Despite the advanced nature of the right to free movement of persons a number of legal problems and political controversies remain to be tackled. These concern firstly, the question as to whether there is truly an Internal

---

[1]  See Arnull (1990).

[2]  Council Directive 90/364/EEC OJ 1990 L 180/26; Council Directive 90/365/EEC OJ 1990 L 180/28; Council Directive 93/96/EEC OJ 1993 L 317/59.

[3]  See Cremona (1995); Peers (1996a).

Market for persons or whether Member States retain a discretion to continue with immigration checks and to ban or deport undesirable people from their territory. The current IGC is considering creating even further competence for the EU to develop cooperation in the intergovernmental sphere relating to justice and home affairs and immigration issues. Secondly, how can the EC/EU develop competence to give immigration and social rights to TCN's? Thirdly, there is the issue of reverse discrimination - can a Member State give its own nationals lesser rights than would be accorded to them under Community law if they had taken advantage of the free movement provisions? Finally, there is the political reality to confront that the Schengen Agreement,[4] operating outside the ambit of Community law, has already created a "frontier free" Europe for the majority of the Member States. Although some Member States have not signed the Agreement or are not full members, by virtue of Article 6 EC the other Schengen Member States must grant similar rights to non-signatory Member States nationals. Fears have been expressed that the Schengen Agreement dilutes some of the rights already available, especially to refugees, under international law.[5] A Working Group under the Chair of Mme Weil has been established to investigate and make proposals to counteract the remaining barriers to the free movement of persons.[6]

## 2.2. LEGAL BASIS OF THE RIGHT TO FREE MOVEMENT

Article 8a EC grants to nationals of one of the EU Member States a right to free movement. It is not yet clear whether Article 8a EC is directly effective since Article 8a(2) EC envisages further implementing legislation to realise this right. The relationship between Article 8a EC and the original rights to free movement based upon the exercise of an economic activity in Articles 48-66 EC must be resolved. In some respects the latter rights are broader since they allow family migration but they are also narrower since they are specifically centered around concepts of work, provision (and receipt) of services and establishment and are hedged with exclusions and derogations. Although the ECJ has stated that it is unnecessary to draw fine distinctions between the concepts of worker, services and establishment[7] it is rather odd

---

[4]   (1991) ILM 73.

[5]   O'Keeffe (1995); Schutte (1991).

[6]   See *Medium Term Social Action Programme 1995-1997* COM (95) 134 final, 13.

[7]   Case 48/75 *Procureur de Roi v Royer* [1976] ECR 497; Case C-363/89 *Roux v Belgium State* [1991] ECR I-273; Case C-19/92 *Kraus v Land Baden-Würtemburg* [1993] ECR

and confusing to find the different rules for each of these categories still in place after the introduction of Article 8a EC. In the Commission's *First Report On Citizenship*[8] the Commission announced that it intended to introduce a new, unitary legal text to codify the existing case law on free movement of persons and residence.

The biggest limitation of the Citizenship provisions is that they crystallise around the right to be a national of a Member State which is left to the Member States to determine.[9] The ECJ has made some inroads into the Member States' sovereignty, however, by drawing a fine distinction between the right to determine nationality questions and the *exercise* of that right under Community law. For example, in *Airola v Commission*[10] the Court ruled that compulsory acquisition of a second nationality in compliance with the nationality law of a Member State may not be recognised for the purposes of Community law. In *Michelleti and others v Delegacion del Gobierno en Cantabria*[11] the Spanish authorities refused to issue a card identifying Michelleti as a Community national since he held both Argentian and Italian nationality and under the Spanish Civil Code the Argentian nationality took precedence. The ECJ ruled that a Member State was not entitled to restrict the effects of the attribution of the nationality of another Member State by imposing an additional condition on recognition of that nationality for the purpose of exercising a fundamental freedom ( in this case the right to free movement to exercise a profession). If a person was able to produce one of the documents referred to in Council Directive 73/148/EEC[12] in order to prove that they were nationals of a Member State, other Member States were not entitled to dispute that status.

---

I-1663. In a later case, Case C-55/94 *Gebhard* [1995] ECR I-4165 the Court states that the three sets of provisions are mutually exclusive with the provisions on the Chapter relating to the free movement of services being subordinate to those on establishment in so far as Article 59(1) EC assumes that the provider and the recipient of the service are "established" in two different Member States and Article 60(1) EC specifies that the provisions relating to services apply only if the provisions relating to establishment do not apply.

[8]   COM(93) 702 final, 5.

[9]   See Greenwood (1988); O'Leary (1992; 1995); Hall (1995); Hall (1996).

[10]   Case 21/74 [1975] ECR 221.

[11]   Case C-369/90 [1992] ECR I-4265.

[12]   OJ 1993 L 172/14.

## 2.3. WORKERS

Article 48 EC is directly effective[13] and grants the right of free movement to workers who have the nationality of one of the Member States and who have crossed an internal frontier in order to take up an offer of employment. The Court has held that the provisions of Community law may apply to the pursuit of professional activities outside of the EU provided the employment relationship retains a sufficiently close link with the Community.[14] The provisions also have an element of extra-territorial effect in that they also cover the situation where a worker is employed outside of the EU but the contract of employment is governed by the law of one of the Member States. This was the situation in *Boukhalfa* v *Bundesrepupublik Deutschland*[15] where a Belgian national was employed in the passport office in the German embassy in Algiers. Her contract of employment was concluded in Algiers where the applicant was already in permanent residence. The contract stated that the terms of the contract would be in accordance with Algerian law. However the applicant paid contributions to a German state pension fund and was subject, to a limited extent, to the German tax system. There was also a clause in her contract giving jurisdiction of any disputes to Bonn and Berlin. Boukhalfa complained that there were discriminatory rules in her contract which gave non-Germans less favourable rights than those local employees with German nationality. The German government defended the discrimination on the grounds that the employment was outside the territorial scope of the EC Treaty (Article 227 EC). The Court found that there was a sufficiently close link to the law of Germany since the contract of employment was in accordance with the Member State's rules which employed her with the stipulation that the conditions of employment were to be determined by Algerian law. At paragraph 17 the Court states "... the prohibition of discrimination based on nationality ... is applicable to all aspects of the employment relationship which are governed by the law of a Member State."

The provisions relating to the free movement of workers were put in place ahead of schedule by 1968. In contrast little headway was made with the right

---

[13]  Article 48 EC has both vertical and horizontal direct effect: Case 167/73 *Commission v France* [1974] ECR 359; Case 36/74 *Walrave and Koch v AUCI* [1974] ECR 1405; Case 13/76 *Dona v Mantero* [1976] ECR 1333; Case C-415/93 *Union Royal Belge des Societies de Football Association ASBL v Bosman* [1995] ECR I-4921.

[14]  Case 237/83 *Prodest v Caisse Primaire d'Assurance Maladie de Paris* [1984] ECR 3153; Case 9/88 *Lopes da Veiga v Staatssecretaris van Financien* [1989] ECR I-2989.

[15]  Case C-214/94 [1996] ECR I-2253.

of establishment and services since in the early years of the Common Market there was disagreement as to how much co-ordination could be achieved. Since the professions are usually highly regulated the problem of coordination was - and still is - a complex one.[16]

## 2.3.1. Concept of Worker

The ECJ ruled that the terms "worker" and "activity as an employed person" must have an EC law meaning otherwise the rules relating to free movement would be frustrated since Member States could fix and modify unilaterally national laws thus excluding certain persons from the free movement provisions.[17] The ECJ has provided a flexible definition of the concept of worker. In *Levin v Staatssecretaris van Justitie*[18] the ECJ included part-time work where the worker supplemented her income from private sources within Article 48 EC. This was extended in *Kempf v Staatssecretaris van Justitie*[19] to include a part-time worker who supplemented his earnings with social assistance provided from public funds. The ECJ has stated that the work must be "effective and genuine." Trainee teachers have also been included within the definition of "worker."[20] In contrast the Court took a more restrictive approach in *Bettray v Staatssecretaris van Justitie*[21] ruling that a German national taking part in a rehabilitation scheme for drug addicts financed from public funds was not a "worker" within the scope of Article 48 EC. It was argued by the Court that the work was not an "effective and genuine activity" since it constituted merely a means of rehabilitation or reintegration into society. People were not selected on their capacity to perform a certain activity. On the contrary, the "work" was chosen in the light of the capabilities of the person on the scheme to re-establish or develop their capacity for work. Here the Court seems to be looking at the reason or purpose for undertaking work. Arguably retraining and the reintegration of people excluded from the labour market, is part of the needs of a smooth functioning Internal Market.

---

[16]  See Laslett (1990/91); Bercusson (1996) 386-396.

[17]  Case 75/63 *Unger v Bestuur* [1964] ECR 1977.

[18]  Case 53/81 [1982] ECR 1035.

[19]  Case 139/85 [1986] ECR 1741.

[20]  Case 66/85 *Lawrie Blum v Land Baden-Württemberg* [1986] ECR 2121.

[21]  Case 344/87 [1989] ECR 1621.

This restrictive ruling might be compared with the generous rulings where workers have left their employment to take up studies and have claimed equality with host state nationals under Article 6 EC and Article 7 of Regulation 1612/68/EEC.[22]

For the last few decades Europe has seen high levels of unemployment and the fight against unemployment was singled out as a priority at the Essen Summit 1994. Again, as a market correcting device, one would expect the principle of free movement to allow individuals to travel within the EU to seek work and optimise their skills. The Member States have been reluctant to encourage this where the burden of unemployment benefits would be transferred between social security budgets. This is seen, for example, in the qualification included in the Rights of Residence Directives that the person claiming the right of residence must have sufficient resources or insurance to avoid becoming a burden on the host state.[23] In the minutes of the Council Meeting when Council Directive 68/360/EEC[24] was adopted the Member States agreed that a person could enter a Member State to look for work for a period of three months provided that he/she did not become a burden on the state. In *Antonissen*[25] the Court ruled that this Declaration was of no legal significance. The Court held that where a potential migrant worker had not found work after the three month period and could not provide evidence that he/she was continuing to seek employment with a genuine chance of being engaged, then a Member State can ask the migrant to leave its territory. The amount of time a person has been unemployed will be a factor in deciding whether it is reasonable to deport an unemployed person.[26] Since these cases were decided before Article 8a EC was introduced it is likely that an unemployed person would be able to remain in the host state for longer, subject to any limitations which are imposed upon the operation of Article 8a EC. In *Commission v Belgium*[27] the ECJ upheld a complaint by the Commission that Belgium was in breach of Article 48 EC and the ruling in *Antonissen* by requiring nationals of other Member States who are seeking work to leave

---

[22] Case C-357/89 *Raulin* [1992] ECR I-1027; Case C-3/90 *Bernini* [1992] ECR I-1071.

[23] Council Directive 90/364/EEC, Article 1; Council Directive 90/365/EEC, Article 1; Council Directive 93/96/EEC, Article 1.

[24] OJ 1968 L 257/13.

[25] Case C-292/89 [1991] ECR I-745.

[26] Case C-171/91 *Tsiotras v Landeshauptstadt Stuttgart* [1993] ECR I-2925.

[27] Case C-344/95 judgment of 20 February 1997.

its territory after a period of three months. Belgium law was also found to contravene Community law by issuing two successive registration certificates instead of a residence permit to people holding employment for at least one year and by requiring payment for those certificates and by asking for payment for certificates granted to seasonal workers.

## 2.3.2. Employment in the Public Service

Article 48(4) EC excludes "employment in the public service" from the scope of Community law. The difficulty is that each Member State has its own particular concept of the "public service" with a wide range of public sector posts falling within national definitions. The ECJ has ruled that the concept of the "public service" in Article 48(4) EC must have a Community law meaning and any criteria applied must be functional, taking account of the nature of the tasks, responsibilities inherent in the post.

In *Sotgiu v Deutsche Bundespost* the ECJ stated that since Article 48(4) EC was a derogation from the principle of free movement it must be interpreted restrictively. The Court ruled that the national rules governing the employment relationship were immaterial. Sotgiu was complaining about the terms on which he was employed and the ECJ ruled that the derogation contained in Article 48(4) EC only applied to access to the public service. The provision cannot be used to justify discriminatory measures against workers once they have been admitted to the public service.[28] The very fact that a worker has been admitted to the public service indicates that those interests which justify the derogation are not at issue.

A decisive step in providing a Community definition of the concept of the public service was taken in *Commission v Belgium (No 1)*. The ECJ provided two criteria[29] to be applied to determine if a post fell within Article 48(4) EC:

*first*: direct or indirect participation in the exercise of powers conferred by public law

*second*: the duties were designed to safeguard the interests of the State or other public authorities.

---

[28] See also Case 225/85 *Commission v Italy* [1987] ECR 2625.

[29] Cf O'Keeffe (1992a) who presumes the criteria are cumulative with Handoll (1988) who argues that they are alternatives.

The test to be applied is, therefore a functional one. In *Commission v France*[30] the post of a nurse in a public hospital was held to fall outside of the scope of Article 48(4) EC. Other cases have involved teaching posts within the framework of civil service schemes,[31] state universities[32] and secondary schools as well as research posts in the Italian National Research Council.

The Commission adopted an Action Plan for elimination of restrictions on the grounds of nationality in access to posts in the public sector.[33] This codifies the Court's case law, listing in general terms categories of posts which fall within the public service exception, such as the police, armed forces, judiciary, tax authorities, diplomatic corps and post which fall outside of Article 48(4) EC such as commercial services, public health services, teaching in state educational establishments and research for non-military purposes in public establishments.

Despite the Commission's campaign to open up the public service discrimination still continues. In *Scholz v Opera Universitaria di Cagliari*[34] a German woman who had acquired Italian nationality through marriage successfully challenged the rejection of her application for a post working in a canteen in an Italian university. Her previous experience in the German public service was not taken into account whereas previous service in an *Italian* public service post would have been taken into account. The ECJ ruled that indirect discrimination had taken place.

There is some speculation as to how far notions of "public service" can survive in the Internal Market and the moves towards ideas of Citizenship of the Union. O'Keeffe has pointed out that the view that only nationals of a Member State can carry out sensitive tasks is based upon a very traditional notion of loyalty to the State, finding its parallel in the denial to foreigners of political rights.[35]

---

[30]  Case 307/84 [1986] ECR 1725.

[31]  Case 66/85 *Lawrie-Blum* [1986] ECR 2121.

[32]  Case 33/88 *Allué and Coonan v Auniversita delgi Studi di Venezia* [1989] ECR 1591.

[33]  OJ 1988 C 72/2. A series of infringement actions have followed: Case C-473/93 *Commission v Luxembourg* nyr; Case C-173/94 *Commission v Belgium* nyr; Case C-290/94 *Commission v Greece* nyr.

[34]  Case C-419/92 [1994] ECR I-505.

[35]  O'Keeffe (1992b).

## 2.4. BEYOND DISCRIMINATION: A MARKET INTEGRATION APPROACH?

The Court has moved beyond a pure non-discrimination approach to an analysis of measures which, although not discriminatory, are nevertheless a hindrance to the principle of free movement. The facts of the *Bosman*[36] case concern the rules governing European football,[37] drawn up by FIFA and UEFA on the transfer of football players. Under the governing bodies' rules a footballer was not free to work out his contract and then go onto the market to conclude a new contract with a new football club without the new club paying a transfer fee. The FIFA/UEFA rules also restricted the number of foreign players who could play in national league football teams. Bosman, a Belgian footballer who had negotiated a new contract with a French football club, was unable to take up the offer of employment because his own club would not forward the relevant transfer documents. He challenged the rules as restricting the employment opportunities of footballers throughout the EU. The Court accepted his argument. It argued that the rules relating to free movement of persons are intended to facilitate the pursuit by EU citizens of occupational activities of all kinds and preclude measures which disadvantage EU citizens from pursuing such occupational activities in another Member State. Thus provisions which *deterred or precluded* an EU citizens from leaving the home state would fall foul of EC law even if they applied irrespective of the nationality of the individual concerned since they constituted an obstacle to the free movement principle.

## 2.5. IMMIGRATION AND SOCIAL RIGHTS OF FAMILY MEMBERS

Article 10 of Regulation 1612/68/EEC allows a migrant worker to bring with him to the host state a fairly extensive list of family members irrespective of their nationality, *ie* they may be third country nationals. The list comprises: the spouse and the descendants under the age of twenty-one of the migrant worker, descendants over the age of twenty-one may also be admitted if they are dependent upon the migrant worker. Dependant relatives in the ascending line of the migrant worker and his/her spouse are also to be admitted. In addition Member States are encouraged to facilitate the admission of any family member not falling within these categories if they are dependent upon the migrant worker or living under his/her roof in the home state. The only proviso

---

[36]  Case C-415/93 [1995] ECR I-4705.

[37]  For a more detailed explanation see Weatherill (1996).

is contained in Article 10(3) of Regulation 1612/68/EEC that the migrant worker must have housing available for the family which is considered as normal for the location. In *Commission v Germany*[38] the Court ruled that this proviso only applies to *first entry* of the migrant's family and cannot be used later to justify the non-renewal of residence permits.

The Court has not been persuaded to expand the categories of family members outlined in Article 10 to include cohabitees. In *Netherlands v Reed*[39] a British national could not rely upon Article 10 to secure a residence permit for her cohabitee in the Netherlands. The Court did accept that since foreigners with a stable cohabiting relationship with a Dutch national were entitled to reside in the Netherlands it would amount to discrimination in breach of Article 6 EC and Article 7(2) of Regulation 1612/68/EEC to deny such social benefits to a Community migrant worker. It remains to be seen if gay/lesbian or transsexual relationships are accepted by the Court as falling within the EC provisions relating to family migration.

Another issue, which has not been explored fully by the Court, is whether a non-EC spouse enjoys the right to remain in the host state after a marriage has ended. This right is enjoyed after the death of a migrant worker by virtue of Regulation 1251/70/EEC.[40] In *Diatta v Land of Berlin*[41] a Senegalese wife of a migrant worker in Germany was living apart from her husband. The couple intended to divorce but the marriage had not been dissolved. The Court pointed out that in order for a spouse to exercise her right to work in the host state under Article 11 of Regulation 1612/68 it may be necessary for couples to live apart. Until the marriage had been annulled the non-EC spouse enjoyed the protection of EC law. A similar approach was taken in *Surinder Singh*[42] where EC law was used against action taken by the home state to deport an Indian spouse whose marriage had broken up when the couple returned to the UK after working in Germany.[43]

---

[38] Case 249/86 [1989] ECR 1263.

[39] Case 59/85 [1986] ECR 1283.

[40] OJ Sp. Ed.1970 L 142/24, 402.

[41] Case 267/83 [1986] ECR 567.

[42] Case C-370/90 [1992] ECR I-4265.

[43] Although the Court does not discuss the issue in this case or in the *Surinder Singh* case discussed below it is presumed that once the marriage is annulled the divorced spouse would not be protected by EC law.

Article 11 of Regulation 1612/68/EEC grants the right to take up an activity as an employed person in the host state to the spouse and children of the migrant worker. In *Gül v Regierungspräsident Düsseldorf*[44] a Cypriot doctor married to a British woman working in Germany was not allowed to practice medicine since the German authorities argued that the practice of medicine was subject to special professional rules. The Court, referring to the fundamental nature of the rules relating to the free movement of persons, found that there was no limitation to the field of activities open to the spouse of a migrant worker. Article 12 of Regulation 1612/68/EEC provides for the right to equal access for the children of a migrant worker to the host state's educational system.

In *Landesamt für Ausbildungsforung Nordrhein-Westfalen v Gaal*[45] the Court ruled that the limitations on age and dependancy found in Article 10 of Regulation 1612/68/EEC could not be read into Article 12 of that Regulation. The Court ruled that the principle of equal treatment found in Article 12 extended to all forms of education, vocational, general and university courses and that the principle required the child of a migrant worker to be able to continue his/her studies in order to be able to complete his/her education successfully. The Court went on to conclude that Article 12 embraced financial assistance for those students who were at an advanced stage in their education even if they were over the age of twenty-one and no longer dependent on their parents.

An important development occurred in *Forcheri v Belgian State*[46] when the *wife* of an Italian worker challenged the "minerval" - the special fee charged to foreign students in Belgium. Forcheri claimed that the fee was contrary to Articles 6 and 48 EC and Article 12 of Regulation 1612/68/EEC. But Article 12 only applies to the *children of the migrant worker*. The Court looked to the fifth recital to the Preamble to Regulation 1612/68/EEC to support the view that it was contrary to EC law where a Member State charged a discriminatory fee against a Community national lawfully established in the host state. The fact that Forcheri was a favoured Community citizen brought her within the scope of EC law. One wonders whether the Court would stretch this reasoning even further if a similar claim was brought by a non-EC spouse?

---

[44] Case 131/85 [1986] 1573.

[45] Case C-7/94 [1995] ECR I-1031.

[46] Case 152/82 [1983] ECR 2323.

Council Directive 77/486/EEC[47] relates to the provision of education facilities for the education of migrant workers' children. Attached to the Directive is a Declaration encouraging the Member States to provide educational facilities for the children of non-EC migrants.[48]

## 2.6. THE RIGHT TO ENTER AND RESIDE IN A MEMBER STATE

Rights of entry and residence of the migrant worker and his/her family to the host state are governed by Council Directive 68/360/EEC.[49]
These rights comprise:

- the right to leave the home state in order for the worker to pursue activities as an employed person in another Member State (Article 2)
- the right to enter the territory of another Member State simply on production of a valid identity card or passport (Article 3(1)). Entry visas may not be demanded except in the case of members of the family who are not Community nationals and Member States are required to accord to such persons every facility for obtaining the necessary visas (Article 3(2)
- the right to obtain a residence permit on production of the document with which the migrant worker entered the host state and a confirmation of engagement from the employer or a certificate of employment (Article 4(3)(a) and (b). This right is not subject to any conditions relating to the kind of employment or the amount of income derived from it.[50]
- the right to obtain a residence permit by members of the family on production of their document of entry, a document proving their relationship with the worker (to be issued by the competent authority of the state of origin) and, if necessary, proving they are dependent on the worker or living under his/her roof in the home state (Article 4(3)(c)(d)(e)).
- the right to a residence permit valid throughout the territory of the host state for a period of at least five years (Article 6)
- the right to automatic renewal of the residence permit (Article 6)

---

[47] OJ 1977 L 199/32.

[48] See Cullen (1996); COM (94) 80 final.

[49] OJ Sp. Ed. 1968 L 257/13.

[50] In Case C-376/89 *Giagounnidis v City of Reutlingen* [1991] ECR I-1069 a migrant worker in Germany held a Greek national identity card of indefinite duration. Under Greek law such a document could not be used in order to leave Greece. The Greek authorities refused to extend his passport and so, in order to extend his residence permit, Giagounidis presented his identity card. The German authorities refused to accept this document. The Court ruled that the sole purpose of the identity card was to establish the identity and the nationality of the person claiming the right of residence.

- the right to break the residence in the host state for six months or fulfil military service without affecting the validity of the residence permit (Article 6(2))
- the right to a residence permit when the migrant worker is temporarily unemployed as a result of illness or accident or involuntary unemployment (Article 7(1)) although when the residence permit is renewed for the first time the period of residence may be restricted to not less than twelve consecutive months if the migrant worker has been involuntary unemployed for more than twelve consecutive months (Article 7(2)). Voluntary unemployment is to be determined by the competent employment office.
- the right of a temporary worker working from three to twelve months to a temporary residence permit for the duration of their employment (Article 6(3)); the right of a seasonal or temporary worker working less than three months to reside without a residence permit (Article 8)

The Court has interpreted these provisions liberally in favour of the migrant worker. In *Procureur du Roi* v *Royer[51]* the Court ruled that the worker's right to reside in the host state is *not* dependent on possession of a residence permit. The right of residence is a fundamental right derived from the Treaty of Rome 1957. The Court also ruled that the right of entry contained in Article 3 included the right to enter and search for work. However in *Antonissen[52]* it was held to be lawful for a Member State to deport a worker if he/she had not found work within months and cannot show that they are continuing to seek work and have a genuine chance of being engaged within a reasonable period of time. In *R v Pieck[53]* the Court ruled that Article 3(2) (which prohibits a Member State from demanding an entry visa or equivalent requirement from a migrant worker) must be interpreted as covering any formality for the purpose of granting leave to enter the territory of a Member State.

## 2.7. INTERNAL FRONTIER CONTROLS

The Commission saw its original objective as doing away with internal frontier controls in their entirety on the completion of the Internal Market.[54] This has not occurred, and some Member States, most notably the United Kingdom, argue that there still is a sovereign right to maintain border controls since the right to free movement of persons is not absolute. In a Communication to the

---

[51] Case 48/75 [1976] ECR 497.

[52] Case C-292/89 [1991] ECR I-745.

[53] Case 157/79 [1980] ECR 2171.

[54] EC Commission, White Paper, *Completing the Internal Market*, COM(85) 310 final, para 27.

Council of Ministers the Commission has argued that Article 7a EC has direct effect.[55] The European Parliament initiated an Article 175 EC action against the EC Commission for failing to present the necessary measures to realise the Internal Market but the President of the Court issued an order withdrawing the case on 11 July 1996 as a result of the Commission issuing a package of proposals.[56] In his Opinion in *Messner*[57] , Advocate General Mischo clearly envisaged that post-1992 Member States could retain some control over foreigners in their territory but entered the caveat that such controls should not restrict the free movement of persons unnecessarily. In *Commission v Belgium*[58] the ECJ ruled that EC law did not prevent a Member State from carrying out checks on residence and establishment permits and requiring such permits to be carried at all times when identical obligations were placed upon its own nationals. But such checks could not be a condition of entry to the Member States and could constitute a barrier to free movement if carried out in a systematic, arbitrary and unnecessarily restrictive manner. In *Watson and Belmann*[59] and *Messner*[60] the Court found that a requirement to register with the Italian authorities within three days of entering Italy with severe penalties imposed for non-compliance did not satisfy the Community principle of proportionality.

---

[55]   EC (92) 877 final, 8 May 1992.

[56]   Case C-445/93. The proposals comprise a proposal on the abolition of internal border controls on all people on the basis of Articles 7a EC and 100 EC COM(95) 347 final; a proposal for a European Parliament and Council Directive amending Directive 68/360/EEC and Council Directive 73/148/EEC, COM(95) 348 final; a proposal for a Council Directive on the right of third country nationals to travel in the Community, COM(95) 348 final. See the Editorial, (1996) 33 CMLRev. 1; Peers (1997a).

[57]   Case C-265/88 [1989] ECR 4209.

[58]   Case 321/87 [1989] ECR 997. See also Case C-68/89 *Commission v Netherlands* [1991] ECR 2637.

[59]   Case 118/75 [1976] ECR 11185.

[60]   Case C-265/88 [1989] ECR 4209.

## 2.8. EMPLOYMENT AND EQUALITY OF TREATMENT

### 2.8.1. The Ban on Discrimination

Articles 6 and 48(2) EC provide for the elimination of all discrimination based on nationality.[61] These provisions have been interpreted narrowly to apply only to people holding the nationality of one of the Member States.[62] A discussion of the moves to bring race discrimination within the ambit of Community law is to be found in Chapter Four. The principle of equality is a fundamental right of Community law and in relation to the ban on nationality discrimination covers both overt and covert (indirect) discrimination.[63]

In *Criminal Proceedings Against Skanavi and Chryssanthakopoulos*[64] the Court ruled that Article 6 EC applied independently only to situations covered by Community law where the Treaty does not lay down a specific prohibition on discrimination. Thus where a specific Treaty provision applies, Article 6 need not be considered. *Skanavi* was a Greek national working in Germany where she failed to exchange her Greek driving licence for a German one within one year of taking up residence as required by Directive 80/1263/EEC. She was prosecuted for driving without a licence and fined 3000 DM. This offence took place after harmonisation measures came into effect on 1 July 1994 by virtue of Directive 91/439/EEC (which repealed Directive 80/1263 from 1 July 1996). In an earlier case, *Choquet*,[65] the Court accepted that national rules relating to the issue and mutual recognition of driving licences by the Member States have an influence on the free movement of persons provisions. However the Court ruled that now harmonisation measures were in place it was *lawful* for a Member State to impose an obligation upon migrants to exchange their driving licences. The Court then went on to consider whether the penalties imposed for failing to exchange a driving licence were compatible with Community law. Looking first at whether treating a person who had failed to carry out an exchange could be treated as a person who was driving without a licence the Court argued that the original

---

[61]  See Sundberg-Weitmann (1977).

[62]  Szyszczak (1992a).

[63]  Case 152/73 *Sotgiu v Deutsche Budespost* [1974] ECR 153; Case 33/88 *Allué and Coonan v Universitia degli Studi di Venezia* [1989] ECR 1591.

[64]  Case C-193/94 [1996] ECR I-929.

[65]  Case 16/78 [1978] ECR 2293.

driving licence from the home state was still valid - in the state where it was issued and in other Member States. Consequently the issue of a new licence in the host state does not grant the right to drive a vehicle in the host state which is directly conferred by Community law but merely evidence of the existence of that right. Thus the obligation to exchange driving licences was merely an administrative requirement. Treating a Community migrant as driving without a licence and the attraction of criminal penalties to the offence was disproportionate and also a barrier to the right to free movement since it would have consequences for employment or the carrying out of professional activities in the host state.

Detailed provisions relating to non-discrimination and equality of treatment are laid down in Regulation 1612/68/EEC. According to Article 3 of Regulation 1612/68/EEC provisions laid down by law, regulation or administrative practices of the Member States shall not apply where they limit applications for, and offers of, employment, or the right of foreign nationals to take up and pursue employment or subject these offers to conditions not applicable in respect of their own nationals. In *Groener v Minister for Education*[66] a Dutch teacher of art was required to demonstrate proficiency in the Gaelic language in order to get a permanent teaching post in a public vocational training college in Dublin. She contended that the requirement was a violation of Article 48(2) EC and Article 3 of Regulation 1612/68/EEC since it was harder for foreign nationals to prove proficiency in Gaelic than it was for Irish nationals to comply with the requirement. The Court accepted that it was possible to justify such a requirement if it could be shown that it was part of a policy for the preservation of the national language and that the requirement satisfied the principle of proportionality.

### 2.8.2. Conditions of Work

Articles 7-9 of Regulation 1612/68/EEC flesh out the non-discrimination principle in relation to migrant workers' rights. The Court has extended these principles to *members of the migrant worker's family*.[67] Article 7(1) covers direct and indirect discrimination[68] in respect of any conditions of employment

---

[66]  Case 379/87 [1989] ECR 3967.

[67]  Case 32/75 *Fiorini v SNCF* [1975] ECR 1085; Case 261/83 *Castelli v ONPTS* [1984] ECR 3199; Case 249/83 *Hoeckx v Centre Public d'Aide Sociale de Kalmthout* [1985] ECR 973.

[68]  Case 15/69 *Wurttembergische Milchverwertung-Sudmilch-AG v Uglioa* [1969] ECR 363; Case 152/73 *Sotgiu v Deutsche Bundespost* [1974] ECR 153.

and work in particular as regards remuneration, dismissal and, if the worker becomes unemployed, reinstatement and re-employment.

### 2.8.3. Tax and Social Advantages

The principle of equal treatment is defined broadly in Article 7 of Regulation 1612/68/EEC to allow the worker - and his/her family to integrate fully into the host Member State.[69] Article 7(2) grants the migrant worker the same social and tax advantages as national workers.[70] Direct and indirect discrimination is caught by the provision.[71] The term "social advantage" has been given a wide definition by the Court and covers social advantages given to workers and their families outside the contract of employment[72] and even advantages granted on a discretionary basis.[73] In *Ministere Public v Even* [74] the ECJ defined "social advantages" as benefits

"which, whether or not linked to a contract of employment, are generally granted to national workers primarily because of their objective status as workers or by virtue of the mere fact of their residence on the national territory and the extension of which to workers who are nationals of other member states therefore seems suitable to facilitate their mobility within the Community."

There are some limits on the scope of Article 7(2). For example, in *Centre Public de l'Aide Sociale de Corcelles v Lebon*[75] the Court ruled that a job seeker is not entitled to social advantages on an equal footing with nationals. Several cases have emerged where people have worked for short periods and then tried to claim the benefits of Article 7(2) in relation to educational and vocational training matters. In *Brown v Secretary of State for Scotland*[76] a student with dual (French/British) nationality had been domiciled in France for

---

[69]  Case C-308/93 *Cabanis-Issarte* [1996] ECR I-2097.

[70]  O'Keeffe (1985); Peers (1997c).

[71]  Case C-111/91 *Commission v Luxembourg* [ 1993] ECR I-817

[72]  Case 32/75 *Fiorini v SNCF* [1975] ECR 1085.

[73]  Case 65/81 *Reina v Landeskreditbank Baden-Württemberg* [1982] ECR 33.

[74]  Case 207/78 [1979] ECR 2019.

[75]  Case 316/85 [1987] ECR 2811.

[76]  Case 197/86 [1988] ECR 3205.

a number of years. He had obtained a place at Cambridge University to study engineering and obtained sponsorship from a firm in Scotland. He worked for the firm for eight months before taking up his university place. The British authorities refused him a maintenance grant. Brown claimed that this was a breach of Article 6 EC and Articles 7(2) and 7(3) of Regulation 1612/68/EEC. The Court ruled that although the term "worker" must be given a Community meaning, Brown was not entitled to be called a "worker" within the meaning of Article 48 EC since he had become a worker exclusively as a result of his university place. In *Lair v University of Hannover*[77] a French woman had worked in Germany on a series of part-time contracts. The Court drew a distinction between a migrant worker who was *involuntarily* unemployed and legitimately resident in the host state and would be entitled to the same treatment as regards reinstatement or re-employment as a national worker and a worker who *voluntarily* gave up work in order to undertake further training in the host state. In the latter situation a maintenance grant would only be available if there was some link between the studies and the previous work experience. The Court pointed out that a person could not abuse the free movement provisions by entering a Member State and working for a short time in order to claim social and tax advantages available to host state nationals. *Lair* thus contains limitations on the right of migrant workers to acquire new skills in order to adapt to changes in the labour market.

In *Raulin*[78] the worker was engaged as an "on-call worker" where work was not actually guaranteed and often the worker did not work at all and was under no obligation to take up work offered. The ECJ ruled that such a form of work did not precede the application of Article 48 EC. It was for the national court to make the necessary findings of fact to decide if the work was effective and genuine or marginal and ancillary. In *Bernini v Minister for Education and Science*[79] the Court ruled that an Italian who had worked for ten weeks in a factory in the Netherlands could be classified as a worker and retained the status of worker when she left the employment and, after a lapse of time, took up a course of study provided that the course of study was linked to the previous employment.

A less generous approach to Article 7(2) of Regulation 1612/68/EEC was taken in *Peter de Vos v Stadt Bielefeld*[80] where a Belgian national was

---

[77] Case 39/86 [1988] ECR 3161.

[78] Case C-357/89 [1992] ECR I-1027.

[79] Case C-3/90 [1990] ECR I-1071.

[80] Case C-315/94 [1996] ECR I-1417.

employed as a doctor by a German local authority. The employer paid contributions to a supplementary old-age and survivors' insurance scheme but these contributions were not paid while the doctor was fulfilling his military service requirements in Belgium. The employer would have been under a duty to pay the contributions for a German employee fulfilling military service requirements. The Court did not find this to be a breach of Article 7(1) or (2) of Regulation 1612/68/EEC. Firstly, because the contributions were not made by virtue of a statutory or contractual obligation but were regarded as an advantage granted by the state as partial compensation for the obligation to perform military service. Secondly, the advantage was essentially linked to the performance of military service which was not accorded to national workers because of their *objective status* as workers or by virtue of their residence on the national territory and thus did not have the essential characteristics of social advantages as defined by the Court in *Even*.[81] This case might be compared with the ruling in *O'Flynn v Adjudication Officer*[82] where an Irish migrant worker in the UK applied for a funeral grant to bury his son in Eire. British law required the funeral to take place in the UK for the grant to be awarded. The Court accepted that the funeral grant fell within Article 7(2) of Regulation 1612/68/EEC and that the rules amounted to indirect discrimination against a migrant worker. The Court did rule, however, that a Member State could fix the amount of the grant by reference to the normal cost of a burial in the host state.

The Commission recently brought an Article 169 EC action against Belgium[83] arguing first, that Belgium's policy of granting "tide over allowances" between education and employment only to persons who had completed their secondary legislation in Belgium discriminated indirectly against the children of migrant workers and was in breach of Article 7(2) of Regulation 1612/68/EEC. Second that the Belgian system for encouraging hiring of the young unemployed breached Article 3(1) of Regulation 1612/68/EEC since the only unemployed who qualified for this programme were those in receipt of the "tide over" allowance. Belgium did not contest the classification of the "tide over allowance" as a "social advantage".[84] The ECJ, in paragraph 29, repeated its formula for finding indirect discrimination

---

[81]  Case 207/78 [1979] ECR 2019.

[82]  Case C-237/94 [1996] ECR I-2617.

[83]  Case C-278/94 *Commission v Belgium* judgment of 12 September 1996.

[84]  See Case 94/84 *Deak* [1985] ECR 1873.

already enunciated in *O'Flynn v Chief Adjudication Officer*,[85] that the condition for satisfying eligibility for the "tide over allowance" was "akin to a condition of prior residence" which could be more easily fulfilled by Belgian nationals. On the second complaint the ECJ ruled that the measures were *unemployment insurance* and not access to employment measures. It was permissible to deny such measures to young, unemployed nationals of another Member State since they had to be classified as "workers" before they could participate in the Community system for co-ordinating unemployment benefits.

### 2.8.4. Trade Union Rights

Article 8 of Regulation 1612/68/EEC grants equality of treatment to migrant workers in relation to membership of trade unions and the exercise of trade union rights.[86] A migrant worker may be excluded from the management of bodies governed by public law but a migrant worker may still sit on workers' representative bodies in such fields. In *Association de Soutien aux Travailleurs Immigres v Chambres des Employes Privés* [87] the association, in its capacity as employer, and with the consent of the three migrant workers concerned had refused to pay contributions to the Chambre des Employes Privés in Luxembourg since the migrant workers had no right to participate in the activities of that organisation. The Court ruled that Article 8(1) of Regulation 1612/68/EEC prohibits national legislation from denying migrant workers the right to vote in elections for members of a professional institute for which they are required to be affiliated and to which they must pay contributions. This is so particularly in the case where the institute is responsible for defending the interests of affiliated workers and exercises a consultative role with regard to legislation. Such rights were recognisable as being comparable with the trade union rights referred to in Article 8.

### 2.8.5. Housing

Article 9 entitles the migrant worker to enjoy all the rights and benefits accorded to national workers in matters of housing, including house owner-

---

[85] Case C-237/94 [1996] ECR I-2617.

[86] See Evans (1979).

[87] Case C-213/90 [1991] ECR I-3507; See also Case C-118/92 *Commission v Luxembourg* [1994] ECR I-1891.

ship. In *Commission v Greece*[88] a restriction on foreigners' rights to own property in Greece was found to infringe the free movement provisions.

### 2.8.6. Access To Vocational Schools and Retraining Centres

Article 7(3) entitles migrant workers access to vocational schools and retraining centres on the same conditions as national workers. In *Brown*[89] and *Lair*[90] the Court interpreted Article 7(3) narrowly to cover only training in vocational establishments.

## 2.9. THE RIGHT TO REMAIN IN THE HOST STATE

Article 48(3)(d) EC grants the right to remain in the host state on retirement of the migrant worker. It is implemented through Regulation 1251/70/EEC[91] which allows a migrant worker and his or her family to remain in the host state after the migrant worker has ceased to work through reasons of incapacity or retirement.

If a worker dies during his or her working life and before acquiring the right to remain in the host state members of the family (as defined in Article 10 of Regulation 1612/68/EEC) may remain in the host state provided the worker resided continuously in the host state for two years prior to his/her death or if she/he died from an accident at work, an occupational disease or if the surviving spouse is a national of the host state who lost that nationality on marriage. In *Fiorini v SNCF*[92] the Court considered a claim from the Italian widow of an Italian migrant worker who had worked in France. The migrant worker had claimed a reduced fare card for the French railway which was granted to parents of large families. After the migrant worker's death the French authorities had denied the widow the concession on the grounds that she was not of French nationality. The Court ruled that although Article 7(1) of Regulation 1612/68/EEC refers to benefits derived from the contract of employment, Article 7(2) covers all tax and social advantages and such rights

---

[88]   Case C-213/90 [1991] ECR I-74.

[89]   Case 316/85 [1988] ECR 3205.

[90]   Case 39/86 [1988] ECR 3161.

[91]   OJ L 1970 L 142/24.

[92]   Case 32/75 [1975] ECR 1085.

continue even after the migrant workers' death where the family has a legal right to remain in the host state.

Under Council Directive 90/365/EEC retired people may also stay in the host state provided that they are financially self-sufficient.

## 2.10. FREEDOM TO PROVIDE SERVICES

More attention has been focused upon freedom of establishment and freedom to provide services since 1992. Service transactions now account for over 64% of Community GDP.[93] As Eeckhout[94] points out, service transactions are extremely complex in their nature, covering the "smokestack services," banking and air transport, to much more uncomplicated activities such as hairdressing and taxi driving. In some services there is very little international exchange. In others the exchange can take place in a number of different ways - by the consumer moving to the service or the service moving to the consumer *or* both the consumer and the service can move, for example, where a service provider uses cross-frontier transport *or* neither the producer of the consumer moves but it is the service itself which travels such as a fax, phone call, television signals.

Fine distinctions between the freedom of establishment and freedom to provide services are not regarded as necessary by the Court in that Member States are not allowed to use differences in the national classification of status to act as an impediment to the free movement principle. For example, in *Roux v Belgian State*[95] the Court states that the categorisation of an economic activity in national social security schemes is unimportant given the underlying similarity of the principles applicable to the free movement of persons and national categorisation of such activities cannot be used to obstruct the principle of free movement.[96] The Court has also made it clear that the free movement provisions should also be interpreted identically in terms of *market access*.[97] However the Court has liberalised the freedom to provide services to a greater degree than it has the freedom of establishment.

---

[93] Eurostat, *Basic Statistics of the Community*, (1995, 32nd ed. OOPEC, Luxembourg) 45.

[94] Eeckhout (1994) 9.

[95] Case C-363/89 [1991] ECR I-273.

[96] Se also Case 48/75 *Procureur de Roi v Royer* [1976] ECR 497.

[97] Case 168/85 *Commission v* Italy [1986] 2945; Case C-58/90 *Commission v Italy* [1991] ECR I-4193.

The two principle barriers to effective integration of services and establishment are the different forms of regulatory rules, especially those governing the professions, between the Member States and secondly different systems of education and vocational training between the Member States. In relation to freedom to provide services the Court has moved beyond the principle of non-discrimination to an idea of "home state control" and mutual recognition of equivalent qualifications - ideas applied also in the area of free movement of goods.[98] This means that a person providing services in another Member State should not have to be regulated twice - once in the home state and again in the host state unless home state control is not adequate. Otherwise the burden of satisfying two regulatory regimes will be a disincentive for a service provider to offer services in another Member State and will increase the cost of those services thus making them less competitive with services provided in the host state. There are some doubts as to whether services can be treated in the same way as goods. Since an analogy can be made between a service provider who moves from one Member State to another Member State the analogy cannot be made with respect to the *service itself* as the service will only materialise in the host state.

The difference between establishment and services is a question of degree. The right of establishment connotes the idea of a person installing him/herself permanently in another Member State whereas freedom to provide services is of a temporary nature. The line between the two areas is drawn in the German "insurance" cases when the Court states that a company would fall within the concept of establishment even if its activities in the host state consisted merely of an office managed by the firm's own staff or an independent staff authorised to act on a permanent basis for the company[99] . In the more recent case of *Gebhard*[100] the Court provides some criteria on which to apply the differentiation between the two Community concepts. Gebhard was a German national authorised to practice as a *Rechtsanwalt* in Germany. He opened chambers in Italy where he described himself as an *avvocato* but after complaints from other lawyers he faced disciplinary proceedings by the Milan Bar. The Court concluded that Gebhard was pursuing his professional activities on a stable and continuous basis from an established professional base and therefore this fell within Article 52 EC. Since the provisions relating to the right of

---

[98] The *"Cassis de Dijon"* principle derived from Case 120/78 *Rewe-Zentral v Bundesmmonopolverwaltung für Brantwein* [1979] ECR 649.

[99] Case 205/84 *Commission v Germany* [1986] ECR 3755.

[100] Case C-55/94 [1995] ECR I-4165.

establishment cover the taking up and pursuit of activities membership of a professional body may be a condition of the taking up and pursuit of such activities. But it could not of itself be constitutive of establishment.

### 2.10.1. Definition of a Service

Article 60(1) EC defines services as those "normally provided for remuneration, in so far as they are not governed by the provisions relating to freedom of movement of goods, capital and persons".[101]  Again the line between the areas may be fine one - to be determined by judicial interpretation. For example, are restrictions on the use of currency within freedom to provide services or capital? Is a magazine offering technical advice a good or a service? Article 60(1) provides us with a non-exhaustive list of examples:

a. activities of an industrial character
b. activities of a commercial character
c. activities of craftsmen
d. activities of the professions

One of the most controversial cases to come before the Court was the issue of whether abortion fell within Article 60 EC. In *SPUC v Grogan* [102]  an injunction had been obtained by the Society for the Protection of the Unborn Child (SPUC) against the officers of the Irish National Union of Students to prevent the Union from distributing information on abortion in other Member States. The Irish High Court had found the dissemination of such information to be contrary to the provisions of the Irish Constitution which protected the right to life of the unborn.[103]  The defendants argued that the ban was contrary to the provisions of Article 59 EC allowing for the free movement of services between the Member States. The Court ruled that a medical termination of a pregnancy fell within Article 60 EC but in this instance there was no breach of Article 59 EC since the students distributing the information were not linked commercially with the supplier of the service. The case has drawn considerable comment[104]  and has been criticised for subordinating the recognition of a

---

[101] See Nicolaides (1989).

[102] Case C-159/90 [1991] ECR I-4685.

[103] The Irish Constitution has subsequently been amended to allow women to obtain an abortion more easily in Ireland.

[104] See Phelan (1992); Coppel and O'Neill (1992; O'Leary (1996).

fundamental human right recognised in one Member State to the economic aims of the Community.

Public services which are provided at below cost price fall outside Article 60 EC.[105]

The non-discrimination principle traditionally focuses upon the nationality - or place of establishment - of the *provider of the service*. But some cases suggest that discrimination *between services* provided between Member States and purely domestic services may breach Article 59 EC. In *Corsica Ferries, France v Direction generale des douanes français*[106] the French government imposed a tax on passengers who arrived in Corsica from other Member States but did not impose a similar tax on passengers who arrived from a French port. The Court considered, that in principle, there was an infringement of the principle of freedom to provide services if a measure discriminated between the provision of services purely within a national context and between services provided between one Member State and another. It could also be argued that such discrimination affects the *recipients* of services. However, in the later case of *Corsica Ferries, Italia v Corpo dei piloti del porto di Genova*[107] the Court suggests that discrimination between the services provided was insufficient; there needs to be discrimination between the *providers* of services for there to be an infringement of Article 59 EC.

The freedom to provide services in another Member State also includes the right to take one's own labour force in order to carry out the service even though the labour force may include TCN's who do not enjoy free movement under EC law. In *Rush Portuguesa Lda v Office National d'Immigration*[108] a Portuguese company won a tender to build a railway in France and wanted to use its own, Portuguese workers to carry out the work even though at this time there was not full freedom of Portuguese nationals to work in another Member State.[109] This was contrary to French law which gave the defendants a monopoly over the engagement of foreign workers. The Court ruled that the

---

[105] Case 263/86 *Humbel v Belgium* [1988] ECR 5365. Cf Case C-109/92 *Wirth v Landeshauptstadt Hannover* [1993] ECR I-6447.

[106] Case C-49/89 [1989] ECR 4441.

[107] Case C-18/93 [1994] ECR I-1783.

[108] Case C-113/89 [1990] ECR I-1417.

[109] Free movement of services provisions came into effect immediately upon Portugal's accession whereas the freedom of movement of workers came into effect after the transitional period.

right to free movement of services involves the right of an undertaking to move with its own employees without immigration restrictions.

In *Van der Elst v Office des Migrations Internationaux*[110] a Belgian was fined under French law for using four Moroccans to carry out a one month demolition contract. The Moroccans had work permits for Belgium but only tourist visas for France. The Court argued that the requirement of work permits for the Moroccan workers increased Van der Elst's costs and hindered his ability to provide services within the meaning of Article 59 EC. The ECJ ruled that requirement was not justified where the TCN's were lawfully resident in another Member State and did not seek access to the labour market of the host state.

By analogy the host state cannot require a service provider to pay social security contributions for his/her employees when they are covered by the legislation of the state of establishment[111] Such ideas are problematic since without a level playing field of employment law and social provisions and where labour costs are a significant factor there is an incentive for firms to establish themselves in the Member States with the lowest labour costs thus giving a comparative advantage to firms offering services in other Member States where labour costs are higher. A Directive on the posting of workers in the framework of the provision of services was adopted in September 1996.[112] It is based upon Articles 57(2) and 66 EC.

### 2.10.2. Rights of Residence and Entry

Secondary legislation has been enacted which mirrors the secondary legislation in relation to the free movement of workers granting rights of residence and entry of equal duration with the period in which the services are provided.[113] Council Directive 75/34/EEC[114] grants the right to remain in the host state Such a right of residence is also available under Council Directive

---

[110] Case C-43/93 [1994] ECR I-3803.

[111] Case C-272/94 *Criminal Proceedings Against Guiot and Climatec SA* [1996] ECR I-1905.

[112] Council Directive 97/71/EC OJ 1997 L 18/1.

[113] Council Directive 73/148/EEC, OJ 1973 L172/14.

[114] OJ 1975 L 14/10.

90/345/EEC[115] provided the retired person has sufficient resources to be independent.

### 2.10.3. Posts Involving the Exercise of Official Authority

Article 66 EC allows the Member State to derogate from the principle of free movement for posts which are connected, even occasionally, with the exercise of official authority.

### 2.10.4. Barriers to the Effective Exercise of Free Movement

The Treaty of Rome 1957 provided for the abolition of existing restrictions to the free movement principle in progressive stages during the transitional period. Under Article 63 EC the Council of Ministers, acting upon a proposal from the Commission, was to draw up a General Programme on the abolition of restrictions on the freedom to provide services and establishment. General Programmes were drawn up in 1961 and although they are not legally binding they have been used as pieces of soft law for interpretative purposes by the Court.[116] The Council of Ministers and the Commission were also assigned the task of issuing Directives for the mutual recognition of diplomas, certificates and other evidence of formal qualifications before the end of the transitional period.[117] This proved to be a difficult task and greater progress was made by the Court declaring Articles 59(1) and 60(3) EC to be directly effective.[118] Some sectoral Directives were achieved with the most success in the medical sector. The Community has abandoned the sectoral approach to the mutual recognition of qualifications and adopted Directives on a general basis for the mutual recognition of qualifications (see below).

In relation to professional rules of conduct the Community has moved beyond the non-discrimination principle[119] and stated that Articles 59 and 60 EC require not only the removal of all discrimination based on nationality but

---

[115] OJ 1990, L 180/28.

[116] See Case 197/84 *Steinhauser v City of Biarritz* [1985] ECR 1819; Case 293/83 *Gravier v City of Liège* [1985] ECR 593.

[117] Article 57(1) EC.

[118] Case 33/74 *Van Binsbergen v Bestuur van de Bedrifssvereniging voor de Metaalnijverheid* [1974] ECR 1229; Case 2/74 *Reyners v Belgian State* [1974] ECR 631.

[119] Case 33/74 *Van Binsbergen* [1974] ECR 1229.

also all restrictions imposed by the host state to persons providing services from another Member State. The Court held that not all legislation or professional rules applying to host state nationals could be applied to a person providing temporary services in its territory. A set of criteria were laid down to allow a Member State to continue with any restrictions.[120] It had to be shown that:

- the rules were necessary for imperative reasons
- relating to the public interest
- the public interest was not met by the rules of the home state
- the same result could not be achieved by less restrictive means

In the Commission's White Paper, *Completing the Internal Market*[121] the idea of a single licence is put forward. This would allow an individual licensed in one Member State to offer services in another Member State with the Community involved in the harmonisation of essential safeguards and standards. These ideas have been employed in the area of financial services.

In *Gouda v Commissariat voor de Media*[122] the Court addressed the question for the first time of whether a *non-discriminatory* restriction can be placed upon the *provision of a service* rather than on who may provide the service. A Dutch law imposed a number of restrictions on advertising by cable network operators providing services exclusively for the Dutch public. The Dutch government argued that the restrictions were necessary to maintain cultural pluralism. The Court ruled that cultural arguments could never be used to justify restrictions being placed on the structure of foreign broadcasters. The Court noted that the restrictions on advertisements only applied to those advertisements intended exclusively for the Dutch public and not to other advertisements. It concluded that the real purpose of the restrictions was not to promote cultural policy but to protect the Dutch body in charge of arranging advertisements with Dutch broadcasters from increased competition. The Court found the restrictions to contravene Article 59 EC.

---

[120] Case 205/84 *Commission v Germany* [1986] ECR 3755.

[121] COM(85) 310 final.

[122] Case C-288/89 [1991] ECR I-4007.

## 2.10.5. Justification of Restrictions

In *Commission v Germany*[123] the ECJ decided to apply the *Cassis de Dijon* style reasoning to services by ruling that in relation to the provision of services in another Member State it was not necessary for the host state to apply the regulatory rules applying to its own nationals unless it could be shown that the host state's regulation was necessary for imperative reasons, relating to the public interest and that the public interest was not already protected by the rules of the Member State of establishment and that the same result could not be obtained by less restrictive means.

In *Criminal Proceedings Against Webb*[124] the manager of a company established and licensed in the UK to provide workers on a temporary basis was prosecuted for having supplied workers in the Netherlands without possessing a licence issued by the Dutch authorities. The Court ruled that the provision of workers was sensitive from an occupational and social point of view so that the aims of preserving the interests of the workforce and ensuring good relations on the labour market were part of a legitimate state policy. Arguably a fourth requirement must also be applied - that the measures respect fundamental human rights.[125]

In *Her Majesty's Custom and Excise* v *Schindler*[126] the Schindler brothers promoted and sold tickets for lotteries organised by the South German Länder. They sent advertisements and application forms for the lotteries through the post from the Netherlands inviting British nationals to take part in these lotteries. The UK prohibited lotteries (with the exception of certain small-scale lotteries) unless prior authorisation had been received from the authorities. Schindler's advertisements were intercepted and confiscated by the British authorities and Schindler claimed that the ban on lotteries was discriminatory and infringed Article 59 EC. The Court ruled that the national legislation was an obstacle to the freedom to provide services. The UK government justified the legislation as preventing crime, protecting gamblers by avoiding stimulating demand in the gambling sector which would have damaging social consequences and to ensure lotteries operated solely for sporting, cultural or charitable purposes and not for personal or commercial profit. The Court accepted this as a valid justification.

---

[123] Case 205/84 [1986] ECR 3755.

[124] Case 279/80 [1981] ECR 3305.

[125] See de Burca (1993).

[126] Case C-275/92 [1994] ECR I-1039.

In *Criminal Proceedings Against Perfili*[127] an Italian provision was challenged which only allowed representatives of litigants to bring a civil claim in criminal proceedings where they had been appointed by a special power of attorney and not where they had been appointed by a general power of attorney. This increased the costs for the litigant since it required the drawing up of an additional document for the action. It also restricted the provision of a service because it prevented a particular form of transaction taking place. The Court ruled that there was no breach of Article 59 EC since nothing restricted the ability of a litigant to appoint a legal representative for actions of this kind.

### 2.10.6. The Official Authority Exception

Article 55 EC states that the provisions of the chapter on freedom of establishment shall not apply to activities which are connected, even occasionally with the exercise of official authority. In *Reyners v Belgium*[128] Advocate General Mayras describes what is understood by the term "official authority" as

> '... that which arises from the sovereignty and majesty of the state for him who exercises it, it implies the power of enjoying the prerogatives outside the general law, privileges of official power and powers of coercion over citizens.'

In *Reyners* the Court was asked whether the legal profession of *avocat* in France should be included within Article 55 EC or only those activities which were connected with the exercise of official powers. The Court ruled that where the official tasks were separable from the rest of the profession's activities then Article 55 should not apply to the profession as a whole. But in the case of the legal profession professional activities even regular and organic including compulsory co-operation with the courts did not fall within Article 55 EC. The Court ruled that this approach left intact the discretion of judicial authority and the free exercise of judicial power.

In an Article 169 EC action the Greek government attempted to argue that the activity of a travel accident expert was covered by Article 55 EC.[129] The Court rejected this contention pointing out that the reports of such experts did not bind the courts and that foreigners could be admitted to the profession and leave the discretion and exercise of judicial power intact. In *Thijssen v*

---

[127] Case C-177/94 [1996] ECR I-161.

[128] Case 2/74 [1974] ECR 631, 664.

[129] Case C-306/89 *Commission v Greece* [1991] ECR I-5863.

*Controledienst voor de Verzekerigen*[130] it was argued that the position of commissioner of insurance companies and undertakings was covered by Article 55 EC. The position covered monitoring companies and reporting on possible infringements of the penal code, the power to prevent insurance companies from implementing certain decisions was not a definitive power and did not affect the power of approval or refusal of the commissioner.

### 2.10.7. Freedom to Receive Services

The ECJ has extended the principle of freedom of movement to cover people moving between the Member States in order to *receive* services. Given the multiplicity of the various forms of services on offer this is potentially an extensive right. The point had been raised by the Commission in *Watson and Belmann*[131] and was developed by Advocate General Mancini in *Luisi and Carbonne v Ministero del Tesoro.*[132] Here two Italians were fined for infringing Italian exchange controls. They wanted to take money out of Italy in order to pay for the provision of services in another Member State. They argued that the Italian provisions were contrary to the rules relating to the free movement of services and the free movement of capital. The Advocate General cited the General Programme for the abolition of the restrictions on the freedom to provide services and Article 1(1) of Council Directive 64/221/EEC which applies to "freedom of movement for employed, self-employed persons *or the recipients of services*" and Article 1(1)(b) of Council Directive 73/148/EEC which requires the Member States to abolish restrictions on the movement and residence of nationals of the Member States "wishing to go to another Member State as recipients of services". The Court ruled that the right to move freely to *receive* services was the corollary of the freedom to provide services. The court included in the list (which presumably is non-exhaustive) of potential recipients of services tourists, persons receiving medical treatment and persons travelling for the purposes of education[133] or business.

---

[130] Case C-42/92 [1993] ECR I-4047.

[131] Case 118/75 [1976] ECR 1185.

[132] Joined Cases 286/82 and 26/83 [1984] ECR 377.

[133] Although note the reluctance of the Court to embrace educational facilities financed from public funds within the definition of a service in Case 263/86 *Humbel v Belgium* [1988] ECR 5365.

In *Cowan v Tresor Public*[134] a British tourist who was mugged on the Paris underground was denied compensation from public funds. Such compensation was only available to French nationals or nationals from a state where there was a reciprocal agreement with France. Cowan argued that this was a form of nationality discrimination, contrary to what is now Article 6 EC. The French government justified its rules by reason of the fact that state compensation was a manifestation of the principle of solidarity which presupposed a closer bond with the state than that of a recipient of services. The Court rejected such arguments stating that when Community law guarantees the freedom for individuals to go to another Member State the protection from harm on the same basis as that accorded to nationals of the host state is a corollary of the right to free movement, even where the compensation is provided from public funds. The Court also dealt with the argument raised by the French government that the compensation procedures at issue were not subject to Article 6 EC because they fell within the law of criminal procedure which was not within the scope of the Treaty of Rome 1957. Although the Court accepted that in principle criminal legislation and the rules of criminal procedure are matters for which the Member States are responsible Community law sets certain limits to their power. In particular, such legislative provisions may not discriminate against persons to whom Community law gives the right to equal treatment or restrict the fundamental freedoms guaranteed by Community law.

The case has been described as creating an "incipient form of citizenship"[135] but is also criticised in that 'Citizenship' often demands duties as well as giving rights. Thus the notion of citizenship rights here is very one-sided. The reasoning of the Court has been subject to even harsher criticism[136] in that the Court stated that the corollary of the right to go to another Member State is the right to be protected from harm on the same conditions as nationals of the host state. Yet Cowan was not seeking protection from harm but *compensation* for the harm suffered. The Court does not establish sufficiently clearly the nature of the link between the receipt of the service and the operation of the non-discrimination principle. Does a Member State have to extend all social and civil rights to the recipient of services that it gives to its own nationals? Although a case has not been before the ECJ, at the national level there have been instances where barriers/restrictions have been placed upon individuals

---

[134] Case 186/87 [1989] ECR 195.

[135] Weatherill (1989).

[136] See Green, Hartley and Usher (1991) 143-144.

wishing to travel to another Member State to obtain medical services in relation to abortion and fertility treatment.

## 2.11. FREEDOM OF ESTABLISHMENT

Article 52 EC provides for the right to take up and pursue activities as self-employed persons and manage undertakings in another Member State on the same terms as host state nationals.[137]  In *R v Secretary of State for Transport ex parte Factortame*[138]  a UK law requiring the owners and operators of shipping vessels to be resident in the UK was considered to be discriminatory on the grounds that it was easier for British nationals to comply with the requirement than foreigners. The Court stated that the right of establishment involves the actual pursuit of an economic activity through a fixed establishment in another Member State for an indefinite period. In *Gebhard*[139] the Court states:

> "... the concept of establishment within the meaning of Treaty is therefore a very broad one, allowing a Community national to participate, on a stable and continuous basis, in the economic life of a member state other than his state of origin and to profit therefrom, so contributing to social and economic penetration within the Community in the sphere of activities as self-employed persons."[140]

The geographical requirement necessary to trigger Article 52 EC is not so much presence in another Member State but the *direction of* activities towards that Member State with a degree of permanence about the activity.[141]  Similar barriers to the right to free movement in the form of educational qualifications and professional regulatory rules of conduct can be potential barriers to exercising the right to freedom of establishment. However because the idea of establishment is of a more permanent nature the principles of home state control are not as easy to apply to establishment as they are to services.

In the absence of implementing legislation, the Court stepped in and implemented the concept of free movement by declaring Article 52 EC directly

---

[137] Everling (1964).

[138] Case C-213/89 [1990] ECR I-2433.

[139] Case C-55/94 [1995] ECR I-4165.

[140] Para 25.

[141] Case 205/84 *Commission v* Germany [1986] ECR 3755.

effective from the end of the transitional period in *Reyners v Belgian State.*[142] In *Steinhauser v City of Biarritz*[143] the Court applied Article 52 EC not only to the taking up on an economic activity in another Member State but also to the *pursuit* of the activity in the host state. The right to equal treatment applied, *inter alia,* to the right to rent premises, the right to enter and to qualify for licences and concessions. In *Commission v Italy*[144] the policy of making social housing and reduced rate mortgages available only to Italian nationals was found to infringe Article 52 EC. The Court reasoned that if complete equality of competition was to be assured facilities which alleviate the financial burden upon the self-employed had to be available on an equal footing.

Article 52 EC prohibits both overt and covert discrimination. In *Segers v Bedrijfsvereiging voor Bank-en Verzekeringswezen*[145] the Dutch social security scheme which denied sickness benefits to directors of foreign registered companies while granting them to the equivalent of a director in Dutch registered companies was found to contravene Article 52 since although the benefits enured to the employees the right of freedom of establishment of companies was thereby restricted.

The most far-reaching extension of the principle of non-discrimination is found in *Halliburton Services BV v Staatssecretaris van Financien*[146] where a German subsidiary of a US company wished to sell its assets in the Netherlands to a Dutch subsidiary. Under Dutch law such a sale would normally be exempt from tax, falling as part of an internal company reorganisation. But this rule did not apply here because the vendor, the German subsidiary, was not incorporated in the Netherlands although the tax was actually levied on the purchaser, the Dutch subsidiary. The Court found the Dutch rules to be contrary to Article 52 EC because they resulted in discrimination against the German subsidiary and the tax on the sale rendered the position of the vendor less favourable - so the terms of the sale to potential purchasers were less favourable.

---

[142] Case 2/74 [1974] ECR 631.

[143] Case 197/84 [1985] ECR 1819.

[144] Case 63/86 [1988] ECR 29. See also Case 305/87 *Commission v Greece* [1989] ECR 1461

[145] Case 79/85 [1986] ECR 2375.

[146] Case C-1/93 [1994] ECR I-1137.

In *Commission v Italy*[147] an Article 169 EC action was brought against Italian laws which required that public authorities had to purchase data-processing systems from companies in which the Italian government had a majority share-holding. The Court noted that the measure favoured Italian companies over companies registered in other Member States.

The non-discrimination principle soon showed that it had its limitations in cases involving secondary establishment where Member States' rules relating to professional conduct requiring a professional to maintain only a single practice. It was argued by the Member States' concerned that such a rule was not discriminatory since it applied to host state nationals and foreigners alike.[148] The Court rejected the use of such rules, pointing out that modern practice and modern telecommunications meant that their justification *per se* could no longer be accepted without an examination of the barriers such rules placed upon the free movement provisions. However, the Court tolerates justification of such rules where they are necessary to protect a legitimate interest which is not unnecessarily restrictive of trade.[149]

The Court has extended the scope of Article 52 EC to cover not only rules which prevent secondary establishment but also which *discourage* it. In *Stanton v INASTI*[150] three directors of a Belgian company who were of British, German and Belgian nationality were employed in Germany. Under Belgian law company directors were categorised as self-employed and were required to pay social security contributions unless they were also employed in Belgium. It was argued that the Belgium laws infringed Article 6 EC and Article 52 EC. By analogy with the *Klopp*[151] reasoning the court held that the rules discouraged a person working in one Member State to work in another Member State in a self-employed capacity. Interestingly here, one of the Directors was of Belgian nationality and so Article 52 EC has been interpreted to cover measures which discourage the right to *leave* a Member State very

---

[147] Case C-3/88 [1989] ECR 4035.

[148] Case 107/83 *Ordre des Avocats au Barreau de Paris v Klopp* [1984] ECR 2971; Case 96/85 *Commission v France* [1986] ECR 1475. For a similar analysis see Case C-351/90 *Commission v Luxembourg* [1992] ECR I-3945.

[149] See Marenco (1991).

[150] Case 143/87 [1988] ECR 3877.

[151] Case 107/83 [1984] ECR 2971. This was a case of a single establishment rule imposed by the French Bar.

similar to the way in which a specific Treaty provision, Article 34 EC, applies to restrictions on the export of goods.[152]

The application of this principle is not without problems. In order to take advantage of the free movement provisions a person must be anchored in one of the Member States. Nationality will give this anchorage to an individual person but for companies Article 58 EC states that the connecting factor for legal persons is their formation in accordance with the law of the Member State in which they were initially established. Member States try to retain this anchorage by setting down requirements that if companies wish to retain their legal personality they must retain their central administration in the state of establishment. Thus if a company wishes to take advantage of Article 52 EC and moves its central administration to the host state it loses the legal personality which enables it to exercise the right to free movement. Such restrictions have been allowed by the *Court in R v HM Treasury ex parte Daily Mail*[153] The Daily Mail wished to transfer its central management from the UK but retain its legal personality in order for it to sell off some shares without being subject to British tax. The UK Treasury would not give permission for the move. The Court did not find that that the UK rules violated Article 52 EC. It pointed out that the Community rules did not invade the prerogative of the Member States to determine, according to national law, the connecting factor required. Thus where connecting factors require the central administration to be located within the home state primary establishment is not feasible for such legal persons. It would still be possible for the legal person to establish secondary establishment - subsidiaries, agents, branches etc. If the rules were interpreted in any other way it would be possible for companies to relocate around the Community seeking out the most beneficial fiscal havens and avoid taxation.

The Court is extending the scope of Article 52 EC to cover not only discriminatory provisions but also national provisions which may hinder the right of establishment. In *Gebhard*[154] the Court repeats a formula now being applied more generally across the economic freedoms:

> ...national measures liable to hinder or make less attractive the exercise of fundamental freedoms guaranteed by the treaty must fulfil four conditions: they must be applied in a non-discriminatory manner; they must be justified by imperative requirements in the general interest; they must be suitable for securing the attainment of the

---

[152] See also in the context of Article 48 EC, Case 415/93 *Bossman* [1995] ECR I-4921.

[153] Case 81/87 [1988] ECR 5483.

[154] Case C-55/94 [1995] ECR I-4165.

objective which they pursue; and they must not go beyond what is necessary in order to attain it.[155]

Yet the Court has not extended Article 52 EC to cover *non-discriminatory* restrictions on the pursuit of an economic activity in another Member State. For example in *Fearon v Irish Land Commission*[156] the Irish Land Commission could make a compulsory acquisition of land where a person or company owning the land had not been resident for more than a year within three miles of that land. The Court held that this provision did not infringe Article 52 EC on the ground that the rule did not discriminate against other Community nationals. It is questionable whether this ruling would still stand today. The rule could amount to covert or indirect discrimination since it would be harder for non-Irish landowners to satisfy its requirement than for Irish nationals to satisfy it. It might also be considered to be a *deterrent* to the right of establishment if Community nationals knew that their private property would be compulsorily purchased if they are not resident in the Member State for a year. Yet the Court has had the opportunity to reconsider the ruling in subsequent decisions and has chosen to stick with it.[157]

In *Commission v Belgium*[158] restrictions were placed upon the provision of clinical biology services by laboratories. The effect of the restrictions was to require those engaged in clinical laboratory testing to maintain their primary establishment in Belgium. The Commission argued that the rules restricted secondary establishment and therefore infringed Article 52 EC. The Court ruled that as long as foreigners were treated in the same way as nationals of the host state there was no infringement of Article 52 EC.

In *Gullung v Conseil de l'ordre des Avocats*[159] a lawyer who held dual French/German nationality applied to register as a *conseil juridique* at the Bar in Mulhouse, France. The Bar refused his registration on the grounds of personal misconduct. Nevertheless Gullung set up office in Mulhouse and the

---

[155] *ibid* para 37.

[156] Case 182/83 [1984] ECR 3677. Cf Protocol 1 TEU 1992: "Property in Denmark - Notwithstanding the provisions of this Treaty, Denmark may maintain the existing legislation on the acquisition of second homes."

[157] See also Case 221/85 *Commission v Belgium* [1987] ECR 719; Case 196/86 *Conradi, Hereth et soc. Metro v Direction de la Concurrence et des Prix* [1987] ECR 4469; See Hedemann - Robinson (1996).

[158] Case 221/85 [1987] ECR 719.

[159] Case 292/86 [1988] ECR 111.

Bar Council ordered its members not to have contact with Gullung. Gullung argued that the requirement of registration contravened Article 52 EC.

Finally a very broad approach to Article 52 EC is seen in *Konstantiinidis v Stadt Altensteig, Standesamt, and Landratsamt Calw, Ordungsamt*[160] where a Greek national working in Germany as a self-employed masseur complained that the incorrect transliteration of his name from the Greek to the Roman alphabet on the civil marriage register was an infringement of Article 52 EC in that it might confuse clients and thereby interfere with the pursuit of his professional activities. The Court ruled that Community law did not prevent the transliteration of Greek names into the Roman alphabet but the method of transliteration was incompatible with Article 52 EC and the unfettered exercise of the right of establishment particularly where it did not provide a remedy for persons whose names were wrongly transliterated. Advocate General Jacobs was prepared to move the free movement principle into the realms of citizenship rights:

> "... a Community national who goes to another Member State as a worker or self-employed person under Articles 48, 52 or 59 of the Treaty is entitled not just to pursue his trade or profession and to enjoy the same living and working conditions as nationals of the host state; he is entitled to assume that, wherever he goes to earn his living in the European Community, he will be treated in accordance with a common code of fundamental values, in particular those laid down in the European Convention on Human Rights. In other words, he is entitled to say 'civis europeus sum' and to invoke that status in order to oppose any violation of his fundamental rights."

## 2.12. RESTRICTIONS ON THE USE OF DIPLOMAS AND QUALIFICATIONS

Qualifications required by Member States regulatory bodies may be a restriction on the taking up and pursuit of an economic activity in another Member State. To qualify twice in the home state and the host state(s) may be a "double burden" and a deterrent to free movement. But since the professions are highly regulated the problem of co-ordinating qualifications was a complex one.[161] A Council Resolution of 6 June 1974 on the mutual recognition of diplomas, certificates and other evidence of formal qualifications[162] set the

---

[160] Case C-168/91 [1993] ECR I-1191.

[161] See Laslett (1990/91).

[162] OJ 1974 C 98/1.

ground for other sectoral Directives. But progress was slow and the sectoral approach was abandoned in favour of a general system for the recognition of higher education diplomas awarded on completion of professional education and training of at least three years' duration.[163] This was followed by Council Directive 92/51/EEC which covers education and training other than the three-year higher-education requirement of Directive 89/48/EEC such as diplomas and certificates.[164]

The Court, however, seems to have driven a coach and horses through this legislation by allowing individuals wishing to establish themselves in another Member State to rely upon the direct effect of Article 52 EC in *Vlassopoulou v Ministerium für Justiz Bundes-und Europaangelegenheiten Baden-Württemberg.*[165] A Greek lawyer had been admitted to the Greek bar in 1982 and then went on to complete a doctorate in Germany. From 1983-1988 she worked for a German law firm and then applied to become a *Rechtsanwalt*. This was refused on the grounds that she did not have the appropriate German qualifications, ie, she needed to have studied law at a German university for two years, completed the First State exams and undergone a period of training. The Court was asked whether it was compatible with Article 52 EC for no account to have been taken of her Greek academic qualifications and her practical experience in Germany.[166] Advocate General Van Gerven discussed the relationship between Article 52 EC and Council Directive 89/48/EEC. Unlike the Directive, Article 52 EC simply required the Member States to take

---

[163] Council Directive 89/48/EEC OJ 1989 L19/16. But even before this legislation was enacted the Court used the direct effect of Article 52 EC to allow individuals to practice a profession in another Member State: Case 71/76 *Thieffry v Conseil de l'Ordre des Avocats á la Cour de Paris* [1977] ECR 765; Case 11/77 *Patrick v Ministre des affaires Culturelles* [1977] ECR 1199. See also case 222/86 *UNECTEF v Heylens* [1987] ECR 4097.

[164] OJ 1992 L 209/25. See Pertek (1992).

[165] Case C-340/89 [1991] ECR I-2357.

[166] Cf. Case C-164/94 *Arantis v Land Berlin* [1996] ECR I-135 where a Greek national with a diploma in geology from a Greek university moved to Berlin to work. He was described as an unskilled assistant by the German authorities and sought a declaration that his Greek diploma was equivalent to a German diploma. The Court ruled that the provisions of Council Directive 89/48/EEC did not cover the situation since the profession of geologist was not regulated in Germany. But the Court ruled that whether the professional activities require a diploma or not the host state authorities must take into account the diplomas, knowledge and qualifications acquired by the person claiming under the free movement provisions. See also Case C-55/94 *Gebhard* [1995] ECR I-4165.

into account qualifications and training already received and only if it were found that these were equivalent to the Member State's requirements could an Community national rely on them. Article 52 EC could not of itself be relied upon to impose an obligation on the state to provide facilities for a Community national to complete an adaptation period which would bring his or her qualifications up to an equivalent level as that demanded by the host state.

Thus the principle of mutual recognition - and of trust and co-operation - which has been developed in relation to the free movement of goods is extended to the free movement of persons. But there are limits to the principle. For example, a Member State may have evidence that the individual does not posses the qualifications it stipulates as necessary.[167]

*Vlassopoulou* concerned the *access* to a profession. Qualifications may also affect the *pursuit* of an activity. In *Kraus v Land Baden-Württemberg*[168] a German who had obtained a Masters degree in law from a Scottish university challenged the requirement that a person needed authorisation from their Land before being able to use higher education titles acquired abroad. The Court observed that qualifications were necessary both for access to a profession and to facilitate more generally the exercise of economic activity. Thus any conditions on the use of a title which hindered or made more difficult the exercise of the economic freedoms fell within the scope of Article 52 EC. The Court did not draw a distinction between those titles necessary for the *access* to a profession and other titles but it did allow Member States to impose non-discriminatory restrictions on the use of titles to prevent fraud and an administrative authorisation for such purposes was compatible with Community law provided it was accessible, susceptible to judicial review, reasons were given for any refusal to approve a title, the administrative costs charged were not excessive and any sanctions imposed for the use of the title without authorisation were not disproportionately heavy.

---

[167] Case 130/88 *Van de Bijl v Staatssecretaris van economische zaken* [1989] ECR 3089.

[168] Case C-19/92 [1993] ECR I-1663.

## 2.13. TAXATION OF THE EMPLOYED AND SELF-EMPLOYED PERSONS

National rules on the taxation of income may have an indirectly discriminatory effect on Community migrants.[169] In *Commission v France*[170] the Court stated that any tax and fiscal regime which discriminated between residents and non-residents could breach the free movement provisions since most non-residents would be foreigners. But such an approach flew in the face of established international practice. One of the basic principles of international tax law is the distinction between taxation based on residence and source taxation. Residence taxation is applied with the idea that residents in a certain state benefit from the economic, social, cultural and physical infrastructure and should contribute to that infrastructure.[171] The Court has allowed the Member States to raise objective justifications for any discrimination that occurred. In *Bachmann v Belgian State*[172] a German national working in Belgium challenged a refusal by the Belgian authorities to allow him to deduct tax from payments on a German life insurance scheme. Such deductions were allowed for Belgian life insurance policies. The Court accepted that the Belgian tax scheme discriminated against foreigners since they were more likely to take out a life insurance policy abroad. The Belgian government defended the scheme on the grounds that the distinction was necessary to preserve the cohesion of their tax order since any payments out of the scheme were taxed and the Belgian authorities had insufficient resources of checking whether companies located outside Belgium were complying with a similar require-ment. The Court accepted this justification but in a subsequent case has refused to allow it to be pleaded where the issue was regulated by a double taxation convention. In *Wielockx v Inspecteur der Directe Belastingen*[173] a self-employed Belgian, residing in Belgium, was not allowed to set up a pension reserve qualifying for reductions in taxation since he received his income from a partnership in a physiotherapy practice in the Netherlands. The Court found these rules giving advantages to resident Dutch citizens to infringe

---

[169] See Wouters (1994a) (1994b); Farmer (1995); Keeling and Shipwright (1995).

[170] Case 270/83 [1986] ECR 273. See also *R v IRC ex parte Commerzbank* [1993] ECR I-4017.

[171] Wattel (1996).

[172] Case C-204/90 [1992] ECR I-249.

[173] Case C-80/94 [1995] ECR I-2493.

Article 52 EC.[174] Here the Court found that fiscal cohesion was secured by a bilateral convention concluded with another Member State.

In another case the Court sought a new line for distinguishing between residents and non-residents. In *Finanzamt Köln v Schumacker*[175] a Belgian national maintained his residence in Belgium but worked in Germany. He paid income tax on his earnings, but on a limited basis, on the grounds that he was a non-resident. This denied him certain benefits which were available to resident tax payers. The Court accepted that national rules based on distinctions of residence were liable to operate to the detriment of non-residents and that non-residents would by and large be foreigners. But the Court then went on to state that "discrimination can arise only through the application of different rules to comparable situations or the application of the same rule to different situations. In relation to direct taxes the Court ruled that the situations of residents and non-residents were not generally comparable since there were objective differences between them from the point of view of the source of the income and the possibility of taking account of their ability to pay tax on their personal or family circumstances. This did not constitute discrimination. But on the facts of this case a non-resident tax payer who received all or almost all of his income in the state where he worked was objectively in the same situation as a resident in that state who was employed on a similar basis there. Both were taxed in that state alone, their taxable income was the same but discrimination arose because the non-resident tax payer did not have his personal and family circumstances taken into account in either his state of employment or his state of residence, consequently his overall tax burden was greater and he would be at a disadvantage when compared with a resident tax payer. In *Schumacker* the Court ruled that since personal and family circumstances were not taken into account in the state of residence the principle of equal treatment required that they be taken into account in the state of employment in the same way as residents. Article 48 EC required equal treatment at the procedural level for non-resident Community nationals. A refusal to grant non-resident Community nationals the benefit of annual adjustment procedures which were available to resident nationals constituted unjustified discrimination. The *Schumacker* ruling states that residents and non-residents are distinguishable only in so far as the state will not have available all the information necessary to take account of the non-residents' overall ability to pay tax, in particular, his/her personal or family circumstances. Subject to this it does not give a Member State a general right to tax

---

[174] See Vanistendael (1996).

[175] Case C-279/93 [1995] ECR I-225.

non-residents higher than residents.[176] The distinction is therefore only relevant in relation to tax which is personal or family related. A Member State may apply a separate regime to those non-residents who do not obtain their income entirely or almost exclusively from that Member State and do not earn sufficient income in the State of residence for personal and family circumstances to be taken into account. The Court leaves open a number of questions such as the percentage of the income the non-resident is earning which is protected in the host state. But the Court has created a new rule in international tax law. Where, as previously, States applied source taxation to non-residents focusing upon the income earned in their territory rather than the *person* earning the income they will be unable to do so for those non-residents earning all or almost all of their income in that state. Instead they must now focus upon the person as someone who should benefit from the social infrastructure that the state has to offer and who should be allowed the appropriate fiscal benefits.

## 2.14. REVERSE DISCRIMINATION

Reverse discrimination is described by Pickup as

"...when a national of a Member State is disadvantaged because he or she may not rely on a protective provision of Community law when a national of another Member State in otherwise identical circumstances may rely on that same provision."[177]

The Court has refused to extend the substantive rights relating to free movement and the principle of non-discrimination to situations which are considered purely internal to a Member State.[178] In other words, a person must trigger the free movement provisions by moving to another Member State before he or she can rely upon EC law. In *R v Saunders*[179] a British national was found guilty to a charge of theft. She was not given a custodial sentence in return for an undertaking to return to Northern Ireland and not return to England or Wales for three years. She broke the undertaking but argued that restriction upon *internal* free movement was contrary to Article 48 EC. The Court ruled that this was a purely domestic matter and the Community law

---

[176] Case 151/94 *Commission v Luxembourg* [1995] ECR I-3685; Case C-107/94 *Asscher v Staatssecretaris van Financien* [1996] ECR I-3089.

[177] Pickup (1986) 137.

[178] Case 298/84 *Iorio v Azienda Autonoma delle Ferrovie dell Stato* [1986] ECR 247.

[179] Case 175/78 [1979] ECR 1129.

could not apply. In *Moser*[180] an ambitious legal argument was raised to challenge a refusal by the German authorities to allow a German national from undertaking postgraduate training on the grounds that he was a member of the Communist party and therefore his loyalty to the German Constitution was questionable. Moser argued that by precluding his application for training the authorities were denying him the opportunity of taking up work in another Member State in the future. Not surprisingly the Court ruled that the matter was a purely internal affair with no connecting factor to EC law. The generous provisions relating to family migration have also been utilised to challenge the restrictive immigration laws on family reunion operated by some Member States. In *Morson and Jhanjan v Netherlands*[181] two Dutch nationals working in the Netherlands were not allowed to use the provisions of Article 10 of Regulation 1612/68/EEC in order to bring their parents (who were of Surinanmese nationality) into the Netherlands since the Court held they had not exercised their rights to free movement under EC law and therefore derived no rights under EC law.

Where a person has triggered the free movement provisions the result may be different. In *Knoors v Secretary of State For Home Affairs*[182] a Dutch plumber worked in Belgium for a number of years and then wished to return to the Netherlands to practice his trade. The Dutch authorities refused to allow him to do so on the grounds that he lacked the necessary qualifications required by Dutch legislation. Under Council Directive 64/427/EEC a Community national who had pursued a trade in the manufacturing or processing industries covered by the Directive for a given number of years in one Member State could have his qualifications experience recognised in other Member States. The court pointed out that in view of the lengthy qualifying periods laid down in the Directive (the length of time varied according to the circumstance but the minimum length was six years) there was little possibility that nationals of the home state would use the Directive to evade the requirements of their own law and that Dutch nationals might be deterred from pursuing their trade in another Member State if they could not return home and continue to use their skills in the home state.

In *R v Immigration Appeal Tribunal and Surinder Singh, ex parte Secretary of State for the Home Department*[183] an Indian national had married a British

---

[180] Case 180/83 [1884] ECR 2539.

[181] Cases 35/82 & 36/82 [1982] ECR 3723.

[182] Case 115/78 [1979] ECR 399.

[183] Case C-370/90 [1992] ECR I-4265.

national. The couple moved to Germany where they both worked for a number of years before returning to the United Kingdom to establish a business. The marriage broke down and the UK authorities issued a deportation notice on the Indian husband before the divorce proceedings were complete. He contested the deportation arguing that he was protected by the immigration rights of spouses under EC law. The Court accepted that the free movement provisions had been triggered and therefore the matter was not wholly internal to a Member State. The Court then went on to state that a potential migrant might be deterred from moving to another Member State if his/ her conditions of entry and residence - and those of his family - to the home state were not equivalent to those he/she would enjoy in the host state.

Issues of reverse discrimination have arisen also in relation to freedom to provide services and establishment. In *Ministre Public v Auer*[184] the French authorities refused to recognise an Italian vetinary qualification obtained by one of their own nationals. The Court ruled that Article 52 EC could only be applied to nationals of another Member State wishing to exercise the freedom of establishment in France. This case would now be decided differently as a result of Council Directive 89/48/EEC and the ruling in *Kraus*.[185]

In *Criminal Proceedings Against Bouchoucha*[186] a French national who had obtained a diploma in osteopathy in the UK was prosecuted for practicing in France without being qualified as a doctor. There were no Community rules relating to osteopathy although Council Directives 75/362 and 75/363 concerned the harmonisation and mutual recognition of medical qualifications without defining the activities of a doctor. The Court ruled that there was nothing to stop a Member State from regulating the activities of osteopaths provided it did not discriminate against its own nationals and those of other Member States. In this situation the Court was obviously aware of the abuse of the free movement provisions in that a Member State had a legitimate interest in preventing its own nationals from evading the national legislation by obtaining a lower standard of qualification in another Member State.

In *Ministerio Fiscal v Lopez Brea*[187] two Spaniards were prosecuted in Spain for carrying out the activities of an estate agent without being properly qualified under Spanish law. The Court ruled that it was open to Spain to require that all estate agents be members of a regulated profession and to

---

[184] Case 136/78 [1979] ECR 437.

[185] Case C-19/92 [1993] ECR I-1663.

[186] Case C-61/89 [1990] ECR I-3551.

[187] Case C-330/90 [1992] I-ECR 323.

reserve the practice of real estate management to members of that profession. *Lopez Brea* was followed in *Portugal v Morais*[188] which concerned the prosecution of a Lisbon driving instructor for taking his pupils outside his district onto the motorway which was contrary to a Portuguese law forbidding driving schools to give driving lessons outside of the district in which they were established. In *Criminal Proceedings against Niño and others*[189] proceedings were brought against four doctors in Italy who having been authorised to practice as doctors had provided complementary treatment in pranotherapy and biotherapy. The Court ruled that it was purely internal issue and that Community law did not apply.

## 2.15. LIMITATIONS JUSTIFIED ON THE GROUNDS OF PUBLIC POLICY, PUBLIC SECURITY, PUBLIC HEALTH

### 2.15.1. Council Directive 64/221/EEC

Under the economic free movement provisions Articles 48(3), 56 and 66 EC allow the Member States to restrict the free movement of persons on the grounds of public policy, public health and public security. These provisions are further defined in Council Directive 64/221/EEC and apply to any action[190] affecting the rights of workers, the self-employed and their families, recipients of services and also to people entitled to rights of residence under Council Directives 90/364/EEC, 90/365/EEC and 93/96/EC.

Council Directive 64/221/EEC[191] contains some general rules on the application of the derogations to the right to free movement and these rules have been subject to further interpretation and clarification by the ECJ. Article 2 of the Directive applies the Directive to all measures concerning entry, issue or renewal of residence permits or expulsion from a Member State taken on the grounds of public policy, public security or public health. These grounds cannot be invoked to serve economic ends. The expiry of the identity card or passport used by the person to enter the host state and obtain a residence permit cannot be used to justify expulsion from the host state (Article 3(3)).

---

[188] C-60/91 [1992] ECR I-2085.

[189] Cases 54 and 91/88 and 14/89 [1990] ECR 3537.

[190] Case 30/77 *R v Bouchereau* [1977] ECR 1999.

[191] OJ 1964 L 56/850.

## 2.15.2. The Narrow Interpretation of the Derogations

In *Van Duyn v Home Office*[192] the Court ruled that certain provisions of Council Directive 64/221/EEC could create vertical direct effect. The Court ruled that the concept of public policy is a Community law concept which must be interpreted strictly but accepted that it may vary from Member State to Member State. In a later case, *Rutili v Minister of the Interier,*[193] the Court added that a Member State cannot restrict the right to free movement of the individual unless the presence of the individual constitutes "a genuine and sufficiently serious threat to public policy". Any restrictions on the right to free movement must be interpreted in accordance with the principle of proportionality. The Court referred to the rights guaranteed under Articles 8 to 11 of the ECHR 1950 and the fact that the only legitimate limitations which could be placed on such rights were those which were necessary for the protection of interests in a democratic society. In *Rutili* the Court was also asked whether Article 48 EC applied only to legislative decisions or whether it also applied to administrative decisions applying the national legislation. The Court ruled that Article 48 EC applied to both forms of decision-making. The court also addressed the right of *internal* free movement, stating that restrictions cannot be imposed on the right of residence or internal free movement of migrant workers except where similar measures are imposed upon the nationals of the host state.

The public policy concept was drawn even more narrowly in *R v Bouchereau*[194] when the Court added that the concept of public policy must always presuppose a genuine and serious threat "affecting one of the fundamental interests of society". In this case the UK government tried to argue that the word "measures" in Articles 2 and 3 of the Directive did not include judicial decisions. The Court ruled that the different language versions of the Directive must be given a uniform interpretation by reference to the general scheme and wording of the Directive. The Court ruled that a judicial decision recommending deportation is a "measure" within the meaning of Article 3 of the Directive.

---

[192] Case 41/74 [1974] ECR 1337.

[193] Case 36/75 [1975] ECR 1219.

[194] Case 30/77 [1977] ECR 1999.

### 2.15.2.(i) Personal Conduct

Any measures taken on the grounds of public policy or public security must be based exclusively on the personal conduct of the individual concerned (Article 3(1)). Article 3(2) provides that previous criminal convictions do not in themselves constitute grounds for invoking the proviso. In order for a Member State to justify the exclusion of an individual the Court has ruled that the "personal conduct" under consideration does not have to be illegal but the host state must have taken steps to register its disapproval of the conduct by considering it to be socially harmful.[195] In *Van Duyn* the Court was asked to consider whether membership of an organisation can be regarded as "personal conduct" within the meaning of Article 3(1). The Court distinguished between past and present conduct. Past association cannot count as personal conduct whereas present association, being a voluntary act, can. The *Van Duyn* case must now be read in the light of the later cases of *Rutili*[196], *R v Bouchereau*[197] and *Adoui and Cornuaille v Belgian State*.[198] The later case concerned the expulsion of French prostitutes from Belgium. Prostitution was not prohibited by Belgian legislation and the Court ruled that a Member State could not deny residence to non-nationals for committing acts which were not subject to repressive or other genuine or effective measures against the host states' nationals. The national court also asked for clarification of general preventative measures under Article 3 of the Directive. In the earlier case of *Bonsignore v Oberstadtdirektor of the City of Cologne*[199] the Court had ruled that a Member State could only use the public policy proviso for breaches of the peace and public security by the individual concerned. In *Adoui* the measures were taken by Belgium because it was anxious to remove foreign prostitutes from its territory because they could promote criminal activities. It was declared that the measures were of a general nature and Belgium had not looked at each case individually to discover if an individual prostitute was indeed a threat to public policy.

The issue of whether a previous criminal conviction can be used by a Member State to show that the individual has a propensity to act in the same

---

[195] Case 41/74 *Van Duyn v Home Office* [1974] ECR 1337.

[196] Case 36/75 [1975] ECR 1219.

[197] Case 30/77 [1977] ECR 1999.

[198] Joined Cases 115 & 116/81 [1982] ECR 1665.

[199] Case 6/74 [1975] ECR 297.

way again in the future was raised in *R v Bouchereau*.[200] The Court ruled that the existence of previous convictions could only be taken into account and used as evidence of personal conduct which constituted a *present* threat to public policy by showing a propensity to act in the same way again. Past conduct alone could constitute a threat to public policy; it was a matter of fact and degree to be decided on an individual basis.

### 2.15.2.(ii). Public Health

The public health derogation is the most tightly defined of the derogations. It may only be used to justify a refusal of entry or the issue of a first residence permit in the host state. Disease and disabilities occurring after a first residence permit has been issued cannot be used to justify a refusal to renew a residence permit or expel a person claiming under the free movement provisions (Article 4(2)). Only the diseases listed in the Annex, List A, to the Directive may be used to justify the application of the public health derogation. These diseases are tuberculosis, syphilis, diseases subject to quarantine as listed in the International Health Regulation No 2 of WHO of 25 May 1951 and other infectious contagious parasitic diseases if they are the subject of provisions for the protection of nationals of the host state. The issue of how to control the spread of AIDS has posed a particular problem for the Member States since any routine testing would be contrary to the free movement provisions.[201]

It should be noted that in List B of the Annex to Council Directive 64/221/EEC the health risks of drug addiction, profound mental disturbance, manifest conditions of psychotic disturbance with agitation, delirium, hallucinations or confusion may threaten public policy or public security.

### 2.16. REMEDIES

Community law also provides a set of general remedies derived from the general principles of Community developed by the Court[202] as well as a set of procedural remedies contained within Articles 5-9 of Council Directive 64/221/EEC.

---

[200] Case 30/77 [1977] ECR 1999.

[201] Hendriks (1990); Pais Macedo van Overbeek (1990).

[202] Arnull (1990).

### 2.16.1. Procedural Rights

### 2.16.1.(i). Temporary Residence:

Article 3(4) of Council Directive 64/221/EEC states that where a migrant's identity card or passport has expired or the nationality of the holder is in dispute, the Member State which issued the identity card or passport must allow its holder to re-enter its territory without formalities. Article 5(1) allows a migrant to remain temporarily in a Member State in order to await a decision granting or refusing a first residence permit. A decision must be taken as soon as possible and not more than six months from the date of application. Article 7 states that where a refusal is given, or where there is a decision to expel a migrant, the migrant shall be allowed, save in cases of urgency, a period of not less than fifteen days (if she/he has not been granted a residence permit) or one month in all other cases in which to leave the Member State.

### 2.16.1.(ii). Reasons

Article 6 provides that a person concerned by an immigration decision shall be informed of the grounds upon which the decision taken is based, unless this is contrary to the interests of the security of the state concerned. This was expanded by the Court in *Rutili v Minister of the Interior*[203] by requiring the authority making the decision to give the migrant a precise and comprehensive statement of the grounds of the decision to allow the migrant to take effective steps to prepare his/her defence.

### 2.16.1.(iii). Rights of Defence

Article 8 provides that a Community migrant must be given the same right to challenge immigration decisions concerning entry, the issue or renewal of a residence permit and deportation as are given to nationals of the Member State to challenge administrative acts in general. Proceedings under Article 8 do not have suspensory effect unless this is the case under national law. But a migrant must be allowed to remain within the Member State long enough to commence proceedings and to state an effective case. Once this has occurred it cannot be inferred from Article 8 that the migrant has the right to remain within the host state for the duration of the proceedings.

---

[203] Case 36/75 [1975] ECR 1219.

## 2.16.1.(iv). Review By a Competent Authority

Where a migrant holds a residence permit and a Member State refuses to renew the residence permit or tries to deport the migrant then Article 9 provides that if the law of the Member State does not make provision for an appeal to a court of law on the merits of the case the immigration authority must, save in cases of emergency, consult the competent authority before taking the decision. The competent authority must be separate from the authority taking the decision and the migrant must have such rights of defence and assistance or representation as provided for in the domestic law of the Member State. After the hearing the competent authority must give its opinion and then the immigration authority can take its decision. The competent authority's opinion must be taken into consideration but it does not bind the immigration authority. The deportation of the migrant must be suspended until a decision on appeal has been given.

Article 9(2) relates to decisions refusing a grant of a residence permit or the deportation of migrant who has not obtained a residence permit. Here the competent authority must be consulted *after* the decision has been taken. In *Pecastaing v Belgian State*[204] the Court ruled that a migrant cannot be deported until the procedure has been completed, save in cases of urgency to be decided by the national authorities.

In the UK where a migrant is convicted of a criminal offence the court sentencing the migrant may recommend deportation. The Home Secretary may make a deportation order and there was no right of appeal against the Home Secretary's deportation order. In *R v Secretary of State ex parte Santillo*[205] the Court ruled that the court which made the recommendation to deport may be regarded as the competent authority for the purposes of Article 9. In *Santillo* there was a lapse of time between the appeal in the case and the deportation order since the migrant was convicted of serious sexual offences and sentenced to eight years' imprisonment with a recommendation to deport at the completion of the sentence. Santillo petitioned the Court of Appeal for leave to appeal against his sentence and the recommendation to deport but leave was refused. Four years later, after earning remission for good conduct, Santillo's prison sentence was coming to an end and the Home Secretary decided to issue a deportation order. Santillo challenged the deportation order and a reference was made to the ECJ. The Court ruled that a lapse of time between the recommendation to deport and the actual order to deport was liable to deprive

---

[204] Case 98/79 [1980] ECR 691.

[205] Case 131/79 [1980] ECR 1585.

the recommendation of its function as an opinion within the meaning of Article 9.

In *Adoui and Cornuaille v Belgian State*[206] the Court was asked a number of questions which related to the composition of the competent authority referred to in Article 9. The Court ruled that the object of Article 9 was to ensure a minimum procedural safeguard for persons against whom an expulsion measure had been adopted. Where any appeal to a court of law against administrative measures relates only to the legal validity of the decision the intervention on the part of the competent authority must make it possible for an examination to be made of the facts and circumstances, including the discretionary factors, on which the measure in question was based before the decision is definitely adopted. The person concerned must be able to put forward to the competent authority his/her arguments in defence and to be assisted or represented in such conditions as to procedure as are provided for in domestic legislation.

The Directive does not state *how* the competent authority is to be appointed. It does not require the competent authority to be a court or to be composed of members of the judiciary. Nor does it require the members of the competent authority to be appointed for a specific period. The essential requirement is that it should be clearly established that the authority is to perform its duties in absolute independence and it is not to be directly or indirectly subject to any control by the authority empowered to take measures provided for in the Directive. As long as this requirement is satisfied it is not contrary to the Directive for the remuneration of the members of the authority to be charged to the budget of the department of the administration of which the authority empowered to take decisions in question forms part or for an official belonging to that administration to serve as secretary to the competent authority.

In *R v Secretary of State For the Home Department ex parte John Gallagher*[207] an Irish national was arrested in the UK under The Prevention of Terrorism (Temporary Provisions) Act 1989 on the grounds that he had been involved in acts of terrorism. Gallagher sought to overturn the exclusion order made against him. Under the 1989 Act he was entitled to make representations and to be interviewed by a person nominated by the Secretary of State. Although informed of these rights, Gallagher consented to his removal from the UK. Later on Gallagher and his lawyers attended a meeting at the British Embassy in Dublin and made oral representations to a person nominated by the Home Secretary for the purpose of interviewing Gallagher and reporting to the

---

[206] Joined Cases 115 & 116/81 [1982] ECR 1665.

[207] Case C-175/94 [1995] ECR 4253.

Home Secretary. The Secretary of State was obliged to reconsider his decision after receiving those representations and the report of the interview. In this case the Secretary of State decided not to revoke the exclusion order and Gallagher sought judicial review of the order. Initial applications for leave to move for judicial review were refused by the High Court but on appeal to the Court of Appeal leave was granted and an Article 177 EC reference made asking, firstly, whether Article 9 of Council Directive 64/221/EEC prohibited the Home Secretary from making an exclusion order before receiving the report of the person nominated to interview Gallagher. Secondly, whether the Directive required that the person appointed to conduct an interview and report to the Home Secretary should be appointed by someone other than the Home Secretary. The Court ruled that, save in cases of urgency, the making of an exclusion order should *follow* and *not precede* the making of representations by, and the interviewing of, a person at risk of exclusion. It went on to conclude that Article 9(1) of Council Directive 64/221/EEC does not preclude the competent authority from being appointed by the same administrative authority taking the decision ordering the expulsion, provided that the competent authority can perform its duties in absolute independence and is not subject to any control by the authority empowered to take measures provided for in the Directive. It is for the national court to determine in each case whether the requirements have been met.

## 2.17. THIRD COUNTRY NATIONALS

A major problem for the development of the Internal Market is that, unlike in the case of free movement of goods, the EU has not been able to create a common external frontier for TCN's wishing to enter the EU. In relation to immigration rights, other legal rights and social benefits, TCNs derive few rights from EC law. Yet TCNs *legally resident* in the EU number, at a conservative estimate, some 10 million.[208] Their status and treatment remains by and large within the competence of the Member States. EEA citizens have the right to free movement within the EU but do not enjoy the rights relating to Citizenship of the Union found in Article 8 EC. The EU has also implemented a number of international agreements which grant some rights to enter the EU and work, the most extensive agreements being Decisions 1/80 and 3/80 concluded by the EC-Turkey Association Council. Although the Court has declared that some of the Articles in these Decisions are legally precise enough to be capable of direct effect even the Court, which we have seen has been liberal in its interpretation of the free movement provisions, has often

---

[208] *Communication on Immigration and Asylum Policies* COM(94) 23, Annex I, 22.

found it difficult to ascribe EC competence in this area. Since the TEU immigration policy in relation to the external frontier has moved on at a far greater speed since immigration issues can be dealt with under the Intergovernmental Pillars of the TEU. The Justice and Home Affairs (JHA) Pillar includes within its remit all controls on people crossing EU external borders, measures to combat drug addiction and international fraud, judicial co-operation in civil and criminal matters, customs and police co-operation. There is little democratic or judicial control over these activities. The EC Institutions have only a small role to play: the Commission has a right of initiative in some areas, although police co-operation and customs are excluded. The European Parliament should be informed of the discussions but this is not a clear obligation. The Court of Justice does not have jurisdiction over this area except in cases where the Council provides for it. Although the Council has the pivotal decision-making function, it is in fact only one of the five negotiating levels (the others being, Coreper, the Article K.4 Committee, steering groups and working parties). Article 110C(6) EC enables the Council of Ministers to determine which TCNs need a visa in order to enter the EU[209] and Article K.9 TEU and 100C(6) EC are *passerelle* provisions providing for the transfer of certain areas relating to immigration policy from the JHA intergovernmental pillar to the decision-making framework of Article 100C EC. While Article 6 EC provides protection against discrimination on the grounds of nationality - without distinction between nationals of an EU Member State and TCNs - the Court has limited its application to nationals of the Member States and, as we shall see in Chapter Four, the EC has very limited competence to enact measures relating to discrimination on the grounds of race, colour, ethnic origin. It is arguable that race discrimination may affect the functioning of the

---

[209] A Regulation laying down a uniform format for visas has been adopted: Council Regulation 1683/95, OJ L 164/1. The list of countries whose nationals must be in possession of a visa when crossing the external borders of the Member States is to be found as an Annex to Regulation 2317/95 OJ 1995, L 234/1. There was some controversy as to whether makes provision for a "positive list" of countries whose nationals are not required to be in possession of a visa when crossing the external frontier of a Member State since a positive list can only be fixed by Article K.3 TEU, see Hailbonner (1994). See also the Council Joint Action on school trips (OJ 1994 L 327/1) and the Council's Joint Action on transit visas for nationals of certain third countries. Rather oddly, the Visa Regulation 231/795 does not cover transit visas whereas the visa format Regulation 1683/95 specifically does. See Peers (1996b). The European Parliament initiated an Article 173 EC action arguing that one of its fundamental prerogatives had been infringed when the Commission's original proposal for Council Regulation 2317/95 was substantially amended by the Council: Case C-392/95 *Parliament v Council*. Advocate General Fennelly delivered an Opinion on 21 March 1997 upholding the Parliament's claim but allowing the Regulation to stand.

Internal Market. Member States may allow firms to use and exploit TCNs thus creating a competitive advantage.[210] Equally, a lack of protection against racial discrimination in the host state may act as a disincentive to migrate.[211]

## 2.18. RIGHTS OF TCNS UNDER EC LAW

### 2.18.1. Non-EC Relatives of Migrant Workers

Under Regulation 1612/68/EEC non-EC relatives of a migrant worker may derive rights under EC law. Such rights include the right to install themselves with the migrant worker in the host state, a conditional right to remain permanently in the host state,[212] admission to the education system on the same conditions as the nationals of the host state, the right to work and access to social security benefits in the host state.[213] Although the cloak of protection of EC law applies while the marriage of a TCN to a migrant worker subsists it is likely to disappear once a marriage has been ended formally.[214] It may be possible to argue that the deportation of a TCN spouse is a breach of the right to family life guaranteed by Article 8 ECHR 1950, especially where he/she is deprived of contact with other family members as a result of the deportation.[215]

### 2.18.2. International Agreements

Under Agreements made between the EU and third states under Article 228 and 238 EC the Member States may be under an obligation to treat nationals of the third states in a way which it is compatible with EC law. Such agreements may be the subject of preliminary rulings and the provisions may be capable of direct effect. The Court has rarely found a breach of the agreements - largely due to the fact that the agreements are limited in the rights

---

[210] See Nielsen and Szyszczak (1994).

[211] Szyszczak (1992a).

[212] The relatives are subject to Article 48(3) EC and Council Directive 64/221/EEC.

[213] See Joined Cases C-297/88 and C-197/89 *Dzodzi v Belgium* [1990] ECR 3783.

[214] Although the court has not stated this explicitly in Cases 267/83 *Diatta v Land of Berlin* [1985] ECR 567 and Case C-370/90 *R v IAT and Surinder Singh ex parte Secretary of State for the Home Department* [1992] ECR I-4265.

[215] *Berrehab v Netherlands* A/138 [1989] ECHR 322. Cf Case 12/86 *Demirel* [1987] ECR 3719.

they grant to TCNs. For example, in *Sevince v Staatssecretaris van Justitie²¹⁶* a Turkish national's application for a new residence permit was rejected. He attempted to argue that the directly effective provisions of the Decisions adopted under the EU Association Agreement with Turkey applied. But the Court ruled that since Sevince's residence permit had been revoked he was no longer in "legal employment" and could not therefore claim rights under the Agreement and the Decisions. In *Bozkurt v Staatssecretaris van Justitie²¹⁷* the applicant worked for a Dutch company as a long distance lorry driver between the Netherlands and the Middle East. He paid tax on his earning in the Netherlands. He was granted a provisional Dutch residence permit which he claimed gave him the right to remain in the Netherlands. Although the Court ruled that legal employment could be established and that such employment necessarily implies the recognition of a right to residence the Court went on to rule that Article 6(2) of Decision 1/80 did not give Bozkurt the right to remain in the Netherlands following an accident at work which rendered him permanently incapacitated for work. In *Demirel v Stadt Schwabisch Gmund²¹⁸* a Turkish woman was ordered to leave Germany after her tourist visa had expired. At that time rights to family reunification were not covered by the EC-Turkey Association Agreement and the Court ruled that the matter was one for domestic law to determine and that the Court did not have jurisdiction to decide if the national rules were compatible with the principles enshrined in Article 8 ECHR 1950.[219]

There are some positive rulings, for example in *Lopes de Veiga*[220] a Portuguese national successfully challenged a refusal of a residence permit by the Dutch authorities. He had been employed on a vessel flying the Dutch flag at the time of Portugal's accession to the EC. Although transitional rules applied to the free movement of workers the Court ruled that the purpose of such rules was to prevent the disruption of national labour markets at the time of Portugal's accession and since the applicant was already employed within a Member State the rules were not applicable. In *Kus v Landeshauptstadt*

---

[216] Case 192/89 [1990] ECR I-3461.

[217] Case C-434/93 [1995] ECR I-1475; See also Case C-285/95 *Kol v Land of Berlin*, pending; Case C-386/95 *Eker v Land Baden-Württemberg*, pending.

[218] Case 12/86 [1987] ECR 3719.

[219] Cf Case C-351/95 *Kadiman* judgment of 17 April 1997.

[220] Case 9/88 [1989] ECR I-2989.

*Wiesbaden*[221] the Court ruled that while Decision 1/80 of the EU-Turkey Association Agreement confers the right to work it must also encompass the right of residence. In *Eroglu v Land Baden-Wurttemburg*[222] the daughter of a Turkish migrant worker joined him in Germany where she studied and then found work. Her application for a residence permit was rejected. Article 7 of Decision 1/80 allows members of the family who have been authorised to join the worker a right to employment (subject to Community preference) after a three year period of legal residence and an unrestricted right to employment after legal residence of five years. In addition children of Turkish workers who have completed a course of vocational training in a Member State have a right of access to employment in that state irrespective of the length of their period of residence as long as one of their parents has been legally employed in that Member State for at least three years. The Court allowed the daughter to rely on this provision. In *Office National de l'Emploi v Kziber*[223] the daughter of a Moroccan national who had retired in Belgium after being a migrant worker there was entitled to rely upon Article 41(1) of the Cooperation Agreement concluded with Morocco in 1976 which provided for equal treatment in the field of social security for Moroccan workers employed in the Member States. The rights expressly mentioned in the Agreement included the aggregation of the periods of insurance, employment and residence in different Member States, the right to family allowances for family members resident in the EU and the right to transfer pensions and other benefits to the state of origin. The Court ruled that social security in Article 41(1) of the Agreement must be understood by means of an analogy with the identical concept in Regulation 1408/71/EEC.[224] The Court concluded that unemployment benefits, although not mentioned expressly in Article 41(1), should be within the scope of the Agreement.

The direct effect of Article 41(1) of the EU-Morocco Co-operation Agreement was utilised in *Yousfi v Belgian State*[225] to counteract discrimination against the son of a Moroccan migrant worker who was denied a disability allowance after an accident at work. It was utilised also in *A. Hallouzi-Choho*

---

[221] Case C-237/91 [1992] ECR I-6781.

[222] Case C-355/93 [1994] ECR I-5113.

[223] Case C-18/90 [1991] ECR I-199.

[224] OJ 1971 L149/2.

[225] Case C-58/93 [1994] ECR I-1353.

*v Bestuur van de Sociale Verzekeringsbank.*[226] Here the Moroccan spouse (who had not been in paid employment) of a Moroccan migrant worker was denied benefits under the transitional arrangements of a Dutch social security law. These benefits were available to Dutch nationals who satisfied certain residence conditions The Dutch government attempted to argue that the transitional arrangements under scrutiny did not cover Regulation 1408/71/EEC and that the pension at issue was a personal right not a derived right. The Court noted that the persons covered by Article 41(1) of the Agreement are not the same as those covered by Article 2 of Regulation 1408/71/EEC and so the case law on Article 2 of Regulation 1408/71/EEC cannot be applied in the context of the Moroccan Agreement.[227] Similar arguments were raised by the Court in *Krid v CNVATS*[228] in the context of Article 39(1) of the Co-operation Agreement between the EEC and Algeria which is identical in wording to Article 41(1) of the Morocco-EEC Agreement. The Court ruled that the refusal to grant the pension was based on the fact that the applicant did not have Dutch nationality and this contravened the principle of Article 41(1) whereby a Member State cannot impose more onerous restrictions on Moroccan nationals employed in the Member State than those applicable to its own nationals. Here, not only the requirement of Dutch nationality was required, but also more onerous conditions of residence or the pursuit of a professional activity which nationals were not required to satisfy.

Most recently the Court has delivered a far-reaching judgment in *Tetik v Land Berlin.*[229] A Turkish national had been legally employed as a seaman on various German ships for eight years obtaining from the German authorities successive residence permits, each for a specific period and limited to employment in shipping. His last permit was valid until 4 August 1988 and stated that it would expire on cessation of his employment in German shipping. Tetik left his post as a seaman and moved to Berlin and applied for an unlimited residence permit to work on the land. The application was refused. Questions were referred to the ECJ on the effect of Article 6 of Decision 1/80 of the Council of the EEC/Turkey Association Agreement. The Court held that Article 6(1) created direct effects and that it granted *not only* the right to respond to a prior offer of employment but also gave the unconditional right

---

[226] Case C-126/95, Judgment of 3 October 1996, nyr.

[227] See Case C-308/93 *Bestuur van de Sociale Verzekeringsbank v Cabanis-Issarte* [1996] ECR I-2097.

[228] Case C-103/94 [1995] ECR I-719.

[229] Case C-171/95, Judgment of 23 January 1997, nyr.

to seek and take up any employment he chose without any possibility of this being subject to priority for workers from the Member States. The Agreement states that "... the contracting parties agree to be guided by Articles 48, 49 and 50 of the [EEC Treaty] for the purpose of progressively securing the free movement for workers between them." Since the Court had ruled in *Antonissen*[230] that Article 48 EC entailed the right of Community nationals to reside in a Member State for the purposes of seeking employment there these principles must, as far as possible , inform the treatment of Turkish workers who enjoyed rights under Decision 1/80. To give full effect to Article 6, therefore, a Turkish worker must, after at least four years of legal employment in a Member State, be entitled to reside in that Member State for a reasonable period while seeking new employment since the right of free access to any paid employment of his choice would be deprived of substance. It was for the national authorities or courts of the host Member State to determine how long a reasonable period should be but it must be sufficient not to jeopardise the Turkish worker's prospects of finding new employment.

## 2.19. TCN IMMIGRATION AFTER THE TEU[231]

In the Commission's White Paper, *Completing The Internal Market*[232] there is the suggestion that during the completion of the Internal Market TCN's who are lawfully resident in the EU should be given rights to live and work in the Member States. But third country immigration matters were placed outside the scope of the SEA 1986 by a General Declaration on Articles 13-19 SEA 1986. The Member States did commit themselves towards cooperation outside the formal Treaty structure on the free movement of persons including TCNs in a Political Declaration on the SEA 1986 allowing the Member States to work on the issue of TCN immigration within the framework of intergovernmental co-operation. A number of common principles for immigration policy have emerged and a number of working groups established to refine the principles. This policy has been criticised by black and ethnic minority groups for its secrecy, lack of democratic input and the objection is raised that immigration matters - including those relating to refugees and asylum seekers are linked

---

[230] Case C-292/89 [1991] ECR I-745.

[231] See Guild (1996); Uçarer and Puchala (1997); Bieber and Monar (1995); d'Oliveira (1995); Hoogenboom (1992), Korella and Twomey (1993).

[232] COM(85) 310 final, paras 15-16.

with other forms of "problems" such as drug trafficking, international terrorism and illegal immigration.

The Commission[233] expressed the view that the logic of the Internal Market implied the elimination of the condition of nationality for the exercise of certain rights and suggested that TCNs should be able to move around the EU freely on the basis of a residence permit which would replace existing visa requirements.[234] The Commission included this idea in a proposal for a Council Decision, based upon Article K.3 TEU for a Convention on the Crossing of External Frontiers.[235] Upon the crossing of an EU frontier all *visiting* TCNs would be allowed to stay within a Member State for three months and all *resident* TCNs would be allowed three months visa-free stays. Longer stays would be subject to national law.[236] This proposal has run into difficulties since there is no consensus between Spain and the UK over the external frontier of Gibraltar. The Commission's Communication on Immigration and Asylum Policies[237] and the White Paper on *European Social Policy* [238]envisaged several new measures to benefit permanently resident TCNs including coverage for health care when travelling in the EU, the right to move abroad for medical treatment, the right to enter other Member States without a visa and priority for job openings in other Member States where no EC national or local TCN was available. It was proposed that full free movement of TCNs should be granted later along with equal treatment in access to employment and social benefits. A package of proposals was unveiled on 12 July 1995.[239] These proposed lifting the requirement for visas for TCN family members, a Directive abolishing internal frontier checks and a Directive on the travel rights of TCNs. The proposed right to travel Directive would grant TCNs substantial new rights: all non-EU citizens *legally* resident in a Member State would be allowed to travel visa-free throughout the EU for three months regardless of

---

[233] Sec (91) 1855 final. See other Communications on Immigration Policy: COM (79) 113; COM(85) 48; SEC (89) 924; SEC (90) 1813;SEC(91) 1855; COM(94) 23.

[234] COM(94) 23, 34.

[235] COM(93) 684.

[236] Note under the existing Schengen Convention arrangements, TCNs are allowed up to three months travel within the Schengen states.

[237] COM (94) 23.

[238] COM (94) 333.

[239] COM (95) 346, 347 and 348. Peers (1997a).

whether or not they are family members of an EU citizen or whether they would otherwise be obliged to obtain a visa. TCNs not resident in a Member State would be entitled to circulate visa-free in any Member State that did not impose a visa requirement. Both rights would be limited only by the obligation to hold a travel document and a residence permit where relevant and the Member States' discretion to impose the public order/public security restrictions on TCNs. A Council Resolution on the status of TCNs in the Member States has already been adopted.[240] This Resolution establishes that the Member States "must make progress in the adoption of measures to facilitate the integration into the host state of TCNs settled in their territory". Such integration is said to contribute to greater security and stability in daily life, work and social peace and therefore a number of principles common to the Member States should be defined. But a number of groups are excluded from the Resolution: family members of EU Citizens, EEA nationals and their families, persons with more favourable status deriving from other agreements between the EC and third states and students. The rights set out in the Resolution cover the right to a residence authorization, but Member States have an option not to grant an unlimited authorization instead they may grant a ten year permit or a permit for the longest period available in national law which should tend to be ten years long. Member States may object to the granting of the permit on public policy or national security grounds. Member States are also entitled to examine the level and stability of the means of existence which the applicant demonstrates in particular whether he/she has health insurance and also the conditions for exercising an occupation.[241] Other rights include the right to travel through the Member States' territory, equivalence with host state nationals in working conditions, trade union membership, public policy on housing, social security, emergency health care and compulsory schooling. It should be possible for them to receive non-contributory benefits.

---

[240] OJ 1996 C 80/2.

[241] Cf Member States may expel an EU citizen after five years residence if he/she is unemployed Article 7(2) Council Directive 68/360/EEC OJ Spec Ed. (II) 1972 402; Article 4(1) Council Directive 73/148 OJ L 1972 172/14. But note a person has a right to remain under Council Directive 90/364 OJ 1990 L 180/26 if he/she has sufficient funds.

There is also a Recommendation on Illegal Immigration and Employment.[242] This Recommendation only exempts EU Citizens and EEA citizens and their families. Thus people covered by the Agreements with third states and also given rights under Articles 59 and 60 EC as a result of *Rush Portuguesa*[243] and *Van der Elst*[244] are excluded. Under the Recommendation identity checks are encouraged where "a person appears to be residing in the country unlawfully" in particular where offences are investigated or prosecuted to ward off threats to public danger or security. To implement the Recommendation, resident rights of apparent unlawful residents must be repeatedly verified when they apply for government benefits with national authorities sharing information to administer the verification process. Member States are encouraged to ask employers to check residence and work permits and to possibly compel them to vet every application with the immigration authorities. Member States are obliged to subject employers to "appropriate penalties" if they employ unauthorised foreign nationals. A central file on all resident foreign nationals is recommended, but not obligatory. Foreign nationals "who have deliberately brought about their illegal position" should be subject to penalties which may fall under criminal law.

Another Recommendation of 27 September 1996, on combating the illegal employment of TCNs[245] implements the 1995 Recommendation in more detail. This Recommendation exempts EU and EEA citizens and their families and also TCNs "in a situation covered by Community law" and any person given more favourable rights in an agreement concluded with the EC or a Member State. But this Recommendation toughens the penalties to be imposed on employers. Illegal trafficking in labour is advised to be criminal offence and the level of the penalty must be effective, persuasive and proportionate.[246]

---

[242] Council Recommendation of 22 December 1995 on harmonizing means of combatting illegal immigration and illegal employment and improving the relevant means of control, OJ 1996 C 5/1. This matter was first raised under the SAP OJ 1976, C 277/2; OJ 1978 C 97/9. See Evans (1994).

[243] Case C-119/89 [1990] ECR 1439.

[244] Case C-43/93 [1994] ECR I-3803.

[245] OJ 1996 C 304/1.

[246] See Peers (1997).

## 2.20. SOCIAL SECURITY FOR MIGRANT[247]

To complement the free movement of persons Article 51 EC addresses the problem of ensuring continuity of social security protection when a person moves between Member States. Article 51 EC empowers the Council to adopt such measures in the field of social security as are necessary to secure the freedom of movement of workers. Three principles guide the measures to be taken:

> *The aggregation principle:* for the purpose of acquiring and retaining the right to benefit and of calculating the amount of benefit there will be aggregation of all periods under the laws of the Member States where the person resides.
>
> *The exportability principle* the payment of benefits acquired under the laws of the Member States to persons resident in another Member State.

As with the free movement of persons programme, the legislation for implementing Article 51 EC was put into effect quickly. The aim of Community law is not to seek *harmonisation* of national social security schemes but rather to *co-ordinate* the diverse national schemes,[248] to prevent a person from being penalised for having moved between the Member States.

The co-ordination principles found in Regulation 1408/71[249] have moved beyond the original aim of facilitating the free movement of persons. In contrast to Regulation 1612/68 it is not necessary to have invoked the right to free movement to utilise the provisions of Regulation 1408/71.[250] The Regulation also addresses the issue of reverse discrimination directly. Wyatt and Dashwood[251] argue that the principle of free movement embraces the right *not* to migrate and in *Kenny v Insurance Officer*[252] the Court states:

---

[247] See generally Pennings (1994).

[248] See van Langendomck (1973); Case C-227/89 *Rönfeldt* [1991] ECR I-323. To date, the ECJ has not provided a definition of "co-ordination". The Member States are free to determine the rules of national social security systems, to decide who is to be insured, benefits to be granted and the principles upon which these benefits are based. EC law will intervene, however, to counteract discrimination based upon sex when Council Directives, 79/7/EEC, 86/378/EEC, 86/613/EEC may be used. See Chapter Four.

[249] OJ 1971 L 149/2.

[250] Case C-2/89 *Kits Van Heyningen* [1990] ECR I-1795.

[251] Wyatt and Dashwood (1993) 326.

[252] Case 1/78 [1978] ECR 1489.

"... it is for the national legislation to lay down the conditions for the acquisition, retention, loss or suspension of the right to social security benefits so long as those conditions apply without discrimination to the nationals of the Member States concerned and to those of other Member States."

Laske summarises the principles underlying the protection to social security rights in the following way:

"... the territorial effect inherent in national social security systems, has been minimised through a policy of co-ordination, allowing independent domestic systems to exist, but modifying those aspects hindering the mobility of persons. In the attempt to create constant protection for migrants, their social security rights are rendered personal rather than territorial."

The scheme of co-ordination of social security systems is not without its critics. The case law of the ECJ has been criticized for breaking the "principle of territoriality" anchoring social security in the Member State, including the suggestion that by facilitating the unlimited export of benefits abroad the EU system is in danger of jeopardizing the very existence of the high level of social security protection in some of the Member States. Laske[253] exposes the EU system to even more searching criticism. She argues that the completion of the Internal Market requires both technical and conceptual changes to the way the protection of social security benefits is addressed in the EU. The Member States have not agreed to allow qualified majority voting under Article 51 EC, thus excluding social security from any further degree of Community competence. The "half-way" house approach has resulted in a complicated system and little has been done to address how new forms of social security protection developed in the Member States have repercussions for the Community system.[254] Yet the idea of creating a new, supra-national system of social security protection for migrants has been rejected as practically impossible economically and socially unnecessary and as politically unacceptable.

A major omission is the lack of co-ordination of occupational and private social security schemes which have grown throughout the EU in recent years. Part II/4 of the Commission's Action Programme to implement the Social

---

[253] See Laske (1993) 515.

[254] Any changes made to national systems are recorded in Annex VI of Regulation 1408/71 and if necessary amendments are made to the EC legislation to accommodate any distortions to the EC system. This results in a complicated web of national and EC legislation.

Charter 1989[255] highlighted the problem but little has been achieved to redress the problem. In July 1991 the Commission issued a Communication[256] recognising that the diversity of schemes across the EU ruled out the possibility of harmonisation of such schemes but raised the possibility of capital transfers for cross-border migrants and cross-border membership schemes. However the resolution of other features of the schemes which disadvantage migrants such as excessively long vesting and waiting periods and the maintenance of acquired rights in pension schemes may be difficult.

Another problem with Regulation 1408/71 is that its coverage of social security is limited to the eight traditional social security areas set out in ILO Convention No. 102.[257] Thus new forms of social security which have emerged are excluded. Equally the exclusion of certain kinds of benefits such as social and medical assistance in Article 4(1) of Regulation 1408/71 (on the grounds that such schemes related to the specific social and economic situation of each Member State) can no longer be supported.

There are also gaps in the personal scope of Regulation 1408/71. Article 2(1) of the Regulation protects the employed and self-employed and their families from losing social security rights if they are nationals of one of the Member States and if they are or have been subject to the social security legislation of one or more Member States. Article 4(4) excludes civil servants (and persons treated as such) subject to special schemes in the Member States, which is a wide exclusion covering a number of public sector jobs. Students and persons who are not insured or persons who are insured voluntarily are also excluded from the scope of the Regulation. Given the moves by the EU to ensure a general right of free movement it is necessary to extend the scope of social security co-ordination to embrace all the people who may want to move freely around the EU.[258]

At present TCNs are also excluded from the scope of Regulation 1408/71 unless they fall within the definition of the claimant's family under Article

---

[255] COM (89) 568 final.

[256] Supplementary Social Security Schemes: the role of occupational pension schemes in the social protection of workers and their implication for freedom of movement, SEC/91/1332 final, Brussels, 22.7.91.

[257] Sickness, maternity, invalidity, old-age and death, accidents at work and occupational diseases, death grants, unemployment, family benefits and family allowances for employed and unemployed persons, benefits for dependent children of pensioners and for orphans.

[258] See the Commission's proposal to extend the personal scope of Regulation 1408/71, COM (91) 528 final.

2(1). However the ECJ has given a limited interpretation of the notion of "family" in *Office National de l'Emploi* v *Josezef Deak*[259] where a Hungarian national living in Belgium with his Italian mother was held not to fall within the personal scope of the Regulation.[260] TCNs are covered in some of the Association Agreements concluded by the EU and third states. The ECJ's approach has been cautious to the interpretation of these Agreements. In the most recent decision, *Z Taflan Met*,[261] various Dutch social security benefits were being withheld from Turkish migrant workers on the grounds that the insured risk did not materialise when the worker was covered by the legislation. Although the Dutch court hearing the claim considered that the applicants could qualify for the social security benefits under Decision 3/80 taken in the framework of the Association Agreement it was uncertain as to whether Decision 3/80 had entered into force as the date of implementation had not been specified. The ECJ ruled that Decision 3/80 entered into force on the date on which it was adopted and had been binding on the contracting parties since that time. The Dutch court also asked if Articles 12 and 13 of the Decision could have direct effect. The ECJ answered in the negative. The Articles were not precisely worded and were intended to be supplemented by a subsequent act of the Council.

## 2.21. THE PRINCIPLES OF CO-ORDINATION

Regulation 1408/71 has as its overriding aim the goal of ensuring that migrant workers and their families should not be disadvantaged as a result of migration to another Member State. Four principles, derived from the Preamble to the Regulation and a purposive interpretation of Articles 48-51 EC underpin the operation of the principle of co-ordination of social security benefits.

Article 3 of Regulation 1408/71 is a concrete application of the *principle of non-discrimination* on the ground of nationality contained in Article 6 EC. Both direct and indirect discrimination is covered.[262]

Only one national system of legislation can apply to a migrant worker at any one time. The fundamental rule is one of *lex laboris*, the system applicable is

---

[259] Case 94/84 [1985] ECR 1873.

[260] Cf Case C-308/93 *Cabanis-Issarte* [1996] ECR I-2097; Case C-126/95 *Hallouzi-Choho*, nyr.

[261] Case C-277/94 judgment of 10 September 1996.

[262] Case 237/78 *CRAM* v *Toia* [1979] ECR 2645; Case C-326/90 *Commission* v *Belgium* [1992] ECR I-5517.

that of the Member State where the worker (or self-employed person) works irrespective of their place of residence or the place of residence of the employer. Where a person ceases an activity in one Member State and does not move to another Member State before a social security risk arises Article 13(2)(f) states that the person shall be subject to the legislation of the Member State in whose territory he/she resides. An exception is also found in Article 14(1) and 14a(1) which provide that where a worker or a self-employed person normally works for a firm in one Member State but is posted to another Member State for up to one year, working for the same firm, the legislation of the original Member State will continue to apply. This rule ensures that the worker does not have to contribute to two social security schemes and eliminates the possibility of not being insured at all. The ECJ has accepted that there may be concurrent application of different schemes provided that workers are entitled to additional benefits for any additional contributions they are required to make.[263] It is possible for the competent authorities of the Member States to agree to provide exceptions to the choice of law rule in the interests of certain workers or categories of workers.[264]

The *principle of aggregation* implies that the host state must take account of periods of insurance completed in other Member States when calculating whether the claimant has satisfied the necessary qualifying conditions for a benefit. Rights in the process of being acquired must be preserved.

The *principle of exportability* preserves rights which have already been acquired. Long-term benefits such as pensions must be paid by the Member State of origin.

### 2.21.1. Supplementary Principles

*Pro-raterisation:* this provides for the equitable distribution of the cost of the benefit between the Member States where the claimant has been insured. This applies largely to long term benefits such as pensions (Articles 40 and 46) and to a limited extent occupational diseases (Article 60). It does not apply to sickness and maternity benefits (Article 18).

*Overlapping of Benefits:* the EC rules can neither confirm or maintain the right to several benefits of the same kind for one and the same period of compulsory insurance (Article 12(1)). However, as a result of the single state principle, (described above) migrants may receive less from the competent state than they would have received if they had not moved. Since the aim of

---

[263] See Case 92/63 *Nonnenmacher* v *Social Verzekeringsbank* [1964] ECR 281.

[264] Article 17.

the EC rules is to eliminate any disadvantages suffered as a result of migration the ECJ ruled in *De Felice*[265] that claimants should be entitled to receive the difference between the sum payable by the competent institution and the sum which would have been paid by the more generous state. Other rulings, such as *Nonnenmacher*[266] suggest that the social security rules should be interpreted to *improve* the position of the migrant.

## 2.22. THE PERSONAL SCOPE OF REGULATION 1408/71

The personal scope of Regulation 1408/71 is defined in relation to persons insured under national legislation rather than in relation to the definitions of free movement of persons outlined in Articles 48, 52 and 59 EC and imple- menting secondary legislation. Thus Article 2(1) provides that Regulation 1408/71 applies to "employed or self-employed persons who are or have been subject to the legislation of one or more Member States and who are nationals of one of the Member States ..... also to members of their families and their survivors." The employed and self-employed are defined further in Article 1(a)(I) as ".... any person who is insured, compulsorily or on an optional continued basis, for one or more of the contingencies covered by branches of a social security scheme for employed or self-employed persons. The ECJ has given a broad interpretation to these provisions.

## 2.23. THE MATERIAL SCOPE OF REGULATION 1408/71

The Regulation applies to all legislation (defined by Article 1(j) to include statutes, regulations and other provisions and all other implementing measures, present or future, relating to the branches and schemes of social security) relating to social security benefits but not social assistance. Article 4(1) provides an exhaustive list of the areas of social security covered by the Regulation.

A major problem is that the Regulation excludes social and medical assistance schemes and to benefit schemes for victims of war and its conse- quences[267] or to special schemes for civil servants.[268] Litigation has arisen

---

[265] Case 128/88 [1989] ECR 923.

[266] Case 92/63 [1964] ECR 281.

[267] Article 4(4).

[268] Case C-443/93 *Vougioukas* v *IRA* [1995] ECR I-4033.

therefore on the definition of these terms. In *Fossi* v *Bundesknappschaft*[269] the Court described social security as "legislation which confers on the beneficiaries a legally defined position which involves no individual and discretionary assessment of needs of person circumstances." Whereas in *Piscitello* v *INPS*[270] social assistance is described as legislation designed to provide benefits for those in need, where eligibility is not dependent on periods of employment, affiliation or insurance but there is some element of individual assessment.[271] Non-contributory benefits of a mixed type may be caught by Regulation 1408/71.[272]

Article 4(2a) introduced a new category of benefits described as special non-contributory benefits which are provided under legislation or schemes other than those provided in Article 4(1) where such benefits are intended to provide supplementary, substitute or ancillary cover against the risks covered by the branches of social security referred to in Article 4(1) or provide specific protection for the disabled. However, Article 10a allows the Member States to provide that special non-contributory benefits are non-exportable.

## 2.24. FUTURE REFORM

Given the political difficulties of reforming the approach taken under Article 51 EC the Commission has adopted two soft law measures to promote social integration and solidarity constituting a limited, but important step, towards harmonisation. Council Recommendation 92/442[273] on the convergence of social policy objectives and Council Recommendation 92/441/EC[274] on common criteria concerning sufficient resources and social assistance have two

---

[269] Case 79/76 [1977] ECR 667.

[270] Case 139/82 [1983] ECR 1427.

[271] See also Council Recommendation 92/441/EEC of 24 June 1992 on common criteria concerning sufficient resources and social assistance in social protection, OJ 1992 L 245/46.

[272] Case C-78/91 *Hughes* v *Chief Adjudication Officer* [1992] ECR I-4839; Case C-356/89 *Newton* v *Chief Adjudication Officer* [1991] ECR I-3107. These benefits relating to family credit and mobility allowance were brought formally within the scope of the Regulation by Regulation 1247/92 OJ 1992 L 136/1.

[273] OJ 1992 L 245/49.

[274] OJ 1992 L 245/46.

objectives in order to realise the aims of Articles 10, 24 and 25 of the Social Charter 1989:

> *firstly*, to secure for workers and retired workers a right to adequate social security benefits and, for the retired, resources to enable them to enjoy a decent standard of living.
> *secondly*, to secure for the unemployed and those reaching retirement age, who are not entitled to a pension sufficient social assistance to satisfy their needs.

The two Recommendations address the *level* of the resources that should be available and provide guidance on the co-ordination of national policies. Member States continue to retain the discretion to prescribe the conditions of access to such benefits, but social benefits must not be discriminatory on the grounds of nationality, race, sex, religion, customs or political opinion and the benefits must be granted according to the principles of fairness. In relation to benefits covering sickness, maternity, unemployment and incapacity for work, the elderly and the family benefits should be available for anyone legally resident in the Member State.

The Commission's White Paper on Social Policy[275] proposes further Recommendations: on the adaptation of social protection schemes to changing family structures through the individualisation of rights and contributions; on the financing of social security, setting out common guidelines to promote better adaptation of social security to employment protection while maintaining solidarity networks and permitting the co-existence of different national systems; long-term care insurance for people who become dependent.

---

[275] COM(94) 333 final.

# CHAPTER THREE

# EDUCATION AND VOCATIONAL TRAINING

## 3.1. LEGAL COMPETENCE

Neither the original EEC Treaty 1957 or the Single European Act 1986 mentioned Community competence in the field of education. Article 128 EEC empowered the Council of Ministers, acting by simple majority vote, to "... lay down general principles for implementing a common vocational training policy capable of contributing to the harmonious development both of the national economies and of the common market." Council Decision 63/266/EEC[1] elaborated the general principles for a Community vocational training policy but there was little legislative activity until the 1980s when a series of ECJ rulings clarified that the Community had competence to develop a vocational training policy and that budgetary provision could be made for the implementation of such programmes. The term 'education' appears for the first time within EC competence as a result of the amendments made by the TEU 1992 in Article 3(p) EC, Article 126 EC and Article 127 EC. However Article C TEU states that:

> "The Union shall be served by a single institutional framework which shall ensure the consistency and the continuity of the activities carried out in order to attain its objectives while respecting and building upon the "acquis communautaire"."

Since Articles 126 and 127 EC are the successors to Article 128 EEC Article C TEU requires that Articles 126 and 127 EC must be interpreted and applied in such a way that Article 128 EEC is respected and built upon. We must, therefore, examine the *acquis communautaire* in relation to the competence of the EC to develop an education policy.

---

[1]  OJ English Special Edition 1963/64, 25.

## 3.2. COMPETENCE PRIOR TO THE TEU

Prior to the TEU, Community competence in the field of education can be discerned in three areas: 1. Education issues were raised under Regulation 1612/68/EEC in relation to rights to facilitate the free movement of workers and for members of their families who wished to study in another Member State. 2. The EC had competence to enact legislation for the mutual recognition of educational and professional qualifications in order to facilitate the free movement of workers under Article 57(1) EC. 3. Legislation was adopted to establish Community schemes in areas such as vocational training, foreign languages, educational exchanges and educational mobility (schemes such as ERASMUS, COMMETT, LINGUA) and to establish a European Training Foundation. This in turn has generated a number of legal base disputes before the ECJ.

### 3.2.1. Education rights in relation to the free movement of persons

Regulation 1612/68/EEC provides rights relating to vocational training in Article 7 which states:

> **1.** A worker who is a national of a Member State may not, in the territory of another Member State, be treated differently from national workers by reason of his nationality in respect of any conditions of employment and work, in particular as regards remuneration, dismissal, and should he become unemployed, reinstatement or re-employment;
> **2.** He shall enjoy the same social and tax advantages as national workers.
> **3.** He shall also, by virtue of the same right and under the same conditions as national workers, have access to training in vocational schools and retraining centres.

And in Article 12:

> The children of a national of a Member State who is or has been employed in the territory of another Member State shall be admitted to that State's general educational, apprenticeship and vocational training courses under the same conditions as the nationals of that state, if such children are residing in its territory.
> Member States shall encourage all efforts to enable such children to attend these courses under the best possible conditions.[2]

---

[2] Council Directive 77/486/EEC on the education of migrant workers' children OJ 1977 L 199/32 was enacted. See also Commission Report on the Education of Migrants' Children in the European Union COM(94)80 final; Cullen (1996).

It was accepted that the Treaty rules alone would not be adequate to ensure the smooth working of the Common Market and therefore legislative powers were assigned to the Community. Where measures in the field of education would ensure the effectiveness of those powers the Community is entitled to enact measures even where no *express* power with regard to education policy has been conferred. These are called *implied* powers[3] and their application is seen in *Casagrande v Landeshauptstadt Munchen*.[4] Here the son of a Italian migrant worker in Germany was denied an educational grant which, under a statute of the Free State of Bavaria, was reserved to German nationals, stateless persons and aliens granted asylum. Under Article 49 EEC the EC has power to adopt "the measures required to bring about, by progressive stages, freedom of movement for workers, as defined in Article 48". The Council of Ministers adopted Regulation 1612/68 on the freedom of movement for workers within the Community on 15 October 1968.[5] The question arose as to whether the EC had exceeded its express powers under Article 49 EEC in enacting Article 12 of the Regulation. The Court found that it had not.

In *Forcheri v Belgium*[6] an Italian spouse of an Italian worker who was employed in Belgium wished to undertake a social work course. She was charged an enrolment fee which was not levied on Belgian students. She claimed that this fee was contrary to Articles 7, 48, 49 EEC. The Court ruled that although education and training policy was not within the competence of the EC, Article 128 EEC empowered the Council of Ministers to lay down general principles for implementing a common vocational training policy. It was held that if a Member State organises educational courses relating in particular to vocational training, to require a national of another Member State lawfully established in the first state an enrolment fee which is not required of its own nationals in order to take part in such courses constitutes discrimination by reason of nationality, which is prohibited by Article 6 EC. Yet as the spouse of a migrant worker, Forcheri derived no independent rights to educational facilities free of discrimination and derived no rights under Regulation 1612/68/EEC since Article 12 of that Regulation only refers to the education rights of the *children* of migrant workers and Article 7 refers to equality in relation to tax, social advantages and vocational training for the *migrant worker*.

---

[3] See Weiler (1991) 2403, 2438 *et seq.*

[4] Case 9/74 [1974] ECR 773.

[5] OJ Sp Ed. 1968(ii) p. 475.

[6] Case 152/82 [1983] ECR 2323.

The Court also used another provision of Regulation 1612/68/EEC, Article 7(2), to cover finance for educational and maintenance costs. These were held to be a social advantage *of benefit to the migrant worker* even though applicable to the child. In *Echternach and Moritz v Netherlands Minister for Education*[7] the Court ruled that the child of a migrant worker retains the status of being a member of the worker's family even when the migrant worker has returned to the state of origin and even if the child temporarily interrupts his or her studies. In *Belgian State v Humbel*[8] the Court ruled that Article 12 of Regulation 1612/68 only applied to children claiming rights in the *host state*. This case concerned the son of a French migrant worker in Luxembourg who wished to study in Belgium. This ruling might be compared with that of *Di Leo v Land Berlin*.[9] Di Leo was an Italian national and the daughter of an Italian migrant worker employed in Germany. She enrolled to study medicine at the University of Sienna and applied for a grant. This was refused since a grant for attendance at an educational establishment abroad could only be awarded to Germans, stateless persons and foreigners granted asylum. Di Leo argued that the German policy was contrary to Article 12 of Regulation 1612/68. The Court ruled that according to its actual wording, Article 12 is not confined to education or training within the host country. The condition of residence, laid down in Article 12 of Regulation 1612/68, is designed to restrict equal treatment as regards the advantages referred to in that Article solely to the children of Community workers who reside within their parents' host country. However, it does not mean that the right to equal treatment depends on the *place* in which the child concerned pursues his/her studies. The Court takes a teleological, purposive approach to further the integration goal of the Community by stating that the freedom of movement must be secured in compliance with the principles of liberty and dignity with the best possible conditions being achieved for the integration of the Community worker's family in the society of the host country. If such integration is to be successful, it is essential for the child of a Community worker who resides with his family in the host Member State to have the opportunity to choose a course under the same conditions as a child of a national of that State.

Similarly in *Matteucci v Communauté Français de Belgique*[10] the Court held that Article 7(2) of Regulation 1612/68 extended to cover grants which would

---

[7]  Cases 389 & 390/87 [1989] ECR 723.

[8]  Case 263/86 [1988] ECR 5365.

[9]  Case C-308/89 [1990] ECR I-4185.

[10]  Case 235/87 [1989] ECR 5589.

enable an EC worker to pursue studies abroad if such grants were made available to nationals.[11]

But the Court has not always provided such a generous interpretation of these provisions. In *Brown v Secretary of State For Scotland*[12] Brown had dual French/British nationality and had been domiciled in France for a number of years. He had worked for nine months for a firm in Scotland as training before commencing a university course at Cambridge. He was denied a maintenance grant and claimed that because he was a migrant worker he was entitled to such a grant on the same footing as British nationals under Article 7 EEC (now Article 6 EC) and Articles 7(2) and (3) of Regulation 1612/68/EEC. The Court ruled that he was a 'worker' within the meaning of Article 48 EC but he was not entitled to a maintenance grant because his employment was merely ancillary to the course of study he wished to undertake, that is, he had become a worker exclusively as a result of his university place. This case might be compared with *Lair v University of Hannover*.[13] A French woman who had worked in Germany on a series of part-time contracts also applied for a maintenance grant to undertake a university course. The Court drew a distinction between a migrant worker who was involuntarily unemployed and legitimately resident in the host state and would be entitled to the same treatment as regards reinstatement or re-employment as national workers and a worker who gave up work in order to undertake further training in the host state. In the latter situation, a maintenance grant would only be available if there was some link between the studies and the previous work experience. It is easy to see why the Court has drawn such a fine distinction - to prevent abuse of the right to non-discrimination in education and training courses but the ruling contains limitations in relation to the restructuring of the labour market, a process which was envisaged by the completion of the Internal Market. In particular it prevents prevent migrant workers from acquiring new skills in order to adapt to such economic changes.

---

[11] See also Case C-7/94 *Landesamt für Ausbidungs Förderung Nordrhein-Westfalen v Lubor Gaal* [1995] ECR I-1031 where the Court held that the definition of a child for the purposes of Council Regulation 1612/68/EEC is not subject to the same conditions of age or dependency as are the rights governed by Article 10(1) and 11 of the Regulation. Here the 'child' was over the age of twenty-one and was not dependent upon the migrant since his father had died and his sole means of support was an orphan's allowance.

[12] Case 197/86 [1988] ECR 3205.

[13] Case 39/86 [1988] ECR 3161.

In *Bernini v Minister van Onderwijs en Wetenschappen*[14] an Italian national who was employed for ten weeks as a paid trainee as part of her occupational training was not precluded from being classified as worker either by the fact that she received low wages or the fact that she only worked a small number of hours per week. However, at paragraph 16, the Court states that when assessing the "genuine and effective" nature of the services a national court may examine whether in all the circumstances the person concerned has completed a sufficient number of hours in order to familiarise themselves with the work. If the worker voluntarily left employment in order to take up a course of full-time study the status of worker would not be lost provided there was a link between the previous employment and the course of study. This link between the studies and the previous occupational activity is again stressed in *Raulin v Netherlands Ministry of Education and Science*.[15] A French woman moved to the Netherlands and was engaged under a contract of employment classified as an 'on call' contract for sixty hours service as a waitress. After five months she began a full-time vocational course and applied to the Dutch authorities for a maintenance grant. This was refused on the grounds that she was not a Dutch national and that she did not hold a residence permit. Raulin argued that she was a worker within the meaning of Article 48 EC and therefore entitled to equality of treatment with Dutch nationals. In applying the test of whether she was a worker under EC law, of looking to see if her work was "genuine and effective", the Court ruled that there must be a consideration of all the occupational activities of the person in the *host* state but not of the activities engaged in elsewhere in the EC. The *duration* of the activities is an appropriate factor to be taken into account. This ruling is a significant concession to the Member States. But is it compatible with the Internal Market? White[16] argues that the ruling raises national boundaries at a time when the completion of the Internal Market should demand that the pattern of work undertaken in a number of Member States could establish the genuine and effective nature of the activities whereas consideration of such activities in the host Member State might suggest much more marginal and ancillary activities.

Council Directive 93/96/EEC[17] granted the right of residence to students exercising the right to vocational training and to certain of their family

---

[14] Case C-3/90 [1992] ECR I-107.

[15] Case 357/89 [1992] ECR 1027.

[16] White (1992) 526.

[17] OJ 1993 L 317/59.

members[18] provided that they have adequate resources so as not to become a burden on the social security schemes of the Member States and are covered by sickness insurance. Prior to Directive 93/96 EEC coming into force the Court in *Raulin v Netherlands Ministry of Education and Science*[19] ruled that the principle of non-discrimination deriving from Article 6 EC and 128 (EEC) granted the right of residence to an EC national who had been admitted to a vocational training course in another Member State for the duration of the course. The right was not contingent upon possession of a residence permit but a Member State could impose some conditions on the right to residence, to minimise public expenditure costs, such as maintenance costs or health insurance. But such conditions must not infringe the principle of equal access to vocational training.

### 3.2.2. EC Competence in the Field of Mutual Recognition of Professional Diplomas

Article 57(1) EC provides that in order to make it easier for persons to take up and pursue activities as self-employed persons, the Council shall, acting in accordance with the procedure referred to in Article 189b, issue Directives for the mutual recognition of diplomas, certificates and other evidence of formal qualificatiòns.Initially the EC pursued a 'harmonisation' or 'co-ordination' sectoral approach. It was necessary to obtain agreement amongst all the Member States on the minimum standard of education or training and usually two Directives would be enacted - one dealing with the general level of education/training and the other listing the qualifications and diplomas awarded in the Member States which satisfied the conditions for recognition. The Council and the Commission took the view that the recognition of professional qualifications necessarily involved an investigation into the *training* curricula of the Member States thus mutual recognition hinged on the harmonization of training curricula - competence deriving from Article 57(2) EC. But such an approach makes deep inroads into the independence of national educational policy in relation to training curricula and while a number of Directives were enacted particularly in the medical professions the approach was slow, piecemeal and not a great success. In 1974 the Council adopted a

---

[18] The category is narrower than that contained in Article 10 of Regulation 1612/68/EEC in that a student may only bring his/her spouse and dependent children to the host state.

[19] Case 357/89 [1992] ECR 1027.

Resolution [20] on the mutual recognition of formal qualifications expressing the hope that future work in the area of mutual recognition would be based upon flexible and qualitative criteria with the Directives resorting as little as possible to prescriptive detailed training requirements.[21] The EC has moved from the sectoral approach to adopting general mutual recognition Directives - the *Cassis de Dijon* approach. An agreement was reached at the Fontainbleau Summit of June 1984 to adopting a general horizontal approach resulting in Council Directive 89/48/EEC of 21 December 1988 on a general system for the recognition of higher education diplomas awarded on completion of professional education and training of at least three years' duration[22] and Council Directive 92/51/EEC of 18 June 1992 on a second general system for the recognition of professional education and training to supplement Directive 89/48/EEC.[23]

If an EC national wishes to pursue a regulated profession in any Member State the competent authorities may not refuse permission provided certain conditions are met. These are that the person has pursued the equivalent of a three year higher education course in the EC and has completed the necessary professional training in order to qualify for the regulated profession in question. If these conditions are satisfied the host state may not refuse permission to practice a profession on the ground of inadequate qualifications. If the duration of the person's training and education is at least one year less than that required in the host state, Article 4(a) of the Directive permits the host State to require certain evidence of professional experience. If the matters covered by the person's education and training differ substantially from those covered by the host state application or if the host state profession comprises specific regulated activities which are not within the profession regulated in the Member State where the qualification was obtained the Member State may require the completion of an adaptation period or an aptitude test. Normally the applicant will have the choice of which to undertake except in the case of professions requiring precise knowledge of national law, when the Member State may stipulate which of the two is required.

The Court seems to have driven a coach and horses through the legislative programme hoever by its ruling in *Vlassopoulou v Ministerium für Justiz,*

---

[20]  OJ 1974 C 98/1.

[21]  See Zilioli (1989).

[22]  OJ 1989 L 19/16;  See *Bull. EC* 6-1988, 11. Pertek (1992)

[23]  OJ 1992 L 209/25.

*Bundes-und Europaangelegenheiten Baden Wurtemberg*.[24] Vlassopoulou qualified as a lawyer in Greece. She sought admission to a German bar on the basis of her qualifications as a Greek advocate and a German doctorate in law without having followed the normal route for admission *viz* basic study of law at a German university, followed by two State examinations separated by a period of practical training. Her application was refused, with the German authorities arguing that Article 52 EC did not give the right to exercise the profession of Rechtsanwaltin on the basis of professional qualifications obtained in Greece. The ECJ ruled that the principle of non-discrimination contained in Article 52 EC would not be observed if national rules did not take account of the knowledge and qualifications obtained by a person in another Member State.. There was therefore a duty of co-operation, underpinned by Article 5 EC, for the Member States to make comparisons of specialised knowledge and abilities in order to allow individuals to exercise the right of free movement guaranteed in Article 52 EC.

What then is the effect of this ruling on Council Directive 89/48/EEC? Advocate General Van Gerven states that the difference between the Directive's provisions and Article 52 EC is that the latter did not of itself give EC nationals the right to establish themselves in any Member State, subject only to the possible requirement of completion of an adaptation period. Article 52 EC only required a Member State to take into account qualifications and training already received and only if it were found that these were equivalent to the Member State's requirements could an EC national place reliance on them. Article 52 EC did not impose an obligation on the Member State to provide facilities for such a person to complete an adaptation period which would raise the qualification/training up to the Member State's level.[25]

In *Kraus v Land Baden-Württemberg*[26] a German law provided that foreign academic titles had to be approved before they could be used in a professional capacity. A fee of 130DM was charged for such approval. German academic

---

[24]  Case C-340/89 [1991] ECR I-235.

[25]  Cf Case C-164/94 *Aranitis v Land of Berlin* [1996] ECR I-135. Here the Land of Berlin had refused to recognise the Greek diploma awarded on the completion of a higher-education geology course as equivalent to a German diploma awarded on completion of a comparable course and consequently to authorise the applicant to use the title attaching to the German diploma. The Court ruled that since there were no laws, regulations or administrative provisions in Germany regulating access to the profession of geologist the profession could not be regarded as a 'regulated profession' within the meaning of Council Directive 89/48/EEC.

[26]  Case C-19/92 [1993] ECR I-1663.

titles needed no special permission. Kraus challenged this policy, arguing that it was incompatible with the free movement of persons. In this case the Court tackles issues of reverse discrimination as well as making an important step towards the convergence of Articles 48, 52, 59 EC. The Court goes out of its way to explain why the case is not just concerned with educational policy but is also within the scope of Articles 48 and 52 EC. The Court points out that although a postgraduate diploma is normally not a pre-condition for taking up a professional activity it may be of advantage in a professional career, enhancing a person's chance of gaining a job and receiving higher remuneration.

A Member State may question the legitimacy of certificates provided by the competent authority in another Member State[27] But if a Member State recognises qualifications obtained outside the EC as equivalent to its own other Member States are not under an obligation to recognise this equivalence.[28] In *Haim v Kassenzahnarztliche Vereinigung Nordrhein* an Italian national who had qualified and practiced as a dentist in Turkey and later practised in Belgium for eight years after the authorities there recognised his qualifications as equivalent to their own. Haim applied to be registered for work within the German national health service but his qualifications were only recognised for work in private practice unless he underwent a further training period. Questions were referred to the Court on the interpretation of Article 52 EC and Article 20 of the Council Directive 78/686.[29] The Court ruled that the competent national authority, in order to verify whether the training period requirement prescribed by the national rules is met, must take into account the professional experience of the plaintiff, including that which he has acquired during his appointment as a dental practioner of a social security scheme in another Member State. In *Tawil-Albertini v Ministre des Affairs Sociales*[30] a French national obtained dental qualifications in the Lebanon. These qualifications were recognised by the Belgian authorities as equivalent to a Belgian qualification. He was also authorised to practice in the UK and Ireland. The French authorities refused Tawil-Albertini permission to practice as a dentist in France. He argued that since his qualification had been recognised as equivalent to Belgian qualifications this should be sufficient to bring his qualification within the Council Directive on the mutual recognition

---

[27] See Case 130/88 *Van de Bijl v Staatsecretaris van Economische Zaken* [1989] ECR 3039.

[28] Case C-319/92 [1994] ECR I-425,

[29] OJ 1978 L 233/1.

[30] Case C-154/93 [1994] ECR I-451.

of dental qualifications even though the Directive did not include any qualifications obtained outside the EC. The Court pointed out that the Directive was based on the guarantees of specific minimum criteria. The co-ordination of training in non-Member States could only be achieved by agreements with individual states but this would not bring such qualifications within the scope of EC Directive and bind the other Member States which did not recognise foreign qualifications.

Although a Recommendation attached to the General Recognition Directive obliges the Member States to take cognisance of qualifications obtained by *EC nationals* in third states there are fears that the EC approach may lead to discrimination against TCNs wanting to work and move between the Member States.

### 3.2.3. EC Competence With Regard to Education Regarded as Vocational Training

As we have seen Article 128 EEC granted only limited competence to the Community to handle matters of educational concern in relation to vocational training, although the ECJ was willing, as the *Forcheri* ruling demonstrates, to expand Community competence, particularly where the matter touched upon the free movement of persons principle.

The ECJ went further in *Gravier v City of Liège* when a French national, who was a student at the Academie Royale des Beaux-Arts, Liège challenged the enrolment fee (minerval) levied on foreign students in Belgium. She contended that the discriminatory fee was contrary to Article 7 EEC [now Article 6 EC] and Article 59 EC. The Court ruled that although educational organization and policy are not as such included in the spheres of Community competence access to, and participation in, courses of instruction and apprenticeship, in particular vocational training, were not unconnected with Community law. The ECJ pointed to Articles 7 and 12 of Regulation 1612/68/EEC and also to Article 128 EEC . In addition it pointed out the particular attention which the Community institutions had given to problems of access to vocational training and its improvement throughout the Community may be seen, moreover, in the 'general guidelines' which the Council laid down 1971 for drawing up a Community programme on vocational training,[31] in the Resolution of the Council and of the Ministers for Education meeting within the Council of 13 December 1976 concerning measures to be taken to improve the preparation of young people for work and

---

[31]  OJ, English Special Edition, Second Series IX, p.50.

to facilitate their transition from education to working life [32] and the Council Resolution of 11 July 1983 concerning the vocational training policies in the European Community in the 1980s.[33] The ECJ thus concluded that the common vocational training policy referred to in Article 128 EEC was gradually being established, constituting an indispensable element of the activities of the Community, whose objectives include, *inter alia,* the free movement of persons, the mobility of labour and the improvement of the living standards of workers.

The Court defined vocational training in paragraph 30 as:

> " ... any form of education which prepares for a qualification for a particular profession, trade or employment or which provides the necessary training and skills for such a profession, trade or employment as vocational training, whatever the age and the level of training of the pupils or students, and even if the training programme includes an element of general education."

The ECJ then found the imposition of different fee structures for Belgian students and other EC students was an infringement of Article 7 EEC (now Article 6 EC). In *Commission v Belgium*[34] the Court upheld the Commission's complaint that the measures introduced by Belgium to comply with the *Gravier* ruling which restricted only two per cent of `outsiders' access to vocational training courses was incompatible with Article 7 EEC.[35]

Legal base/competence questions were raised in *Commission v Council*[36] in an application for annulment under Article 173 EC of Council Decision 87/327/EEC adopting EC action scheme for the mobility of university students (ERASMUS).[37] The Council, by unanimous vote, had added Article 235 EEC to Article 128 EEC. Article 235 EEC can only be used where no other provision of the Treaty gives the Community institutions the necessary power to adopt the measure in question[38] The ECJ noted that the contested decision

---

[32] OJ 1976 C 308/1.

[33] OJ 1983 C 193/2.

[34] Case 42/87 [1988] ECR 5445.

[35] Further definitions of vocational training were given in Case 24/86 *Blaizot v University of Liège* [1988] ECR 379; Case 263/86 *Belgian State v Humbel* [1988] ECR 5365.

[36] Case C-242/87 [1989] ECR 1425.

[37] OJ 1987 L 166/20.

[38] Case 45/86 *Commission v Council* [1987] ECR 1493.

concerned not only the sphere of vocational training but also that of scientific research, the Council did not have the power to adopt it pursuant to Article 128 EEC alone and thus was bound, before the SEA entered into force, to base the decision on Article 235 EEC as well. Another dimension to the legal base for education policy was raised in *European Parliament v EC Council*.[39]

Here the European Parliament challenged Council Directive 90/366/EEC granting rights of residence to students and their families on the grounds that the Commission's initial choice of legal base (Article 7(2) EEC ,now Article 6(2) EC) was correct and that the Council was wrong to alter the legal base to Article 235 EEC. Referring to its ruling in *Raulin*[40] the ECJ underlined the fact that the right to equal treatment in relation to the conditions of access to vocational training applies not only to requirements imposed by the educational establishment in question, such as registration fees, but also to any measure liable to hinder the exercise of that right. It is obvious that a student who is admitted to a course may be unable to follow it if he has no right to reside in the Member State where the course is being held. It followed that the principle of non-discrimination in relation to the conditions of access to vocational training which derive from Articles 7 [now Article 6 EC] and 128 EEC mean that a national of a Member State who has been admitted to a course of vocational training in another Member State enjoys the right to reside in the latter State for the duration of the course. After this ruling it is possible to argue that the non-discrimination principle developed in relation to finance for education and maintenance grants in cases such as *Echternach and Moritz* could be applied to *all* students.

### 3.2.4. Is Education a Service?

In *Gravier* the Court was asked whether students receiving vocational training in a Member State other than their own were recipients of services within the meaning of Article 59 EC. The Court did not address the question but in a later ruling, *Belgium v Humbel*,[41] the Court took the view that such services were not *remunerated* within the meaning of Article 60 EC. The State in establishing and maintaining such a system was not engaging in a gainful activity but fulfilling duties towards its own population in the social, cultural and educational fields withe system funded from public funds. The fact that

---

[39] Case C-295/90 [1992] ECR I-4193.

[40] Case 357/89 [1992] ECR 1027.

[41] Case 263/86 [1988] ECR 5365.

pupils or their parents may sometimes pay enrolment fees or contribute to the operating expenses of the system did not detract from this fact. But in *Wirth v Landeshauptstadt Hannover*[42] the Court ruled that even though most institutions of higher education were financed from public funds, those institutions which sought to make a profit and which were financed mainly out of private funds could fall within the definition of services contained in Articles 59 and 60 EC. However it is arguable that it is not always easy to draw the distinction between the economic motives of such activities.

### 3.2.5. The Community Charter of the Fundamental Social Rights of Workers 1989

Further attention was paid to vocational training in The Community Charter of the Fundamental Social Rights of Workers 1989. Title I, 15 states:

> "Every worker of the European Community must be able to have access to vocational training and to benefit therefrom throughout his working life. In the conditions governing access to such training there may be no discrimination on grounds of nationality.
>
> The competent public authorities, undertakings or the two sides of industry, each within there own sphere of competence, should set up continuing and permanent training systems enabling every person to undergo retraining more especially through leave for training purposes, to improve his skills or to acquire new skills, particularly in the light of technical developments."

### 3.3. COMMUNITY COMPETENCE IN THE FIELD OF EDUCATION AFTER THE TEU

There was a gradual shift of balance towards the development of Community vocational training policy through educational institutions as a matter of educational policy, so that from the mid-1980s onwards we find a proliferation of Community vocational training programmes, such as the ERASMUS programme, which created a platform for Community intervention into the further and higher education systems of the Member States.[43] This evolution towards a double-track approach to vocational training, with an *education* track as well as an employment policy track, was decisively confirmed by the TEU 1992. On the employment policy front, Article 123 EEC was amended to make

---

[42]  Case C-109/92 [1993] ECR I-6447.

[43]  Freedland (1996).

148

it explicit that vocational training and retraining were the particular means by which the Social Fund was to facilitate adaptation to industrial changes and changes in production systems.

Additionally a new Treaty chapter was created, entitled "Education, Vocational Training and Youth". This conferred powers and imposed duties on the Community, which were quite distinct from those relating to the Social Fund, in respect of the development of education (Article 126 EC) and vocational training (Article 127 EC). The importance of Article 127 EC is not, however, in the enlargement of the overall competence of the Community in respect of vocational training, but in the way that it locates some of that competence in the field of education policy rather than employment policy.

The relationship between Articles 127 EC and 128 EC is of major importance[44], since the content of the Community powers which they delineate is not identical, and neither is the way in which those powers are exercised. The decision-making procedure with regard to education is `co-decision' (Article 189B EC), whereas that with regard to vocational training is `cooperation' (Article 189C EC). The demarcation line between education and vocational training has been made more difficult to draw by the fact that the dynamic interpretation which the Court has given to the expression `vocational training' in connection with Article 128 EEC has caused a number of educational curricula activities to be regarded as vocational training. In the context of the *acquis communautaire* the terms `education' and `vocational training' are therefore no longer mutually exclusive, although not all forms of vocational training are provided in an educational context. Now, all forms of education which were not classified as `vocational training' and falling within Article 128 EC will be covered by the new Article 126 EC. This will include pre-school, primary education, general secondary education and university courses for people wishing to improve their general knowledge rather than prepare themselves for an occupation. Indeed it is arguable that Article 126 EC has become the *lex generalis* with Article 127 the *lex specialis*.[45] The question remains as to whether Articles 126 EC and 127 EC exhaustive or can Article 235 EC still be used to give the EC competence in matters excluded from the scope of these Articles?[46] Lenaerts[47] predicts that the ECJ will be asked to rule

---

[44]  Laenerts (1994).

[45]  See Council Decision 94/819/EC of 6 December 1994 OJ 1994, L 340/8 establishing an Action Programme for the Implementation of an EC Vocational Training Policy, (the `Leonardo Decision').

[46]  Compare the Resolution of the European Parliament:Resolution A3-0139/92 of 15 May 1992 on education and training policy in the run-up to 1993, OJ 1992 C 150/366, 368,

on a number of legal base disputes, possibly initiated by the European Parliament.

The Leonardo Decision[48] is regarded as a key instrument in the new EC policy towards education and vocational training. Article 3 lays down a common framework of objectives for EC action. Freedland [49]calls it `a new constitution for EC vocational training policy in all but name.' Tthere is now a tendency to see vocational training policy as a matter of educational, rather than employment, policy. This is seen in the Leonardo Decision and also the Education White Paper.[50] Freedland argues that important dimensions of the question, of the scope and purpose of vocational training are lost or downplayed if employment policy is not given sufficient emphasis.

Finally, Article 57(2)EC has been amended requiring a unanimous vote in the Council (on a proposal from the Commission and after consulting the European Parliament) in order to enact Directives `the implementation of which involves in at least one Member State amendment of the existing principles laid down by law governing the professions with respect to training and conditions of access for natural persons'.

---

1.2 "[The European Parliament] considers that the fields of action referred to in Arts. 126 and 127 are not exhaustive but are rather in the nature of examples, and that the new Treaty forms a solid basis, while respecting the areas of responsibility of the Member States and/or regions, for action in the areas referred to and in other areas in which action proves necessary, to bring about the necessary cohesion between measures to be taken in the field of education and training by the Community and in the political sphere by the Member States."

[47] Lenaerts (1994).

[48] Council Decision of 6 December 1994 establishing an action programme for the implementation of a European Community vocational training policy 94/819/EC OJ 1994 L 340/8.

[49] Freedland (1996). Cf Lane (1993).

[50] European Commission White Paper on Education and Training. *Teaching and Learning - Towards the Learning Society*, Luxembourg, 1996.

# CHAPTER FOUR

# EQUAL TREATMENT AND EQUAL OPPORTUNITIES

## 4.1. EQUAL PAY

### 4.1.1. Historical Background

Article 119 EC contains a broad legal obligation to implement the principle of equal pay for equal work. [1] As we have seen in Chapter One, it was left to individuals to breathe life into the equal pay concept through a series of cases in the 1970s and 1980s. In two early cases brought by Community officials the ECJ side-stepped the question of the direct enforceability of Article 119 EC by determining the issue of sex discrimination according to the general principles of law. [2] It was the *Defrenne* litigation which gave the impetus for further Community intervention, bringing about further references from other national courts and the elevation of the principle of equal treatment into one of the fundamental rights protected by Community law. [3]

### 4.1.1.(i) Defrenne v Belgian State (No. 1)[4]

Defrenne was an air hostess compelled to retire at the age of 40. She brought an action alleging sex discrimination on the ground that male cabin crew could work until the normal pension age and thereby receive full pension rights. She brought an action for breach of contract against her employer, the airline Sabena, and an application for the annulment of the Royal Decrees setting out the special rules governing retirement in the aviation industry. The novelty of the claim lay in the fact that Defrenne was attempting to use Article 119 EC

---

[1]   See Barnard (1996).

[2]   Case 20/71 *Sabbatini v European Parliament* [1972] ECR 345; Case 32/71 *Chollet v European Commission* [1972] ECR 363.

[3]   Arnull (1990); Docksey (1991).

[4]   Case 80/70 [1971] ECR 345.

directly before the Belgian courts and against a private party. The Belgian Conseil d'État referred 3 questions to the ECJ:

> 1. Does the retirement pension granted under the terms of the social scheme financed by contributions from workers, employers and the state subsidy, constitute a consideration which the worker receives indirectly in respect of his employment from his employer?
> 2. Can the rules establish a different age-limit for retirement of men and women workers?
> 3. Do air hostesses and stewards in civil aviation do the same work?

The ECJ adopted a restrictive approach to the first question by ruling that a retirement pension established within the framework of a social security scheme laid down by legislation did not fall within the scope of Article 119 EC. The Court therefore did not address the second and third questions. This ruling created problems for the inter-relationship of contractual and general social security benefits, particularly as the partial privatisation of many social security issues took place throughout the EU in the 1980s and, as we shall see, the ECJ has been forced to modify its position.

### 4.1.1.(ii) Defrenne v Sabena (No.2)[5]

The second *Defrenne* case is one of the most significant cases in Community law. The Belgian Cour du Travail referred a number of questions to the ECJ which were addressed in an ambitious but also ambiguous way. *Firstly*, the ECJ ruled that Article 119 EC was capable of creating both *vertical* and *horizontal* direct effect. The Resolution[6] adopted by the Member States in 1961 was not capable of modifying the legal obligations contained in Article 119 EC and the Article was enforceable in the original signatory states from 1 January 1962 and in the first Accession states[7] from 1 January 1973. The Irish and UK governments made submissions to the ECJ pointing out the financial problems of back-dating equal pay claims and the ECJ accepted these arguments by stating that the equal pay principle could not be relied upon in the national courts before the date of the ruling (8 April 1976) unless an equal pay claim had already been started in the national courts before that date.

---

[5] Case 43/75 [1976] ECR 455.

[6] *Bulletin of the EC* 1962 No 1, 7-9.

[7] Denmark, the UK and Ireland.

*Secondly,* the ECJ added a further limitation to the content and scope of Article 119 EC by limiting direct effect to *"direct and overt discrimination"* which can be identified solely with the aid of criteria based upon equal work and equal pay. Article 119 EC did not produce direct effect in relation to *"indirect and disguised discrimination"* which could only be identified by reference to more explicit implementing legislation at either the Community or national level. The idea of what was meant by "indirect discrimination" in this context proved to be ambiguous and in *Worringham and Humphreys v Lloyds Bank Ltd.*[8] the ECJ spoke of Article 119 EC applying:

> "... to all forms of discrimination which may be identified solely with the aid of the criteria of equal work and equal pay referred to by the Article in question, without national or Community measures being required to define them with greater precision in order to permit their application."[9]

But even this did not resolve all matters since although it had been clarified that indirect discrimination could fall within the scope of Article 119 EC the ruling in *Jenkins v Kingsgate (Clothing Productions) Ltd.*[10] seemed to suggest that it was necessary to show an *intention* to discriminate. The matter was finally clarified by Advocate General Darmon in *Bilka-Kaufhaus GmbH v Weber*[11] where he explained that Article 119 EC was not confined to deliberate discrimination but the absence of discriminatory intent on the part of the employer was not enough to justify a finding that the conduct was contrary to Article 119 EC.

*Thirdly,* the ECJ adopted a teleological approach to the interpretation of Article 119 EC. The Court argued that Article 119 EC fulfilled a two-fold function:

- an *economic* function to avoid the distortion of competition; *and*
- a *social* function to fulfil the purposes of Article 117 EC and the Preamble to the Treaty of Rome 1957

This double aim was evidence of the fact that the principle of equal pay formed part of the foundations of the Community and could be used for "equalisation upwards": ie the lower wages of women should be raised to the level of the

---

[8] Case 69/80 [1981] ECR 767.

[9] Para 23.

[10] Case 96/80 [1981] ECR 911.

[11] Case 170/84 [1986] ECR 1607.

higher wages of the male comparator. The question of whether all social policy law should be seen in a similar way has created a number of problems especially in the field of social security where the Member States have argued that public expenditure constraints necessitate lowering levels of social security in order to achieve equalisation of benefits.

*Finally,*the ECJ ruled that it was the duty of the national courts to scrutinise discrimination:

> "... arising directly from legislative provisions or collective labour agreements, as well as cases in which men and women receive unequal pay for equal work which is carried out in the same establishment or service, whether private or public"[12]

Thus the Member States' policies were not immune from judicial scrutiny in determining whether or not Article 119 EC had been infringed.[13]

### 4.1.1.(iii) Defrenne v Sabena (No.3)[14]

The final *Defrenne* case was a reference from the Belgian Cour de Cassation concerning the financial consequences of the different retirement ages for male and female employees in the aviation industry. At this time the Equal Treatment Directive[15] was not in force and so the issue of a "working condition" relating to retirement ages was discussed solely in the context of Article 119 EC. The ECJ ruled that the retirement age condition did not fall within Article 119 EC since Article 119 EC was based upon the close connection which exists between the nature of the services provided and the amount of remuneration for those services and therefore the matter fell within *national* not Community competence:

> "... at the period under consideration Community law contained only the provisions in the nature of a programme laid down by Articles 117 and 118 of the Treaty, which relate to the general development of social welfare, in particular as regards conditions of employment and working conditions."[16]

---

[12] Para 40.

[13] Case 171/88 *Rinner-Kühn v FWW Spezial-Gebäudereinigung GmbH & Co Kg* [1989] ECR 2743.

[14] Case 149/77 [1978] ECR 1365.

[15] Council Directive 76/207/EEC, OJ 1976 L 39/40.

[16] Para 31.

The Court did, however, repeat its view that the elimination of sex discrimination formed one of the fundamental principles of Community law, drawing inspiration from international labour law conventions:

"The Court has repeatedly stated that respect for fundamental personal rights is one of the general principles of Community law, the observance of which it has a duty to ensure. There can be no doubt that the elimination of discrimination based on sex forms part of those fundamental human rights. Moreover, the same concepts are recognised by the European Social Charter of 18 November 1961 and by Convention No 111 of the International Labour Organisation of 25 June 1958 concerning discrimination in respect of employment and occupation."[17]

### 4.1.2. Article 119 EC and the Equal Pay Directive 75/117/EEC

As we have pointed out in Chapter One, the concept of equal pay contained in Article 119 EC was deliberately narrower than the "equal pay for work of equal value" concept contained in ILO Convention No. 100. The *Defrenne* litigation and the SAP 1974-76 provided the impetus for further initiatives in the equal treatment field, the first being an Equal Pay Directive to supplement Article 119 EC. While the ECJ[18] has argued that the purpose of the Directive was designed to facilitate the practical application of Article 119 EC and that it in no way altered the scope of the content of the equal pay principle there are suggestions that the Directive was intended to broaden the equal pay principle.[19]

The Member States were given only one year in which to introduce the provisions of the Directive. From the number of infringement actions taken in the subsequent years it is clear the Member States were unable and unwilling to do this, finding it difficult to adapt their pay bargaining structures to accommodate the Community obligations. Although Article 1 refers to the use of job classification schemes it does not make them compulsory and it does not

---

[17] Para 26.

[18] Case 96/80 *Jenkins v Kingsgate (Clothing Productions) Ltd.* [1981] ECR 911, para 22. Cf Forman (1982); Arnull (1986). Note also in the infringement action against the UK, Case 61/81 *Commission v UK* [1982] ECR 2601 the UK government argued that its original legislation introduced to meet the requirements of Article 119 EC also fulfilled the obligations of the Equal Pay Directive but the ECJ rejected these submissions. See also the Opinion of Advocate General VerLoren van Theemaat in Case 143/83 *Commission v Denmark* [1985] ECR 427.

[19] See Szyszczak (1985); Editorial Comments, (1974) 11 *Common Market Law Review* 1. Cf Burrows (1980).

make reliance upon the concept of equal value dependent upon job classification. Article 7 of the Directive imposes a duty upon the Member States to bring national and Community law to the attention of all employees "by all appropriate means, for example at their place of employment". Articles 2-6 introduce other obligations to ensure that the right to equal pay is effective particularly by the provision of appropriate remedies. The ECJ has built upon the concept of effective remedies in its case law. There is now a Directive going through the SPA on the reversal of the burden of proof in sex discrimination claims.

In *Commission v Denmark*[20] the ECJ ruled that where collective bargaining was the dominant form of regulation the Member State was nevertheless under a duty to provide effective protection for all workers particularly non-union workers and in employment sectors where collective bargaining did not cover or fully guarantee the principle of equal pay. Relying upon the general principles of law, the principle of legal certainty and protection of individuals the Court went on to rule that *all* workers, and in particular those not covered by a collective agreement required an unequivocal statement of the rights flowing from Council Directive 75/117/EEC so that national courts would be in a position to ensure that the obligations were being observed.

### 4.1.3. The Concept of Pay

Article 119 EC acknowledges that under modern contracts of employment the concept of pay is complex and is not confined to wages but also to

> "... any other consideration, whether in cash or in kind, which the worker receives, directly or indirectly, in respect of his employment from his employer."

In *Barber v GRE*[21] the ECJ ruled that *each* benefit received under a contract of employment must be paid in a non-discriminatory basis. This would ensure transparency enabling a national court to review pay schemes.

---

[20] Case 143/83 [1985] ECR 427.

[21] Case C-262/88 [1990] ECR I-1889.

The concept of pay has embraced sick pay[22] survivor's benefits,[23] bridging pensions,[24] travel concessions,[25] additional statutory redundancy payments, [26] special bonus payments,[27] pay to attend training courses[28] and rules governing the classification of salary grades. [29] In *Gillespie v Northern Health and Social Services Board*[30] the ECJ ruled that the benefit paid by an employer under legislation or collective agreements to a woman on maternity leave constitutes pay since it is consideration paid by the employer either by virtue of legislative provisions or the contract of employment whose purpose is to ensure that income is received even though the employee is not performing any work at the time of its receipt.

The *Defrenne* litigation emphasised the nexus between a person's employment and pay and the problems of the interaction with social security schemes.[31] The *First Defrenne* case did not, however, discuss the relationship of occupational social security schemes and Article 119 EC and this question has occupied the ECJ in a number of references. It was not until *Beune*[32] that the ECJ really got to grips with the problem and specified the criteria necessary to identify state social security schemes. The ECJ ruled that a pension scheme directly governed by statute is a strong indication that the benefits provided by the scheme are social security benefits and not pay. If the scheme applies to general categories of workers where no element of collective bargaining is involved the benefits available under it are not likely to be deemed pay even

---

[22] Case 171/88 *Rinner-Kühn* [1989] ECR 2743.

[23] Case 109/91 *Ten Oever* [1993] ECR I-4879.

[24] Case C-132/91 *Birds Eye Walls* [1993] ECR I-5579.

[25] Case 12/81 *Garland v BRE* [1982] ECR 359.

[26] Case C-173/91 *Commission v Belgium* [1991[ ECR I-67.

[27] Case 58/81 *Commission v Luxembourg* [1982] ECR 2175.

[28] Case C-380/90 *Bötel* [1992] ECR I-3589.

[29] Case C-184/89 *Nimz* [1991] ECR I-297.

[30] Case C-342/93 [1996] ECR I-475.

[31] See Case C-305/95 *Plapied and Gallez* pending asking if flat-rate supplementary family allowances paid by an employer fall within Article 119EC.

[32] Case C-7/93 [1994] ECR I-4471.

where the scheme is funded by the contributions of workers, employers and possibly the public authorities.

In *Worringham v Lloyds Bank Ltd.*[33] the Court ruled that supplements paid to male employees' gross salaries to compensate them for payments made to a pension fund infringed the principle of equal pay in Article 119 EC. Discrimination occurred since gross salary rates were used to calculate other benefits and social advantages such as redundancy payments, unemployment benefits, credit facilities. Furthermore the deducted supplements were repaid if a male employee left the employment. The Court accepted that the discriminatory consequences brought the payments within the ambit of Article 119 EC. In a subsequent case, *Liefting v Directie van het Academish Zienkenthuis*[34] the Court ruled that the employer's share in the financing of statutory social security schemes (composed of employer and employee contributions) does not fall within Article 119 EC but amounts of compensation included in the calculation of *gross* pay, which determine the calculation of other salary-related benefits, may fall within Article 119 EC, even though, as in this case, they are paid immediately into a pension fund. A different approach was taken in *Newstead v H.M. Treasury and Department of Transport.*[35] The disparity here was in *net* pay, rather than *gross* pay, of a civil servant's salary. A deduction of 1.5% was made from male civil servants' pay to finance a widows' pension scheme. These deductions were refunded with interest on the death or retirement of unmarried male civil servants. In a lengthy piece of litigation the ECJ ruled that the pension scheme fell within the scope of Article 118 EC since it was a *substitute* for the general old-age pension scheme. Since the deduction produced results in the *net* salaries and did not affect gross pay on which other salary-related benefits were calculated there was no discrimination within the meaning of Article 119 EC. In a staff case, *Razzouk and Beydoun v Commission,*[36] the ECJ ruled that a failure to provide a survivor's pension in the Community Staff Regulations infringed one of the general principles of Community law.

The Court has taken significant steps towards linking state and occupational social security schemes and Article 119 EC. In *Bilka-Kaufhaus v Weber*[37] a

---

[33]  Case 69/80 [1981] ECR 767.

[34]  Case 23/83 [1984] ECR 3225.

[35]  Case 192/85 [1987] ECR 4753. See also Case C-200/91 *Coloroll* [1994] ECR I-4389.

[36]  Joined Cases 75 and 117/82 [1984] ECR 1509.

[37]  Case 170/84 [1986] ECR 1607.

pension scheme was adopted in accordance with German legislation but originated in a collective agreement and incorporated into the individual contract of employment. The occupational pension *supplemented* the state pension scheme and was financed solely by employer contributions. Unlike the *Worringham* and *Liefting* schemes the pension did not form part of the employee's gross pay. The ECJ ruled that the pension scheme fell within Article 119 EC and that a long service requirement for part-time workers could mount to *indirect discrimination* unless it could be justified. In *Rinner-Kühn v FWW Spezial-Gebaudereiningung GmbH & Co Kg*[38] the Court ruled that the exclusion of part-time workers from a sick pay scheme financed by the employer could also amount to indirect discrimination even though the exclusion of part-time workers from the scheme was sanctioned by German legislation.

The real bomb shell came in *Barber v Guardian Royal Exchange Assurance Group.*[39] Here there was a non-contributory pension scheme "contracted out" of the general pension arrangements ( and therefore a substitute for the state scheme). Under the normal terms of the pension scheme (which formed part of the employee's contract of employment) the pensionable age was 65 for men and 60 for women. Barber had transferred into the GRE scheme as a result of GRE's acquisition of another company and this company had lower pension ages of 62 for men and 57 for women. The GRE pension provided for an immediate pension to be payable if an employee retired at any time in the 10 years before normal pensionable age. Barber was made redundant at the age of 52 in 1980. The severance terms of his contract provided that men aged at least 55 and women aged at least 50 whose contract had been terminated on the grounds of early retirement or redundancy were entitled to an immediate pension. For employees aged below those threshold ages the severance terms provided for an entitlement to a deferred payment at the normal pensionable age and an enhanced statutory redundancy payment. Barber was granted a deferred pension and a severance payment. He brought a claim for discrimination arguing that a woman in a similar position would have received a pension. The Court ruled that Article 119 EC applied to the benefits paid by an employer to a worker in connection with a compulsory redundancy, whether paid under a contract of employment, by virtue of legislation or on a voluntary basis. The severance payment was explained as facilitating the adjustment to new circumstances as a result of the termination of employment which provides the worker with a source of income during the period in which the

---

[38]  Case 171/88 [1989] ECR 2743.

[39]  Case C-262/88 [1990] ECR I-1889.

worker was seeking new employment. Article 119 EC covered any consideration, whether immediate or future, received, albeit indirectly by the worker in respect of employment by the employer. The UK government had argued that a statutory redundancy payment fell within Article 118 EC and not Article 119 EC but the Court reiterated the view held in *Defrenne (No.2)* that Article 119 EC also applies to discrimination which, although arising from legislative provisions, applies to the worker by reason of the existence of an employment relationship. Thus statutory or *ex gratia* payments were not excluded from the scope of Article 119 EC even when they reflected considerations of social policy.

The Court considered the effect of *Defrenne (No.1)* on the contracted out pension scheme. It was held that contracted-out pensions were not caught by the ruling in *Defrenne (No.1)* but were the outcome of either an agreement between the employer and workers or of a unilateral decision by the employer and financed either solely by the employer or by contributions from employers and workers without any subsidisation from public funds. As such, the pension schemes formed part of the consideration offered to workers by the employer. Furthermore, such pension schemes only applied to workers employed by certain undertakings and were not compulsorily applicable to general categories of workers as envisaged in *Defrenne (No.1)*. Such pension schemes had to be established in conformity with national legislative rules but were governed by their own rules. The ECJ held that even if the contributions paid and benefits provided are in part a substitute for the general statutory scheme they may give greater benefits than the statutory scheme. Therefore their economic function is similar to that of *supplementary* pension schemes, the benefits under which had already been held by the Court to fall within Article 119 EC in *Bilka Kaufhaus*. The Court ruled that it was a breach of Article 119 EC to impose an age condition based on different pensionable ages in the national statutory social security scheme. The application of the principle of equal pay must be ensured in respect of each element of remuneration in order to ensure transparency of the pay system.

The most problematic aspect of the *Barber* ruling is the temporal limitation imposed by the ECJ. The ruling applied to claims brought after the date of the ruling - 17 May 1990 - except where legal proceedings or an equivalent claim had been initiated prior to 17 May 1990. The justification for the temporal ruling was that in the light of the state [40] and occupational[41] Social Security Directives, Member States and the parties concerned were reasonably entitled

---

[40]  Council Directive 79/7/EEC, OJ 1979 L 6/24.

[41]  Council Directive 86/378/EEC, OJ 1986 L 225/40.

to consider that Article 119 EC did not apply to pensions paid under contracted-out schemes and therefore it was permissible to have different rules in this area. There was a strong desire not to "... upset retroactively the financial balance of many contracted-out schemes".[42] A Protocol[43] was attached to the TEU 1992 explaining the temporal limitation of *Barber*:

> "For the purposes of Article 119 ... benefits under occupational social security schemes shall not be considered as remuneration if and insofar as they are attributable to periods of employment prior to 17 May 1990, except in the case of workers or those claiming under them who have before that date initiated legal proceedings or introduced an equivalent claim under the applicable law."

Subsequent case law has allowed for further clarification of the temporal limitations of the *Barber* ruling. In *Bilka-Kaufhaus v Weber*[44] the Court ruled that Article 119 EC applied to *access* to an occupational pension scheme. In *Vroege v NCIV*[45] the Court applied this principle to an occupational pension scheme which excluded part-time workers. If a greater number of workers from one sex are affected by the rule and the employer cannot objectively justify the rule by factors unrelated to sex then indirect discrimination may be found. In *Fisscher v Voorhuis Hengelo*[46] the ECJ recognised that the exclusion of married women from the membership of an occupational pension scheme amounted to discrimination based directly on sex and in contravention of Article 119 EC. There is no temporal limitation in relation to *access* to occupational security schemes.

As we shall see, the Court, in cases brought under the Equal Treatment Directive had suggested that the fixing of pensionable ages relating to the conditions of access to occupational pension schemes could be reviewed for sex discrimination under the ETD despite the implications such factors would have for pay.[47] In *Barber* the ECJ found that it was contrary to Article 119 EC to impose an age condition which differed according to sex in respect of a

---

[42]  Para 44.

[43]  See Curtin (1993); Hervey (1993).

[44]  Case 170/84 [1986] ECR 1607.

[45]  Case C-57/93 [1994] ECR I-4541.

[46]  Case C-128/93 [1994] ECR I-4583.

[47]  Case C-19/81 *Burton* [1982] ECR 555; Case 152/84 *Marshall* [1986] ECR 723; Case 151/84 *Roberts* [1986] ECR 703.

contracted out pension scheme, even where, as in this case the factor was based on the differences found in the statutory pension scheme.

In *Moroni*[48] and *Coloroll*[49] the Court extended the *Barber* principles to supplementary, non-contracted out occupational pension schemes. By bringing this issue within the ambit of Article 119 EC, which has both vertical and horizontal direct effect, the ECJ widened the scope of the application of the equality principle.[50]

The issue of the temporal limitation of Article 119 EC was discussed in *Ten Oever*[51] - a case decided before Protocol No 2 to the TEU came into effect. The ECJ opted for an interpretation of *Barber* which applied the principle of equal treatment to *benefits payable in respect of periods of service after 17 May 1990*. The Court justified this interpretation since with pensions there is a time lag between the *accrual* of entitlement to the pension which occurs gradually throughout the employee's working life and the *actual payment* which is deferred. Also influential in the Court's reasoning was the way in which occupational pensions are funded and the accounting links between an individual's periodic contributions and the amount of pension paid.

Another problem which has faced the Court is whether, to secure equality under Article 119 EC, a man's occupational pension scheme terms should be raised to the higher level of the female comparator - in accordance with the *Second Defrenne*[52] ruling or whether it was permissible for the Member State to achieve equality by taking away the more favourable terms of the woman's occupational pension scheme: ie *levelling down*. Levelling down occurred in *Smith v Advel Systems*[53] and the ECJ responded by identifying 3 different situations. In respect of periods of service prior to 17 May 1990 the *Barber* ruling excluded the application of Article 119 EC to pension benefits payable in respect of those periods. In respect of periods after 17 May 1990 where discrimination existed and a scheme had not adopted equalization measures the Court rule that *levelling up* must occur.[54] In respect of periods after the entry

---

[48]  Case C-110/91 [1993] ECR I-6591.

[49]  Case C-200/91 [1994] ECR I-4389.

[50]  See Ellis (1994).

[51]  Case C-109/91 [1993] ECR I-4879.

[52]  Case 43/75 [1976] ECR 455.

[53]  Case C-408/92 [1994] ECR I-4435.

[54]  See C-184/89 *Nimz* [1991] ECR I-297.

into force of rules to eliminate discrimination the Court ruled that Article 119 EC does not preclude *levelling down* measures on the argument that Article 119 EC requires merely *equality of pay* and does not specify the *amount* of pay. In *Smith v Advel* the ECJ ruled out the possibility of phasing in equality measures.

In *Ten Oever*[55] the ECJ established that Article 119 EC may cover survivors' benefits paid under an occupational pension scheme. The Court justified their inclusion since the entitlement to the benefit is consideration from the dead workers' membership of the scheme, the pension being vested in the survivor by reason of the employment relationship. Although the temporal limitation of *Barber* applies to survivor's benefits a survivor may rely upon the direct effect of Article 119 EC to assert his/her rights since the survivor is the only person with a vested interest.

The Court has ruled, however, that the use of different actuarial factors in funded and defined-benefit schemes fell outside of the scope of Article 119 EC.[56] Although the ECJ acknowledged that the payment of a periodic pension fell within the definition of pay for the purposes of Article 119 EC the Court explained that the commitment does not necessarily link in to the funding arrangements, including the selection of actuarial factors, utilized to secure the payment of the pension. Additional voluntary contributions paid by employees to increase benefits under an occupational pension scheme are not within the scope of Article 119 EC since they are paid into a separate fund administered by the occupational pension scheme.[57]

In *Barber v GRE*[58] the ECJ ruled that Article 119 EC applied to an occupational pension scheme established as a trust and administered by trustees who were independent of the employer since Article 119 EC applies to consideration received *indirectly* from the employer.

In *Coloroll*[59] the ECJ ruled that trustees of a pension scheme are under a duty to do everything within the scope of their powers to ensure compliance with the equal treatment principle. Here a worker transferred pension rights from one occupational pension scheme to another as a result of change of job. The ECJ ruled that the second scheme was obliged to increase the benefits it

---

[55] Case C-109/91 [1993] ECR I-6591.

[56] Case C- 152/91 *Neath* v *Hugh Steeper* [1993] ECR I-6935.

[57] Case C-200/91 *Coloroll* [1994] ECR I-4389

[58] Case C-262/88 [1990] I-1889.

[59] Case C-200/91 [1994] ECR I-4389.

undertook to pay him when accepting the transfer so as to eliminate the effects which were in conflict with Article 119 EC due to the inadequacy of the capital transferred because of discrimination under the first scheme in relation to benefits payable in periods of service subsequent to 17 May 1990.

The Court ruled that if securing the principle of equality is beyond the powers of trustees then employers and trustees are under a duty to use all means available under domestic law, for example, recourse to the courts particularly where the involvement of the courts is necessary to amend the provisions of the pension scheme or trust deed.

The Council adopted a Directive on 20 December 1996, Council Directive 96/97/EC[60] amending the earlier occupational social security Directive, 86/378/EEC[61] in order to take account of the ECJ's case law under Article 119 EC.

### 4.1.3.(i) Benefits in Kind

Article 119 EC does not only apply to *contractual* benefits but covers payments in kind such as travel concessions.[62] In *Nimz v Freie und Hansestadt Hamburg*[63] the ECJ regarded payments paid for seniority as pay.

### 4.1.3.(ii) Benefits Arising From A Collective Agreement

In *Danfoss*[64] a claim was brought on behalf of a group of female workers who earned on average 7% less than male workers covered by the relevant collective agreement. While the same *basic* wage was applied, the employer supplemented it according to a number of criteria including flexibility, professional training and long service. There was no clarification of how and when the criteria were being used. The ECJ ruled that in order for there to be transparency in the wage determination process a partial reversal of the burden of proof should take place in such cases putting the onus upon the employer to explain the wage determination process. This was justified by reference to

---

[60] OJ 1997 L 46/20.

[61] OJ 1986 L 225/40.

[62] Case 12/81 *Garland v British Rail Engineering* [1982] ECR 359; Case C-249/96 *Grant v S.W. Trains* pending.

[63] Case C-184/89 [1991] ECR I-297.

[64] Case C-33/89 [1990] ECR I-2591.

Article 6 of Council Directive 75/117/EEC, that, without the knowledge of *how* the criteria would be applied, the complainants would be denied access to an effective remedy.

In *Kowalska v Freie und Hansestadt Hamburg*[65] the ECJ applied Article 119 EC to a discriminatory provision of a German white collar public service collective agreement. Employees normally working less that 38 hours per week were excluded from a severance payment on retirement. The ECJ held that the severance pay constituted "pay" within the terms of Article 119 EC and, that since a higher proportion of part-time workers were women, indirect discrimination would occur unless the terms could be justified. Similarly in *Nimz v Freie und Hansestadt Hamburg*[66] the ECJ applied Article 119 EC to a collective agreement under which employees with at least 3/4 of normal full time work were treated more favourably than employees working between ½ and 3/4 of normal working hours. Here the national court was anxious for guidance on the application of Article 119 EC and respect for the principle of the social partners' autonomy. The Court viewed the problem solely from the perspective of the supremacy of Community law, ruling that it would be incompatible with the principle of supremacy of Community law[67] if a national court refused to grant supremacy of Community law over the provisions of a collective agreement.

The interaction of statutory obligations and collective agreements is explored in *Commission v Belgium*.[68] Belgium was found to breach of Article 119 EC by retaining legislation which excluded female workers over the age of 60 from the benefit of additional redundancy payments provided for in a collective agreement.

In *Arbeiterwohlfahrt der Stadt Berlin e. v Bötel*[69] the issue of compensation paid for attending staff training courses in relation to the activities of staff committees was raised. Part-time workers did not receive compensation corresponding to their full working time and often had to spend extra time, beyond their normal working hours, in order to complete such training courses. Since a higher proportion of women than men worked part-time indirect discrimination was raised. The ECJ ruled that it was contrary to Article 119 EC

---

[65]  Case C-33/89 [1990] ECR 2591.

[66]  Case C-184/89 [1991] ECR I-297.

[67]  See Case 106/78 *Simmenthal v Amministrazione delle Finanze* [1978] ECR 629.

[68]  Case C-173/91 [199] ECR I-673.

[69]  Case C-360/90 [1992] ECR I-3589.

and Council Directive 75/117/EEC to limit such compensation on the basis of individual work time tables. In *Lewark*[70] the Court was asked to reconsider its position but refused to do so.[71]

### 4.1.4. The Range of Comparisons under Article 119 EC and Council Directive 75/117/EEC

The ECJ has stated that for the purposes of comparison under Article 119 EC the comparators must be in identical situations.[72] Here the employer paid a bridging pension to a man aged between 60 and 65 but female employees received a reduced pension because they were in receipt of the state pension. The ECJ ruled that no discrimination occurred since the objective premise was to treat people in different situations differently. Similarly in *Gillespie v Northern Health and Social Services Board*[73] a complaint was brought that women on maternity leave receiving maternity pay under the terms of a collective agreement (which was more favourable than the statutory system) suffered from discrimination because their pay had been reduced while on maternity leave and they could not take advantage of a back-dated pay rise. The ECJ ruled that the women on maternity leave were in a special position requiring them to be afforded special protection. This situation was not comparable either with that of a man or a woman actually at work.

The ECJ has been asked to determine the temporal and spatial scope of Article 119 EC and the Equal Pay Directive. In *Macarthys Ltd. v Smith*[74] a woman brought an equal pay claim comparing her pay and her work with that of her male predecessor. The ECJ ruled that there was no limitation that the posts being compared should be contemporaneous - the test of comparability should be entirely qualitative in character. But the Court was not prepared to entertain hypothetical comparisons since these would fall outside the direct effect of Article 119 EC. There are arguments that *Macarthys v Smith* should not be read too literally since it is apparent from *Defrenne (No.2)* that the ECJ

---

[70] Case C- 457/93 [1996] ECR I-243.

[71] Cf Case C-399/92 *Helmig* [1994] ECR I-5727 where part-timers did not receive the higher rate of over-time pay until they worked in excess of the normal hours of full-time workers. The ECJ ruled that no discrimination occurred since part-timers and full-timers were treated the same.

[72] Case C-132/92 *Birds Eye Walls Ltd. v Roberts* [1993] ECR I- 5579.

[73] Case C-342/93 [1996] ECR I-475.

[74] Case 129/70 [1979] ECR 1275.

envisaged a wide potential for Article 119 EC[75] and there are indications in Advocate General Van Theemaat's Opinion in *Commission v UK*[76] that wider comparisons may be permissible under Article 119 EC. In his Opinion in *Commission v Denmark*[77] the Advocate General expresses doubts about the use of a single work place as a basis for equal pay comparisons.[78]

In *Murphy v An Bord Telecom Eireann*[79] the ECJ did allow spatial comparisons to be brought with a named comparator in the same company where the work of the female applicant was of greater value than that performed by the male worker. But the Court ruled that the applicant could only obtain *equal pay;* a claim for a greater amount of pay on a proportional basis to the value of the work was not admissible.

In *Royal Copenhagen*[80] the ECJ provided criteria for identifying the comparator group. It ruled that the groups under comparison must encompass a relatively large number of workers and all the workers who can be said to be in a comparable situation, taking into account factors such as the nature of the work, the training requirements and the working conditions. The national court must ensure that any differences are not due to purely fortuitous or short-term factors or to differences in the individual output of workers concerned. Thus groups formed in an arbitrary manner would not be permissible. In this case the ECJ then seems to conflate the tests for equal value and the justification for any differences in pay since the ECJ then moves on to state that if the groups are comparable it is for the national court to decide whether in the light of the work done and the conditions under which it is performed the work is of equal value or whether there are any objective factors unrelated to discrimination which can justify the pay differential.

---

[75] See Curtin (1989).

[76] Case 61/81 [1982] ECR 2601. See also the Commission's submissions which endorsed the Dutch system of wage review which provides for wider comparisons.

[77] Case 143/83 [1985] ECR 427.

[78] See also COM(94) final, 6.

[79] Case 157/86 [1988] ECR 673.

[80] Case C-400/93

### 4.1.5. Equal Work and Job Evaluation Schemes

In *Rummler v Dato Druck GmbH*[81] the applicant challenged the classifications used in the framework wage-rate agreement for the German printing industry. She argued that her work should have been placed in a different category since she was obliged to lift heavy weights which for women represented heavy physical work. The Court ruled that Article 1 of Council Directive 75/11/EEC does not preclude the use of factors such as physical effort which may favour one sex provided that overall the job evaluation scheme does not discriminate on grounds of sex. In order for a job evaluation scheme not to be discriminatory as a whole it must, in so far as the tasks carried out in the undertaking permit, take into account criteria for which workers of each sex may show particular aptitude. The criteria for governing the classification of pay must ensure that the work which is objectively the same attracts the same rate of pay whether it is performed by a man or a woman. While the concept of equal pay for work of equal value is not contingent upon a job evaluation scheme where such a scheme has been introduced it is not the final determinant of the issue. The ECJ has also ruled that an assessment of a particular job may be carried out without the employer's consent through adversary proceedings.[82]

### 4.1.6. Defences To Equal Pay Claims

Article 119 EC and the Equal Pay Directive ban discrimination "based on sex". In *Macarthys v Smith*[83] the Court ruled that it was possible to pay successive male and female employees different rates of pay based on objective factors such as age, skill, seniority, qualifications, provided that such factors were not a form of indirect discrimination. Whether a particular factor is discriminatory is a question of fact for the national court to decide.

In *Jenkins v Kingsgate (Clothing Productions) Ltd.*[84] The Court refused to acknowledge that a difference in pay between full-time and part-time work amounted to sex discrimination *per se* unless it could be shown that it was in reality an indirect way of reducing the pay of part-time workers on the ground that that group of workers was composed exclusively or predominantly of

---

[81] Case 235/84 [1986] ECR 2101. Cf Fredman (1992).

[82] Case 61/81 *Commission v UK* [1982] ECR 2601.

[83] Case 129/79 [1979] ECR 1275.

[84] Case 96/80 [1981] ECR 911.

women. In *Bilka-Kaufhaus*[85] the ECJ clarified the defence to indirect discrimination claims by stating that an objective justification for the wage differential must be made out and supplied a test for the national courts to apply:

"... the national court finds that the measures chosen ... correspond to a real need on the part of an undertaking, are appropriate with a view to achieving the objective pursued and are necessary to that end."[86]

This is an "economic objectives" test based upon the principle of proportionality. It should be noted in *Bilka-Kaufhaus* that the Court stressed that Article 119 EC does not have the effect of requiring employers to organise occupational pension schemes (or other aspects of pay) to accommodate family responsibilities. *Rinner-Kühn*[87] extended the objective justification to cover policy underlying the occupational sick pay established by the German government. The test seems to have been relaxed here. In relation to state policy a "necessary aim" must be shown. However the German government's generalised statements on the position of part-time work were not considered concrete enough to provide an objective justification for the exclusion of part-time workers from the sick pay provisions.

The principles of *Bilka-Kaufhaus* were applied to the specific criteria used to justify the wage differentials in *Danfoss*.[88] Where incremental payments were used to reward flexibility the ECJ held that when these payments were used to reward the *quality* of the work carried out the criteria must be neutral as regards sex. Where the application of criteria resulted in unfairness to women the outcome could only be explained by the fact that the criteria had been applied in an abusive manner, since it was inconceivable that the work carried out by female workers would be generally of a lower quality. If the increments were paid to reward adaptability to variable work schedules or the place of work the employer could justify such increments in accordance with the test set out in *Bilka-Kaufhaus*. Similarly increments paid for vocational training could be justified using the test propounded in *Bilka-Kauhaus*. *Danfoss* was regarded as disappointing in that in relation to increments payable relating to seniority the ECJ recognised the adverse impact such payments had

---

[85]  Case 170/84 [1986] ECR 1607.

[86]  Para 36.

[87]  Case 171/88 [1989] ECR 2743.

[88]  Case C-109/88 [1989] ECR 3199.

upon female workers but ruled that since seniority nearly always had an effect upon the way a worker carries out his/her duties there was no need to justify seniority payments. In the later case of *Nimz*[89] the Court modified its ruling on the lawfulness of seniority payments and ruled that the objectivity of the seniority criterion must depend on all the circumstances of the particular case, in particular the relationship between the nature of the work performed and the experience gained from the performance of the work.[90]

In *Enderby v Frenchay Health Authority and the Secretary of State For Health*[91] the ECJ ruled that where there was "apparent discrimination" ie when a measure distinguishing between employees on the basis of their hours of work has in practice an adverse impact on substantially more members of one or other sex the measure must be regarded as being contrary to Article 119 EC unless the employer can show it can be objectively justified on objective factors. In the later case of *Royal Copenhagen*[92] the ECJ ruled that in relation to a piece-work pay scheme a prima facie case of discrimination did not arise solely because significant statistics disclose appreciable differences between the average pay of two groups of workers, since those statistics might be attributable to differences in output. But where the individual pay consisted of both a fixed element and a variable element and it was not possible to identify the factors which determined the rates used to calculate the variable amount the employer had to show that the differences were not due to sex discrimination. But it was for the national court to determine if the conditions had been met to shift the burden of proof. More recently, in cases under the State Social Security Directive, *Nolte*[93] and *Megner and Scheffel*[94] the Court gave Member States a broad margin of discretion to determine matters of social policy applying a test of reasonableness, even where it was alleged that the measures had an indirectly discriminatory effect on women.

---

[89] Case C-184/89 [1991] ECR 297.

[90] See Case C-243/95 *Hill* pending on the justification for incremental increases which have a disparate impact on female job sharers.

[91] Case C-127/92 [1993] ECR I-5535.

[92] Case C-400/93 [1995] ECR I-1275.

[93] Case C-317/93 [1995] ECR I-4625.

[94] Case C-444/93 [1995] ECR I-4625.

### 4.1.7. The Social Policy Agreement

Article 6(1) and (2) of the SPA annexed to the EC Treaty by the Social Policy Protocol of the TEU 1992 repeats Article 119 EC but adds in Article 6(3) the possibility of forms of positive action to be introduced in order to achieve equal pay. This provision must now be interpreted in the light of the ECJ's ruling on forms of positive action permissible under the Equal Treatment Directive in the *Kalanke*[95] ruling.

### 4.1.8. Memorandum On Equal Pay For Work of Equal Value

In June 1994 the Commission adopted a Memorandum on Equal Pay For Work of Equal Value.[96] This document showed that while all the Member States have incorporated the equal pay principle into national law there has been little effective progress in achieving equal pay in practice. All the Member States have an earnings gap: Italy having the narrowest gap of 82.7% and Ireland having the largest gap of 65.1%. The reasons put forward for the continued pay differentials are: occupational segregation, job classification schemes, variations in employment structures and rewards systems. The Commission sees the development of non-discriminatory job evaluation schemes as an essential step forward. It also recognises that in addition to the existing legal mechanisms for enforcing equal pay other measures are required. For example:

- the improvement of baseline data on women and pay, including accurate comparative pay data with men. Member States should undertake and improve the systematic collection of information on gender pay and occupational segregation.
- improving the dissemination of information
- practical and legal training

### 4.1.9. Code of Conduct

The Commission has also issued a Code of Conduct on the implementation of the equal pay for work of equal value principle.[97] Essentially the Code proposes two aims:

---

[95] Case C-450/93 [1995] ECR I-3051.

[96] COM (94) 6 final.

[97] COM (96) 336 final.

(1) that negotiators at all levels, whether on the side of the employers or the unions, who are involved in the determination of pay systems, should carry out an analysis of the remuneration system and evaluate the data required to detect sexual discrimination in the pay structures so that remedies can be found;

(2) that a plan for follow up should be drawn up and implemented to eliminate any sexual discrimination evident in the pay structures.

### 4.1.10. Further Amendments[98]

In the Irish Presidency's draft proposals for amendments to the EC Treaty some attention is paid to the issue of equality of men and women. It is proposed to supplement Article 2 EC to include as one of the Community's objectives:

> The Community shall ... promote ... a high level of employment and social protection, equality between men and women, the raising of the standard of living and quality of life, and economic and social cohesion and solidarity among member states.

Article 3 would be supplemented with a new paragraph

> In all activities referred to in this Article, the Community shall aim to eliminate inequalities and to promote equality between men and women.

It is also proposed that Article 119 EC be amended to read as follows with an additional paragraph::

> "Each Member state shall during the first stage ensure and subsequently maintain the application of the principle that men and women should receive equal pay for ... work of equal value.
> The Council, acting by a qualified majority on a proposal from the Commission and after consulting the European Parliament and the Economic and Social Committee, shall adopt measures to ensure the application of the principle of equal opportunities and equal treatment of men and women in matters of employment and occupation, including the principle of equal pay for work of equal value.
> With a view to ensuring full equality in practice in working life, this article shall not prevent a member state from maintaining or adopting measures providing for specific advantages in order to make it easier for the under-represented sex to pursue a vocational activity or to prevent or compensate for disadvantages in professional careers."

The Irish presidency also proposed that gender-neutral language should be incorporated into the Treaty wherever this was appropriate.

---

[98] CONF 2500/96, Brussels 5 December 1996.

## 4.2. EQUAL TREATMENT

The equal pay principle was complemented by Council Directive 76/207/EEC[99] which was based upon Article 235 EC. Referring to the Social Action Programme 1974-76, the Directive introduces the principle of equal treatment as regards access to employment, vocational training, promotion and working conditions. The principle of equal treatment is defined in Article 2, embracing direct and indirect discrimination, and covering marital or family status. There are derogations where sex is a determining factor of a particular job and where there are special provisions protecting women during pregnancy and maternity or measures taken to secure positive action. Social security matters were left outside the scope of the Directive.

Article 3 applies the equal treatment principle to all conditions of employment covered by the Directive - selection criteria, access to all jobs and posts, whatever sector of industry, and to all occupational levels. Member States are under a duty to amend any laws, regulations or administrative provisions which are contrary to the Directive and to make provision for the amendment or nullification of discriminatory provisions in collective agreements, rules of undertakings and professional associations. In an infringement action against the UK[100] it was argued that the non-binding character of collective agreements in the UK took the agreements outside of the scope of Council Directive 76/207/EEC. The ECJ rejected these submissions. By looking at the obligations imposed by Article 4 the Court ruled that *all* collective agreements were covered by the Directive irrespective of their legal effect since they have important consequences for the employment relationship.

Articles 6 and 7 impose an obligation upon the Member States to ensure that employees have access to the judicial process to assert their rights under the Directive. Article 8 imposes an obligation upon the Member States to ensure that employees are aware of their rights under the Directive.

### 4.2.1. Different Retirement Ages

Article 5 of the Directive has generated much litigation and received an expansive interpretation from the ECJ.[101] The consequences of differences in

---

[99] OJ 1976 L 39/40.

[100] Case 165/82 *Commission v United Kingdom* [1983] ECR 3431.

[101] Article 5 states: "Application of the principle of equal treatment with regard to working conditions, including the conditions governing dismissal, means that men and women shall be guaranteed the same conditions without discrimination on

retirement ages based on the state pension age have provided the ECJ with a number of references on the relationship between Article 5(1) and the exclusion of discrimination based on different state pension ages contained in Article 7(1)(a) of Council Directive 79/7 EEC and the deferment of the equalisation of state pension ages in Article 9(a) of Council Directive 86/378/EEC. In *Burton v British Railways Board*[102] it was alleged that there was discrimination contrary to Article 5(1) where a female employee could take a voluntary severance payment at the age of 55 while male employees were only entitled to such payments at the age of 60. Both qualifying ages were linked to the state pension age. The Court ruled that it was not contrary to Council Directive 76/207/EEC to provide unequal access to such payments since Article 1(2) of Council Directive 76/207/EEC and Article 7(1) of Council Directive 79/7/EEC excluded the determination of minimum pensionable ages and retirement pensions and the consequences of such rules from the equal treatment principle. However, the Court ruled that the term "dismissal" should be given a broad interpretation. This idea was taken up in *Marshall v Southampton and South West Hampshire Area Health Authority (Teaching)*[103] where the Court drew a distinction between the *pension* age and the *retirement* age. The case concerned the compulsory retirement of a female employee at the age of 62 - the normal retirement policy being linked to the state pension age of 60 for women and 65 for men. *Burton* was distinguished by the ECJ treating the question of *dismissal* separately from the issue of the exclusion of *state pension ages* from the equal treatment principle. Thus the consequences of the determination of pension age did not override the application of Article 5(1). An employee could not be dismissed merely because she satisfied the requirements for a state pension.

The limitations of *Burton* are seen in *Roberts v Tate and Lyle Industries Ltd.*[104] This case, like *Burton*, concerned access to early retirement benefits. Here the early retirement scheme was made available to all employees aged 55 and over. Mrs Roberts was aged 53 and she claimed that discrimination occurred since she was within 10 years of normal retirement age but, unlike the situation of a man, she had no right to an immediate pension. The Court ruled that the grant of a pension to workers adopted irrespective of the sex of the worker in order to guarantee all workers the same rights. In contrast in *Beets-*

---

grounds of sex,"

[102] Case 19/81 [1982] ECR 555.

[103] Case 152/84 [1986] ECR 723.

[104] Case 151/84 [1986] ECR 703.

*Proper v F. van Lanschot*[105] the ECJ ruled that it was an infringement of the Directive when different ages for the dismissal of men and women had been chosen in relation to a difference in retirement age.

### 4.2.2. Night Work

The issue of protective legislation, in the form of laws preventing women from working at night was discussed in two cases in the context of a 1987 French law on the flexibilization of working time which introduced a general derogatory mechanism from the female prohibition of nightwork (Article L.213-1 Labour Code).[106] The issue of national prohibitions or restrictions upon women working at night is complicated by the fact that France, and at some point all the Member States with the exception of the UK, had ratified the ILO Convention No 89 of 1948 which prohibits nightwork by women. A Protocol attached to this Convention was approved in 1990 which authorises derogations from the ban on nightwork by means of collective bargaining, subject to consultation with worker representatives and verification by a competent authority. Before the ratification of this Protocol the Commission had invited the Member States who adhered to the ILO Convention No 89 to denounce it.[107] In *Ministère Public v Stoeckel*[108] a manager of a video and cassette packaging company was charged with having employed women on night work in contravention of the French Labour Code. In defence the manager claimed that the French law was contrary to Article 5 ETD and the judgment of the Court in *Commission v France*.[109] The French government defended its law by arguing that the prohibition on night work was qualified by numerous derogations and was consistent with the general aims of protecting female employees alongside special considerations of a social nature such as the risks of assault and the greater burden of domestic duties borne by women in society. In examining these defences the ECJ ruled that it was not evident, except in cases of pregnancy and maternity, that the risks incurred by women by working at night were different from those incurred by men. If it was assumed that the risk of assault was greater at night than by day suitable

---

[105] Case 262/84 [1986] ECR 773.

[106] Kilpatrick (1996); Sciarra (1996).

[107] A new non-discriminatory convention (No 171) was passed in 1992.

[108] Case 345/89 [1991] ECR I-4047.

[109] Case 312/86 [1988] ECR 3559.

measures could be adopted to handle this risk without jeopardising the fundamental principle of equal treatment. In relation to the claim that another purpose of the French law was to redress the inequalities in domestic responsibilities the Court reiterated a view expressed in the earlier case law that the purpose of the ETD is *not* to settle questions as to the organisation of the family or to alter the allocation of domestic responsibilities within the family.[110]Turning to the numerous derogations from the prohibition on nightwork the Court found these to be inadequate to give effect to the equal treatment principle contained in the Directive particularly since the Directive itself did not provide for any general principle excluding women from nightwork the derogations in themselves could be a source of discrimination. Thus the Court found the French law to be in breach of Article 5. The Court did not address the issue of the existence of the ILO Convention No 89.

In *Levy*[111] a pork products manufacturer, who was also prosecuted for having employed women at night, contended that the French law was incompatible with Article 5 ETD and that the ETD was not incompatible with the ILO Convention. A third reference came from the Liège Labour Court[112] concerning a woman who lived in Belgium but who had worked at night in the hotel and catering industry in Luxembourg. On moving to Liège she stopped working and applied for unemployment benefit. The job centre (ONEM) refused to grant the unemployment benefit on the ground that she had declared that she was no longer prepared to work at night for family reasons. ONEM's decision was declared to be unjustified on the grounds that Belgium legislation prohibited women from working between midnight and 6am. The Belgian law laid down a general prohibition of night work for men and women but contained different systems of derogation for men and women. The derogations for women were determined by legislation and for men by the administrative authorities. ONEM appealed against this decision and a reference was made to the ECJ as to the compatibility of the Belgian law restricting women's working hours with Article 5 ETD. The Court in *Levy* and *Minne* stated that a national court is obliged to ensure that full effect is given to Article 5 ETD and must not apply any contrary provisions of national legislation unless the application of such a provision is necessary in order to ensure that the Member State fulfils its obligations arising out of an agreement concluded with a non-

---

[110] Case 184/83 *Hoffmann v Barmer Ersatzkasse* [1984] ECR 3047; Case 318/86 *Commission v France* [1988] ECR 3559.

[111] Case 158/91 *Ministère Public et Direction du travail et de l'emploi v Levy* [1993] ECR I-4287.

[112] Case C-13/93 *ONEM v Minne* [1994] ECR I-371.

Member State before the entry into force of the EEC Treaty 1957. The reasoning of *Stoeckel* was then applied, with the Court ruling that Article 5 ETD precludes a Member State from maintaining divergent systems of derogations from the ban on night working for men and women. Belgium has now enacted new legislation giving equality for men and women in nightwork.[113]

### 4.2.3. The Concept of Sex Discrimination

In *Petra-Kirshammer-Hack v Nurhan Sidal*[114] the Court considered the exclusion of small businesses employing 5 or less employees from the national system of protection against unfair dismissal was indirectly discriminatory as being contrary to Articles 2(2) and 5(1) ETD. The Court ruled that discrimination would only exist if it were established that small businesses employ a considerably greater number of women than men but on the facts furnished for the Court no such evidence emerged. In any event, an employer would be able to raise a justification for the claim on the principles laid down in *Bilka-Kaufhaus.*

In *Meyers v Adjudication Officer*[115] the Court was asked to rule as to whether family credit - a social security benefit designed to encourage workers who are poorly paid to continue working and meet family expenses - fell within the scope of the ETD. The UK government contended that the measure was a social security provision excluded from the scope of the ETD by Article 1(2). The Court has held that Article 1(2), being a derogation from the fundamental principle of equality, should be narrowly construed.[116] Thus a benefit does not become excluded from the scope of the ETD because it is formally part of the social security system. A benefit may fall within the scope of the ETD if it addresses access to employment, including vocational training and working conditions.

An expansive interpretation of sex discrimination was applied in *P v S and Cornwall CC*[117] where the applicant had been dismissed after undergoing

---

[113] (1997) 279 *European Industrial Relations Review and Report* 24.

[114] Case C-189/91 [1993] ECR I-6185.

[115] Case C-116/94 [1995] ECR I-2131.

[116] Case 151/84 *Roberts v Tate & Lyle Industries Ltd* [1986] ECR 703; Case 152/84 *Marshall (No. 1)* [1986] ECR 723.

[117] Case C-13/94 [1996] ECR I-2143.

gender realignment surgery. Advocate General Tesauro urged the Court to be courageous. Although accepting that the wording of the ETD indisputably referred to the traditional man/woman dichotomy the Advocate General argued that where unfavourable treatment of a transsexual was related, to or caused by, a change of sex there was discrimination by reason of sex, or on grounds of sex. To say that P had not been discriminated against on the grounds of sex was a "quibbling formalistic interpretation and a betrayal of the true sense of that fundamental and inalienable value which is equality." Referring to the right not to be discriminated against on grounds of sex as "one of the fundamental human rights whose observance the Court has a duty on ensure"[118] the Court made the dramatic statement that

> "To tolerate such discrimination would be tantamount, as regards such a person, to a failure to respect the dignity and freedom to which he or she is entitled, and which the Court has a duty to safeguard."[119]

The Court still retained a basis of comparison for deciding if discrimination had occurred by making a comparison with the treatment of the transsexual with persons of the sex to which he or she was deemed to belong before undergoing gender reassignment.

### 4.2.4. Derogations from The Equal Treatment Principle

Article 2 (2)-(4) contains a number of derogations from the equal treatment principle.

### 4.2.4.(i) Sex as a Genuine Occupational Qualification

Article 2(2) allows for exclusions where the sex of the worker is a determining factor in the job. In *Commission v UK*[120] the Court rejected the Commission's complaint that the refusal to allow men full access to training in midwifery was not in breach of Article 2 since the occupation fell within a sphere "in which respect for the patient's sensitivities is of particular importance."[121] But in accordance with Article 9(2) the position was to be kept under review. In

---

[118] Para 19.

[119] Para 22.

[120] Case 165/82 [1983] ECR 3431.

[121] *Ibid* para 18.

relation to the exclusion in UK law, exempting employers with fewer than 6 staff from the scope of national discrimination law, this was found *not* to be in line with Article 2(2). But in relation to the exemption for private households the Court accepted that the exception might be permissible where the principle of respect for private life was relevant.

In *Commission v Germany*[122] the Court dismissed allegations that the German government had failed to implement Council Directive 76/207/EEC in the public service and the independent professions. In relation to the complaint that Germany had failed to define the scope of the derogations from the equal treatment principle in Article 2(2) the Court ruled that it was for the Member States to complete a verifiable list, in whatever, form and to notify it to the Commission. Since Germany had not adopted measures to create even a minimum of transparency the Court concluded that the Commission had been prevented from exercising effective supervision and had made it difficult for individuals to defend their rights.

Articles 2(2) and 2(3) were considered in *Johnston v Chief Constable of the Royal Ulster Constabulary*[123] a complaint was brought by a female officer in the full-time reserve of the RUC challenging the practice of not allowing female officers to receive firearms training or to carry firearms. The Chief Constable argued that if female officers were armed it would increase the risk of assassination and it would be a departure from the ideal of an unarmed police force. Furthermore, it would hinder the valuable  work of female officers in the social field. The first issue addressed by the ECJ was whether sex could be a determining factor of the job within Article 2(2). The Court looked at the specific context of a police officer in Northern Ireland, a situation in which there were frequent assassinations, and concluded that the requirements of public safety might justify the exclusion of women from handling firearms but any derogations from the principle of equal treatment should be interpreted strictly and justified according to the principle of proportionality:

"The principle requires that derogations remain within the limits of what is appropriate and necessary for achieving the aim in view and requires the principle of equal treatment to be reconciled as far as possible with the requirements of public safety which constitutes the decisive factor as regards the context of the activity in question."

The Court was eager to point out that women should not be excluded from a particular employment

---

[122] Case 248/83 [1985] ECR 1459.

[123] Case 222/84 [1986] ECR 1651.

"... on the ground that public opinion demands that women be given greater protection than men against risks which affect men and women in the same way and which are distinct from women's specific needs of protection ..."[124]

Article 2(2) was discussed further in *Commission v France*[125] in an infringement action concerning the recruitment practices for head warders of small prisons and 5 categories of the national police force for which separate recruitment and special allocations were organised for men and women. The Court used the concept of transparency to judge the validity of the derogations from the equal treatment principle. It was held that the Commission should be in a position to supervise the derogations and the derogations must be capable in principle of being adapted to social developments. The Court held that Article 2(2) covered the highest grades of the prison service and it was legitimate to restrict the position to a member of one sex. But for the categories of police officer it was not sufficiently clear or transparent why sex was a determining factor for specific activities. While the French government could rightly argue that there were good reasons for recruiting head warders from experienced prison staff. The post was managerial and did not involve contacts with prisoners which might rightly justify the same restrictions imposed on prison officers. The French government could have avoided the problem by organising their departments differently by creating, for example, a separate *corps* for prison governors or by including the post of prison governor in the management *corps*.

### 4.2.4.(ii) Protection of Pregnant Women

There have been ECJ rulings on another exclusion, Article 2(3), which allows for special protection to be afforded to women in relation to pregnancy and maternity. An infringement action was brought against Italy for breach of Articles 5 and 6 of the Directive for failing to grant parental leave to adoptive fathers on the same terms as leave granted to adoptive mothers.[126] The Court accepted the justification that the difference in treatment was based upon a legitimate concern to assimilate as far as possible the conditions of entry of the adopted child to the adoptive family as those of the arrival of a new-born baby during the very delicate initial period. The Court was even less responsive to

---

[124] Para 44.

[125] Case 318/86 [1988] ECR 3559.

[126] Case 163/82 *Commission v Italy* [1983] ECR 3273.

paternity leave in *Hofmann v Barmer*[127] where a father's request to take over the extended period of maternity leave granted to mothers was rejected on the grounds that maternity leave was a legitimate form of special conditions granted to women for physiological, biological reasons to recover from childbirth and secondly to protect the special relationship that exists between a woman and her child from being disturbed by the multiple burdens of bonding, childcare and the simultaneous pursuit of employment.[128] The Court was not willing to take Community law into the realms of altering "the division of responsibility between parents." Despite these rulings both Italy and Germany amended their domestic laws to accommodate forms of parental leave.[129]

Articles 2(1) and 3(1) have come under consideration in a number of cases relating to pregnancy discrimination *against* women. In *Dekker v Stichting Vormingscentrum voor Jong Volwasseneen*[130] an employer refused to hire a woman because she was pregnant and the employer's insurer would not reimburse the maternity payments payable during maternity leave. The employer argued that it would be impossible to pay for a replacement during the period of maternity leave and as a result the undertaking would be short-staffed. The Court ruled that the refusal to engage a pregnant woman on the ground that she was pregnant constitutes a form of *direct* discrimination on the grounds of sex. Proof of such discrimination is not contingent upon a comparison with the treatment of a male employee. The Court stressed that the primary liability for a breach of Council Directive 76/207/EEC was upon the employer and that he/she cannot rely upon exemptions, exclusions or justifications available in national law to justify discrimination against a pregnant employee.

In contrast the Court[131] ruled that an illness originating in pregnancy or confinement was not covered by Council Directive 76/207/EEC once an employee had exhausted the period of maternity leave set by the Member State. Then the special rules relating to pregnancy ended and one had to compare the treatment of the woman with the way a man would be treated in similar circumstances. In this case the employee had been dismissed after

---

[127] Case 184/83 [1984] ECR 3047.

[128] Ibid, para 25.

[129] Docksey (1991). See now Council Directive 96/34, OJ 1996 L 145/4.

[130] Case C-177/88 [1990] ECR I-3941.

[131] Case C-179/88 *Hertz v Dansk Abejdsgiverforening* [1990] ECR I-394.

exhausting the period of maternity leave and sickness leave (the latter being available to male and female employees). The Court went on to rule that where an illness occurred *after* the period of maternity leave it was unnecessary to distinguish between an illness which originated in pregnancy, childbirth or confinement from any other illness. Since both men and women were liable to be ill the national court should look to see whether the woman has been dismissed on the ground of absence due to ill health under the same conditions as a man. If the answer was in the negative then there was direct discrimination on the grounds of sex. It was considered unnecessary to consider whether women were absent more often due to illness and consequently whether there was any indirect discrimination.

Not content with the ruling by the ECJ that discrimination on the grounds of pregnancy is caught by Council Directive 76/207/EEC the national courts have continued to make references to the Court in order to distinguish the *Dekker* ruling. In *Webb v EMO Air Cargo (UK) Ltd*.[132] The House of Lords asked the ECJ to rule on whether it was contrary to the ETD for an employer to dismiss a pregnant woman who had recently commenced work, initially to cover another maternity leave but with the prospect of being retained as a permanent employee. The employer argued that the employee was required for a specific purpose (to cover a period of maternity leave) and that he would have dismissed a man engaged for a specific purpose who required leave for medical or other reasons at the crucial time. Both the Advocate General and the Commission put forward the submission that in some circumstances *direct* discrimination could be justified, despite the fact that in *Dekker*, the Court was adamant that direct discrimination can never be justified.

Particular emphasis seems to have been placed upon the fact that Webb was taken on as a *permanent* employee with the immediate task of covering for another employee's maternity leave. At paragraph 27 the ECJ states:

> "In circumstances such as those of Mrs Webb, termination of a contract for an indefinite period on grounds of the woman's pregnancy cannot be justified by the fact that she is prevented, on a purely temporary basis, from performing the work she has been engaged."

In another pregnancy dismissal case, decided shortly before *Webb*, *Habermann-Beltermann v Arbeiterwohlfahrt, Bezirksverband*[133] the Court seems to underline the fact that sex discrimination was found because the employee was a permanent employee and that a different result might occur if

---

[132] Case C-32/93 [1994] ECR I-3567.

[133] Case C-421/92 [1994] ECR I-1657.

there was only a temporary contract. Here the applicant had been engaged under a contract to work only at night in a home for the elderly. Soon after starting her contract the employee became ill and was found to be pregnant, the pregnancy having commenced before her employment. Under German law pregnant women were not allowed to carry out night work thus making the contract void (for contravening the German statute) or voidable by the employer due to mistake. The Court accepted that while the Member States had a wide discretion to lay down provisions for the *protection of* pregnant women under Article 2(3) ETD the prohibition against night work in German law took effect for only a limited period in relation to the total length of the employment contract. Therefore to allow that the contract to be avoided or found to be invalid due to a temporary inability to perform the work would undermine the effectiveness of the ETD and would be contrary to its objective of protecting pregnant women.

### 4.2.4.(iii) Positive Action

In contrast, the Court interpreted the derogation restrictively in two cases involving positive action measures. In *Commission v France*[134] a French law permitted collective agreements and individual employment contracts to grant special advantages to employees because of any family responsibilities. Such advantages included the extension of maternity leave, leave when a child was ill, extra pension points for second and subsequent children, the payment of allowances to women for childcare costs. The French government defended the provisions as falling within Article 2(3) and (4). In relation to Article 2(4) the French government argued for an expansive interpretation embracing social measures relating to the sharing of family responsibilities which would affect women's equal opportunities in the workplace. The Commission objected to the provisions arguing that the preservation of "special" rights for women was contrary to the principle of equal treatment dictated by the Directive. The Court agreed with the Commission. It ruled that it was permissible to use national measures which were discriminatory in appearance but are intended to eliminate or reduce inequality which already exists in social life but it was held that the French government had failed to show that its provisions would in fact reduce the perceived inequalities which existed.

---

[134] Case 312/86 [1988] ECR 6315. More (1993).

The case which has generated most controversy, however, is *Kalanke v Freie Hansestadt Bremen*.[135] Here a man challenged a soft form of positive action introduced by the State of Bremen in the public sector. Where there were less than 50% of employees of one sex in the relevant personnel group and a male and female candidate were equally qualified for a post then automatic priority would be given to the member of the under-represented sex. Advocate General Tesauro found the Bremen law to infringe Article 2(4) of the ETD. His Opinion is unusual in that he refers extensively to American legal precedents to reach his conclusions. He argued that positive action under the ETD cannot be used to secure equal results. It must be directed at removing the obstacles preventing women from having equal opportunities, for example, by tackling educational guidance and vocational training. Numerical - and hence only formal equality - is seen by him as an "incontestable violation of a fundamental value of every civil society: equal rights, equal treatment for all". The Court, following the Advocate General, found the Bremen law to be in breach of the ETD. The immediate reaction to the ruling was series of shock waves around the EU, particularly since the Community had been keen to encourage positive action measures.[136] There are two possible interpretations of the ECJ's ruling. One is very narrow, confining the ruling to the content of the Bremen law - the Court assumed that because there was no safeguard clause in the Bremen law which protected the best male applicant from individual hardship it led to automatic preferential treatment for women. A wider reading of the ruling can be found in paragraphs 16 and 22 where the Court refers to a results approach:

> 16. A national rule that, where men and women who are candidates for the same promotion are equally qualified, women are automatically to be given priority in sectors where they are under-represented, involves discrimination on grounds of sex.
> 22. National rules which guarantee women absolute and unconditional priority for appointment or promotion go beyond promoting equal opportunities and overstep the limits of the exception in Article 2(4) of the Directive.

To stem the panic, the Commission issued a Communication to the Council and the European Parliament on the interpretation of the *Kalanke* ruling, proposing the following amendment to Article 2(4) ETD.

---

[135] Case C-450/93 [1995] ECR I-3051. Szyszczak (1996); Schiek (1996); Prechal (1996).

[136] See the Council Recommendation on the promotion of positive action for women, 84/635/EEC, OJ 1984 L331/34. Vogel-Polsky (1989); Serdjenian (1994).

4. This Directive shall be without prejudice to measures to promote equal opportunity for men and women, in particular by removing existing inequalities which affect the opportunities of the under-represented sex in the areas referred to in article 1(1). Possible measures shall include the giving of preference, as regards access to employment or promotion, to a member of the under-represented sex, provided that such measures do not preclude the assessment of the particular circumstances of an individual case.

The Commission takes the view that quota systems which fall short of being rigid and automatic are still lawful. The Communication also provides a list of positive action measures which are lawful:

- quotas linked to the qualifications required for the job, as long as they allow account to be taken of particular circumstances which might, in a given case, justify an exception the principle of giving preference to the under-represented sex;
- for promoting women, prescribing the proportions and the time limits within which the number of women should be increased, but without imposing an automatic preference rule when individual decisions on recruitment and promotion are taken;
- an obligation *of principle* for an employer to recruit or promote by preference a person belonging to the under-represented sex; in such a case, no individual right to be preferred is conferred on any person;
- reductions in social security contributions which are granted to firms when they recruit women who return to the labour market, to perform tasks in sectors where women are under-represented;
- other positive action measures focussing on training, professional orientation, the re-organisation of working time, childcare etc.

The Commission has a vested interest in maintaining the viability of positive action since its Fourth Medium-Term Action Programme on Equal Opportunities for Men and Women[137] contains proposals to use positive action schemes. The Court will have the opportunity to reconsider the position of positive action again in the reference in *Hellmut Marschall v Land Nordrhein-Westfalen*[138] which seeks clarification of whether a form of positive action with an individual hardship rule is compatible with Article 2(4) ETD.

### 4.2.5. Effective Remedies

Article 6 states that:

---

[137] Com (95) 381 final.

[138] Case C-409/95, OJ 1996 C 46/11 pending.

Member states shall introduce into their national legal systems such measures as are necessary to enable all persons who consider themselves wronged by failure to apply to them the principle of equal treatment within the meaning of Articles 3, 4 and 5 to pursue their claims by judicial process after possible recourse to other competent authorities.

In *Von Colson and Kamann v Land Nordrhein-Westfalen*[139] the Court ruled that Article 6 did not create direct effect but, nevertheless, argued that the full implementation of Article 6 does entail that the sanctions chosen for a breach of the Directive must be such as to guarantee real and effective judicial protection and have a real deterrent effect on the employer.

The principle of effective judicial protection was elevated into one of the general principles of Community law in *Johnston v The Chief Constable of the RUC*.[140] In this case the Court referred to Articles 6 and 13 of the ECHR 1950 and the Joint Declaration of the respect for fundamental human rights issued by the Institutions 1977 to confirm the significance of the right to an effective judicial remedy in Community law.

In *Dekker*[141] the Court implied that when sanctions, as opposed to the substantive rights, in a Directive are at issue there is a duty upon the national courts to set aside national provisions incompatible with the Directive even when the litigation involves a private employer. This point was explored further in *Marshall v South West Hampshire Area Health Authority (No. 2)*.[142] When Marshall took her case back to the UK courts for an assessment of her compensation she faced a statutory cap on the amount of compensation which could be awarded which she argued did not provide an effective remedy.[143] The ECJ also ruled that interest should be available on the award since the effluxion of time had decreased the real value of her compensation.[144] In the more recent ruling of *Nils Draehmpaehl* v *Urania Immobilienservice ohG*[145]

---

[139] Case 14/83 [1984] ECR 1891.

[140] Case 222/84 [1985] ECR 1651.

[141] Case C-177/88 [1990] ECR I-3941. See Nielsen (1992).

[142] Case C-271/91 [1993] ECR I-4367; See Fitzpatrick and Szyszczak (1993). Cf Case C-66/95 *Sutton* judgment of 22 April 1997, nyr.

[143] The Industrial Tribunal assessed her compensation at £19,405 but the statutory maximum she could be awarded was £6,250.

[144] Cf Case C-66/95 *Sutton* judgment of 22 April 1997, nyr.

[145] Case C-180/95, judgment of 22 April 1997, nyr.

the Court ruled that it was contrary to Articles 2(1) and 3(1) of the ETD to make provisions relating to compensation subject to a requirement of fault. It went on to rule, however, that national law could impose a ceiling upon the amount of compensation available provided that the remedy was real and effective.

A number of research reports have been commissioned by the Community on the implementation of the equal treatment programme at the national level revealing the inadequacies of the application of the equal treatment programme and the inadequacy of national remedies.[146]

## 4.3. STATE SOCIAL SECURITY[147]

The Commission's first draft of the Equal Treatment Directive included social security matters within its remit but in the final version of the Directive social security was omitted from the text largely as a result of pressure from the UK.[148] The Commission originally envisaged that occupational and state social security matters should be dealt with in one Directive but instead the two areas have been dealt with in separate Directives which contain *lacunae* and envisage further implementing measures.[149]

---

[146] *Inter alia:* Rubenstein, M., *The Dignity of Women at Work: A Report on the Problem of Sexual Harassment in the Member States of the European Community* V/412/1/87-EN; Fitzpatrick, B., *The Impact of EEC Sex Discrimination Law on Collective Agreements: A Comparative Report* (EC Commission, 1990); *Report of the Commission to the Council on the Application as at 12 February 1978 of the Principle of Equal Pay for Men and Women*, COM(78) 711 final; Corcoran, J. and Donnelly, E. *Report of a Comparative Analysis of the Provisions for Legal Redress in Member States the EEC in Respect of Article 119 of the Treaty of Rome and the Equal Pay, Equal Treatment and Social Security Directives* V/564/84-EN Def; Landau, E. *The Rights of Working Women in the European Community* (EC Commission 1985); von Pronzyski, F. *Implementation of the Equality Directives*, V/151/86-EN; Fitzpatrick, B., Gregory, J. and Szyszczak, E. Blom, J. Fitzpatrick, B. Knegt, R. and O'Hara, U. *The Utilisation of Sex Equality Litigation Procedures in the Member States of the Community*, DGV Brussels, 1995, V/782/96-EN. See also McCrudden (1993); Fitzpatrick (1992); Szyszczak (1997).

[147] See McCrudden (1994).

[148] See Hoskyns (1996).

[149] A third Directive has not materialised, OJ 1988 C 95/4.

### 4.3.1. Council Directive 79/7/EEC[150]

Atkins and Luckhaus[151] argue that the tension between the social and economic objectives of the Community and the perceived need to restrain public expenditure to ensure economic growth is a crucial factor influencing the drafting of Council Directive 79/7/EEC and the subsequent decisions of the Court. The Directive was adopted on 23 December 1984 but Article 8 gave the Member States a 6 year transitional period in which to implement its provisions.

### 4.3.1.(i) The Personal Scope of the Directive

Article 2 of the Directive states that the Directive shall apply to the "working population" this is described as including self-employed persons, and

> 2... workers and self-employed persons whose activity is interrupted by illness, accident or involuntary unemployment and persons seeking employment - and to retired or invalided workers and self-employed persons."

In paragraph 22 of the ruling in *Drake v Chief Adjudication Officer*[152] the ECJ gave a broad interpretation to the concept of the "working population". The concept was

> "... based on the idea that a person whose work has been interrupted by one of the risks referred to in Article 3 belongs to the working population ... Mrs Drake ... has given up work solely because of the risks listed in Article 3 ..."

In three references from the Dutch social security court the question was raised as to whether women who had not worked in the paid labour market for a number of years prior to retirement age could be included in the concept of the "working population". The ECJ ruled that the women were housewives, one had never participated in the paid labour market, and that the Directive applied to persons in work, seeking work or involuntarily out of work. The Directive did not apply to persons who had not made themselves available for employment or had ceased to be available for a risk other than those outlined in

---

[150] OJ 1979 L 6/24.

[151] Atkins and Luckhaus (1988). See also Hoskyns and Luckhaus (1989).

[152] Case 150/85 [1986] ECR 1995.

Article 3(1)(a): illness, invalidity, old age, an accident at work, occupational disease or unemployment.[153]

The ECJ has included within the definition of the "working population" people described as engaged in "minor employment" consisting of less than 15 hours' work per week and attracting remuneration of less than one seventh of the average monthly salary.[154]

In *Van Damme*[155] the ECJ ruled that the definition of the "working population" is very broad since it covers any worker, including persons who are merely seeking employment. Thus a person who, in the year preceding the commencement of incapacity for work did not receive a certain income from or in connection with work does not necessarily fall outside the scope of the *ratione personae* of the Directive.

The *Drake* ruling might be compared with that of *Züchner v Handelskrankenkasse (Ersatzkasse) Bremen*[156] where the ECJ ruled that Article 2 of the Directive did not cover a person who undertakes, as unpaid work, the care of a handicapped spouse where the carer had not given up paid work or interrupted efforts to find employment in order to undertake the caring responsibility.

### 4.3.1.(ii) The Material Scope of the Directive

Article 3(1) of the Directive states that the principal of equal treatment shall apply in statutory social security schemes which provide protection against the following risks:

- sickness
- invalidity
- old age
- accidents at work and occupational diseases
- unemployment

---

[153] Joined Cases 48/88 *Achterberg te Riele v Sociale Verzekeringsbank,* Case 106/88 *Bersen-Gustin v Sociale Verzekeringsbank,* Case 107/88 *Egbers-Reuvers v Sociale Verzekeringsbank* [1989] ECR 1963. See also Case C-31/90 *Johnson v Chief Adjudication Officer* [1991] ECR I-3723.

[154] Case C-317/93 *Nolte v Landesverischerungsansalt Hannover* [1995] ECR I-4625; Case C-444/93 *Megner and Sheffel v Innungskrankenkasse Rhein hessen-Pflaz* [1995] ECR I-4741.

[155] Case C-280/94 [1996] ECR I-179.

[156] Case C-77/95 Judgment of 7 November 1996.

The principle of equal treatment also applies to social assistance schemes intended to replace or supplement the above schemes.[157] In *Drake v Chief Adjudication Officer,*[158] the ECJ, applying a broad purposive interpretation, included a benefit payable to a *carer* within the scope of Article 3. But a more restrictive view was taken in *R v Secretary of State for Social Security ex parte Florence Simithson,*[159] a case concerning housing benefit. Housing benefit was paid to people whose real income was lower than a notional income known as the "applicable amount". One of the factors which could be taken into account in order to determine the "applicable amount" was the "higher pensioner premium" which was applicable, *inter alia,* to persons aged between 60 and 80 years who lived alone and were in receipt of one or more social security benefits including an invalidity pension. An invalidity pension was payable until the pension age was reached (60 years for women, 65 years for men). If a person passed the pension age and continued in regular employment the invalidity pension could be paid for a further 5 years beyond the pension age. Anyone who had retired and was below the age of 65 (for women) or 70 (for men) could elect to withdraw from the pension scheme in order to obtain an invalidity pension. Ms Smithson was aged 67 and had received invalidity benefit until she reached the age of 60 then she received her retirement pension. She also received housing benefit but did not fulfil the criteria to receive the "higher pensioner premium". Her complaint was that a man under the age of 70 with a similar physical condition would be able to claim an invalidity pension and would therefore be eligible for the "higher pensioner premium". The ECJ held that although the mode of payment was not decisive as regards the identification of a benefit in order to fall within the scope of the Directive a benefit had to be *directly and effectively* linked to the protection of one of the risks specified in Article 3(1) of the Directive. The Court pointed out that Article 3(1)(a) did not refer to statutory schemes which were intended to guarantee any person whose real income was lower than a notional income (calculated on the basis of certain criteria) a special allowance to meet housing costs.

Similarly in *Jackson and Cresswell* v *Chief Adjudication Officer*[160] the Court ruled that a general benefit aimed at people with insufficient resources to provide for their own needs fell outside the scope of the Directive. The

---

[157] Article 3(1)(b).

[158] Case 150/85 [1986] ECR 1995. See Luckhaus (1986).

[159] Case 243/90 [1992] ECR I-467.

[160] Joined Cases C-63/91 and C-64/91 [1992] ECR I-4737.

cases involved claims by single mothers who lost benefits as a result of deductions for child-minding expenses. Jackson had been in receipt of supplementary benefit which was withdrawn when she began a course of vocational training and received a weekly allowance from the Manpower Services Commission. Childminding expenses were not deducted from the latter benefit whereas they had been from the former. Cresswell had been in receipt of income support but this was not paid to persons who were regarded as being in "remunerative work" for more than 24 hours per week. Cresswell commenced working part-time for less than 24 hours per week. Child-minding expenses were not deductible from those in part-time work whereas they had been when she was in receipt of full income support. Claims, alleging indirect discrimination, were brought against the UK rules alleging they were in breach of Council Directives 79/7/EEC and 76/207/EEC.[161] The Court ruled that Council Directive 79/7/EEC did not refer to a statutory scheme which provided persons with means below a legally defined limit with a special benefit designed to enable them to meet their own needs. This was despite the fact that the recipient was in one of the situations covered by Article 3, ie, unemployment. Since the benefits in question exempted claimants from the obligation to be available for work these benefits were not directly and effectively linked with protection against the risks of unemployment.

### 4.3.1.(iii) Scope of the Equal Treatment Principle

Article 4 outlines the scope of the equal treatment principle as meaning:

> "no discrimination whatsoever on grounds of sex either directly, or indirectly by reference in particular to marital or family status, in particular as concerns:
> - the scope of the schemes and the conditions of access thereto,
> - the obligation to contribute and the calculation of contributions,
> - the calculation of benefits including increases due in respect of a spouse and for dependents and the conditions governing the duration and retention of entitlement to benefits."

Article 4(2) allows for special protection to be accorded to women on the grounds of maternity. The aims of the Directive were limited. It seems to have succeeded in removing some of the areas of discrimination against married women. But the Directive is unable to help those people excluded from national social schemes to accrue independent entitlement largely because of

---

[161] The ECJ dismissed the application of Council Directive 76/207/EEC since the benefits did not provide *access* to employment but provided income support. Cf Case C-116/94 *Meyers v Chief Adjudication Officer* [1995] I-2131.

its focus upon social security schemes protecting against loss of employment based on risk.[162]

Article 4 has direct effect in the national courts. In *McDermott and Cotter v The Minister for Social Welfare and the Attorney General*[163] a successful challenge was made to the Irish social security arrangements whereby a married woman received less unemployment benefit and for a shorter period than men and single women. The Irish government attempted to comply with the Directive by repealing the discriminatory provisions but failed to make the amendments fully retrospective to 23 December 1984 - the end of the transitional period for the Directive's implementation. The Irish legislation came into force on 15 May 1986 and only those married women who had received unemployment benefit within the period of 78 days prior to 15 May 1986 were able to rely upon the new provisions. The Irish government argued that Article 4 did not contain a clear and precise obligation and was conditional upon national implementing measures. The Dutch government, intervening, argued that the variety of alternative mechanisms to achieve the principle of equal treatment denied Article 4 of the ability to create direct effect. The Court rejected such arguments: Article 4 was sufficiently precise, clear and unconditional to create direct effect even though the choice of implementing mechanisms was left to the Member States. The Member States could not restrict or impose conditions on the application of the equal treatment principle. Where the Directive had not been implemented fully by 23 December 1984 an individual could rely upon Article 4 in the national courts. The Court supplied criteria for assessing whether the equal treatment principle had been complied with: in the absence of national implementing measures women had the right to be treated in the same manner and to have the same system applied to them as men in the same situation.

The issue of levelling up, retroactivity and the issue of unjust enrichment were addressed in *Cotter and Others v Minister for Social Welfare and others*.[164] The ECJ ruled that if married men had automatically received increases in social security benefits in respect of a spouse and children deemed to be dependants without having to prove actual dependency married women without actual dependants were also entitled to those increases even if, in some cases, this would result in a double payment of the increases.

---

[162] See Sohrab (1994; 1996); Whiteford (1997).

[163] Case 286/85 [1987] ECR 1453.

[164] Case 286/85 [1987] ECR 1453; Case C-377/89 *Cotter and McDermott* [1991] ECR I-1155.

After the ruling in *McDermott and Cotter* the Irish government enacted legislation to implement the Directive, the legislation coming into force in May 1986. Mrs Emmott, a married woman with two dependant children applied for the backdating of a disability benefit on an equal footing with that of a male beneficiary to 23 December 1984. The Minister for Social Welfare responded to this request by stating that since the matter was still the subject of litigation in the second *Cotter* reference no decision in relation to her claim could be taken. Litigation began in the High Court and the court gave leave for the recovery of the unpaid benefits but this leave was granted without prejudicing the right of the government to raise the issue that the claim was time-barred. The ECJ was asked to rule on whether it was contrary to the general principles of Community law for the authorities of the Member States to rely upon national procedural rules in order to restrict or refuse a claim based upon Community law. The ECJ ruled[165] that the Member States were required to ensure the full application of Directives in a sufficiently clear and precise manner so that where Directives were intended to create rights for individuals, individuals should be able to ascertain the full extent of those rights and where necessary rely upon such rights before the national courts. The Court pointed out that the direct effect of Community law was of a second resort, it was only in specific circumstances, in particular where a Member State had failed to take implementing measures or the measures taken were not in conformity with the Directive that the issue of direct effect arose. As long as a Directive had not been transposed properly into national law individuals would not be able to ascertain the full extent of their rights. This state of uncertainty would exist even where the ECJ had delivered a ruling upon the point of Community law at issue. Only the proper transposition of the Directive would bring the state of uncertainty to an end. Thus, until such time as a Directive had been properly transposed into national law a Member State cannot rely upon national limitation periods in order to defend the claims brought against it.

In April 1985 the Dutch government reformed its social security provisions abolishing rules which prevented married women from receiving unemployment benefit. The legislation was retroactive to 23 December 1984 but it adopted a "levelling down" approach (ostensibly to limit public expenditure costs in order to guarantee financial cover) by reducing the level of unemployment benefit payable to men. The duration of the unemployment benefit was also limited for unemployed people under the age of 35 years. In *The Netherlands v FNV*[166] the ECJ took a broad brush approach to the determina-

---

[165] Case C-208/90 [1991] ECR I-4269.

[166] Case 71/85 [1986] ECR 3855.

tion of the equal treatment principle, ruling that Article 4 was directly effective from 23 December 1984 and from that date until the adoption of the new legislation in April 1985 married women were entitled to claim unemployment benefit on the same terms as single women and married men.

Another discriminatory aspect of the Dutch amending legislation was questioned in *Dik and others v College van Burgemeester en Wethouders der gemeente Arnheim/College van Burgemeester en Wethouders der Gemeente Winterswijk*.[167] Married women who became unemployed before 23 December 1984 had no right to receive unemployment benefit after 23 December 1984. This rule perpetuated the discrimination found in the old provisions relating to entitlement to unemployment benefit. The ECJ ruled that this rule affected vested rights which individuals had acquired under the direct effect of Article 4.

Discrimination in transitional provisions was tackled also in *Borrie-Clarke v Chief Adjudication Officer*[168] where the UK had abolished its non-contributory invalidity pension (NCIP) and introduced a new benefit Severe Disablement Allowance (SDA) from 20 November 1984. Under the NCIP a married woman was obliged to show that she was incapable of performing "normal household duties" as well as satisfying other criteria to prove disability. The SDA was available from 29 November 1984 for claimants under the age of 35, over the age of 50 and all persons in receipt of NCIP. For all other claimants SDA was available from 28 November 1985 (or the date when the claimant reached the age of 50 years). As in *Dik*, there was perpetuation of past discrimination in that married women who were not entitled to NCIP before 19 November 1984 were not entitled to the SDA. The ECJ ruled that a national court should look to see how a married man would be treated under similar circumstances. In *Borrie-Clarke* a married man was automatically entitled to the SDA, therefore it could be shown that the equal treatment principle had been infringed.

In *Caisse d'Assurance Sociale pour Travailleurs Independants "Integrity" v Rouvray*[169] a dispute arose over a Belgian law which allowed married women, widows and students to be exempt from the payment of social security contributions. It was argued that this was contrary to the principle of equal treatment contained in Article 4 of the Directive. The ECJ ruled that Article 4 must be interpreted as precluding national legislation which reserves to

---

[167] Case 80/87 [1988] ECR 1601.

[168] Case 384/85 [1987] ECR 2865.

[169] Case C-373/89 [1990] ECR 4243.

married women, widows and students the possibility of being assimilated to persons not liable to pay any social security contributions without the possibility of a similar exemption being granted to married men or widowers satisfying the same conditions.

### 4.3.1.(iv) Indirect Discrimination[170]

The first case of indirect discrimination to arise under the Directive was *J W Teuling-Worms v Bedrijfsvereniging voor de Chemische*[171] which concerned a contributory invalidity benefit. Supplements were allowed to the benefit for dependants but these supplements were calculated on the basis of a previous law which was overtly discriminatory. The ECJ accepted that a system of social security benefits in which supplements not directly based on the sex of the beneficiary but which take into account the marital status and family situation of the claimant would be caught by Article 4(1) where a considerably smaller proportion of women than men could qualify for the supplement. The system could be justified by reasons unrelated to sex. The ECJ held here that the aim of the measures was to ensure adequate minimum subsistence and that the supplements were necessary to meet the additional burdens borne by the claimants. Thus even though a greater number of men than women qualified for the supplement there was no infringement of the Directive.

The Court also stated that Community law does not prevent a Member State from justifying the control of public expenditure taking into account the fact that claimants with dependant children or spouses have greater needs than single claimants. Thus legislation which restricts a guarantee of benefits equivalent to a statutory minimum wage previously available to all workers suffering incapacity but altered to cover claimants with a dependant spouse or child on a low income was compatible with Article 4(1). The principles of proportionality and necessity derived from *Bilka-Kaufhaus*[172] were to be applied to both the methods chosen and the ultimate objective of the social security legislation.

---

[170] For a comprehensive discussion see Bieback, K-J. *Indirect Discrimination Within The Meaning of Directive (CE) 79/7 in the Social Security Law of the EC Member States* (Commission, Brussels, V/1333/96-EN, February 1996).

[171] Case 30/85 [1987] ECR 2497.

[172] Case 170/84 [1986] ECR 1607.

Part-time work was discussed in *Ruzius-Wilbrink v Bestuur van de Bedrijsvereniging*[173] which concerned a challenge to Dutch legislation which provided for allowances for incapacity to work at the level of minimum subsistence income except where the wage previously earned by the disabled worker was lower than the minimum subsistence allowance because the work had been part-time. The ECJ ruled that this could amount to indirect sex discrimination which was capable of being objectively justified on grounds unrelated to sex.

The Advocate General Lenz was willing to accept that the conditions could disadvantage women but, like the Court, accepted that the Dutch government was entitled to offer specific protection to people who had maintained themselves from earned income. Thus the policy was unrelated to sex discrimination.

The ECJ dismissed a complaint brought under Article 169 EC against Belgium[174] where Belgium successfully argued that its social security provisions were aimed at ensuring that families would have a minimum subsistence level of income. The Commission's allegation that indirect discrimination arose because a greater number of men than women benefited from the scheme was refuted by the ECJ repeating its *Teuling* reasoning that Community law did not prevent a Member State from controlling its public expenditure by taking into account the fact that the needs of beneficiaries with a dependant(s) was greater than that of a single person.

The ECJ has used the requirement of a "necessary aim" of the social policy objectives of a Member State from *Rinner-Kühn* but seems to have exercised greater restraint in assessing the legality of Member States' social security laws against Community law than it has in the employment field[175] and has not applied the principle of proportionality specifically even though it is used in ECJ's case law.[176]

In *De Weerd*[177] the ECJ ruled that national legislation requiring the receipt of a benefit for incapacity for work subject to a condition of having received

---

[173] Case C-102/88 [1989] ECR 4311.

[174] Case 229/89 *Commission v Belgium* [1991] ECR I-2205.

[175] Herbert (1994); Bieback (1996).

[176] See Case 30/85 *Teuling* [1987] ECR 2497, para 18; Case 102/88 *Ruzius-Wilbrink* [1989] ECR 4311; Case 229/89 *Commission v Belgium* [1991] ECR 2203, para 26; Case C-343/92 *Roks* [1994] ECR I-571.

[177] Case C-343/92 [1994] ECR I-571

income from work in the year prior to the beginning of the incapacity affected more women than men fell within Article 4(1) of the Directive. The ECJ stated that Article 4(1) precludes the application of national measures which although stated in neutral terms affect more women than men unless the measure is based on objectively justified factors unrelated to any discrimination on grounds of sex. Thus if the measures reflect a legitimate aim on the part of the state and are shown to be necessary and appropriate they be justified. But budgetary considerations do not justify a difference in treatment. Budgetary considerations may be taken into account, however, when making the continuance of entitlement to social security benefit dependent on certain conditions.[178]

In *Van Damme*[179] the ECJ was asked to interpret its earlier ruling in *De Weerd* as to whether national law could not be justified at all or only that the national law could not be justified on budgetary grounds. The ECJ confirmed the latter interpretation. Here the Dutch government's argument that a social policy aim was being pursued in guaranteeing a minimum income to people who had given up work on the grounds of incapacity, even though conditions of access gave rise to allegations of indirect discrimination and the scheme replaced a national insurance scheme which reduced the number of people who were eligible for the new benefit.

The concept of objective justification was raised in *Megner and Scheffel*.[180] Here workers described as being in "minor employment" working less than 15 hours per week and earning one-seventh of the average monthly salary were excluded from the statutory old age insurance scheme and were exempt from paying contributions to the unemployment benefit scheme.

It was alleged that the German scheme created indirect discrimination since more women than men were affected by the exclusion. The ECJ cited the test for objective justification set out in *De Weerd* and went on to state that in the current state of Community Law it was left to the discretion of the Member States to choose the measures most appropriate to fulfill their social policy aims. This point had been made in *De Weerd* and *Commission v Belgium*. The ECJ then ruled:

"It should be noted that the social and employment policy aim relied on by the German government is objectively unrelated to any discrimination on the grounds of

---

178 See also Case C-137/94 *Richardson* [1995] ECR I-3407; Case C-280/94 *Van Damme* [1996] ECR I-179.

179 Case C-280/94 [1996] ECR I-179.

180 Case C-444/93 [1995] ECR I-4741.

sex and that, in exercising its competence, the national legislative was reasonably entitled to consider that the legislation in question was necessary in order to achieve that aim."

This more relaxed approach is seen in subsequent cases. In *Laperre v Bestuurscommissie Beroeps zaken in de Provincie Zuid-Holland*[181] conditions relating to access to a non-means tested social security benefit were alleged to create indirect discrimination. The Dutch government defended the scheme by stating that it was intended to bring unemployed people back to work without interfering with the savings of those with "modest assets".

### 4.3.2. Exceptions and Derogations

The Directive excludes survivors' benefits and family benefits - other than those which are increased for dependants of the beneficiaries covered in Article 3(1)(a) - from its scope.[182] It also excludes occupational pension schemes[183] and schemes relating to maternity provision.[184] Article 7 lists a set of exceptions, the most significant being provisions which relate to the determination of the pension age for the purposes of granting old age pensions and retirement pensions. In *R v Secretary of State For Social Security ex parte Equal Opportunities Commission*[185] the EOC challenged the UK state pension scheme which differentiated between men and women - women could receive a state pension at the age of 60 whereas men had to wait until they were 65. This meant that men had to pay contributions for a greater number of years . The ECJ ruled that although Article 7(1)(a) does not refer expressly to discrimination in respect of an obligation to contribute such discrimination was necessary to achieve the objective of Article 7(1). The derogations to the Directive reflected the progressive nature of the task of achieving equality in state social security systems. However, in the subsequent case of *R v Secretary of State For Social security ex parte Thomas*[186] where a challenge was made to the refusal to grant disablement and invalid care allowances to people who

---

[181] C-8/94 [1996] ECR I-273.

[182] Article 3(2).

[183] Article 3(3).

[184] Article 4(2).

[185] Case C-9/91 [1992] ECR I-4297.

[186] Case C-328/91[1993] ECR I-2147.

had reached state pension age the Court reiterated a fundamental point that any exceptions/derogations to the equal treatment principle must be interpreted restrictively. Forms of discrimination provided for in benefit schemes other than old-age or retirement must be objectively justified. It must be shown that discrimination is necessary to avoid disrupting the complex financial equilibrium of the social security system or to ensure consistency between retirement pension schemes and other benefit schemes. In *Van Cant*[187] a Belgian law was challenged which provided for different methods of calculating pensions for men and women even though the state pension age was equal. The ECJ ruled that once the national system took the step of abolishing the difference in state pension ages Article 7(1)(a) could not be relied upon to justify maintaining a difference in calculating the retirement pension.

Another discrepancy which arose as a result of different state pension ages was that women in the UK were allowed free medical prescriptions from NHS sources from the age of 60 but this concession was not granted to men until the age of 65. In *R v Secretary of State* for *Health ex parte Richardson*[188] the ECJ ruled that the concessions fell within the scope of Article 3(1) of the Directive and were not permitted under Article 7(1)(a). Although the concessions were not strictly speaking social security benefits they were part of a statutory scheme providing direct and effective protection against one of the risks covered by the Directive, namely sickness.

In *Atkins v Wrekin DC and Department of Transport*[189] a concessionary travel scheme which allowed men over the age of 65 and women over the age of 60 reduced fares on public transport was challenged as being contrary to the Directive. The ECJ repeated its formula from *Richardson* that in order for a benefit to fall within the scope of the Directive it must constitute the whole or the part of a statutory scheme providing protection against one of the specified risks or a form of social assistance having the same objective. But here the benefit did not fulfil the conditions: it was granted at the discretion of the local authority and did not form direct and effective protection against one of the risks listed in Article 3(1). The fact that the recipient fell within one of the risks outlined in Article 3(1) was not sufficient to bring the benefit within the scope of the Directive. The ECJ did, however, state that the way a benefit was

---

[187] Case C-154/92 [1993] ECR I-381.

[188] Case C-137/94 [1995] ECR I-3407.

[189] Case C-228/94 [1996] ECR I-3633.

granted was not decisive for the purposes of deciding if it fell within the scope of the Directive.

### 4.3.3. Remedies

In *Emmott*[190] the ECJ ruled that national time limits cannot begin to run until a Member State has transposed a Directive properly. The Court has ruled subsequently that the *Emmott* ruling is not a general rule but is justified by the particular circumstances of the case since the time bar resulted in depriving *Emmott* of any opportunity to rely on the Directive.[191]

The issue of a duty to pay interest on arrears of social security benefits arose in *R v Secretary of State For Social Security ex parte Eunice Sutton*[192] where the English High Court referred a question as to the availability of interest on arrears of social security benefits not paid under obligations enforceable under Council Directive 79/7/EEC. The applicant argued that interest should be available by analogy with the interpretation given to Article 6 of Council Directive 76/207/EEC in *Marshall (No 2)*.[193] The ECJ ruled that the arrears of social security benefits

> "... in no way constitute reparation for loss of damage sustained and the reasoning of the Court in its judgment in *Marshall II* cannot be applied...".[194]

Sutton also claimed that since the UK had failed to transpose the Directive properly she had suffered loss on account of the belated payment of the social security benefit she was entitled to since inflation had eroded its real value. The ECJ ruled that in an action for damages against the state for failure to transpose the Directive correctly the principles enunciated in *Francovich*[195]and the subsequent case law left it for the national court to determine liability.

---

[190] Case C-208/90 [1991] ECR I-4269.

[191] Case C-338/91 *Steenhorst-Neerings* [1993] ECR I-5475; Case C-410/92 *Johnson (No 2)* [1994] ECR I-5483. See Szyszczak, (1997); O'Keeffe (1996).

[192] Case C-66/95 Judgment of 22 April 1997, nyr.

[193] Case C-271/91 [1993] ECR I-4367.

[194] Para 24.

[195] Joined Cases C-6 and 9/90 [1991] ECR I-5357.

## 4.4. OCCUPATIONAL SOCIAL SECURITY

The *Barber* ruling drove a coach and horses through the Occupational Social Security Directive 86/378/EEC[196] which was intended to complement the State Social Security Directive. The original Directive has now been amended by Council Directive 96/97/EC[197] which was adopted on 20 December 1996. Its aim is to amend Council Directive 86/378/EEC in the light of *Barber* and the subsequent case law. The Directive is based on Article 100 EC. Article 1 of Council Directive 96/97/EEC defines occupational social security schemes as:

> "... schemes not governed by Directive 79/7/EEC whose purpose is to provide workers, whether employees or self-employed, in an undertaking or group of undertakings, area of economic activity, occupational sector or group of sectors with benefits provided by statutory social security schemes or to replace them, whether membership of such schemes is compulsory or optional."

Article 7 excludes certain schemes from the Directive's coverage:

- individual contracts for self-employed workers
- schemes for self-employed workers having only one member
- insurance contracts to which the employer is not a party, in the case of salaried workers
- optional provision of occupational schemes offered to participants individually to guarantee them either additional benefits or a choice of date on which the normal benefits for self-employed workers will start or a choice between several benefits.
- occupational schemes in so far as benefits are financed by contributions paid by workers on a voluntary basis

Article 1 also states that the Directive does not preclude an employer granting to persons who have already reached the retirement age for an occupational pension, but not for a statutory pension, a *supplementary* pension, the aim of which is to equalize the amount of pension payable to both sexes. Article 1(1) is intended to replace Article 2 of Council Directive 86/378/EEC.

The Directive will now apply to members of the working population, including self-employed persons, persons whose activity is interrupted by illness, maternity, accident or involuntary unemployment and persons seeking employment, retired, disabled workers and those claiming under them in accordance with national law and/or practice.

---

[196] OJ 1986 L 225/40.

[197] OJ 1997 L 46/20.

Article 1(3) replaces Article 6 of Council Directive 86/378/EEC. It defines provisions contrary to the principle of equal treatment where they are based on direct or indirect sex discrimination, family or marital status. Article 1(3) then provides a list of provisions caught by the Directive:

(a)　determining the persons who may participate in an occupational scheme;

(b)　fixing the compulsory or optional nature of participation in an occupational scheme;

(c)　laying down different rules as regards the age of entry into the scheme or the minimum period of employment or membership of the scheme required to obtain the benefits thereof;

(d)　laying down the different rules, except as provided for in points (h) and (i), for the reimbursement of contributions when a worker leaves a scheme without having fulfilled the conditions guaranteeing a deferred right to long-term benefits;

(e)　setting different conditions for the granting of benefits or restricting such benefits to workers of one or other of the sexes;

(f)　fixing different retirement ages;

(g)　suspending the retention or acquisition of rights during periods of maternity leave or leave for family reasons which are granted by law or agreement and are paid by the employer;

(h)　setting different levels of benefit, except in so far as may be necessary to take account of actuarial calculation factors which differ according to sex in the case of defined-contribution.

In the case of funded defined-benefit schemes, certain elements (examples of which are annexed) may be unequal where the inequality of the amounts results from the effects of the use of actuarial factors differing according to sex at the time when the scheme's funding is implemented;

(i)　setting different levels for workers' contributions;

setting different levels for employers' contributions, except:

- in the case of defined-contribution schemes if the aim is to equalise the amount of the final benefits or to make them more nearly equal for both sexes,

- in the case of funded defined-benefit schemes where the employer's contributions are intended to ensure the adequacy of the funds necessary to cover the cost of the benefits defined.

Management bodies of pension schemes which have a discretion to grant benefits are caught by the Directive

Article 1(4) replaces Article 8 of Council Directive 86/378/EEC and obliges the Member States to take the necessary steps to implement the principle of equal treatment in occupational social security schemes by 1 January 1998. But rights and obligations relating to periods of membership of occupational schemes prior to revision will remain in force.

Article 1(5) allows for the deferment of the equal treatment principle in relation to

- determination of pensionable age for the granting of old-age/retirement pensions and the possible implications for other benefits until either equality is achieved in statutory schemes or prescribed by an EC Directive
- survivors' pensions until Community law establishes the principle of equal treatment in statutory schemes
- the application Article 6(1)(i) (setting different levels for workers' contributions) to take account of the different actuarial calculation factors, at the latest until 1 January 1999.

A new Article 9a will allow men and women to claim a flexible pensionable age under the same conditions.

Article 1(7) of Council Directive 96/97/EC supplies a new Annex giving examples of elements which may be unequal in respect of funded defined-benefit schemes referred to in Article 6(h):

- conversion into a capital sum of part of a periodic pension
- transfer of pension rights
- a reversionary pension payable to a dependant in return for the surrender of part of a pension
- a reduced pension where the worker opts to take early retirement.

Article 2 states that any measure implementing the Directive must, as regards paid workers, cover all benefits derived from periods of employment subsequent to 17 May 1990 and such measures shall apply retroactively to 17 May 1990. But for any persons who have instituted legal proceedings or raised an equivalent claim under national law the implementation measures must apply retroactively to 8 April 1976 - the date of the *Second Defrenne*[198] case applying the direct effect of Article 119 EC. The implementing measures must cover all benefits relating to periods of employment from that date.

Article 2(2) allows national time limits to apply provided they are not less favourable than those applying to similar actions under domestic law and do not render the exercise of Community rights impossible in practice.

There is a short implementation period to this Directive - the Member States must implement it by 1 July 1997.

## 4.5. EQUAL TREATMENT OF THE SELF-EMPLOYED

A Directive was enacted applying the principle of equal treatment to the self-employed and their spouses.[199] Dubbed "the farmer's wife directive" it was

---

[198] Case 43/75 [1976] ECR 455.

[199] Council Directive 86/613/EEC, OJ 1986 L 359/5.

intended to give protection to spouses who worked in a family business. But it also applies to spouses who form a company. It applies to a number of aspects of working conditions such as "the establishment, equipment or extension of a business or the launching or extension of any form of self-employed activity including financial activities."[200] The Directive states that if a Member State provides for a contributory social security scheme for the self-employed a spouse who participates in the activities of the self-employed worker should be able to join the scheme voluntarily.[201] The Directive also encourages the Member States to recognise the work performed by spouses in the circumstances recognised by the Directive.

Article 8 requires the Member States to examine the conditions under which a female self-employed worker and the wife of a self-employed worker may have access to services supplying temporary replacements and benefits under a social scheme in the event of interrupting their work as a result of pregnancy and motherhood. Article 9 obliges the Member States to allow those who consider that their rights have been infringed under the Directive to pursue their claims by judicial process. The Directive's transitional period ended on 30 June 1989 and the Council had intended to review its application by 1 July 1993 but no action was taken.

## 4.6. SOFT LAW MEASURES IN THE EQUAL TREATMENT FIELD

The Member States have been willing to adopt a number of soft law measures in the field of equal treatment showing their commitment to the ideal but recognising that not enough consensus exists to adopt measures which create individual rights.

### 4.6.1. Action Programmes

There have been four Action programmes on equal opportunities.[202] These Action Programmes set out goals to be achieved within a given period as well as providing a framework for developing Community policy. The current Action Programme, the Fourth Medium-Term Action Programme on Equal

---

[200] Article 4.

[201] Article 7.

[202] See *Bulletin of the EC,* Supp 1/82; *Bulletin of the EC,* Supp 3/86; COM (90) 449 final; COM (95) 381 final.

Opportunities for Women and Men (1996 - 2000),[203] was adopted by a Council Decision[204] on 22 December 1995 and came into operation, on a reduced budget, on 1 January 1996.[205] The Programme has 6 objectives:

(1)   promoting equality in the economy
(2)   the reconciliation of working and family life
(3)   a better balance in the decision making process
(4)   promoting the active exercise of citizenship rights by women who are nationals of *or resident in*, the EU
(5)   mainstreaming
(6)   supporting implementation, monitoring and assessment of the Action Programme.

The Fourth Action Programme dovetails with the new approach to social policy issues outlined in Chapter One and the Medium Term Social Action Programme.[206]Concrete proposals for legislative action are minimal. Consolidation of progress to date is linked to the launching of debates on key issues with consultation, identification and transposition of good practice, encouragement of innovation and motivation as key messages.

Promoting equality in the economy will be tackled by the integration of women's issues into all aspects of employment planning and the 'information society' and by tackling the issue of desegration of labour markets. It is envisaged that positive action programmes will have a role to play in these strategies.[207]

The Commission refers to the implementation of its Memorandum on Equal Pay 1994[208] and pledges itself to implementing its ideals with the wide dissemination of the EU Code of Practice.[209] The Commission also pledges to adapt its own public procurement practices with a view to promoting equal opportunities. Mainstreaming is given greater prominence in this Programme

---

[203] COM (95) 381 final.

[204] OJ 1995 L 335/37.

[205] Szyszczak (1996).

[206] COM (95) 134.

[207] Cf Case C-450/93 *Kalanke* [1995] ECR I-3051 and the Commission's Communication of 27 March 1996, COM (96) 88.

[208] COM (94) 6.

[209] COM (96) 336.

as well as a higher profile to monitoring and the evaluation of equal opportunities policy.[210] This is designed to reduce the fragmentation which has occurred in previous Action Programmes.

The Programme focuses upon ways women are able to exercise their legal rights under Community law and offers support for exchanges of information, conferences. Legislation is promised in the areas of the reversal of the burden of proof, part-time work, revision of Council Directive 86/613/EEC (on self-employed persons), work towards transforming the sexual harassment procedures initiated in the 1991 Recommendation on the protection of the dignity of women and men in the workplace into a binding Community instrument,[211] work towards revising the occupational social security Directive[212] in the light of ECJ's case law and a Communication on the individualization of social security rights.

### 4.6.2. Sexual harassment

Research has been undertaken[213] on the legal protection afforded to victims of sexual harassment in the EU. The Commission and also the Parliament[214] proposed that a Directive on sexual harassment should be adopted but the Council merely passed a Resolution on the protection of the dignity of women and men at work.[215] This was followed by a Commission Recommendation 92/131/EEC and a Code of Conduct.[216] A proposal for a Directive on sexual

---

[210] The Commission's White Paper on Social Policy (COM (94) 333) promised an annual equality report. The first one, *Equal Opportunities Between Women and Men in the European Union*, COM (96) 650 has been distributed to all relevant authorities and will be the subject of a debate in the Parliament and the Council. The report is intended to be a monitoring instrument.

[211] OJ 1992 L 49/1.

[212] See now Council Directive 96/97/EEC OJ 1997 L 46/20.

[213] Rubenstein, M. *The Dignity of Women At Work: A Report on the Problem of Sexual Harassment in the Member States of the European Communities* (October 1987, ISBN 92-825-8764-9). See generally Elman (1996).

[214] OJ 1986 C 176/79.

[215] OJ 1990 C 157/2.

[216] OJ 1992 L 49/1. *How To Combat Sexual Harassment At Work: A Guide To Implementing the Commission Code of Practice* (OPEC, 1993, ISBN 92-826-5225-4).

harassment is at the second stage of consultation with the social partners under the SPA.

### 4.6.3. Childcare and Parental Leave

The issue of enabling men and women to reconcile their occupational and family obligations is one which permeates the Commission's Action programmes. There has been a Council Recommendation on child care[217] and in 1995 the social partners drew up an agreement on parental leave under the SPA procedures. This agreement was adopted in the form of a Directive by the Council.[218] In the Preamble to the Parental Leave Directive there are two references to the Social Charter 1989 - to paragraph 16 on equal treatment for men and women and to the fact that the Social Charter 1989 recognizes the fight against all forms of discrimination especially that based on sex, colour, race, opinions and creeds. Reference is also made to Article F(2) TEU and respect for fundamental human rights. The Directive states in Article 1 that its purpose is to put into effect the parental leave agreement concluded under the SPA processes between the general cross-industry organisations (UNICE, CEEP and ETUC). The framework agreement sets out *minimum* requirements for parental leave, distinct from maternity leave and for time off work on the grounds of *force majeure*. It is left for the Member States and the social partners to establish the conditions of access and detailed application of the minimum requirements in accordance with the situation in each Member State. he agreement applied to all workers, male and female who have an employment contract or employment relationship defined by the law, collective agreement or practices in force in each Member State. The agreement grants an *individual* right to parents, male and female, to parental leave on the grounds of birth or the adoption of a child to enable them to take care of the child for at least three months until a given age up to 8 years. In principle, in order to promote equal opportunities, it is considered that the right to parental leave should be granted on a non-transferable basis.

The conditions for parental leave are defined as *minimum requirements* to be implemented by the Member States through legislation and/or collective agreements. The Member States may introduce more favourable conditions. It is therefore left to the national system to:

---

[217] Recommendation 92/241/EEC OJ 1992 L 123/16.

[218] Council Directive 96/34/EC, OJ 1996 L 145/4.

- decide whether parental leave is granted on a full-time/part-time basis, in a piecemeal way or in the form of a time-credit system;
- to make entitlement to parental leave subject to a period of work qualification and/or a length or service qualification (which shall not exceed one year);
- adjust conditions of access and detailed rules for applying parental leave to the special circumstances of adoption;
- establish notice periods to be given by the worker to the employer when exercising the right to parental leave, specifying the beginning and the end of the period of leave.
- define the circumstances in which an employer, following national requirements for consultation, is allowed to postpone the grant of parental leave for justifiable reasons related to the operation of the undertaking.[219] Any problems arising from the application of this provision should be handled through national procedures;
- authorize special arrangements to meet the operational and organization requirements of small undertakings.

Member States and/or the social partners must take the necessary measures to protect workers against dismissal related to an application for parental leave. At the end of a period of parental leave workers shall have the right to return to the same job or, if that is not possible, an equivalent/similar job which is consistent with their employment contract/employment relationship. Any rights acquired, or in the process of being acquired, on the date on which parental leave begins shall be maintained *as they stand* until the end of parental leave when these rights, including any changes arising from national leave, collective agreement or practice shall apply.

The Member States and/or the social partners, shall define the *status* of the employment contract/employment relationship for the period of parental leave. All matters relating to social security in relation to the Parental Leave Agreement are to be determined at the national level with underlying consideration of the importance of the continuity of entitlements, particularly health care.

In addition to parental leave at the time of the birth/adoption of a child Member States and/or the social partners are to introduce measures to allow time off work on the grounds of *force majeure* for urgent family reasons in cases of sickness/accident making the immediate presence of the worker indispensable. This entitlement may be limited to a certain amount of time per year and/or per case.

---

[219] For example, where work is of a seasonal nature, where a replacement cannot be found within the notice period, where a significant proportion of the workforce applies for parental leave at the same time, where a specific function is of strategic importance.

The Final Provisions state quite firmly that the introduction of the Parental Leave Agreement shall not constitute valid grounds for reducing the general level of protection afforded workers in the areas covered by the Agreement. Neither will it prejudice the rights of the Member States and/or the social partners to develop different provisions in the light of changing circumstances (including the introduction of non-transferability) provided the minimum requirements are observed. This dynamic is secured by a provision (Clause 4(3)) allowing the European level social partners to agree complementary provisions to the Agreement in the light of particular circumstances.

The Member States are under an obligation to implement Council Directive 96/34/EC by 3 June 1998. They must ensure that the social partners implement any necessary collective agreements by this date. Given the complexity of implementing this duty an additional year's grace is given for this method of implementation where there are particular difficulties.

Although any grievances/disputes arising under the Agreement are to be dealt with according to national procedures there is a provision (Clause 4 (6)) stating that, without prejudice to the role of the Commission, national courts and the ECJ, any matter relating to the interpretation of the Agreement at *European level* should, in the first instance, be referred by the Commission to the signatory partners who will give an opinion. If one of the signatory parties so requests, the signatories partners will review the Agreement five years after the date of the Council Decision adopting the Agreement (3 June 2001).

The Directive is, of course, innovative on the increased role played by the social partners in its formation - and it would seem - in its implementation. But it only improves upon the situation in 3 Member States - Ireland, Belgium and Luxembourg and is silent on the most contentious issue: income during the period of parental leave.

### 4.6.4. *Broadening the Basis of the Non-Discrimination/Equality Principle*

Despite its relative success the equal treatment programme has been subject to much criticism in recent years. The criticism focussing upon the narrow, market-oriented focus of the programme and the ECJ's use of "market-ideology" in its reasoning.[220] This has led to debates as to how a broader, more holistic approach[221] might be taken to address, not only issues of inequality between men and women within the EU, but also how to tackle other inequalities. As we have seen in Chapter One, the EU has adopted "social

---

[220] Hoskyns (1986); Fredman (1992; 1996) Fenwick and Hervey (1995);

[221] See McGlynn ((1996); Everson (1996); Ward (1996); Hervey (1996).

exclusion" as one of its priorities for social policy and used macro-economic policy initiatives and the Structural Funds to implement this goal. Recent years have seen debates as to how to broaden the appeal of the EU through improvements in communication, transparency and democratic participation in decision-making. Growing importance is attached to creating a constitutional order which recognises, *inter alia,* certain basic individual rights either by broadening the ambit of equality law generally or to creating a general non-discrimination clause in the EC Treaty with a similar function to that of Article 6 EC. In Chapter One we have discussed the ways in which social policy issues in general might be addressed through the use of a broader set of human/social rights guarantees. In this Chapter we look specifically at the issue of broadening the ambit of equality/ anti-discrimination standards.[222] We begin by looking at some specific areas where there has been some Community activity and move on to look at the broader more general discussions of introducing wider human rights/citizenship/non-discrimination provisions.

### *4.6.4.(i) Sexual Orientation*

Political pressure from the gay liberation movement throughout Europe has led to the modification of a number of Member States' laws and cases brought under the ECHR 1950. Pressure has been brought to bear on the EU to include a ban on sexual orientation discrimination but to date no legislation has been enacted.[223] In a report prepared by the European Human Rights Foundation and presented to the Commission it was proposed to include protection from discrimination on the grounds of sexual orientation as one of the rights to be included in a Community Bill of Rights The Squarcialupi Report 1984 on sexual discrimination in the workplace suggested that the European Parliament should initiate measures to protect the gay community of the EU and this was followed by a Resolution[224] of the European Parliament requesting the Commission to:

- submit proposals to prevent discrimination in employment on grounds of sexual orientation
- take steps to induce the WHO to delete homosexuality from its International Classification of Diseases

---

[222] See Bell and Waddington (1996).

[223] See Waaldijk and Clapham (1993).

[224] EP Debates, 13 March 1984, No 1-311/1, 19. See also OJ 1994 C 61/40.

- identify discrimination related to sexual orientation in national laws relating to housing and other social issues

The Commission has argued that the only possible legal base to introduce measures relating to sexual orientation discrimination would be Article 235 EC and it would be unlikely to achieve unanimity in the Council.[225] Tatchell [226] records that Commission began an informal dialogue with gay and lesbian groups and this proved instrumental in including sexual orientation as one of the grounds of sexual harassment in the Code of Practice on Sexual Harassment attached to the Commission's Recommendation on the Protection of the Dignity of Women and Men At Work.[227] Although the Commission has continued to show support for Parliament's attempts to keep sexual orientation issues on the political agenda no firm legislation has emerged.[228] It is interesting to note that the inclusion of sexual orientation in the Preamble to the Parental Leave Directive was dropped by the Council in the final draft.[229]

It is arguable that the fundamental right to private life, as protected by Article 8 ECHR 1950 and recognised by the Court in *X v Commission*[230] could be used to protect aspects of discrimination based on sexual orientation. There are two reference before the ECJ on sexual orientation issues. The first, *Grant v South West Trains*[231] concerns the question of an employer refusing to give travel concessions to the partner of a lesbian employee where such concession are available to married and cohabiting heterosexual couples. The case is based upon Article 119 EC, where after the ruling in *Garland v BRE*[232] there is no doubt that concessionary rail fares fall within the scope of "pay". The crucial issue is the question referred by the Industrial Tribunal in the UK as to

---

[225] Commissioner Ivor Richard Debates of the European Parliament No 1-311/17, 13 February 1984). See also the Written Answer from Commissioner van den Broeck, OJ 1995 C 326/40.

[226] Tatchell (1992).

[227] OJ 1992 49/1.

[228] See European Parliament Report on Equal Rights For Homosexuals and Lesbians in the European Community, Document A3-0028/94.

[229] Council Directive 96/34/EC OJ 1996 L 145/4.

[230] Case C-404/92P [1994] ECR I-4737.

[231] C-249/96 pending.

[232] Case 12/81 [1982] ECR 359.

whether, for the purposes of Article 119 EC, "discrimination based on sex" includes discrimination based upon sexual orientation. If this question is answered in the affirmative the possibility of further litigation under the Equal Treatment Directive on other forms of discrimination against gay and lesbian workers is bound to materialise but the impact of including sexual orientation discrimination within Article 119 EC will also create more interest in pay-related issues such as dependant's pensions.

The second case, also from the UK, relates to the discrimination faced by gay and lesbian personnel in the armed forces.[233] Here a judicial review action was sought challenging the total ban on gay and lesbians in the armed services in the UK with compatibility of the obligations contained in the ETD.

Even if these cases are successful there is still the need for a residual clause relating to sexual orientation to cover aspects of discriminatory treatment not covered by Article 119 EC and the equal treatment programme - for example in the area of free movement of persons.

### 4.6.4.(ii) Disability

EU's response to disability[234] has been tentative with the focus upon on the *social* and *economic* integration of disabled persons through the adoption of soft law.[235] The EU has used Articles 128 EC and 235 EC to initiate programmes the most recent being the HELIOS.[236] The ESF has been used to fund projects such as the Horizon Fund aimed at supporting research into technology and the TIDE[237] programme.

Article 26 of the Social Charter 1989 addressed disability:

"All disabled persons, whatever the origin and nature of their disablement, must be entitled to additional concrete measures aimed at improving their social and professional integration. These measures must concern, in particular, according to the capacities of the beneficiaries, vocational training, ergonomics, accessibility, mobility, means of transport and housing."

---

[233] Case C-xx/xx *Perkins* pending.

[234] See Waddington (1995).

[235] See Council Recommendation and Guideline on the Employment of Disabled People in the European Community, OJ 1986 L 225/43.

[236] Handicapped People in the European Community Living Independently in an Open Society.

[237] Technology Initiative for Disabled and Elderly People.

In its Action Programme to implement the Social Charter the Commission argued that and also recognised the need for *positive action measures*

> "The social and economic integration of disabled people is an important element of the social dimension of the single market... It is not only a question of social justice. It is also an economic issue in so far as their occupational integration in a regular working environment may often represent an asset for the Community.
> ... disabled people have the same right as all other workers to equal opportunity in training and employment, and ... special measures are needed at Community and national level if these are to be achieved."

Article 2 of the SPA annexed to the EC Treaty includes the *integration of persons excluded from the labour market* as an area which may be dealt with by qualified majority voting.

These standards are ambivalent as to whether there is a *right* to equality of treatment. On the one hand some provisions set a standard of *equality of regard* to the position of disabled people in that any provisions which are made for them must reflect their individual situation. In some ways this goes further than the equal treatment standard for sex discrimination, recognising *substantive* rather than formal equality. But the standards are set in provisions of soft law which do not have the same legal force as Directives. In reality the most substantive measures have been taken within the Commission's HELIOS[238] programmes but while these provide special programmes and funding opportunities they do not provide enforceable individual rights.

In the responses received to the Commission's Green Paper on Social Policy[239] a number of issues relating to disability were raised and the Commission argued for the introduction of a specific clause dealing with disability in the EC Treaty in the subsequent White Paper.[240] Only recently has the Commission adopted a Communication on equality of opportunity for people with disabilities, setting out a rights-based approach.[241] The Dublin Presidency's draft for a new general non-discrimination clause does not include disability as a specific area but instead suggests the use of Articles 127 or 100a EC to tackle the specific issue.

---

[238] COM (96) 406 final.

[239] COM (93) 551.

[240] COM (94) 33.

[241] COM (96) 406 final. See also Amended Proposal For a Council Recommendation For A Parking Card For People With Disabilities COM (97) 76 final.

### 4.6.4.(iii) Race Discrimination

Finding a legal and economic base to tackle race discrimination within the EU has proved problematic with the attempts by the Commission to bring the interests of TCNs under the protective wing of EC law meeting opposition from the Council of Ministers.[242] In 1986 a Joint Declaration Against Racism and Xenophobia was signed by the Commission, Council and Parliament.[243]One of the major criticisms of the Social Charter 1989 was that only a passing reference to race discrimination was made in the Preamble. Initiatives in this area have been largely at the instigation of the European Parliament resulting in some soft law measures. In its Resolution[244] on a day to commemorate the Holocaust the Parliament called upon the Commission to examine how, with due respect for the principle of subsidiarity, the Union might act against racism, xenophobia, anti-semitism and denial of the Holocaust at a European level.

In a Resolution[245] on Racism, xenophobia and anti-semitism the Parliament argued that if Community competence in this area was created an interim monitoring body should be established. In a more recent Resolution[246] on Racism, xenophobia and anti-semitism the Parliament supported the idea of incorporating into the EC Treaty provisions concerning the condemnation of racism, xenophobia and anti-semitism and the extension of Article 6 EC to prohibit *all* forms of discrimination.

In July 1996 the Council agreed a Resolution declaring 1997 the Year Against Racism.[247] The goals are to:

-   highlight the threat posed by racism to the respect of fundamental rights and to the economic and social cohesion of the EU
-   to encourage reflection and discussion on matters to combat racism;
-   to promote the exchange of experience and dissemination of information and good practice and effective strategies to combat racism
-   to make known the benefits of immigrant integration policies;

---

[242] Szyszczak (1992a).

[243] OJ 1986 C 158/1.

[244] OJ 1995 C 166/132.

[245] 1995 OJ C 166/32. See the Commission's study of the feasibility of a Racism Monitoring Centre (687 1/ 1/96, RAXEN 18).

[246] OJ 1995 C 151/56.

[247] OJ 1996 C 237/1.

- to turn to good account the experience of persons actually affected or likely to be affected by racism, xenophobia and antisemitism.

### 4.6.4.(iv) Older People

Throughout the EU demographic trends reveal an ever increasing section of the population past retirement age. The Social Charter 1989 provided that:

" 24. Every worker of the European Community must, at the time of retirement, be able to enjoy resources affording him or her a decent standard of living.
25. Every person who has reached retirement age but who is not entitled to a pension or who does not have other means of subsistence, must be entitled to sufficient resources and to medical and social assistance specifically suited to his needs."

The Commission has issued various communications and drafted an Action Programme providing for pilot projects, exchanges of information between groups representing the elderly. In 1990 the Council issued a Decision[248] on Community action for the elderly which included designating 1993 as the European Year of the Elderly and of Solidarity Between Generations. In the White Paper, *Social Policy - A Way Forward*,[249] the Commission proposed to issue a Decision for further EU-wide action.

The Council and Representatives of the Governments of the Member States adopted a Resolution on the Employment of Older Workers.[250] It has two underlying principles:

*first*, increased efforts are necessary to adjust the conditions in which workers in the latter part of their working lives work and are vocationally trained, taking account of the competiveness of undertakings;
*second*, older workers must benefit from adequate resources and from measures to prevent their exclusion from the labour market.

The Resolution calls upon the Member States *and* the social partners to:

- encourage work to be organised in a way which allows the jobs of older workers to be adapted to make the best use of their experience
- to endeavour to ensure that older workers have sufficient resources through compensation for those who have lost their jobs and by financing early retirement

---

[248] Council Decision 91/49/EEC, OJ 1991 L 28/29; Council Decision 92/440/EEC OJ 1992 L 245/43.

[249] COM (94) 333, 52.

[250] OJ 1995 C 228/1.

- to make use of early retirement, especially in the case of workers who have spent many years in arduous work
- to facilitate phased retirement by developing possibilities of part-time work for older workers while respecting the principle of equal treatment, in particular as regards access to social protection.

The Member States are asked to take appropriate measures to eliminate any obstacles to the employment of older workers, to make employers aware of individual or collective consequences of dismissing older workers, to facilitate the return to work of older long-term unemployed people through financial aid for recruitment and genuine vocational training. Where the State acts as employer it should set positive examples.

In the proposals for a set of fundamental social rights put forward by Hepple, Sciarra and Weiss[251] age discrimination is included and the Comité des Sages' proposal includes age discrimination in their list of rights to be protected. The Dublin Presidency's draft of the revised EC Treaty, also includes within the proposed Article 6, a broad reference to "age" as one of the protected categories.

### 4.6.4.(v) Use of Existing Community Law: Human Rights Standards

We have seen in this Chapter One and in Chapter Two how the ECJ has used the general principles of Community law to elevate the free movement of persons and the equal treatment of men and women into a fundamental right of Community law.[252] Human rights standards are recognised as general principles of Community law and a number of Citizenship and human/social rights standards are already included as objectives of the EU. For example, Article B TEU includes as one of the objectives of the Union.

"... to strengthen the protection of the rights and interests of the nationals of its Member States through the introduction of a citizenship of the Union".

And a limited set of embryonic, but positive, Citizenship rights may be found in Articles 8 a-e EC. Article 8e EC specifically recognises the dynamic process of building upon these rights. A direct reference to human rights standards lies in the requirement that the justice and home affairs matters outlined in Article K.1. be dealt with in compliance with the ECHR 1950 and the Refugee Convention 1950

---

[251] *Fundamental Social Rights: Proposals for the European Union*, 1995.

[252] See Szyszczak (1995).

Article F(2) TEU states that the Union:

"... shall respect fundamental rights, as guaranteed by the European Convention for the Protection of Human Rights and Fundamental Freedoms ... and as they result from the constitutional traditions common to the Member states, as general principles of Community law."

This Article codifies the Court's case law, but somewhat paradoxically, Article L TEU tells us that Article F TEU is not justiciable. There are hints that the ECJ does not consider Article L TEU as totally restrictive. For example, in *Bosman*[253] the Court states at paragraph 79:

"As regards the arguments based on the principle of freedom of association, it must be recognised that this principle, enshrined in Article 11 of the European Convention for the Protection of Human Rights and Fundamental Freedoms and resulting from the constitutional traditions common to the Member States, is one of the fundamental rights which, as the Court has consistently held and is reaffirmed in the preamble to the Single European Act and in Article F(2) of the Treaty on European Union, are protected in the Community legal order."

Similarly we see the Court addressing the importance of upholding human rights in the Community legal order in *Opinion 2/94 Accession by the Community to the European Convention for the Protection of Human Rights and Fundamental Freedoms*[254] at paragraph 32:

"It should first be noted that the importance of respect for human rights has been emphasised in various declarations by the member states and of the Community Institutions ...Reference is also made to respect for human rights in the preamble to the Single European Act and in the preamble to, and in Article F(2), the fifth indent of Article J.1.(2) and Article K.2.(1) of the Treaty on European Union. Article F provides that the Union is to respect fundamental rights, as guaranteed, in particular, by the Convention. Article 130u(2) EC provides that Community policy in the area of development co-operation is to contribute to the objective of respecting human rights and fundamental freedoms."

Although not legally binding, one of the recitals to the Social Charter 1989 reads:

"Whereas, in order to ensure equal treatment, it is important to combat every form of discrimination, including discrimination on grounds of sex, colour, race, opinions and

---

[253] Case C-415/93 [1995] ECR I-4921.

[254] [1996] ECR I-1759.

beliefs, and whereas, in a spirit of solidarity, it is important to combat social exclusion..."

### 4.6.4.(vi) Amendment of the Treaty

Other ways in which the non-discrimination principle could be broadened is by way of a radical amendment to the EC Treaty to include either a very broad non-discrimination principle, modelled upon Article 6 EC, or, a limited "wish list" of particular areas of discrimination where there is political consensus throughout the EU that such forms of discrimination should be addressed through legal measures. The Commission established a "Comité des sages" which produced a report entitled "For A Europe of Civic and Social Rights" which was considered at a meeting in Brussels in March 1996 at a Social Policy Forum attended by some 1000 representatives of government and non-government organisations. The report proposed that the current IGC should consider incorporating fundamental social and civic rights into the Treaty in the form of a Bill of Rights which would have the immediate force of law but would be considered in more detail at a later stage. One right would be a ban on discrimination of any form on the basis of race, colour, sex, language, religion, political or other opinion, national or social origin, membership of a national minority, wealth, birth, disability or any other situation.

In the Dublin draft for a new Treaty there are proposals to strengthen the human rights provisions of the Treaty as well as introduce a new Article 6a EC which would read as follows:

"Within the scope of application of this Treaty and without prejudice to any special provisions contained therein, the Council acting unanimously on a proposal from the Commission and after consulting the European Parliament, may take appropriate action to prohibit discrimination based on sex, racial, ethnic or social origin, religious belief, disability, age or sexual orientation."

There is also a reference to incorporating specific measures to take account of persons with a disability, for example, in Article 127 EC or 100a EC.

# CHAPTER FIVE

## EMPLOYMENT RIGHTS AND ECONOMIC POLICIES

### 5.1. THE INTERPLAY BETWEEN ECONOMIC AND SOCIAL POLICIES

The EU has always had economic policy objectives but it was not until the amendment of the EC Treaty by the Treaty on the European Union (TEU) that social and labour market policy was established as an independent policy area in Art 3 EC.

In July 1994, the Commission published its White Paper on European Social Policy[1] containing its proposals for the future direction of social policy. It argued for a new mix between social and economic policy insisting that competitiveness and social progress could flourish together. It was argued that Europe needed, above all, an adaptable, educated and motivated workforce, something which only social policy could create. The main themes of the White Paper were employment, how to develop the legislative base, and the vital need for a society in which all were active, all could contribute.

The Social Action Programme 1995-97[2] prepared by Directorate General V on Employment and adopted following the TEU declares the economic and social dimensions to be interdependent. There cannot, according to the programme, be social progress without competitiveness and economic growth. Conversely, it is not possible to ensure sustainable economic growth without taking the social dimension into account. Social progress and social solidarity must form an integral part of the European approach to competitiveness. A new balance must be achieved between the economic and social dimensions, in which they are treated as mutually reinforcing, rather than conflicting, objectives.

---

[1]   COM(94)333.

[2]   COM (95) 134.

## 5.2. THE CONCEPT OF ECONOMIC ACTIVITIES

In the infringement case against the UK[3] concerning the Transfer of Undertakings Directive[4] one of the Commission's complaints was a requirement in the UK law that the undertaking be in the nature of a commercial venture. According to the Commission - and on this point it was not contradicted by the UK - the term "commercial venture" was interpreted as referring to the investment of capital with a view to making profits and accepting the risk of losses. That definition of "undertaking" was, in the Commission's view, too restricted in view of the fact that Directive 77/187/EEC applies to all undertakings, even those which do not aim to be profit-making. This point is supported by the Court's judgment in *Redmond*,[5] which concerned the transfer of activities of a foundation financed wholly out of public funds.

In its defence, the UK pointed out that Directive 77/187/EEC was adopted on the basis of Article 100 EC, which authorizes the Community legislature to issue Directives "for the approximation of such provisions laid down by law, regulation or administrative action in Member States as directly affect the establishment or functioning of the common market". According to the UK, the scope of Directive 77/187/EEC cannot be more extensive than that allowed under the Treaty base. National rules concerning the transfer of undertakings can directly affect the establishment or functioning of the Common Market only to the extent to which they relate to the transfer of undertakings or parts thereof which constitute part of the economic activity of the transferor and/or the transferee. They can have such an effect only if they render more difficult the establishment of undertakings in other Member States or give rise to unequal conditions of competition between the Member States. With regard to the establishment of undertakings, non-profit-making bodies are excluded under the EC Treaty (Articles 58 and 66 EC).

In its reply, the Commission stated that it agreed with the UK that the Directive, on the ground that it is based on Article 100 EC, is concerned only with economic activities. That, however, does not mean that a non-profit-making body must be excluded from the scope of the Directive, so long as it is engaged in economic activities. The Commission considered that the UK's criticism of the judgment in *Redmond* was unjustified. The activities of the

---

[3]  Case C-382/92 *Commission* v *UK* [1994] ECR I-2435.

[4]  77/187/EEC, OJ 1977 L 61/26.

[5]  Case C-29/91 *Dr Sophie Redmond Stichtung* v *Hendrikus Bartold et al* [1992] ECR I-3189.

foundation in that case were of an economic nature, in the sense that the same type of activity could equally have been carried on by a profit-making body; moreover, there was no reason why one type of organization should have a competitive advantage over another by virtue of being excluded from the scope of the Directive. The Commission therefore concluded that all undertakings within the meaning of Community law (which therefore have by definition an economic nature) fall within the scope of Directive 77/187/EEC and must for that reason be covered by national law implementing it.

Advocate General Van Gerven discussed the issue at length in his Opinion in the infringement action. He stated that the underlying principle must be that the EC treaty, by virtue of the fundamental provision in Article 2 EC, covers "economic activities" "throughout the Community" and that the Community, in order to promote a harmonious (and henceforth also a balanced) development of those activities, has as its task to establish a Common Market. The court has consistently conferred a broad meaning on the term "economic activities". As early as its judgment in *Donà*,[6] the Court held that:

"the pursuit of an activity as an employed person or the provision of services for remuneration must be regarded as an economic activity within the meaning of article 2 of the Treaty".

In order for an activity to be described as economic, it is thus evident that it must be performed for remuneration. It is clear from the Court's judgment in *Lawrie-Blum*[7] that the decisive importance does not attach to the sector within which the activity is performed or even the legal provisions under which it takes place. In its case law on the provision of services, the Court has defined the term "remuneration". It follows from the judgment in *Steymann*[8] that the element of remuneration, in the sense of economic consideration, does not necessarily presuppose the existence of a profit-making motive. In that case, which concerned *inter alia* the question of the extent to which unwaged work performed by a member of a religious sect could be regarded as an economic activity within the meaning of the EC Treaty, the Court ruled:

"in so far as the work, which aims to ensure a measure of self-sufficiency for the Bhagwan community, constitutes an essential part of participation in that community,

---

[6]   Case 13/76 *Gaetano Donà* v *Mario Mantero* [1976] ECR 1333.

[7]   Case 66/85 *Lawrie Blum* v *Land Baden Würtemberg* [1986] ECR 2121.

[8]   Case 196/87 *Steymann v Staatssecretaris van Justititie* 1988] ECR 6159.

the services which the latter provides to its members May be regarded as being an indirect quid pro quo for their work."

It follows from the foregoing that the economic activities covered by the EC Treaty must not be confined to those performed with a view to making profit or with the acceptance of commercial risks. On the contrary, the term covers all activities performed directly or indirectly for remuneration in the sense of economic consideration.

In the absence of a specific definition in the Directive itself, that term must cover all undertakings which pursue an economic activity within the meaning of the EC Treaty and not only profit-making undertakings (although this will be the case in most instances). Under this interpretation, which is consistent with the judgments in *Redmond*[9] and *Watson Rask*,[10] there is no breach of the legal basis of the Directive, in view of the fact, that the expression "Common Market" covers, pursuant to Article 2 EC, the entire panoply of economic activity within the community.Advocate General Van Gerven concluded:

"The conclusion which I draw from the foregoing is that the scope of directive 77/187 covers all undertakings which pursue an economic activity within the meaning of article 2 of the EC treaty and not only those which operate with a view to making profit. As the version of regulation 2(1) of the 1981 regulations, prior to the 1993 legislative amendment, included only the latter undertakings within the expression "undertaking", the United Kingdom has failed in that regard to fulfil its obligations under the treaty and the Commission' s application must be upheld."

## 5.3. ARTICLES 30 - 36 EC

As long as no harmonization of technical and marketing standards has taken place, the free movement of goods is governed by the provisions laid down in Articles 30-36 EC. Article 30 EC prohibits quantitative restrictions on imports and all measures having an equivalent effect. In *Dassonville*[11] the ECJ ruled that all trading rules enacted by Member States which are capable of hindering, directly or indirectly, actually or potentially, intra-Community trade are to be considered as measures having an effect equivalent to quantitative restrictions.

---

[9]   Case C-29/91 *Dr Sophie Redmond Stichtung* v *Hendrikus Bartold et al* [1992] ECR I-3189.

[10]   Case C-209/91 *Anne Watson Rask and Kirsten Christensen* v *ISS Kantineservice A/S* [1992] ECR-I-5755.

[11]   Case 8/74 [1974] ECR 837.

### 5.3.1. The "Cassis" Case Law

Until the *Keck* judgment,[12] it was a well established and fundamental principle that a measure does not lie outside the scope of Article 30 EC simply because it applies without distinction to domestic and imported products. In *Cassis de Dijon*[13] the ECJ delimited lawful derogations from the scope of Article 30 EC. The ECJ ruled that in the absence of common rules, obstacles to free movement within the Community resulting from disparities between the national laws relating to the marketing of a product must be accepted in so far as those provisions may be recognized as being necessary in order to satisfy *mandatory requirements* relating in particular to the effectiveness of fiscal supervision, the protection of public health, the fairness of commercial transactions and the defence of the consumer. These categories are not closed.[14]

*Cassis de Dijon* is also authority[15] for the rule that there is a presumption that goods which have been lawfully marketed in another Member State will comply with the mandatory requirements of the importing Member State. Under Article 100B EC, which was inserted into the EC Treaty by the Single European Act 1986, the Council of Ministers, acting in accordance with Article 100A EC, may decide that provisions in force in one Member State shall be recognised as being equivalent to those applied by another Member State.

It is obvious that national technical or marketing requirements may be measures having an equivalent effect.[16] Such requirements are now in the process of being harmonized under Article 100A EC leading to Article 30 EC becoming less important with regard to the working environment discussed further in Chapter Eight.

One can ask whether Article 30 EC applies to national employment law, for example, working time provisions and other subject matter dealt with under Article 118A EC or if such provisions come under the derogations from Article

---

[12]   Joined Cases C-267/91 and C-268/91 [1993] ECR I-6097.

[13]   Case 120/78 [1979] ECR 649.

[14]   Case 302/86 *Commission v Denmark* [1988] ECR 4607.

[15]   Cf the EC Commission's Communication concerning the consequences of the *Cassis de Dijon* judgment, OJ 1980 C 256/2.

[16]   There is an abundant case law and literature on the interpretation of Articles 30-36 EC, see further Oliver (1996) and Steiner (1992).

30 EC following from the *Cassis de Dijon* principle allowing mandatory requirements or Article 36 EC.

In general terms the answer is that working environment provisions either fall outside of the scope of Article 30 EC because they do not affect cross-country trade or will be lawful as a "mandatory requirement" within the meaning of *Cassis de Dijon* or as part of "public health" provisions in Article 36 EC.

The ECJ's case law on mandatory requirements and Article 36 EC does not, however, reserve certain matters to the exclusive jurisdiction of Member States but permits national law to derogate from the principle of the free movement of goods to the extent that such derogation is and continues to be justified.[17] Where harmonisation measures to ensure the protection of the working environment have been adopted at Community level and establish Community procedures to ensure the working environment recourse to Article 36 EC or the "mandatory requirements" is no longer justified.

The ECJ has considered the permissibility of rules prohibiting nightwork in bakeries in *Oebel.*[18] The Court found that Articles 30 and 34 EC do not apply to national rules which prohibit the production of ordinary and fine baker's ware and also their transport and delivery to individual consumers and retail outlets during the night up to a certain hour.

In *Torfaen*[19] the ECJ ruled on a provision in the (then) English Shop's Act prohibiting the sale of certain products on Sunday. The Court referred to *Cinéthèque,*[20] where it held, with regard to a prohibition of the hiring of video-cassettes applicable to domestic and imported products alike, that such a prohibition was not compatible with the principle of the free movement of goods provided for in Article 30 EC unless any obstacle to Community trade thereby created did not exceed what was necessary in order to ensure the attainment of the objective in view and unless that objective was justified with regard to Community law.

National rules governing the opening hours of retail premises reflect certain political and economic choices in so far as their purpose is to ensure that working and non-working hours are so arranged as to accord with national or

---

[17] Case 35/76 *Amministrazione delle Finanze dello Stato* v *Simmenthal SpA* [1976] ECR 1871.

[18] Case 155/80 [1981] ECR 1993.

[19] Case 145/88 *Torfaen Borough Council v B&Q plc* [1989] ECR 3851.

[20] Joined Cases 60 and 61/84 *Cinéthèque SA and Others* v *Fédération nationale des cinémas francais* [1985] ECR 2618.

regional socio-cultural characteristics, and that, in the present state of Community law, is a matter for the Member States. Furthermore, such rules are not designed to govern the patterns of trade between Member States. The Court found that Article 30 EC does not apply to such provisions. In *CGT*[21] and *André Marchandise*[22] the Court likewise found that Article 30 EC does not preclude provisions restricting Sunday work. In the latter case the ECJ also ruled that Articles 3(f), 5, 34, 59-66 and 85 EC do not prohibit restrictions on work on Sundays.[23]

### 5.3.2. Keck and Mithouard

In its judgment of 24 November 1993 in *Criminal proceedings against Bernard Keck and Daniel Mithouard*[24] the ECJ stated that it is established by the case law beginning with *"Cassis de Dijon"*[25] that, in the absence of harmonization of legislation, obstacles to free movement of goods which are the consequence of applying, to goods coming from other Member States where they are lawfully manufactured and marketed, rules that lay down requirements to be met by such goods (such as those relating to designation, form, size, weight, composition, presentation, labelling, packaging) constitute measures of equivalent effect prohibited by Article 30 EC. This is so even if those rules apply without distinction to all products unless their application can be justified by a public-interest objective taking precedence over the free movement of goods.

By contrast, contrary to what had previously been decided, the ECJ held in *Keck* that the application to products from other Member States of national provisions restricting or prohibiting certain selling arrangements is not such as

---

[21] Case C-312/89 *Union departmentale des syndicats CGT de l'Aisne v Conforama et al* [1991] ECR 997.

[22] Case C-332/89 [1991] ECR 1027.

[23] In three judgments from December 1992, ie before *Keck* the ECJ confirmed this view on Sunday trading. See Case C-306/88 *Rochdale Burrough Council v Stewart John Anders* [1992] ECR I-6457, Case C-304/90 *Reading Borough Council v Payless Diy Limited, Wickes Building Supplies Limited, Great Mills (South) Limited, Homebase Limited, B & Q Plc* [1992] ECR I-6493 and Case C-169/91 *Council of the City of Stoke-on-Trent, Norwich City Council v B & Q Plc* [1992] ECR I-6635.

[24] Joined Cases C-267/91 and C-268/91 [1993] ECR I-6097.

[25] Case 120/78 *Rewe-Zentral v Bundesmonopolverwaltung für Branntwein* [1979] ECR 649.

to hinder directly or indirectly, actually or potentially, trade between Member States within the meaning of the *Dassonville* judgment,[26] so long as those provisions apply to all relevant traders operating within the national territory and so long as they affect in the same manner, in law and in fact, the marketing of domestic products and of those from other Member States.

Provided that those conditions are fulfilled, the application of such rules to the sale of products from another Member State meeting the requirements laid down by that State is not by nature such as to prevent their access to the market or to impede access any more than it impedes the access of domestic products. Such rules therefore fall outside the scope of Article 30 EC.

### 5.3.3. After Keck and Mithouard

The consequences of the ECJ's ruling in *Keck* is still a matter of dispute.[27] Advocate General Jacobs argued in *Société d'Importation Edouard Leclerc-Siplec* v *TF1 Publicité Sa and M6 Publicité Sa*[28] that

> "41. The question then is what test should be applied in order to determine whether a measure falls within the scope of Article 30. There is one guiding principle which seems to provide an appropriate test: that principle is that all undertakings which engage in a legitimate economic activity in a Member State should have unfettered access to the whole of the Community market, unless there is a valid reason for denying them full access to a part of that market. In spite of occasional inconsistencies in the reasoning of certain judgments, that seems to be the underlying principle which has inspired the Court's approach from Dassonville through "Cassis de Dijon" to Keck. Virtually all of the cases are, in their result, consistent with the principle, even though some of them appear to be based on different reasoning."

After the *Keck* ruling, the ECJ has again considered questions as to whether prohibition of certain kinds of Sunday and public-holiday trading is a violation

---

[26]  Case 8/74 [1974] ECR 837.

[27]  See further Oliver (1996) 100 ff.

[28]  Case C-412/93 [1995] ECR I-179.

of Article 30 EC.[29]   The Court based its judgment on *Keck* and its earlier Sunday trading case law and held that

"24 There is no evidence that the aim of the rules at issue is to regulate trade in goods between Member States or that, viewed as a whole, they could lead to unequal treatment between national products and imported products as regards access to the market. In this connection, it must be reiterated that national rules whose effect is to limit the marketing of a product generally, and consequently its importation, cannot on that ground alone be regarded as limiting access to the market for those imported products to a greater extent than for similar national products. As the Court stated in paragraph 13 of Keck and Mithouard, the fact that national legislation may restrict the volume of sales generally, and hence the volume of sales of products from other Member States, is not sufficient to characterize such legislation as a measure having an effect equivalent to a quantitative restriction.

25 Moreover, the Court has repeatedly recognized that national legislation such as that at issue pursues an aim which is justified under Community law, and that national rules restricting the opening of shops on Sundays reflect certain choices relating to particular national or regional socio-cultural characteristics. It is for the Member States to make those choices in compliance with the requirements of Community law (see Case C-169/91 B & Q [1992] ECR I-6635, paragraph 11).

26 The Court went on to rule in that case that Article 30 of the Treaty is to be interpreted as meaning that the prohibition it lays down does not apply to national legislation prohibiting retailers from opening their premises on Sundays.

27 No new factor has emerged in these proceedings which might justify an assessment different from that made by the Court in the judgments in Punto Casa and PPV and B & Q."

The reply given to the national court was therefore that, on a proper construction, Article 30 EC does not apply to national rules on the closing times of shops applicable to all traders exercising an activity on national territory and

---

[29]   Joined Cases C-418/93, C-419/93, C-420/93, C-421/93, C-460/93, C-461/93, C-462/93, C-464/93, C-9/94, C-10/94, C-11/94, C-14/94, C-15/94, C-23/94, C-24/94 and C-332/94 *Semeraro Casa Uno Srl* v *Sindaco del Comune di Erbusco, Semeraro Mobili SpA* v *Sindaco del Comune di Erbusco, RB Arredamento Srl* v *Sindaco del Comune di Stezzano, Citt Convenienza Milano Srl* v *Sindaco del Comune di Trezzano sul Naviglio, Citt Convenienza Bergamo Srl* v *Sindaco del Comune di Stezzano, Centro Italiano Mobili Srl* v *Sindaco del Comune di Pineto, Il 3C Centro Convenienza Casa Srl* v *Sindaco del Comune di Roveredo in Piano, Benelli Confezioni SNC* v *Sindaco del Comune di Capena, M. Quattordici Srl* v *Commissario straordinario del Comune di Terlizzi, Societ Italiana Elettronica Srl (SIEL)* v *Sindaco del Comune di Dozza, Modaffari Srl* v *Sindaco del Comune di Trezzano sul Naviglio, Modaffari Srl* v *Comune di Cinisello Balsamo, Cologno Srl* v *Sindaco del Comune di Cologno Monzese, Modaffari Srl* v *Sindaco del Comune di Osio Sopra, M. Dieci Srl* v *Sindaco del Comune di Madignano* and *Consorzio Centro Commerciale "Il Porto"* v *Sindaco del Comune di Adria* judgment of 20 June 1996, nyr.

affecting in the same way in law and in fact the marketing of national products and products from other Member States.

## 5.4. COMPETITION LAW AND LABOUR LAW

The relationship between EU labour law and competition law, in particular Article 86 EC has been addressed in a number of cases. In *Klaus Höfner and Fritz Elser* v *Macrotron Gmbh*[30] the ECJ held that a public employment agency engaged in the business of employment procurement may be classified as an undertaking for the purpose of applying the Community competition rules since, in the context of competition law, that classification applies to every entity engaged in an economic activity, regardless of its legal status and the way in which it is financed.

As an undertaking entrusted with the operation of services of general economic interest, a public employment agency engaged in employment procurement activities is, pursuant to Article 90(2) EC, subject to the prohibition contained in Article 86 EC, so long as the application of that provision does not obstruct the performance of the particular task assigned to it. A Member State which has granted it an exclusive right to carry on that activity is in breach of Article 90(1) EC where it creates a situation in which that agency cannot avoid infringing Article 86 EC. That is the case, in particular, where the following conditions are satisfied:

- the exclusive right extends to executive recruitment activities;
- the public employment agency is manifestly incapable of satisfying demand prevailing on the market for such activities;
- the actual pursuit of those activities by private recruitment consultants is rendered impossible by the maintenance in force of a statutory provision under which such activities are prohibited and non-observance of that prohibition renders the contracts concerned void;
- the activities in question may extend to the nationals or to the territory of other Member States.

In *Merci Convenzionali Porto di Genova* v *Siderurgica Gabrielli*[31] the ECJ held that Italian legislation which reserved dock work to Italian nationals was contrary to Article 48(2) EC and could not be justified on the basis of the public service exception in Article 48(4) EC. Although the simple fact of

---

[30]  Case C-41/90 [1991] ECR I-1979.

[31]  Case C-179/90 *Merci Convenzionali Porto di Genova spa* v *Siderurgica Gabrielli Spa* [1991] ECR I-5889.

creating a dominant position by granting exclusive rights within the meaning of Article 90(1) EC is not as such incompatible with Article 86 EC, a State is in breach of those two provisions if the undertaking in question, merely by *exercising* the exclusive rights granted to it, cannot avoid abusing its dominant position or when such rights are liable to create a situation such that it is induced to commit such abuses.

This is the case when an undertaking to which a monopoly to perform dock work has been granted is induced either to demand payment for services which have not been requested, to charge disproportionate prices, to refuse to have recourse to modern technology or to grant price reductions to certain consumers and at the same time to offset such reductions by an increase in the charges to other consumers. A national measure which has the effect of facilitating the abuse of a dominant position capable of affecting trade between Member States is normally incompatible with Article 30 EC in so far as it has the effect of making more difficult and hence of impeding the importation of goods from other Member States. Even within the framework of Article 90 EC, the provisions of Articles 30, 48 and 86 EC have direct effect and give rise for individuals to rights which the national courts must protect.

Dock work is not, in principle, a service of general economic interest exhibiting special characteristics, as compared with the general economic interest of other economic activities, which might bring it within the field of application of Article 90(2) EC. In any case, the fact that the public authorities have entrusted an undertaking with the operation of services of general economic interest does not, by virtue of the aforesaid provision, absolve it from compliance with the rules EC unless the application of those rules may obstruct the performance of the particular tasks assigned to it and unless the interests of the Community are not affected.

### 5.4.1. Merger Control

#### 5.4.1.(i). Must social objectives be taken into consideration in the Commision's merger control?

In the scheme of the Merger Control Regulation,[32] the primacy given to the establishment of a system of free competition may in certain cases be reconciled, in the context of the assessment of whether a concentration is compatible with the Common Market, with the taking into consideration of the social effects of that operation if they are liable to affect adversely the social

---

[32]  4064/89/EEC, OJ 1989 L 395/1.

objectives referred to in Article 2 EC. The Commission may therefore have to ascertain whether the concentration is liable to have consequences, even if only indirectly, for the position of the employees in the undertakings in question, such as to affect the level or conditions of employment in the Community or a substantial part of it. Article 2(1)(b) of Regulation 4064/89/EEC requires the Commission to draw up an economic balance for the concentration in question, which may, in some circumstances, entail considerations of a social nature, as is confirmed by the thirteenth recital in the Preamble to the Regulation, which states that "the Commission must place its appraisal within the general framework of the achievement of the fundamental objectives referred to in Article 2 EC, including that of strengthening the Community's economic and social cohesion, referred to in Article 130a". In that legal context, the express provision in Article 18(4) of the Regulation, giving specific expression to the principle stated in the nineteenth recital that the representatives of the employees of the undertakings concerned are entitled, upon application, to be heard, manifests an intention to ensure that the collective interests of those employees are taken into consideration in the administrative procedure.

In 1989, the Opinion of the Economic and Social Committee on the social consequences of cross-frontier mergers[33] stated:

> "Since, independently of [the European Company Statute], there is a need for information and participation rights for employees' representatives in connection with cross-frontier concentrations between undertakings, a Community framework should be devised for this. This framework ought to be based on national arrangements for employee representation, and provide for regular information and consultation of employees' representatives at European level".

On this occasion the Economic and Social Committee criticised the fact that the merger Regulation[34] is not accompanied by social policy law provisions and the Committee suggested that the Commission's approval of mergers under the Regulation be made conditional upon the establishment of a European Works Council in the undertaking. So far this suggestion has not been followed by the Commission but it has power under the Regulation to introduce such a requirement as a condition of approving cross-border mergers.

---

[33]  OJ 1989 C 329/35.

[34]  4064/89/EEC, OJ 1989 L 395/1.

### 5.4.1.(ii). Can trade unions take annulment actions against a Commission decision declaring a merger compatible with the Common Market?

Under Article 173 EC a natural or legal person can institute proceedings for the annulment of a decision addressed to another person only if that decision is of direct and individual concern to him.

In *Comité Central D' Entreprise de la Societé Génerale des Grandes Sources and Others v Commission*[35] and *Comité Central d'Entreprise de la Société Anonyme Vittel and Comité d'Etablissement de Pierval and Féderation Génerale Agroalimentaire v Commission*[36] the Court of first Instance held that a Commission decision on the compatibility with the Common Market of a concentration, taken pursuant to the Merger Control Regulation,[37] is of *individual* concern, within the meaning of Article 173(4) EC, to the representatives, recognized in national law, of the employees of the undertakings in question, simply because that regulation expressly mentions them among the third parties showing a sufficient interest to be heard by the Commission during the procedure for examination of the planned concentration, regardless of whether they have actually taken part in that procedure.

On the other hand, in principle and in the absence of exceptional circumstances, it is not of *direct* concern to them. Firstly, a decision authorizing a concentration, after an examination from the point of view of Community competition law, does not in itself have any effect on the own rights of the representatives of the employees of the undertakings concerned, which, as provided for by the relevant provisions of Community law, will be applicable in accordance with the provisions of national law on the occasion of the transfer of the undertaking as a result of the concentration. Secondly, it does not directly affect the interests of the workers concerned, since, as follows from Directive 77/187/EEC on the safeguarding of employees' rights in the event of transfers of undertakings (discussed in detail in Chapter Six), the concentration cannot itself bring about a change in the employment relationship as regulated by the contract of employment and collective agreements.

However, since the representatives of the employees have been given procedural rights by Regulation 4064/89/EEC and those rights can in principle

---

[35] Case T-96/92 *Comité Central D' Entreprise de la Societé Génerale des Grandes Sources and Others v Commission* [1995] ECR II-1213.

[36] Case T-12/93 *Comité Central d'Entreprise de la Société Anonyme Vittel and Comité d'Etablissement de Pierval and Féderation Génerale Agroalimentaire v Commission* [1995] ECR II-1247.

[37] 4064/89/EEC, OJ 1989 L 395/1.

be given effect to by the Community judicature only at the stage of review of the lawfulness of the Commission' s final decision, those representatives must be afforded a remedy limited to the defence of their procedural rights, and must therefore be recognized as entitled to bring proceedings against that decision for the specific purpose of having the Community judicature examine whether or not the procedural guarantees which they were entitled to assert during the administrative procedure[38] have been infringed. When that remedy is exercised, only a substantial breach of the procedural rights of the employees' representatives, as opposed to a plea based on substantive breach of the rules laid down in Regulation 4064/89/EEC, may lead to annulment of the Commission' s decision.

### 5.4.1.(iii). Interim measures

In *Comité Central D' Entreprise de la Societé Génerale des Grandes Sources and Others* v *Commission*[39] a trade union made an application for interim measures to suspend the operation of a decision authorizing a concentration between undertakings. The Court of First Instance held that if, in proceedings for interim measures, it is claimed that the application is manifestly inadmissible, it is for the judge hearing the application for interim measures to establish that the application reveals *prima facie* grounds for concluding that there is a certain probability that it is admissible.

Where suspension of the operation of a Commission decision authorizing, under Regulation 4064/89/EEC, a concentration between undertakings, sought by the bodies representing the workforce of one of them, would amount to suspending the authorization given throughout the course of the proceedings before the Court and therefore to upset the functioning of the undertakings concerned, and where the grant of the interim measures applied for in the alternative would prolong the existence of a dominant position liable to entail irreversible repercussions on competition in the sector concerned, which the conditions and obligations imposed by the decision are specifically intended to bring to an end, it is incumbent on the judge hearing the application for interim measures to balance all the interests involved. Accordingly, account must be taken not only of the applicants' interests and of the Commission's interest in restoring effective competition but also of the interests of third parties, in particular the undertakings concerned, in order to obviate both the

---

[38] Under Article 18 of Regulation 4064/89/EEC, OJ 1989 L 395/1.

[39] Case T-96/92 R *Comité Central D' Entreprise de la Societé Génerale des Grandes Sources and Others* v *Commission* [1992] ECR II-2579.

creation of an irreversible situation and serious and irreparable damage to any of the parties to the proceedings or to a third party or to the public interest.

In such circumstances, the grant of the measures applied for can be justified only if it appears that, without them, the applicants would be exposed to a situation liable to endanger their future. In the case at issue, the contested decision could not in the view of the ECJ have repercussions on the rights of the employees of the undertakings concerned or expose them to the risk of a loss such as to justify intervention by the judge hearing the application for interim measures. The ECJ referred in this context to Articles 3 and 4 of Directive 77/187/EEC on transfers of undertakings, according to which the transferor' s rights and obligations under a contract of employment or an employment relationship are transferred to the transferee. The transfer of undertakings Directive is discussed further in Chapter Six.

In *Peralta*[40] the ECJ held that Articles 3(f), 7, 30, 48, 52, 59, 62, 84 and 130R EC and Regulation 4055/86/EEC, applying the principle of freedom to provide services to maritime transport between Member States and between Member States and third countries, do not preclude the legislation of a Member State from prohibiting all vessels, regardless of the flag which they fly, from discharging harmful chemical substances into its territorial waters and its internal waters, or from imposing the same prohibition on the high seas only on vessels flying the national flag, or, finally, in the event of infringement, from penalizing masters of vessels who are nationals of that State by suspending their professional qualification.

## 5.5. STATE AID

Article 92(1) EC prohibits any aid granted by a Member State or through state resources in any form whatsoever which distorts or threatens to distort competition by favouring certain undertakings or the production of certain goods, in so far as it affects trade between Member States. Under Article 92(2) and (3) EC state aid is, however, lawful in certain circumstances, for example aid having a social character, granted to individual consumers, provided that such aid is granted without discrimination related to the origin of the products concerned, aid to make good the damage caused by natural disasters or other exceptional occurrences, aid to promote the economic development of areas where the standard of living is abnormally low or where there is serious underemployment, aid to facilitate the development of certain economic

---

[40] Case C-379/92 *Criminal Proceedings against Matteo Peralta* [1994] ECR I-3453.

activities or of certain economic areas, where such aid does not adversely affect trading conditions to an extent contrary to the common interest.

Under Article 93 EC, the Commission shall keep under constant review all systems of aid existing in the Member States. For state aid to be lawful the prior consent of the Commission is required, see further Article 92(3) EC.

The interplay between Article 92 EC on state aid and provisions relating to labour law has been the subject of rulings from the ECJ.

### 5.5.1. State Aid to Set Up Training Schemes and Infrastructure

In *Matra SA* v *Commission*[41] where Matra claimed annulment of a Commission decision accepting a Portuguese aid scheme, Portugal had, in accordance with Article 93(3), notified to the Commission an aid scheme for Newco, an undertaking set up by Ford and VolksWagen in equal shares, for the establishment of a factory for multi-purpose vehicles at Setbal in Portugal for the period from 1991 to 1995. The aid notified consisted of a regional subsidy and also envisaged a training programme for employees organized jointly by the Portuguese Government and Newco, costing ESC 36 000 million, of which 90% was to be financed by the Portuguese Government, and various investments in infra-structure relating to road construction, water and electricity supply and waste-processing. Following a complaint lodged by Matra on 26 June 1991 alleging infringements of Article 92 EC et seq by the Portuguese Government and of Article 85 EC by Ford and VolksWagen, a meeting took place between the Commission and Matra at which the latter was heard and the Commission explained why the procedure under Article 93(2) EC had not been initiated. On 16 July 1991 the Commission informed the Portuguese Government that it had no objections to the aid scheme notified. By order of 4 December 1991, the President of the ECJ dismissed Matra's application for suspension of operation of the Commission's decision.[42]

The ECJ held in the annulment case[43] that the Commission enjoys a wide discretion under Article 93(3) EC, the exercise of which involves assessments of an economic and social nature which must be made within a Community context. In its review of legality under Article 173 EC, the ECJ must therefore restrict itself to determining whether the Commission has exceeded the scope

---

[41]  Case C-225/91 [1993] I-3203.

[42]  Case C-225/91R *Matra* v *Commission* [1991] ECR I-5823.

[43]  Case C-225/91 [1993] I-3203.

of its discretion by a distortion or manifest error of assessment of the facts or by misuse of powers or abuse of process.

The procedure under Article 85 EC et seq and that under Article 92 EC et seq are independent procedures governed by specific rules, with the result that, when the Commission is called upon to take a decision on the compatibility of State aid with the Common Market, it is not obliged to await the outcome of a parallel procedure initiated under Regulation 17/62/EEC, once it has reached the conclusion, based on an economic analysis of the situation and without any manifest error in the assessment of the facts, that the recipient of the aid is not in contravention of Articles 85 and 86 EC.

### 5.5.2. Small Businesses

In *Petra Kirsammer-Hack* v *Nurhan Sidal*[44] the ECJ held that the exclusion of small businesses from a national system of protection of workers against unfair dismissal, with the effect that employers are not obliged to pay compensation in the event of socially unjustified dismissals or to bear the legal expenses incurred in proceedings concerning the dismissal of workers, does not constitute aid within the meaning of Article 92(1) EC. Such a measure does not entail any direct or indirect transfer of State resources to those businesses but derives solely from the legislature' s intention to provide a specific legislative framework for working relationships between employers and employees in small businesses and to avoid imposing on those businesses financial constraints which might hinder their development.

### 5.5.3. International Shipping

In *Firma Sloman Neptun Schiffahrts AG* v *Seebetriebsrat Bodo Ziesemer der Sloman Neptun Schiffahrts AG*[45] the Court ruled that the application by a Member State to merchant vessels entered in its International Shipping Register of a system enabling seafarers who are Third Country Nationals (TCN's) and have no permanent abode or residence in that Member State to be subjected to working conditions and rates of pay which are not covered by the law of that Member State and are considerably less favourable than those applicable to seafarers who are nationals of that Member State does not constitute State Aid within the meaning of Article 92(1) EC. The Court

---

[44]   Case C-189/91 [1993] ECR I-6185

[45]   Joined Cases C-72/91 and C-73/91[1993] ECR I-887. See Nielsen and Szyszczak (1994a).

explained that, in its view, a system of that kind does not seek, through its object and general structure, to create an advantage financed from State resources, that is, one which would constitute an additional burden for the State or for public or private bodies designated or established by the State, since its only purpose is to alter, in favour of shipping undertakings, the framework within which contractual relations are formed between those undertakings and their employees. The consequences of this with regard to the basis for the calculation of social security contributions and tax revenue, determined on the basis of low rates of pay, are inherent in the system and are not a means of granting a particular advantage to the undertakings concerned.

In its reference in *Neptun*, the Arbeitsgericht Bremen argued that allowing German shipowners to pay wages of only 20% of German wages resulted in German shipowners being exempted from 80% of the compulsory social contributions which under German social security legislation is levied upon the undertakings and calculated on the basis of the wages. The fact that this system operated more at the expense of the workers than of the state could not make it lawful. In its submissions the German government defended Paragraph 21(4) of the Flaggenenrechtsgesetz on the argument that it was intended to ensure the competitivity of German merchant vessels on an international basis by the reduction of labour costs.

The Commission argued in favour of a violation of Article 92 EC stressing that the state of Germany lost revenue from income taxes by allowing German shipowners to underpay Philipine, as compared with German, seamen. This loss of income for the German state results in a distortion of competition in favour of German shipowners since only German undertakings could enter the German ISR. The fact that most Member States to whom shipping is important behave in the same way as Germany does not remedy the unlawfulness of German State Aid. In this respect the Commission referred to ground 24 of the ECJ judgment in *Firma Steinike und Weinlig v Federal Republic of Germany*[46] where the Court held that any breach by a Member State of an obligation under the treaty in connexion with the prohibition laid down in Article 92 EC cannot be justified by the fact that other Member States are also failing to fulfil this obligation. The effects of more than one distortion of competition on trade between Member States do not cancel one another out but accumulate and the damaging consequences to the Common Market/Internal Market are increased.

In *Neptun* the ECJ pointed out that Article 92(1) EC declared any aid granted by a Member State (or through state resources in any form whatsoever) which distorted or threatened to distort competition by favouring certain

---

[46] Case 78/76 [1977] ECR 595.

undertakings or the production of certain goods, in so far as it affected trade between the Member States, to be incompatible with the Treaty. But only benefits granted *directly or indirectly* out of State resources fell within Article 92(1) EC. The distinction between aid granted by the State and aid through State resources was intended to include in the definition of aid not only aid granted directly by the State but also aid granted by public or private bodies appointed or created by the State. Thus it was necessary to conduct an inquiry as to whether or not the benefits from a system such as that applicable to the ISR were to be regarded as an aid out of State resources.

Looking at the object and general structure of the ISR the ECJ concluded that it did not seek to create an advantage amounting to an additional burden for the State but only to alter for the benefit of shipping undertakings the framework in which contractual relations were drawn up between the undertakings and their employees. The resulting consequences, ie the different basis of calculation for social security contributions and any loss in tax revenue were inherent in the system and did not constitute a means of affording the undertakings concerned a specific advantage. Thus a system such as the ISR did not constitute a State Aid within the meaning of Article 92(1) EC.

## 5.6. EMPLOYMENT PROTECTION AND PUBLIC PROCUREMENT

Labour law and public procurement law represent two different approaches to European contract law. European labour law is a prime example of social contract law[47] while procurement law is of a more commercial nature. The two areas of law interrelate. They complement each other and in some respects they may even be contradictory.

Seen in isolation procurement law is rather narrowly aimed at fulfilling economic purposes of a commercial nature. The primary objectives of the Union's public procurement policy are:

- to create competitive conditions in which public contracts are awarded without discrimination through the choice of the best bid submitted;
- to give suppliers access to a single market with major sales opportunities;
- and to ensure the competitiveness of European suppliers.

In contrast, labour law is based on a dual economic and social objective. In the White Paper, *Growth, Competitiveness, and Employment. The Challenges and*

---

[47] Wilhelmsson (1995) and Nielsen (1996).

*Ways Forward Into the 21st Century*,[48] issued by the Directorate General for the Internal Market it is argued that procurement should be targeted to promoting sustainable growth:

> "The dynamics of the internal market can be channelled into generating optimal resource use in the Community : firstly, sound competition on a level playing field affords a better chance of generating the necessary technological changes and renewal of capital stock; secondly, *public procurement rules could be explicitly tailored to sustainable objectives*; thirdly, the internal relocation of economic activities will contribute to the most efficient exploitation of environmental resources inside the Community as well as to a reduction of the excessively high environmental pressures in some areas. The same argument  applies, of course, to the enlargement of the Community."[49]

In its Green Paper of 27 November 1996 on *Public Procurement* the Commission emphasizes that the foundations of the Community's open procurement rules are to be found in the EC Treaty, particularly in those provisions which guarantee the free movement of goods, services and capital, establish fundamental principles (equality of treatment, transparency and mutual recognition) and prohibit discrimination on grounds of nationality. It is to be noted that Treaty provisions on free movement of workers or other labour related Treaty provisions are not explicitly mentioned. Article 48 EC is one of those provisions which prohibit discrimination on grounds of nationality. But the free movement provisions of the EC Treaty do not constitute the foundation of EU labour law to nearly the same degree as they do in respect of procurement law. EU labour law consists mainly of provisions of a substantive nature whereas public procurement law - apart from the general provisions on free movement, the ban on discrimination on grounds of nationality in the EC Treaty and selection and award criteria - primarily concerns procedureal matters and remedies and sanctions. This difference makes the two areas of law complementary in a number of situations. In tendering procedures the procedural rules of procurement law can and must be observed alongside many substantive employment provisions, for example concerning the working environment.

---

[48]  COM(93) 700 final.

[49]  Emphasis added.

## 5.6.1. Procurement Directives

The substantive rules in the EC Treaty on free movement are, in matters of public procurement, complemented with 4 directives coordinating tendering procedures in respect of supplies, works, services and utilities[50] and 2 remedy directives.[51] The legal basis of these directives are the harmonization provisions relating to the free movement provisions, ie Art 100A EC (corresponding to Art 30 EC on free movement of goods) as regards the supplies Directive; Art 57,2 (corresponding to Art 52 EC on freedom of establishment), Art 66 EC (corresponding to Art 59 EC on free movement of services) and Art 100A as regards the works Directive; Art 57,2 and Art 66 as regards the service Directive; and Articles 57(2), 66, 100A and 113 EC as regards the utilities Directive.

The procurement directives contain procedural and remedial provisions aimed at ensuring transparency and equal treatment of different tenderers. There is free choice for the contracting authority or contracting entity between two different tender procedures: open procedures or restricted procedures. There are detailed provisions on selection of candidates to be invited to submit tenders in restricted procedures; on exclusion of potential contractors or service providers and on proof of professional and technical capability and of economic and financial standing.

Award of contracts will usually have to be made on the basis of either the lowest price or the economically most advantageous tender. There is no definition in the Directives of the concept of »economically most advantageous tender«, in particular no indication as to whether non-commercial criteria are lawful or not.

---

[50] 93/36/EEC, OJ 1993 L 199/1, coordinating procedures for the award of public supply contracts, 93/37/EEC, concerning the coordination of procedures for the award of public works contracts, 92/50/EEC, OJ 1992 L 209/1, relating to the coordination of procedures for the award of public(services), 93/38/EEC, OJ 1993 L 199/94, coordinating the procurement procedures of entities operating in the water, energy, transport and telecommunications sectors.

[51] 89/665/EEC, OJ 1989 L 395/33, on the coordination of the laws, regulations and administrative provisions relating to the application of review procedures for the award of public supply and public works contracts and 92/13/EEC, OJ 1992 L 76/14, coordinating the laws, regulations and administrative provisions relating to the application of Community rules on the procurement procedures of entities operating in the water, energy, transport and telecommunications sectors.

### 5.6.2. Legal obligations relating to wages, employment protection and working conditions binding in the locality where a works contract is being performed

To prevent social dumping contracting authorities and contracting entities may be called upon to implement various aspects of social policy when awarding their contracts.

As examples of the pursuit of social policy objectives, one can mention legal obligations relating to wages, employment protection and working conditions binding in the locality where a works contract is being performed. Such an obligation may follow from national law which may be derived from international law obligations. Historically, labour law aspects of public procurement were first addressed within the context of ILO which adopted the Labour Clauses (Public Contracts) Convention No 94 in 1949. The Convention requires public contracts to include clauses ensuring working conditions:

> "Article 2: 1. ...not less favourable than those established for work of the same character in the trade or industry concerned in the district where the work is carried on
> (a)   by collective agreement or other recognised machinery of negotiation between organisations of employers and workers...
> 2. Where the conditions of labour referred to in the preceding paragraph are not regulated in a manner referred to therein in the district where the work is carried on, the clauses to be included in contracts shall ensure to the workers concerned wages (including allowances), hours of work and other conditions of labour which are not less favourable than
> (a)   those established by collective agreement or other recognised machinery of negotiation, by arbitration, or by national laws or regulations, for work of the same character in the trade or industry concerned in the nearest appropriate district; or
> (b)   the general level observed in the trade or industry in which the contractor is engaged by employers whose general circumstances are similar".

Recommendation No 84 of 1949 concerning Labour Clauses in Public Contracts provides in Article 2:

> "Labour clauses in public contracts should prescribe, either directly or by reference to appropriate provisions contained in laws or regulations, collective agreements, arbitration awards or other recognised arrangements.... (wages, hours, holidays and sick leave)".

The freedom to supply services in another Member State also includes the freedom to use one's own labour force in order to carry out the service. This issue arose in *Rush Portuguesa Limitada D'Immigration*[52] which involved a Portuguese company specialising in construction work. Member States are free to make national labour law provisions mandatory and require foreign service providers to comply with them on the condition that the same requirement is put on domestic employers.

### 5.6.3. Selection, exclusion and qualification of candidates

One may also ask the question as to whether it is lawful to exclude an otherwise qualified tenderer because of non-compliance with a labour clause in a public contract performed earlier[53] and to what extent employment criteria can be used as proof of professional and technical capability and of economic and financial standing. Experience, which is one of the relevant criteria in the procurement directives,[54] is a qualification which is often vested in the personnel.

Provisions which have been included in all the Directives offer an initial possibility for pursuing social objectives by allowing contractors or suppliers to be excluded where they have been convicted of an offence concerning their professional conduct or have been found guilty of grave professional misconduct. These rules clearly also apply where the offence or misconduct involves an infringement of legislation designed to promote social objectives. In these cases, then, the provisions in question indirectly allow contracting authorities to pursue such objectives by excluding from contract award procedures candidates who have failed to comply with such legislation.

Another possibility is to require successful tenderers to comply with social obligations when performing contracts awarded to them, for example obligations aimed at promoting the employment of women or the protection of certain disadvantaged groups. Contract performance conditions are allowed only where they do not result in direct or indirect discrimination against tenderers from other Member States. Sufficient transparency must also be ensured by mentioning the conditions in the contract notices or contract documents.

---

[52] Case C-113/89 [1990] ECR I 1417. See also Joined Cases 62 and 63/81 *Seco SA v Establissement d'Assurance contre la Vieillesse et l'Invalidite* [1982] ECR 223, Case C-43/93 *Raymond vander Elst* v *Office des Migrations Internationales* [1994] ECR I-3803 and Case C-272/94 *Criminal Proceedings against Michel Guiot and Climatec SA* [1996] ECR I-1905.

[53] Cf ILO Convention No 94 Article 5.

[54] See for example the Works Directive 93/37/EEC, OJ 1993 L 199/54 Article 27.

It is the Commission's view that the Directives do not currently allow social considerations to be taken into account when it comes to checking the suitability of candidates or tenderers on the basis of the selection criteria, which relate to their financial and economic standing or their technical capability.

### 5.6.4. Economically most advantageous tender

A closer examination of the question as to whether and to what extent the award criterion »economically most advantageous tender« precludes a contracting authority from taking employment criteria into account is particularly important in this context, ie the freedom or otherwise of contracting entities to pursue non-commercial policies by means of public or utilities procurement. Employment related criteria may consist in requirements that certain employment conditions, typically those normally applicable at the place of work, must be observed by a contractor or service provider operating under a public contract, or they may consist in requirements concerning the composition of the work-force. It is for example conceivable that a contracting authority may wish to give preference to its own nationals, or that it may wish to promote a certain labour market policy, for example, the employment of unemployed, ethnic minorities, the under-represented sex, etc. It is the Commission's view in the abovementioned *Green Paper* that the Directives do not currently allow social considerations to be taken into account when it comes to awarding contracts on the basis of the award criteria laid down in the Directives, which must relate to the economic qualities required of the supplies, works or services covered by the contract whereas the Commission is of the opinion that, in the case of contracts falling below the thresholds for application of the Directives, purchasers may include social preferences in the award criteria, provided that they are extended without discrimination to all Community nationals with the same characteristics.

This view is, however, not supported by the case law of the ECJ.[55] The ECJ has delivered a number of judgments on public procurement. In *Beentjes*[56] questions arose in proceedings between Gebroeders Beentjes BV and the Netherlands Ministry of Agriculture and Fisheries in connection with a public invitation to tender for a public works contract in connection with a land consolidation operation. In the main proceedings, Beentjes, the plaintiff, claimed that the decision of the awarding authority rejecting its tender,

---

[55]   Martín (1996).

[56]   Case 31/87 *Gebroeders Beentjes BV* v *The Netherlands* [1988] ECR 4635.

although it was the lowest, in favour of the next-lowest bidder had been taken in breach of the provisions of the abovementioned directive. The contracting authority had preferred a tenderer who was able to employ long-term unemployed and the contested issue was whether this was lawful under the procurement rules.

The ECJ held with regard to the award of a public works contract falling within the scope of Directive 71/305/EEC[57] that the condition relating to the employment of long-term unemployed persons is compatible with the Directive if it has no direct or indirect discriminatory effect on tenderers from other member states of the community. An additional specific condition of this kind must be mentioned in the contract notice.

The *Beentjes* case is a well known example of employment related terms in contracts concluded as a result of a tendering procedure. Another example is the general conditions of the Øresund Link contract. The conditions contain the following provisions:

> »2.1.6. All key personnel of the contractor shall be fluent in English.
>
> 2.1.7. The Contractor shall not replace any key personnel identified in the Contract without the approval of the Owner.
>
> 2.1.8. Should the continued employment of any person in connection with the Contract, or any subcontract, be considered by the Owner to be prejudicial to the interests of the Øresund Link project, that person shall be immediately removed from the Works upon the direction of the Owner. The Contractor shall not be entitled to any claim as a result of the implementation of such direction.
>
> 2.6.2.1. ..The Contractor's Representative shall until completion of the works be resident in the Copenhagen or Malmö area«

It may be argued that if employment criteria are lawful as contract terms then it will be economically most advantageous to accept a bid from the tenderer which is best equipped to comply with it or at least that a tenderer which cannot fulfil the criteria is thereby disqualified.

### 5.6.5. Transfer of Undertakings through Tendering Procedures

Finally, the question arises as to whether a transfer of a works or service contract as a result of tender competition amount to a transfer of an undertaking within the meaning of Directive 77/187/EEC. When tendering for public service contracts the successful tenderer may under the Transfer of Undertakings directive have to continue the employment of the staff on the same

---

[57]  That Directive has been replaced by 93/37/EEC but the problem remains the same.

conditions (wages, hours, etc) as the previous employer. This issue is discussed further in Chapter Six.

## 5.7. PRIVATE INTERNATIONAL LAW AND POSTING OF WORKERS

Issues relating to disparities in labour costs - for Community and non-Community migrant labour - raise problems for the maintenance of fair competition within the Internal Market and for the operation of Community enterprises in the international arena which are not yet fully regulated by Community law.[58]

These disparities may give rise to "forum shopping" and choice of law clauses aimed at circumvening employment protection legislation.

### 5.7.1. The Brussels Convention

In 1968, the Brussels Convention on Jurisdiction and the Enforcement of Judgments in Civil and Commercial Matters was signed.[59] In the case of a legal dispute venues can be established in several member states both under national law and under the Judgment Convention.

### 5.7.2. Choice of Law. The Rome Convention

In 1972, the Commission proposed a Regulation on conflicts of laws in employment relationships within the Community.[60] In view of the Opinions of the Economic and Social Committee and the European Parliament, an amended proposal was presented in 1976.[61] In 1972, the Commission also submitted a Preliminary Draft Convention on the Law Applicable to Contractual and Non-Contractual Obligations which among other matters contained provisions on the choice of law in employment relations. The draft Regulation on the choice of law in employment relations has never been adopted, whereas the draft

---

[58]  Szyszczak (1992).

[59]  OJ 1972 L 299/1. See for a commentary to the Brussels Convention by P. Jenard O J 1979 C 59/1.

[60]  JO 1972 No C 49/26. The text of the draft Regulation is also published in Rabels Zeitschrift für ausländisches und internationales Privatrecht, 1973, 585.

[61]  COM (75)653. This text is reprinted in Bulletin of Comparative Labour Relations, Deventer 1976, 288.

Convention in an amended form (omitting the non-contractual obligations) was signed in Rome in 1980 as the European Communities' Convention on the Law Applicable to Contractual Obligations.[62] The main difference between the draft Regulation on the choice of law in employment relations and the Rome Convention on the Law Applicable to Contractual Obligations relates to the degree to which party autonomy is permitted. The draft Regulation outlawed party autonomy in most cases in employment matters and provided for the law of the place of work to be mandatory.

The Rome Convention allows party autonomy as the main rule in all contractual matters including employment relations and collective agreements. Article 3 of the Convention provides that a contract shall be governed by the law chosen by the parties. However, in individual employment contracts the employee is protected by the mandatory rules of the law which would govern the individual employment contract in the absence of a choice of law by the parties, see Article 6 of the Convention. According to Article 6(2) this is the law of the country in which the employee habitually carries out his work or, if the employee does not habitually carry out his work in any one particular country, the law of the country in which the place of business through which he was engaged is situated. If it appears from the circumstances of the case that the contract is more closely connected with the law of another country the contract shall be governed by the law of that country.

Article 4 of the Convention contains the general rule that contracts shall be governed by the law of the country with which they are most closely connected.

Individual employment contracts are, according to Article 6(2), prima facie governed by the law of the country in which the employee habitually carries out his work or, if the employee does not habitually carry out his work in any one particular country, the law of the country in which the place of business through which he was engaged is situated. The prima facie rule in Article 6 is a presumption of some strength. It applies unless it appears from the circumstances of the case that the contract is more closely connected with the law of another country. In that case the contract shall be governed by the law of that country.

The German Act of 1989 establishing the International Shipping Register which was at issue in *Neptun*[63] amended the Flaggenrechtsgesetz (Law on the right to fly the flag) by inserting a new Paragraph 21(4) on the right of the

---

[62] OJ 1980 L 266/1.

[63] Joined Cases C-72/91 and C-73/91[1993] ECR I-887. See Nielsen and Szyszczak (1994a).

parties to employment contracts and collective agreements to choose the applicable law. It stipulated that the sole fact that a ship flied the German flag and was enlisted in the German ISR did not make it mandatory to apply German law to the contracts of employment of seamen not having their domicile or habitual residence in Germany. It further stipulates that collective agreements covering such employment relationships and entered into with foreign trade unions were not governed by German collective labour law unless expressly provided for in the collective agreement. This legislation was - as also pointed out by the German Government - in accordance with the general framework of the rules of conflict of law in private international law. In the case which gave rise to the referral to the ECJ a collective agreement was entered into between an employers' organisation on behalf of the German shipowner Sloman Neptun and a Philipine trade union. In this collective agreement[64] there was a choice of law clause in Article 26 in favour of Philipine law.

### 5.7.3. The Posting of Workers Directive

The "opt out" for social policy provisions secured by the UK in the Social Charter 1989 and the Social Policy Protocol and Agreement annexed to the EC Treaty have caused concern. To this end, in order, to minimise one of the effects of "social dumping", the European Commission in 1991 proposed a Directive[65] which was amended in 1993[66] concerning the posting of workers in the framework of provision of services which would give employees posted to another Member State the protection of the host state's labour laws rather than those of the sending state.

After considerable controversy a Directive on Posting of Workers[67] based in the provisions on freedom of establishment and freedom to provide services was, finally, adopted in 1996. This Directive is a derogation from the Rome Convention. It makes a 'hard core` of protective rules in the host country mandatory for the provider of the services notwithstanding the duration of the worker's posting. According to Article 20 of this Convention which lays down

---

[64] It is reprinted in Schwemmler, Margot: Das Internationale Seeschiffartsregister (ISR) der Bundesrepublik Deutschland als arbeitsrechtliches Konfliktfeld unter besonderer Berücksichtigung des Rechts der Europäischen Gemeinschaften, Bremen 1991.

[65] COM(91)230, OJ 1991 C 225/6.

[66] OJ 1993 C 187/5.

[67] 96/71/EC, OJ 1997 L 18/1.

the principle of precedence of Community law the Directive on Posting of Workers supercedes the law generally applicable under the Rome Convention 1980.

### 5.7.3.(i). Scope of the Directive

The Directive applies to undertakings established in a Member State which, in the framework of the transnational provision of services, post workers to the territory of a Member State to the extent that the undertakings take one of the following transnational measures:

(a)  post workers to the territory of a Member State on their account and under their direction, under a contract concluded between the undertaking making the posting and the party for whom the services are intended, operating in that Member State, provided there is an employment relationship between the undertaking making the posting and the worker during the period of posting; or

(b)  post workers to an establishment or to an undertaking owned by the group in the territory of a Member State, provided there is an employment relationship between the undertaking making the posting and the worker during the period of posting; or

(c)  being a temporary employment undertaking or placement agency, hire out a worker to a user undertaking established or operating in the territory of a Member State, provided there is an employment relationship between the temporary employment undertaking or placement agency and the worker during the period of posting.

### 5.7.3.(ii). Mandatory Application of Minimum Employment Protection in the Host State

Article 3 is the main provision of the Directive. It provides that Member States shall ensure that, whatever the law applicable to the employment relationship, the undertakings covered by the Directive must

(1) guarantee workers posted to their territory the terms and conditions of employment covering the following matters which, in the Member State where the work is carried out, are laid down:
- by law, regulation or administrative provision, and/or
- by collective agreements or arbitration awards which have been declared universally applicable within the meaning of paragraph 8, insofar as they concern the activities referred to in the Annex:
(a)  maximum work periods and minimum rest periods;

(b)   minimum paid annual holidays;

(c)   the minimum rates of pay, including overtime rates; this point does not apply to supplementary occupational retirement pension schemes;

(d)   the conditions of hiring-out of workers, in particular the supply of workers by temporary employment undertakings;

(e)   health, safety and hygiene at work;

(f)   protective measures with regard to the terms and conditions of employment of pregnant women or women who have recently given birth, of children and of young people;

(g)   equality of treatment between men and women and other provisions on non-discrimination.

In the case of initial assembly and/or first installation of goods where this is an integral part of a contract for the supply of goods and necessary for taking the goods supplied into use and carried out by the skilled and/or specialist workers of the supplying undertaking, the Directive does not apply if the period of posting does not exceed eight days, except as regards temporary employment undertakings.

## 5.8. GENDER EQUALITY

Originally equal pay was addressed for competitive reasons to prevent distortion of competition because some Member States respected the principle of equal pay more than others.[68] Today the EU context has shifted from preventing distortion of competition to promoting European Union ideals. In the 4th Medium Term Action Programme on Equal Opportunities for Women and Men (1996-2000)[69] it is stated, that equal treatment for women and men is a basic principle in law and equal opportunities form an integral part of democratic citizenship. The Council Decision of 22 December 1995 on the programme provides for a mainstreaming strategy, ie the integration of gender equality considerations into all policies both at EU and Member States level:

Article 2
Principle of integrating the equal opportunities dimension in all policies and activities (mainstreaming)
The programme is intended to promote the integration of equal opportunities for men and women in the process of preparing, implementing and monitoring all policies and

---

[68]   Hoskyns (1996).

[69]   Adopted by Council Decision of 22 December 1995, OJ 1995 L 335/1; Szyszczak (1996).

activities of the European Union and the Member States, having regard to their respective powers

Article 3. Aims
1. The programme shall support Member States' efforts in the area of equal opportunities
2. The programme has the following aims:
(a)    to promote integration of the equal opportunities dimension in all policies and activities;
(b)    to mobilize all the actors in economic and social life to achieve equal opportunities
(c)    to promote equal opportunities in a changing economy, especially in the fields of education, vocational training and the labour market;
(d)    to reconcile working and family life for men and women;
(e)    to promote a gender balance in decision-making;
(f)    to make conditions more conducive to exercising equality rights.

This widening of the context of EU equality from a narrow economic one to a broader framework of European citizenship facilitates the integration of employment considerations into economic policies.

Member States retain, however, a considerable freedom to set their standards of social security. In *Commission* v *Belgium*[70] the ECJ thus held that a system of unemployment or invalidity benefits under which the amount of benefit is determined by taking into account both the existence of persons dependent on the beneficiary and any income received by such persons is in conformity with EC law when that system seeks to secure for families a minimum replacement income, and grants to persons cohabiting with a spouse or children without income increases not exceeding the amount of the burdens which may reasonably be imputed to the presence of those persons. Since such a system corresponds to a legitimate objective of social policy and the means deployed to that end are appropriate and necessary, it is justified by reasons unrelated to discrimination on grounds of sex.

The ECJ even allows a narrow interpretation of the prohibition against sex discrimination in matters of social security (discussed in Chapter Four). In *Inge Nolte* v *Landesversicherungsanstalt Hannover*[71] the Court ruled that Directive 79/7/EEC must be interpreted as not precluding national provisions under which employment regularly consisting of fewer than 15 hours' work a week and regularly attracting remuneration of up to one-seventh of the average

---

[70]   Case C-229/89 [1991] ECR I-2205.

[71]   Case C-317/93 [1995] ECR I-4625. See also *Ursula Megner and Hildegard Scheffel* v *Innungskrankenkasse Vorderpfalz, Now Innungskrankenkasse Rheinhessen-Pfalz* [1995] ECR I-4741.

monthly salary is excluded from the statutory old-age insurance scheme, even where they affect considerably more women than men, since the national legislature was reasonably entitled to consider that the legislation in question was necessary in order to achieve a social policy aim unrelated to any discrimination on grounds of sex.

## 5.9. THE EUROPEAN SOCIAL FUND (ESF)

The ESF is a component of the EU's "Structural Funds" which also include the European Regional Development Fund and the Cohesion Fund. The volume of these funds was doubled between 1988 and 1993, and is set to double again by 1999. In the 1994-99 period, the ESF's share of the total ECU 156 billion allocated to the funds will be around ECU 47 billion. Around 45% of spending is concentrated in seven "absolute priority" zones containing altogether about one sixth of the Union's working population.

Priorities for the ECU 5.6 billion spent by the ESF in 1995 were converting regions seriously affected by industrial decline and combating long-term unemployment. The Funds general aims include:

- helping the long-term unemployed back into work
- helping the youth unemployed to enter the jobs market
- support the integration of people excluded from employment e.g. women and the disabled
- equality of employment opportunities between men and women
- helping workers to adapt to industrial change and to changes in production systems
- strengthen and improve education and training systems.

# CHAPTER SIX

## EMPLOYMENT PROTECTION

The Social Action Programme 1974-76[1]elaborated several objectives in relation to protecting workers' rights but as we pointed out in Chapter One only three Directives materialised before the adoption of the Social Charter 1989, providing protection in situations relating to collective redundancies, takeovers and insolvencies. Following the Social Charter 1989 the Directive on collective redundancies was amended and Council Directive of 14 October 1991 on an employer's obligation to inform employees of the conditions applicable to the contract or employment relationship was adopted.[2]

### 6.1. COLLECTIVE REDUNDANCIES

The plans to harmonise collective redundancies materialised as a result of a report drawn up by the Commission and sent to the Council of Ministers in July 1972.[3]This Report analysed the provisions within the Member States on the protection of workers in the event of dismissal. It noted the disparity between the provisions in the Member States and recognised the desirability of harmonising these provisions in order to fulfil the aims of Article 117 EEC. The proposals emerging from this Report formed the basis of the provisions contained in the Social Action Programme 1974-76. The disparity between the Member States ranged from the influential role of workers' representatives in Germany where the Works Council legislation operated in redundancy situations to the significant role of public bodies in France and the Netherlands which had sole responsibility to authorise redundancies.

In the Commission's original draft proposal for a Directive the core protections offered were:

---

[1]  (1974) *Bulletin af the EC*, Supplement 2/74, OJ 1974 C 13/1.

[2]  91/533/EEC, OJ 1991 L 288/32.

[3]  (1972) *Bulletin of the EC* (No 9) para 42.

- compulsory consultation with workers' representatives about collective dismissals
- compulsory notification of impending redundancies to public authorities
- powers on the part of public authorities to postpone or prohibit dismissals in certain circumstances.

Freedland argues

"The progress from the first draft to the final directive was a long and tortuous one involving extensive disagreements between the Member States both as to the substance of the proposals and as to the extent of the harmonisation requirement to be imposed."[4]

One major stumbling block was the proposal to allow public authorities to prohibit collective redundancies and in the final version of the Directive a compromise optional provision was adopted.

Council Directive 75/129/EEC[5] on the approximation of the laws of the Member States relating to collective redundancies was based upon Article 100 EEC. The Preamble to the Directive states that it is important that greater protection should be afforded to workers in a collective redundancy situation while taking into account the need for the balanced economic and social development within the Community. It is pointed out that, despite increasing convergence of attitudes towards collective redundancies, there are still differences between the various provisions governing the regulation of such redundancies within the Member States and these differences may directly affect the functioning of the Common Market.

Several parts of the Social Charter and the Commission's Action Programme[6] may affect the operation of collective redundancies. For example, Article 10 guarantees the right of every worker to adequate social protection and Articles 17 and 18 relate to information, consultation and participation of workers. Article 18(iii) specifically refers to collective redundancies. In Part 3 of the Commission's Action Programme entitled "Improvement of Living and Working Conditions" the Commission points to the loophole of Article 1(2)(d), excluding termination of an establishment's activities by judicial decision from the scope of Council Directive 75/129/EEC. Noting the passage of time, socio-

---

[4]  Freedland (1976) 27.

[5]  Article 4 Council Directive 75/129/EEC OJ L 1975 48/29.

[6]  COM(89)568 final, Brussels 25 November 1989.

economic changes and the establishment of the Internal Market the Commission proposes a revision of the Directive:

"There will most certainly be cases of trans-frontier restructuring which, justified though they may be, will have to be accompanied by appropriate information and consultation. A response at Community level appears the most appropriate approach especially since the directive should apply in cases where the decision concerning collective redundancies is taken by a decision-making centre or an undertaking located in another Member State."

A formal proposal was presented to the Council of Ministers in 1991[7] and Council Directive 92/56/EEC[8] amending Directive 75/129/EEC on the approximation of the laws of the Member States relating to collective redundancies was adopted on 24 June 1992. The 1992 Directive broadens the scope of the Community provisions on collective redundancies and strengthens the information and consultation requirements.

The Commission has proposed a codification of the Collective Redundancies Directives.[9] The purpose of this codification is only to clarify the law by making it more easily accessible to the users.

### 6.1.1. Definitions and Scope of Council Directive 75/129/EEC and Directive 92/56/EEC

The Directives determine the scope of collective redundancies but leaves the Member States to choose between criteria laid down in Article 1(1):

"(a) "collective redundancies" means dismissals effected by an employer for one or more reasons not related to the individual workers concerned where, according to the choice of the Member States, the number of redundancies is:
- either, over a period of 30 days:
(1)  at least 10 in establishments normally employing more than 20 and less than 100 workers;
(2)  at least 10 per cent of the number of workers in establishments normally employing at least 100 but less than 300 workers;
(3)  at least 30 in establishments normally employing 300 workers or more;
- or, over a period of 90 days, at least 20, whatever the number of workers normally employed in the establishments in question;"

---

[7]  OJ 1991 C 310/5.

[8]  OJ 1992 L 245/3.

[9]  COM(96)620, OJ 1996 C373/ 4.

Council Directive 92/56/EEC added the following subparagraph to paragraph 1:

> "For the purpose of calculating the number of redundancies provided for in the first subparagraph of point (a), terminations of an employment contract which occur to the individual workers concerned shall be assimilated to redundancies, provided that there are at least five redundancies."

The scope of the collective redundancies Directive is thus expanded by the 1992 amendment through the provisions on how the relevant numbers are calculated. A further and very important expansion of the scope is achieved by deleting the exception for redundancies following from a judicial decision.

Article 1(2) of Council Directive 75/129/EEC lists a number of exclusions to the scope of the Directive:

> "(a)   collective redundancies affected under contracts of employment concluded for limited periods of time or for specific tasks except where such redundancies take place prior to the date of expiry or the completion of such contracts;
> (b)   workers employed by public administrative bodies or by establishments governed by public law (or, in Member States where this concept is unknown, by equivalent bodies);
> (c)   the crews of sea-going vessels;
> (d)   workers affected by the termination of an establishment's activities where that is the result of a judicial decision."

Council Directive 92/56/EEC provides for subparagraph 2(d) to be deleted. The "old" exception for redundancies resulting from a judicial decision applied mainly to situations of bankruptcy, winding up and the like. The abolition of this exclusion marks a major change in the 1975 Directive which may give grounds for questioning whether the judgment of the ECJ on the scope of Article 1 of Council Directive 75/129/EEC in *Dansk Metalarbejderforbund and Specialarbejderforbundet i Danmark* v *H Nielsen & Søn, Maskinfabrik A/S*, in liquidation[10]can still be considered an expression of the current state of the law. In that case the company informed the bankruptcy court that it was suspending payment of its debts. Two trade unions asked the company to provide a bank guarantee for the future payment of wages but no guarantee was forthcoming and on the advice of the trade union the workers stopped work. On 21 March 1980 the Company informed the competent Danish Employment Office that it was considering dismissing all its workers. On 25 March 1980 it was declared insolvent (on its own application) and on 26 March 1980 the workers were given due notice of dismissal.

---

[10]   Case 284/83 [1985] ECR 553.

The ECJ referred to the exclusion of redundancies resulting from a judicial decision as part of its reason for not accepting the workers' cessation of work as a redundancy within the meaning of the Directive:

"Moreover, as the Commission rightly observes, the effect of the interpretation proposed by Specialarbejderforbundet i Danmark would be that any employer who ceased to trade as a result of insolvency and who failed to notify the public authority of any projected collective redundancy would incur the penalties laid down by national law, since he would not have foreseen collective redundancies in sufficient time. Such an interpretation would run counter to the wording of Article 1(2), which excludes from the scope of the directive collective redundancies caused "by the termination of an establishment's activities where that is the result of a judicial decision."[11]

The Danish Law on the Procurement of Employment and Unemployment Insurance, Chapter 5A was the implementing legislation for Council Directive 75/129/EEC. Under this law the trade unions claimed special allowances *in lieu* of the failure to give notice 30 days in advance of a proposed collective redundancy. In the event of an employer's insolvency the Wage-earners' Guarantee Fund would be responsible for the payment of an allowance. The Danish Supreme Court (Højesteret) referred two questions to the ECJ. First, whether in the circumstances of the case, the cessation of work by the workers constituted a repudiation of their contract amounting to a dismissal attributable to the employer and thereby falling within Council Directive 75/129/EEC. The second question related to whether the employer ought to have contemplated collective redundancies within the meaning of Council Directive 75/129/EEC, on announcing that it was suspending payment of its debts, since that announcement was followed by the winding up of the company and the collective redundancy of the workers.

On the first question, the Commission, the Wage-earners' Guarantee Fund and the Specialarbejderforbundet i Danmark pointed out that it was impossible to stretch Article 1(1)(a) of Council Directive 75/129/EEC to embrace the termination of the employment by *employees*. Collective redundancies were defined as dismissals effected by an employer. However, the Specialar-bejderforbundet i Danmark was prepared to argue that the objective of the Directive was to strengthen the protection of workers in the event of collective dismissal. This implied that the termination of the workers' employment on the ground that payment of wages was no longer guaranteed should be treated as a dismissal effected by the employer.

---

[11] *Ibid* para 16.

The ECJ ruled that such an argument cannot be accepted. The Directive does not affect the employer's freedom to effect or refrain from effecting collective dismissals. Its sole object is to provide for consultation with the trade unions and for notification of the competent public authority prior to such dismissals. Article 2(2) provides that consultation with the trade unions must, at least, cover "ways and means of avoiding collective redundancies or reducing the number of workers affected, and mitigating the consequences." Article 4 provides that projected collective redundancies notified to the competent authority are to take effect only after a particular period has elapsed. The competent public authority is to use that period to seek solutions to the problems raised by the projected collective redundancies. As the Guarantee Fund and the Commission had observed, to treat termination of their employment by the workers in the manner advocated by Special-arbejderforbundet i Danmark would give the workers the possibility of bringing about dismissals against the will of the employer and without the employer being in a position to discharge his or her obligations under Articles 2 and 3 of the Directive. It would lead to a result precisely contrary to that sought by the Directive, namely to avoid or reduce collective redundancies.

On the second question, the Specialarbejderforbundet i Danmark contended that the effectiveness of the Directive would be impaired if employers were not obliged to foresee collective redundancies as soon as they encountered serious financial difficulties. The Commission and the Wage-earners' Guarantee Fund pointed out that there was no implied obligation to foresee collective redundancies. The Directive does not stipulate the circumstances in which an employer must contemplate collective redundancies and it does not affect employers' freedom to decide whether and when plans for a collective redundancy must be formulated. The Directive merely states that the employer must consult trade unions when collective redundancies are contemplated and the employer must inform the public authority of projected redundancies. The Commission pointed out that to use the interpretation advanced by the Special-arbejderforbundet i Danmark would expose an employer to penalties where it did not foresee collective redundancies in time. Such an interpretation would run counter to Article 1(2) which excluded redundancies caused. The ECJ followed this line of argument and ruled that Council Directive 75/129/EEC only applied where the employer had in fact contemplated collective redundancies or had drawn up a plan for collective redundancies.

The scope of Article 1 of Council Directive 75/129/EEC was also considered by the ECJ in *Commission v Belgium*.[12]During the course of the infringe-

---

[12]  Case 215/83 [1985] ECR 1039.

ment proceedings the Belgium Government amended its laws and the ruling was limited to two complaints. The first was that Belgian law did not cover collective redundancies arising from the closure of an undertaking where the closure did not come about as the result of a judicial decision. The second complaint related to the exclusion of ship repairers, port workers and manual workers in the building industry from the Belgian provisions purporting to implement the Directive.

On the first complaint the Belgian Government maintained that the distinction drawn in Belgium between the closure of undertakings and collective redundancies was due to historical factors. In Belgium the vast majority of closures of undertakings likely to lead to collective redundancies would come about as a result of a judicial decision. Thus, as a result of Article 1(2)(d), outlined above, these redundancies would be excluded from the scope of Council Directive 75/129/EEC. The ECJ nevertheless upheld the Commission's complaint. Even if a small number of collective redundancies were covered

"... that does not relieve the Kingdom of Belgium of its duty to provide workers with the protection envisaged by the Directive in the event of collective redundancies arising from such closures."[13]

On the second complaint the ECJ held that the list of exclusions contained in Article 1(2) was exhaustive. The Commission had conceded that Article 1(2)(a) would exclude workers engaged on a day-to-day basis or where the contract was a fixed term or task contract but only on condition that the Directive would apply to such workers where a collective redundancy took place prior to the date of expiry or completion of the contract of employment. Thus the ECJ held that the Belgian rules unlawfully excluded such workers from the benefits of the Directive. In the case of ship repairers and port workers the Belgian Government had argued that such workers' "natural mobility" and the fact that they were covered by a special social security scheme justified the exclusion of such workers from the Directive's provisions. The ECJ rejected this contention, emphasising the binding nature of Community law:

"The Court has consistently held that the Member States must fulfil their obligations under Community directives in every respect and may not plead provisions, practices

---

[13] *Ibid* para 17.

or circumstances existing in their internal legal system in order to justify a failure to comply with those obligations."[14]

Furthermore, alternative forms of protection, such as the provision of special social security schemes for the ship repairers and port workers were not acceptable ways of securing (presumably, the harmonisation) objectives of Community Law.

### 6.1.2. Consultation Procedure

In *Dansk Metalarbejderforbund and Specialarbejderforbundet i Danmark*[15] the ECJ stated that the sole object of Council Directive 75/129/EEC was:

"... to provide for consultation with the trade unions and for notification of the competent public authority prior to such dismissals."[16]

Section II of Council Directive 75/129/EEC lays down certain requirements as to the nature of consultations which should take place with workers' representatives "with a view to reaching an agreement" (Article 2(1)). The consultations should, at least, cover ways and means of avoiding collective redundancies or of reducing the number of workers affected and mitigating the consequences (Article 2(2)).

In the infringement case against the United Kingdom[17] the ECJ held that despite the limited character of the harmonization of rules in respect of collective redundancies which Directive 75/129/EEC was intended to bring about, national rules which, by not providing for a system for the designation of workers' representatives in an undertaking where an employer refuses to recognize such representatives, allow an employer to frustrate the protection provided by Articles 2 and 3 of Directive 75/129/EEC must be regarded as contrary to the provisions of that directive.

According to Article 1(1)(a) of Directive 75/129, the directive applies to collective redundancies in the sense of dismissals for one or more reasons not related to the individual workers concerned, including dismissals resulting from new working arrangements within an undertaking unconnected with its

---

[14]  *Ibid* para 25.

[15]  Case 284/83 [1985] ECR 553.

[16]  *Ibid* para 10.

[17]  Case C-383/92 *Commission* v *United Kingdom* [1994] ECR I-2479.

volume of business. Its scope cannot for that reason be limited to cases of redundancy defined as resulting from a cessation or reduction of the business of an undertaking or a decline in demand for work of a particular type.

National rules which merely require an employer to consult trade union representatives about proposed dismissals, to "consider" representations made by such representatives and, if he rejects them, to "state his reasons", whereas Article 2(1) of the Directive requires the workers' representatives to be consulted "with a view to reaching an agreement" and Article 2(2) lays down that such consultation must "at least, cover ways and means of avoiding collective redundancies or reducing the number of workers affected, and mitigating the consequences", fail correctly to transpose Directive 75/129.

Where a Community Directive does not specifically provide any penalty for an infringement or refers for that purpose to national laws, regulations and administrative provisions, Article 5 EC requires the Member States to take all measures necessary to guarantee the application and effectiveness of Community law. For that purpose, while the choice of penalties remains within their discretion, they must ensure in particular that infringements of Community law are penalized under conditions, both procedural and substantive, which are analogous to those applicable to infringements of national law of a similar nature and importance and which, in any event, make the penalty effective, proportionate and dissuasive.

In the case where an employee may be entitled to payment of various amounts under his/her contract of employment and by reason of its breach, an award which may be set off against such amounts cannot be regarded as sufficiently deterrent for an employer who, in the event of collective redundancies, fails to comply with his/her obligations under Directive 75/129/EEC to consult and inform his/her workers' representatives.

Council Directive 92/56/EEC develops the information and consultation requirements further. Article 2 of the old Council Directive 75/129/EEC is replaced by the following:

"1. Where an employer is contemplating collective redundancies, he shall begin consultations with the workers' representatives in good time with a view to reaching an agreement.
2. These consultations shall, at least, cover ways and means of avoiding collective redundancies or reducing the number of workers affected, and of mitigating the consequences by recourse to accompanying social measures aimed, inter alia, at aid for redeploying or retaining workers made redundant.
Member States may provide that the workers' representatives may call upon the services of experts in accordance with national legislation and/or practice.

After the 1992 amendment of the Directive it is thus specified that the possible mitigation should be through social measures.

In order for the workers' representatives to be able to make constructive proposals the employer must supply them with all relevant information. The minimum information which employers must provide to workers' representatives was expanded by the 1992 amendment to include the categories of workers normally employed and to be made redundant, the criteria to be employed in selecting workers for redundancy and the method for calculating any non-statutory redundancy payments. Directive 92/56/EEC provides in Article 2(3):

> 3. To enable workers' representatives to make constructive proposals, the employers shall in good time during the course of the consultations:
> (a) supply them with all relevant information and
> (b) in any event notify them in writing of:
>> (i) the reasons for the projected redundancies;
>> (ii) the number of categories of workers to be made redundant;
>> (iii) the number and categories of workers normally employed;
>> (iv) the period over which the projected redundancies are to be effected;
>> (v) the criteria proposed for the selection of the workers to be made redundant in so far as national legislation and/or practice confers the power therefore upon the employer;
>> (vi) the method for calculating any redundancy payments other than those arising out of national legislation and/or practice.
> The employer shall forward to the competent public authority a copy of, at least, the elements of the written communication which are provided for in the first subparagraph, point (b), subpoint (i) to (v).

### 6.1.3. Groups of Undertakings

According to Article 2(4) of the 1992 Directive the obligations laid down in Article 2, paragraphs 1, 2 and 3 apply irrespective of whether the decision regarding collective redundancies is being taken by the employer or by an undertaking controlling the employer.

In considering alleged breaches of the information, consultation and notification requirements laid down by the Directive, account shall not be taken of any defence on the part of the employer on the ground that the necessary information has not been provided to the employer by the undertaking which took the decision leading to collective redundancies.

This provision clarifies the legal position in case of redundancies in groups of companies. It may be seen as the main change of the Directive.[18] Its aim is to ensure that the Directive's provisions apply in complex business structures.

In *Rockfon A/S* v *Specialarbejderforbundet i Danmark*[19] the ECJ held that Article 1(1)(a) of Directive 75/129, on the approximation of the laws of the Member States relating to collective redundancies, is to be interpreted as meaning that it does not preclude two or more interrelated undertakings in a group, neither or none of which has decisive influence over the other or others, from establishing a joint recruitment and dismissal department so that, in particular, dismissals on grounds of redundancy in one of the undertakings can take place only with that department's approval. The sole purpose of Directive 75/129EEC is partial harmonization of collective redundancy procedures and its aim is not to restrict the freedom of undertakings to organize their activities and arrange their personnel departments in the way which they think best suits their needs.

The term "establishment" appearing in Article 1(1)(a) of Directive 75/129/EEC on the approximation of the laws of the Member States relating to collective redundancies must be understood as meaning, depending on the circumstances, the unit to which the workers made redundant are assigned to carry out their duties. It is not essential, in order for there to be an establishment, for the unit in question to be endowed with a management which can independently effect collective redundancies. To make the definition of "establishment", which is a concept of Community law and cannot be defined by reference to the laws of the Member States, dependent on the existence of such a management within the unit would be incompatible with the aim of the Directive since that would allow companies belonging to the same group to try to make it more difficult for the Directive to apply to them by conferring on a separate decision-making body the power to take decisions concerning redundancies and by this means they would be able to escape the obligation to follow certain procedures for the protection of workers, such as their right to be informed and consulted. Problems relating to information and consultation in groups of companies are discussed further in Chapter Seven.

### 6.1.4. Procedure for Collective Redundancies

Section III of the Directive outlines the content and scope of the obligations to notify collective redundancies to the competent public authorities in the

---

[18]  Cf *European Industrial Relations Review* 226, October 1992 24.

[19]  Case C-449/93 [1995] ECR I-4291.

Member States. Article 3(1) provides that employers shall notify the competent public authorities in writing of any projected redundancies. This notification must contain all the relevant information concerning the projected redundancies and the consultations with workers' representatives provided for in Article 2 of the Directive with the exception of the information on redundancy payments. The workers' representatives are to be given a copy of this notification and they may send comments on it to the competent public authority. The projected collective redundancies notified to the public authority may not take effect earlier than 30 days after the date of notification. This provision is without prejudice to the provisions governing individual rights with regard to notice of dismissal. In Article 3(1) the following subparagraph is added after the first subparagraph by Council Directive 92/56/EEC:

"However, Member States may provide that in the case of planned collective redundancies arising from termination of the establishment's activities as a result of a judicial decision, the employer shall be obliged to notify the competent public authority in writing only if the latter so requests."

The notification period may be reduced by the Member States (Article 4(1)). Where the initial period of notification is shorter than 60 days Member States may grant the competent public authority the power to extend the initial period to 60 days following notification of the proposed collective redundancy where the problems relating to the redundancy are unlikely to be solved within the initial period. In addition the Member States may grant the competent public authority wider powers of extension. The employer must be informed of the extension and the grounds for it before the expiry of the initial 30 day period (Article 4(3)). In Article 4, the following paragraph was added after paragraph 3:

"Member States need not apply this Article to collective redundancies arising from termination of the establishment's activities where this is the result of a judicial decision."

Article 5 also allows the Member States to apply or introduce laws, regulations or administrative provisions which are more favourable to workers.

In an infringement action brought against Italy, the Italian Government attempted to argue that Council Directive 75/129/EEC was adequately, if not more favourably, implemented through collective agreements.[20] In certain sectors, notably agriculture and commerce, the Italian Government conceded that the Italian legislation underpinning collective bargaining was not as

---

[20] Case 91/81 [1982] ECR 2133.

comprehensive as the provisions of the Directive. The ECJ also pointed out that Italian collective agreements did not require employers to notify in writing proposed collective redundancies, there was no duty to notify the collective redundancies to competent public authorities and that there was no obligation upon public authorities to intervene in order to seek solutions to the problems raised by the projected collective redundancies. Thus the core notification provisions of Article 3 of the Directive were not met. As Article 4(2) of the Directive states, the object of notification and involvement of public authorities is to seek solutions (and presumably ameliorate the problems) to the wide range of legal, social and economic issues connected with large-scale redundancy situations.

The binding nature of Article 169 EC judgments is shown in the second infringement action taken against Italy.[21] The Italian Government had argued that the economic and social situation in Italy demanded that economic policy should be directed towards maintaining the level of employment and that it was inappropriate to direct legislative activity towards regulating collective redundancies during an emergency situation which had to be dealt with in order to safeguard employment. The ECJ confirmed the binding nature of Community law:

"Article 171 of the EEC Treaty does not lay down a time-limit within which a judgment must be complied with. However, it is well-established that the implementation of a judgment must be commenced immediately and must be completed as soon as possible."[22]

The ECJ found that there had been unreasonable delay in this situation and re-iterated its views that a Member State may not plead provisions, practices or circumstances existing in its internal legal system in order to justify failure to comply with obligations and time-limits laid down in Directives. The right of an individual to claim damages against a Member State decided in *Francovich and Bonifaci v Italy*[23] is discussed in Chapter One. In the TEU Article 171 EC is amended so as to provide for a lump sum or a penalty payment to be paid by a Member State which fails to comply with a judgment of the ECJ.

---

[21]  Case 131/84 *EC Commission* v *Italy (No.2)* [1985] ECR 3531.

[22]  *Ibid* para 7.

[23]  Joined Cases C-6/90 and C-9/90 [1991] ECR I-5357. See Szyszczak (1992b).

The notification requirements of Council Directive 75/129/EEC were also at issue in *Commission* v *Kingdom of Belgium*.[24]Under Belgian law a distinction was drawn between the concept of closure of an undertaking and a collective redundancy. As a result redundancies arising from a closure of an undertaking were governed by a law not designed to implement the obligations contained in Council Directive 75/129/EEC. The scope of the obligation to notify under this law was narrower than the scope of the obligations laid down in Articles 3 and 4 of the Directive. The Belgian government argued that the vast majority of closures of undertakings were regulated by judicial decision and therefore outside the scope of the Directive (Article 1(2)(d)). The ECJ held that, despite this, the Directive had not been fully implemented in Belgium and

> "...that Belgian law does not offer a sufficient degree of legal certainty as regards the protection of workers envisaged by the Directive."[25]

## 6.2. TRANSFER OF UNDERTAKINGS

### 6.2.1. Purpose of Directive 77/187/EEC

Directive 77/187/EEC [26] applies to the transfer of an undertaking, business or part of a business to another employer as a result of a legal transfer or merger. The Directive is intended to safeguard the rights of workers in the event of a change of employer by making it possible for the worker to continue to work for the transferee under the same conditions as those agreed with the transferor. As the Court stated in its judgment in *Knud Wendelboe m fl* v *L J Music,*[27]it is intended to ensure, as far as possible, that the employment relationship continues unchanged with the transferee, in particular by obliging the transferee to continue to observe the terms and conditions of any collective agreement (Article 3(2)) and by protecting workers against dismissals motivated solely by the fact of transfer (Article 4(1)).

---

[24]  Case 215/83 [1985] ECR 1039.

[25]  Para 19.

[26]  See generally Legnier (1977).

[27]  Case 19/83 [1985] ECR 457.

The Directive must be interpreted in accordance with this purpose but a linguistic interpretation is complicated by the fact that the different language versions are not totally identical.[28] In *Wendelboe*, the ECJ was asked:

"Does the Council directive of 14 February 1977 on the approximation of the laws of the Member States relating to the safeguarding of employees' rights in the event of transfers of undertakings, business or parts of businesses require the Member States to enact provisions under which the transferee of an undertaking becomes liable in respect of obligations concerning holiday pay and compensation to employees who were not employed in the undertaking on the date of transfer?"

The ECJ held that it follows from a textual interpretation of the provision in the various language versions, that the Directive refers only to the rights and obligations of workers whose contract of employment or employment relationship is in force on the date of the transfer and not to those who have ceased to be employed by the undertaking in question at the time of the transfer. This is apparent from the fact that in the Dutch, French, German, Greek and Italian versions the phrase "existing on the date of the transfer" relates unequivocally to the expression "contract of employment or ... employment relationship" and that, in the English and Danish language versions, the same interpretation is in any event possible.

In *Foreningen af Arbejdsledere i Danmark v A/S Danmols Inventar*[29] the ECJ stressed that Directive 77/187/EEC is intended to achieve only partial harmonization essentially by extending the protection guaranteed to workers independently by the laws of the individual Member States to cover the case where an undertaking is transferred. Its aim is to ensure, as far as possible, that the contract of employment or the employment relationship continues unchanged with the transferee so that the employees affected by the transfer of the undertaking are not placed in a less favourable position solely as a result of the transfer. However, it is not intended to establish a uniform level of protection throughout the Community on the basis of common criteria.

---

[28] *Ibid* Para 9. On problems relating to differences between different language versions see Case 283/81 *CILFIT* [1982] ECR 3415; Case 19/83 *Wendelboe* [1985] ECR 457 and Case 135/83 *Abels* [1985] ECR 469.

[29] Case 105/84 [1985] ECR 2639.

### 6.2.2. Mandatory

In *Foreningen af Arbejdsledere i Danmark* v *Daddy's Dance Hall A/S*[30] the ECJ held that the Directive is mandatory on each point so that it cannot be derogated from on one point to the disadvantage of the employee even if the contract seen as a whole is in the favour of the employee.

According to the Court, it is not permissible to derogate from the rules in a manner unfavourable for the employees and hence the implementation of the rights conferred on employees may not be made subject to the consent of either the transferor or the transferee nor the consent of the employees' representatives or the employees themselves, with the sole reservation, as regards the workers themselves, that, following a decision freely taken by them, they are at liberty, after the transfer, not to continue the employment relationship with the new employer.[31] In this event it is for the Member States to determine what the fate of the employment contract or employment relationship should be. Notably, they may provide in such circumstances that the contract must be regarded as terminated either by the employee or by the employer. They may also provide that the contract be maintained with the transferor.[32]

According to Article 7 the Directive does not affect the right of Member States to apply or introduce laws, regulations or administrative provisions which are more favourable to the employees.

### 6.2.3. Scope

The Directive applies "where and insofar as the undertaking, business or part of the business to be transferred is situated within the territorial scope of the Treaty" (Article 1.2) or a member country of the European Economic Area (Norway, Iceland, Liechtenstein).

The Directive applies to the *transfer* of any type of undertaking, business or part of a business, whether public or private, to another employer. Transfers involving sea-going vessels are specifically excluded by the Directive. The fact that an undertaking is engaged in non-profit-making activities is not sufficient to remove the undertaking from the scope of the Directive. In the infringement case against the UK[33] the ECJ held that

---

[30]  Case 324/86 [1988] ECR 739.

[31]  Case 362/89 *d'Urso* [1991] ECR-I-4105.

[32]  Case 132/91 *Katsikas* [1992] ECR-I-6577.

[33]  Case C-382/92 [1994] ECR I-2435.

2. Article 1(1) of Directive 77/187 on the approximation of the laws of the Member States relating to the safeguarding of employees' rights in the event of transfers of undertakings precludes a Member State from restricting the application of the national rules transposing the directive to transfers of profit-making undertakings. A body may be engaged in economic activities and be regarded as an "undertaking" for the purposes of Community law even though it does not operate with a view to profit.

The *persons* the Directive aims to protect are persons with a contract of employment or persons in an employment relationship as defined by the employment law of the Member States at the time of the transfer.

The ECJ has held that it is for the national courts to establish to what extent the persons concerned are to be regarded as employees and that, consequently, whether or not an employment contract or employment relationship exists on the date of transfer must be established on the basis of the provisions of national law.[34]

The Directive does not apply to the transfer of rights and obligations in respect of persons who were employed by the transferor on the date of transfer but, of their own free will, do not continue to occupy an employee's post with the transferee.[35]

### 6.2.4. Key Concepts

Article 2 provides that for the purposes of the Directive:

(a) "transferor" means any natural or legal person who, by reason of a transfer within the meaning of Article 1(1), ceases to be the employer in respect of the undertaking, business or part of the business;

(b) "transferee" means any natural or legal person who, by reason of a transfer within the meaning of Article 1(1), becomes the employer in respect of the undertaking, business or part of the business;

(c) "representatives of the employees" means the representatives of the employees provided for by the laws or practice of the Member States, with the exception of members of administrative, governing or supervisory bodies of companies who represent employees on such bodies in certain Member States.

---

[34] Case 105/84 *A/S Danmols Inventar* [1985] ECR 2639.

[35] Case 19/83 *Wendelbo* [1985] ECR 457.

### 6.2.4.(i) Concept of Employee

In *Danmols*[36] the ECJ was asked whether the expression "employee" in Council Directive 77/187/EEC must be interpreted to mean that it is sufficient for the person concerned to have been an employee of the transferor or whether he must also occupy a position as employee with the transferee. It was further asked whether, if the person concerned must also be an employee of the transferee, the expression "employee" contained in the Directive covers a person who has a 50 per cent interest in the company in question.

The parties to the main proceedings and the Commission suggested that the first question should be answered in the negative. This followed both from a linguistic interpretation of the provision and from an interpretation based upon the objective of the Directive. The actual wording of the provision in question shows that it applies only where there is a change of employer, in other words, where the person concerned continues as an employee of the transferee. This conclusion was, in their view, supported by reference to the aim of the Directive, which is to ensure the continuity of the employment relationship of the employee *vis-à-vis* the person acquiring the undertaking.

The ECJ held that the protection which the Directive is intended to guarantee is redundant where the person concerned decides of his/her own accord not to continue the employment relationship with the new employer after the transfer. This is the case where the employee in question terminated the employment contract or employment relationship of his/her own free will with effect from the date of the transfer, or where that contract or relationship is terminated with effect from the date of the transfer by virtue of an agreement voluntarily concluded between the worker and the transferor or the transferee of the undertaking. In that situation Article 3(1) of the Directive does not apply.

In regard to the second question the plaintiff in the main proceedings claimed that the term "employee" means a person who works for an employer and is subject to the instructions and orders of that employer. Such a definition does not apply to a person who carries out work for a company in which he or she holds a large percentage of the shares. The defendant in the main proceedings, on the other hand, maintained that the term "employee" within the meaning of Directive 77/187/EEC does extend to a person who holds shares in, or is a member of the Board of Directors of, the company by which he or she is employed, provided that he or she does not occupy a dominant position on that Board.

---

[36] Case 105/84 *A/S Danmols Inventar* [1985] ECR 2639.

The ECJ held that Directive 77/187/EEC may be relied upon only by persons who are, in one way or another, protected as employees under the law of the Member State concerned. If they are so protected, the Directive ensures that their rights arising from a contract of employment or an employment relationship are not diminished as a result of the transfer.

In reply to the second question it was held therefore that the term "employee" within the meaning of Directive 77/187/EEC must be interpreted as covering any person who, in the Member State concerned, is protected as an employee under national employment law. It is for the national court to establish whether this is the case.

### 6.2.4.(ii) Concept of transfer

The Directive applies to a transfer which takes place as a result of a legal transfer or merger.

### 6.2.4.(ii)a Transfer operations associated with insolvency proceedings

According to the ECJ the Directive does not impose on the Member States the obligation to extend the rules laid down therein to transfers taking place in the context of insolvency proceedings instituted with a view to the liquidation of the assets of the transferor, without prejudice to the national legislator's right to decide otherwise.[37]

The ECJ held in *H B M Abels* v *The Administrative Board of the Bedrijfsvereniging voor de Metaalindustrie en de Electrotechnische Industrie*[38] that the Directive does not apply to the transfer of an undertaking where the transferor has been adjudged insolvent and the undertaking in question forms part of the assets of the insolvent transferor, although the Member States are at liberty to apply the principles of the Directive to such a transfer on their own initiative.

In the *Danmols*[39] case the ECJ held that the mere fact that the transfer of an undertaking has occurred after the transferor has suspended payments of his/her debts is not enough to exclude the transfer from the scope of the Directive, which applies to a transfer which is effected in the course of a procedure or at a stage prior to the commencement of liquidation proceedings.

---

[37] Case 135/83 *Abels*; Case 179/83 *FNV*; Case 186/83 *Botzen*; Case 362/89 *d'Urso*.

[38] Case 135/83 [1985] ECR 469.

[39] Case 105/84 *A/S Danmols Inventar* [1985] ECR 2639.

The Court has also ruled that the Directive does not apply to transfers of undertakings made as part of a creditor's arrangement procedure of the kind provided for in the Italian legislation on compulsory administrative liquidation but that it does apply when, in accordance with a body of legislation such as that governing special administration for large undertakings in critical difficulties, it has been decided that the undertaking is to continue trading for as long as that decision remains in force.[40]

By contrast, the Directive does apply to the transfer of an undertaking, business or part of a business to another employer in the context of proceedings of the type "surséance van betaling" (suspension of payments) under Dutch law, as such proceedings may allow the continuation of business.

The fact that the transfer of an undertaking, business or part of a business takes place after the suspension of payments by the transferor is not in itself sufficient to exclude such transfers from the scope of the Directive. Furthermore, the Directive applies to undertakings in which a state of crisis has been recognised.[41]

### 6.2.4.(ii)b No Direct Contractual Link between the Transferor and Transferee

In *Landsorganisationen i Danmark for Tjenerforbundet i Danmark v Ny Mølle Kro*[42] and *Harry Berg and Johannes Theodorus Maria Busschers v Ivo Martin Besselsen*[43] it was held that the Directive also applies to a transfer which occurs as a result of a repudiation of a contract. The ECJ held a similar view in *Dr Sophie Redmond Stichtung* v *Hendrikus Bartold et al*[44]G and in *Anne Watson Rask and Kirsten Christensen* v *ISS Kantineservice A/S.*[45] In *Jørn Ulstein & Per Otto Røiseng* v *Asbjørn Møller*[46] the EFTA Court expressed the same view.

---

[40]   Case C-362/89 *d'Urso* [1991] ECR I-4105

[41]   Case 472/93 *Spano* [1995] ECR I-4321.

[42]   Case 287/86 [1987] ECR 5465.

[43]   Case 144 and 145/87 [1988] 2559.

[44]   Case C-29/91 [1992] ECR-I-3189.

[45]   Case C-209/91 [1992] ECR-I-5755.

[46]   Case E-2/96, judgment of 19 December 1996 nyr.

### 6.2.4.(iii) Change of Employer

For the Directive to apply there must be a transfer to another employer. The Directive does not apply when the majority of shares in a limited company is acquired by another company.

In *Landsorganisationen i Danmark for Tjenerforbundet i Danmark* v *Ny Mølle Kro*[47]the ECJ considered the question whether the words "transfer to another employer as a result of a legal transfer or merger" in Article 1(1) of the Directive cover the situation in which, following the lessee's breach of a lease agreement, the owner of a leased undertaking rescinds that agreement and subsequently takes over the running of the undertaking. The answer was in the affirmative.

In *Foreningen af Arbejsledere i Danmark* v *Daddy's Dance Hall A/S*[48]the following question was also answered in the affirmative:

"(1) must Article 1(1) of Council Directive 77/187/EEC... be interpreted as meaning that the directive applies where a non-transferable lease of a business is terminated and as a result, without there being any interruption in the running of the business, the owner leases the business to a new lessee, who re-employs the staff, who had been given notice but had not left their employment, and buys the former lessee's stock?"

### 6.2.4.(iv) Part of an Undertaking

The Directive also applies to the transfer of a part of an undertaking. In *Arie Botzen et al* v *Rotterdamsche Droogdok Maatschappij BV*[49]the ECJ held that the Directive must be interpreted as not covering the transferor's rights and obligations arising from a contract of employment or an employment relationship existing on the date of the transfer and entered into with employees who, although not employed in the transferred part of the undertaking, performed certain duties which involved the use of assets assigned to the part transferred or who, while being employed in an administrative department of the undertaking which had not itself been transferred, carried out certain duties for the benefit of the part transferred.

---

[47]  Case 287/86 [1987] ECR 5465.

[48]  Case 324/86 [1988] ECR 739

[49]  Case 186/83 [1985] ECR 519.

In its judgment in *Redmond*,[50] the Court pointed out that whenever in the case of an undertaking - here, a foundation established under Dutch law to assist victims of drug abuse - only part of its activities (in particular only the provision of help, but not social or recreational functions) are transferred to another undertaking, that does not necessarily mean that the Directive is inapplicable. The Court pointed out that the mere fact that those social and recreational activities "constituted an independent function does not suffice to rule out the application of the aforementioned provisions of the Directive."

### 6.2.4.(v) Economic Identity

As the Court stated in its judgment in *Merckx*,[51] it is settled case-law that the decisive criterion for establishing whether there is a transfer for the purposes of the Directive is whether the entity in question retains its economic identity, as indicated *inter alia* by the fact that its operation is actually continued or resumed.[52] In order to determine whether that condition is met, it is necessary to consider all the facts characterizing the transaction in question, including the type of undertaking or business, whether or not the business' s tangible assets, such as buildings and movable property, are transferred, the value of its intangible assets at the time of the transfer, whether or not the majority of its employees is taken over by the new employer, whether or not its customers are transferred and the degree of similarity between the activities carried on before and after the transfer and the period, if any, for which those activities were

---

[50] Case 29/91 *Dr Sophie Redmond Stichtung* v *Hendrikus Bartold et al* [1992] ECR I-3189

[51] Case C-171/94 *Albert Merckx and Patrick Neuhuys* v *Ford Motors Company Belgium SA* [1996] ECR 1253.

[52] At the time of writing there are 24 judgments from the ECJ and 4 from the EFTA Court on the interpretation of Directive 77/187/EEC. The ECJ has dealt with the concept of transfer in Article 1 of the Directive in a number of cases, in particular, Case 186/83 *Botzen* v *Rotterdamsche Droogdok Maatschappij* [1985] ECR 519, Case 24/85 *Spijkers* v *Benedik* [1986] ECR 1119, Case 287/86 *Landsorganisationen i Danmark for Tjenerforbundet i Danmark* v *Ny Mølle Kro* [1987] ECR 5465; Case 324/86 *Tellerup* v *Daddy's Dance Hall* [1988] ECR 739; Case 101/87 *Bork International* v *Foreningen af Arbejdsledere i Danmark* [1988] ECR 3057; Case C-29/91 *Redmond Stichting* v *Hendrikus Bartol* [1992] ECR I-3189, Case C-392/92 *Schmidt* [1994] ECR I1311, Case C-209/91 *Watson Rask and Christensen* [1992] ECR I-5755, Case C-48/94 *Rygaard* v *Strø Mølle Akustik* [1995] ECR I-2745, Joined Cases C-171/94 and C-172/94 *Merckx and Neuhuys* v *Ford Motors Company Belgium* [1996] ECR I-1253 and Case C-13/95 *Ayse Süzen* v *Zehnacker Gebäudereinigung GmbH Krankenhausservice* judgment of 11 March 1997, nyr.

suspended. All those circumstances are merely single factors in the overall assessment which must be made and cannot therefore be considered in isolation. The undertaking must thus have preserved its business identity. The ECJ has dealt with this criterion in some 10 cases and the EFTA court in 3.

The ECJ addressed the issue of economic identity for the first time in *Jozef Maria Antonius Spijkers* v *Gebroeders Benedik Abattoir C V and Alfred Benedik en Zonen B V*[53] where it held that a transfer of an undertaking does not occur simply because the assets of the undertaking are disposed of. It is necessary to consider whether the business was disposed of as a going concern, as would be indicated, *inter alia*, by the fact that its operation was actually continued or resumed by the new employer with the same or similar activities. In *Spijkers* the ECJ considered the following questions:

> (1) is there a transfer within the meaning of Article 1(1) of Council Directive no 77/187/EEC where buildings and stock are taken over and the transferee is thereby enabled to continue the business activities of the transferor and does in fact subsequently carry on business activities of the same kind in the buildings in question?
> (2) does the fact that at the time when the buildings and stock were sold the business activities of the vendor had entirely ceased and that in particular there was no longer any goodwill in the business prevent there being a transfer as defined in question 1?
> (3) does the fact that the circle of customers is not taken over prevent there being such a transfer?

The ECJ ruled[54] that Article 1(1) of Directive 77/187/EEC must be interpreted to the effect that the expression "transfer of an undertaking, business or part of a business to another employer" envisages the case in which the business in question retains its identity. In order to determine whether those conditions are met, it is necessary to consider all the facts characterizing the transaction in question, including

- the type of undertaking or business,
- whether or not the business' tangible assets, such as buildings and movable property, are transferred,
- the value of its intangible assets at the time of the transfer,
- whether or not the majority of its employees are taken over by the new employer,
- whether or not its customers are transferred
- the degree of similarity between the activities carried on before and after the transfer and
- the period, if any, for which those activities were suspended.

---

[53]  Case 24/85 [1986] ECR 1119

[54]  *Ibid* para 13.

All those circumstances are merely single factors in the overall assessment which must be made and cannot therefore be considered in isolation. It is for the national court to make the necessary factual appraisal, in the light of the criteria for interpretation set out above, in order to establish whether or not there is a transfer in the sense indicated above.

The requirement that the undertaking must have preserved its economic identity was also dealt with in *Landsorganisationen i Danmark for Tjenerforbundet i Danmark* v *Ny Mølle Kro.*[55]In that case the Court held that the directive:

> "envisages the case in which the business retains its identity inasmuch as it is transferred as a going concern, which may be indicated in particular by the fact that its operation is actually continued or resumed by the new employer, with the same or similar activities ".

In *P. Bork International A/S under konkurs* v *Foreningen af arbejdsledere i Danmark, og Jens E. Olsen, Karl Hansen m fl. samt HK* v *Junckers Industrier A/S*[56] the question posed by the Danish Højesteret was:

> "does Council Directive 77/187/EEC... apply where the lessor of the buildings, plant and machinery used for the operation of an undertaking, after giving notice bringing the lease to an end or upon termination thereof and the undertaking' s cessation of operations, retakes possession of the leased property and thereafter transfers it to a third party who shortly afterwards resumes the operation of the undertaking without engaging new staff, inasmuch as the transferee takes on again, without there being an agreement on the subject either with the former lessee or with the transferor or between those two parties, just over half of the employees who were employed in the undertaking by the former lessee?"

The Court held that the fact that in such a case the transfer is effected in two stages, inasmuch as the undertaking is first re-transferred from the lessee to the owner and the latter then transfers it to the new owner, does not prevent the Directive from applying, provided that the undertaking in question retains its identity, as it does if it is a going concern whose operation is actually continued or resumed by the new employer, with the same or similar activities. In order to determine whether those conditions are met, it is necessary to consider all the circumstances surrounding the transaction in question, including, in particular, whether or not the undertaking' s tangible and intangible assets and the majority of its employees are taken over, the degree

---

[55] Case 287/86 [1987] ECR 5465

[56] Case 101/87 [1988] ECR 3057.

274

of similarity between the activities carried on before and after the transfer and the period, if any, for which those activities ceased in connection with the transfer.

As regards the last criterion, it was pointed out, as the Court had already held in *Ny Mølle Kro,*[57] that the fact that the undertaking in question was temporarily closed at the time of the transfer and therefore had no employees certainly constitutes one factor to be taken into account in determining whether a business was transferred as a going concern. However, the temporary closure of an undertaking and the resulting absence of staff at the time of the transfer do not of themselves preclude the possibility that there has been a transfer of an undertaking within the meaning of Article 1 (1) of the Directive. That is true, in particular, in circumstances such as those of this case, where the undertaking ceased to operate only for a short period which coincided, moreover, with the Christmas and New Year holidays.

In *Schmidt*[58] the national court in its two questions sought to ascertain whether the cleaning operations of a branch of an undertaking can be treated as part of a business within the meaning of the Directive and whether it is possible to do so where the work was performed by a single employee before being transferred by contract to an outside firm.

The ECJ ruled, *inter alia*, that the protection provided by the Directive applies, by virtue of Article 1(1), where the transfer relates only to a business or part of a business, that is to say, a part of an undertaking. In those circumstances the transfer relates to employees assigned to that part of the undertaking since, as the Court held in its judgment in *Botzen*[59] an employment relationship is essentially characterized by the link between the employee and the part of the undertaking or business to which he/she is assigned to carry out his/her duties. It went on to state:

"14. Thus, when an undertaking entrusts by contract the responsibility for operating one of its services, such as cleaning, to another undertaking which thereby assumes the obligations of an employer towards employees assigned to those duties, that operation may come within the scope of the directive. As the court held at paragraph 17 of its judgment in Watson Rask and Christensen, .. the fact that in such a case the activity transferred is for the transferor merely an ancillary activity not necessarily

57 Case 287/86 *Landsorganisationen i Danmark for Tjenerforbundet i Danmark* v *Ny Mølle Kro* [1987] ECR 5465.

58 Case C-392/92 *Christel Schmidt* v *Spar- und Leihkasse der Früheren Ämter Bordesholm, Kiel und Cronshagen* [1994] ECR 1311.

59 Case 186/83 *Arie Botzen et al* v *Rotterdamsche Droogdok Maatschappij BV* [1985] ECR 519.

connected with its objects cannot have the effect of excluding that operation from the scope of the directive."

In *Ledernes Hovedorganisation, Acting on behalf of Ole Rygård v Dansk Arbejdsgiverforening, Acting on behalf of Strø Mølle Akustik A/S*[60] the ECJ held that Article 1(1) of Directive 77/187/EEC must be interpreted as *not covering* the transfer by an undertaking to another undertaking of one of its building works with the view to its completion, by merely making available to the new contractor certain workers and materials for completing the work in question. The term "transfers of undertakings" assumes that what is transferred is a stable economic entity whose activity is not limited to performing one specific works contract.

In *Süzen*[61] the ECJ was asked whether the Directive applies to a situation in which a person who had entrusted the cleaning of his premises to a first undertaking terminates his contract with the latter and, for the performance of similar work, enters into a new contract with a second undertaking without any concomitant transfer of tangible or intangible business assets from one undertaking to the other.

The Court stated as it has done in a number of cases that in order to determine whether the conditions for the transfer of an entity are met, it is necessary to consider all the facts characterizing the transaction in question, including in particular the type of undertaking or business, whether or not its tangible assets, such as buildings and movable property, are transferred, the value of its intangible assets at the time of the transfer, whether or not the majority of its employees are taken over by the new employer, whether or not its customers are transferred, the degree of similarity between the activities carried on before and after the transfer, and the period, if any, for which those activities were suspended. All those circumstances are merely single factors in the overall assessment which must be made and cannot therefore be considered in isolation. The mere fact that the service provided by the old and the new awardees of a contract is similar does not therefore support the conclusion that an economic entity has been transferred.

The Court also ruled that an entity cannot be reduced to the activity entrusted to it. Its identity also emerges from other factors, such as its workforce, its management staff, the way in which its work is organized, its operating methods or indeed, where appropriate, the operational resources

---

[60]  Case C-48/94 [1995] ECR I-2745.

[61]  Case C-13/95 *Ayse Süzen* v *Zehnacker Gebäudereinigung GmbH Krankenhausservice* judgment of 11 March 1997, nyr.

available to it. The mere loss of a service contract to a competitor cannot, therefore, by itself indicate the existence of a transfer within the meaning of the Directive. In those circumstances, the service undertaking previously entrusted with the contract does not, on losing a customer, thereby cease fully to exist, and a business or part of a business belonging to it cannot be considered to have been transferred to the new awardee of the contract.

It must also be noted that, although the transfer of assets is one of the criteria to be taken into account by the national court in deciding whether an undertaking has in fact been transferred, the absence of such assets does not necessarily preclude the existence of such a transfer.

The national court, in assessing the facts characterizing the transaction in question, must take into account among other things the type of undertaking or business concerned. It follows that the degree of importance to be attached to each criterion for determining whether or not there has been a transfer within the meaning of the Directive will necessarily vary according to the activity carried on, or indeed the production or operating methods employed in the relevant undertaking, business or part of a business. Where in particular an economic entity is able, in certain sectors, to function without any significant tangible or intangible assets, the maintenance of its identity following the transaction affecting it cannot, depend on the transfer of such assets.

Since in certain labour-intensive sectors a group of workers engaged in a joint activity on a permanent basis may constitute an economic entity, it must be recognized that such an entity is capable of maintaining its identity after it has been transferred where the new employer does not merely pursue the activity in question but also takes over a major part, in terms of their numbers and skills, of the employees specially assigned by his predecessor to that task. In those circumstances, the new employer takes over a body of assets enabling him to carry on the activities or certain activities of the transferor undertaking on a regular basis. The Court ruled:

'...that the directive does not apply to a situation in which a person who had entrusted the cleaning of his premises to a first undertaking terminates his contract with the latter and, for the performance of similar work, enters into a new contract with a second undertaking, if there is no concomitant transfer from one undertaking to the other of significant tangible or intangible assets or taking over by the new employer of a major part of the workforce, in terms of their numbers and skills....'

## 6.2.5. Safeguarding of Employees' Rights

Article 3 of the Directive provides:

1. The transferor's rights and obligations arising from a contract of employment or from an employment relationship existing on the date of a transfer within the meaning of Article 1(1) shall, by reason of such transfer, be transferred to the transferee.

Member States may provide that, after the date of transfer within the meaning of Article 1(1) and in addition to the transferee, the transferor shall continue to be liable in respect of obligations which arose from a contract of employment or an employment relationship.

2. Following the transfer within the meaning of Article 1(1), the transferee shall continue to observe the terms and conditions agreed in any collective agreement on the same terms applicable to the transferor under that agreement, until the date of termination or expiry of the collective agreement or the entry into force or application of another collective agreement.

Member States may limit the period for observing such terms and conditions, with the provision that it shall not be less than one year.

3. Paragraphs 1 and 2 shall not cover employees' rights to old-age, invalidity or survivors' benefits under supplementary company or inter-company pension schemes outside the statutory social security schemes in Member States.

Member States shall adopt the measures necessary to protect the interests of employees and of persons no longer employed in the transferor's business at the time of the transfer within the meaning of Article 1(1) in respect of rights conferring on them immediate or prospective entitlement to old-age benefits, including survivors' benefits, under supplementary schemes referred to in the first subparagraph.

### 6.2.5.(i) Contract or Employment Relationship in Existence

The employment contract or the employment relationship must be in existence on the date of the transfer. This requirement has given rise to a number of Danish cases under Article 177 EEC[62] probably because the Danish implementing legislation is worded in a different way. In *Wendelboe*, the ECJ was asked:

"Does the Council Directive... require the Member States to enact provisions under which the transferee of an undertaking becomes liable in respect of obligations concerning holiday pay and compensation to employees who were not employed in the undertaking on the date of transfer?".

The ECJ held that it follows from a textual interpretation of that provision in the various language versions that it refers only to the rights and obligations of workers whose contract of employment or employment relationship is in force on the date of the transfer and not to those who have ceased to be employed by the undertaking in question at the time of the transfer.

---

[62] See in particular: Case 19/83 *Wendelboe* [1985] ECR 457; Case 287/86 *Ny Mølle Kro* [1987] ECR 5465; Case 101/87 *Bork* [1988] ECR 3057.

The existence or otherwise of a contract of employment or an employment relationship on the date of the transfer within the meaning of Article 3(1) of the Directive must be established on the basis of the rules of national law, subject however, to observance of the mandatory provisions of the Directive and, more particularly, Article 4(1) thereof, concerning the protection of employees against dismissal by the transferor or the transferee by reason of the transfer. It is for the national court to decide, on the basis of those factors, whether or not, on the date of the transfer, the employees in question were linked to the undertaking by virtue of a contract of employment or employment relationship.

### 6.2.5.(ii) Automatic transfer of the employer's obligations

In *Harry Berg and Johannes Theodorus Maria Busschers* v *Ivo Martin Besselsen*[63] the ECJ considered the question whether the Directive provides for an automatic release of the transferor from obligations arising from the contract of employment even in cases where the employees object to that. The ECJ replied in the affirmative. The Court ruled that according to the first subparagraph of Article 3(1) of the Directive "the transferor's rights and obligations arising from a contract of employment or from an employment relationship existing on the date of the transfer... shall, by reason of such transfer, be transferred to the transferee." the second subparagraph of this provision states that : "member states may provide that, after the date of the transfer... and in addition to the transferee, the transferor shall continue to be liable in respect of obligations which arose from a contract of employment or an employment relationship ". An analysis of Article 3(1) and, more particularly, the relationship between the first and second subparagraphs of this paragraph show that the transfer of an undertaking entails the automatic transfer from the transferor to the transferee of the employer's obligations arising from a contract of employment or an employment relationship, subject to the right of Member States to provide for joint liability of the transferor and transferee following the transfer. It follows that, unless the Member States avail themselves of this possibility, the transferor is released from his/her obligations as an employer solely by reason of the transfer and that this legal consequence is not conditional on the consent of the employees concerned. The ECJ confirmed this view in *Grigorios Katsikas et al* v *Angelo Konstantinidis et al.*[64]

---

[63]  Cases 144 and 145/87 [1988] ECR 2559.

[64]  Joined Cases C-132/91, C-138/91 and C-139/91 [1992] ECR I-6577.

### 6.2.5.(iii) Collective and Individual Rights

In *Landsorganisationen i Danmark for Tjenerforbundet i Danmark* v *Ny Mølle Kro*[65] the ECJ was asked by the Danish Labour Court:

> (4)    Must Article 3(2) of the Directive be interpreted as meaning that the transferee must continue to observe the terms of a collective agreement binding the transferor regarding pay and working conditions notwithstanding the fact that at the time of the transfer no employees were employed by the undertaking?

The ECJ reformulated the question as meaning that the Arbejdsretten (the Labour Court) essentially asked whether Article 3(2) of Directive 77/187/EEC must be interpreted as obliging the transferee to continue to observe the terms and conditions agreed in any collective agreement in respect of workers who were not employed by the undertaking at the time of its transfer.

According to Landsorganisationen i Danmark (the Danish Confederation of Trade Unions) that question should be answered in the affirmative. On the other hand, Dansk Arbejdsgiverforening (the Danish Confederation of Employers), the United Kingdom and the Commission emphasized that only persons who are employed by the undertaking at the time of the transfer may take advantage of the Directive, and not persons who are engaged after the transfer.

The Court held, as it had previously stated, in its judgment in *Foreningen af Arbejdsledere i Danmark* v *Danmols Inventar*,[66] that the purpose of the Directive is to ensure, as far as possible, that the contract of employment or employment relationship continues unchanged with the transferee, in order to prevent the workers concerned from being placed in a less favourable position solely as a result of the transfer. It is therefore consistent with the scheme of the Directive to interpret it as meaning that unless otherwise expressly provided, it may be relied on solely by workers whose contract of employment or employment relationship is in existence at the time of the transfer subject, however, to compliance with the mandatory provisions of the Directive concerning protection of employees from dismissal as a result of the transfer.

It followed that Article 3(2) of the Directive is intended to ensure the continued observance by the transferee of the terms and conditions of employment agreed in a collective agreement only in respect of workers who

---

[65]    Case 287/86 [1987] ECR 5465.

[66]    Case 105/84 [1985] ECR 2639.

were already employed by the undertaking at the date of the transfer, and not as regards persons who were engaged after that date.

For those reasons the reply to the fourth question was that Article 3(2) of Directive 77/187/EEC, properly construed, does not oblige the transferee to continue to observe the terms and conditions agreed in a collective agreement in respect of workers who were not employed by the undertaking at the time of the transfer.

### 6.2.6. Dismissal

Article 4(1) of the Directive provides that "the transfer of an undertaking, business or part of a business shall not in itself constitute grounds for dismissal by the transferor or the transferee". However, that provision is not to "stand in the way of dismissals that may take place for economic, technical or organizational reasons entailing changes in the workforce".

If the contract of employment or the employment relationship is terminated because the transfer within the meaning of Article 1(1) involves a substantial change in working conditions to the detriment of the employee, the employer shall be regarded as having been responsible for termination of the contract of employment or of the employment relationship.

### 6.2.7. Information and Consultation

### 6.2.7.(i). Employee Representatives

The Directive was not intended to bring about global harmonization of the national systems of employee representation in the firm. However, in the infringement case against the UK[67] the ECJ held that

> 1. Despite the limited character of the harmonization of rules in respect of the safeguarding of employees' rights in the event of transfers of undertakings which Directive 77/187 was intended to bring about, national rules which, by not providing for a system for the designation of employees' representatives in an undertaking where an employer refuses to recognize such representatives, allow an employer to frustrate the protection provided for employees by Article 6(1) and (2) of Directive 77/187, must be regarded as contrary to the provisions of that directive.

It is thus necessary for a Member State to have some kind of employee representation in order to comply with the Directive. If the business preserves its autonomy, status and function, as laid down by the laws, regulations or

---

[67] Case C-382/92 [1994] ECR I-2435

administrative provisions of the Member States, the representatives or the representation of the employees affected by the transfer within the meaning of Article 1(1) shall also be preserved.

The first subparagraph shall not apply if, under the laws, regulations, administrative provisions or practice of the Member States, the conditions necessary for the re-appointment of the representatives of the employees or for the reconstitution of the representation of the employees are fulfilled.

If the term of office of the representatives of the employees affected by a transfer within the meaning of Article 1(1) expires as a result of the transfer, the representatives shall continue to enjoy the protection provided by the laws, regulations, administrative provisions or practice of the Member States.

### 6.2.7.(ii). Information

According to Article 6 the transferor and the transferee shall be required to inform the representatives of their respective employees affected by a transfer within the meaning of Article 1(1) of the following:

- the reasons for the transfer,
- the legal, economic and social implications of the transfer for the employees,
- measures envisaged in relation to the employees.

The transferor must give such information to the representatives of his/her employees in good time before the transfer is carried out. The transferee must give such information to the representatives of his/her employees in good time, and in any event before his/her employees are directly affected by the transfer as regards their conditions of work and employment.

### 6.2.7.(iii). Consultation

If the transferor or the transferee envisages measures in relation to his/her employees, he or she shall consult his/her representatives of the employees in good time on such measures with a view to seeking agreement.

Member States whose laws, regulations or administrative provisions provide that representatives of the employees may have recourse to an arbitration board to obtain a decision on the measures to be taken in relation to employees may limit the obligations laid down in paragraphs 1 and 2 to cases where the transfer carried out gives rise to a change in the business likely to entail serious disadvantages for a considerable number of the employees.

The information and consultations shall cover at least the measures envisaged in relation to the employees. The information must be provided and consultations take place in good time before the change in the business as referred to in the first subparagraph is effected. Member States may limit the obligations laid down in paragraphs 1, 2 and 3 to undertakings or businesses which, in respect of the number of employees, fulfil the conditions for the election or designation of a collegiate body representing the employees. Member States may provide that where there are no representatives of the employees in an undertaking or business, the employees concerned must be informed in advance when a transfer within the meaning of Article 1(1) is about to take place.

Whereas the obligation to provide information is general, the consultation obligation is limited. This obligation exists when the transferor or transferee envisages measures in relation to his/her employees (Article 6.2), for example a reduction in the size of the workforce. Consultation takes place "with a view to seeking agreement". The Court of Justice has interpreted a similar provision in Directive 75/129/EEC (collective redundancies) as not creating an obligation with regard to results.[68] This consultation must be made "in good time" with the employees' representatives. In the infringement case against the UK[69] the ECJ held that

3. National rules which merely require a transferor or transferee envisaging measures in relation to employees affected by a transfer to consult the representatives of trade unions recognized by him, to take into consideration any representations made by them, to reply to those representations and, if he rejects them, to provide reasons, whereas Article 6(2) of Directive 77/187 on the approximation of the laws of the Member States relating to the safeguarding of employees' rights in the event of transfers of undertakings imposes an obligation to consult representatives of the employees "with a view to seeking agreement", fail correctly to transpose that directive.

4. Where a Community directive does not specifically provide any penalty for an infringement or refers for that purpose to national laws, regulations and administrative provisions, Article 5 of the Treaty requires the Member States to take all measures necessary to guarantee the application and effectiveness of Community law. For that purpose, while the choice of penalties remains within their discretion, they must ensure in particular that infringements of Community law are penalized under conditions, both procedural and substantive, which are analogous to those applicable to infringements of national law of a similar nature and importance and which, in any event, make the penalty effective, proportionate and dissuasive.

---

[68] Case 284/83 [1985] ECR 553.

[69] Case C-382/92 [1994] ECR I-2435

In cases where awards are also due by reason of infringements of the rules on redundancies, compensation which may be set off against such awards cannot be regarded as sufficiently deterrent for employers who fail to comply with their obligation under Article 6 of Directive 77/187 to inform and consult their employees' representatives.

### 6.2.8. Memorandum Explaining the Acquired Rights of Workers

The Commission published in March 1997[70] a Memorandum on Acquired Rights of Workers in Cases of Transfers of Undertakings, with a view to increasing information and guidance on the application of Community law, taking into account the large number of cases which have come before the Court.

### 6.2.9. Future amendments

In the Action Programme relating to the Social Charter 1989 the Commission proposes amendments to the transfer of undertakings Directive. The Commission adopted a proposal in September 1994 to clarify the Directive.[71] This proposal is currently before the Council of Ministers.

### 6.3. INSOLVENCY

An attempt to harmonize the Member States' protection of workers' rights in the event of insolvency of an employer was made in Council Directive 80/987/EEC.[72]In the Preamble it is pointed out that the differences in protection offered by the Member States may directly affect the functioning of the Common Market and this justifies the use of Article 100 EEC as the legal base for the Directive.

The transitional period for this Directive ended on 23 October 1983. The ECJ has held that the Directive may not be relied upon to protect workers affected by an insolvency which took place before 23 October 1983.[73]

---

[70] COM(97)85. It may be found on the Internet http://europa.eu.int/rapid/. In paragraph 11.3.2 of the Medium-Term Social Action Programme (1995-1997) the Commission declared its intention to produce this Memorandum.

[71] COM(94)300, OJ 1994 C 274/10.

[72] OJ L 283/80.

[73] Joined Cases C-140/91, C-141/91, C-278/91 *Suffritti, Fiori, Giacometti, Dal Pane and Baletti v Instituto Nazionale della Providenza Sociale* [1992] ECR I-6337.

### 6.3.1. Scope of Council Directive 80/987/EEC

Section 1 defines the scope of the Directive and provides some definitions of the kind of insolvency situation to which it applies. An insolvency situation is defined in Article 2 in two ways. First, where a request has been made for the opening of proceedings involving the employer's assets according to national law in order to satisfy the claims of creditors and which make it possible to take into account the rights of workers protected in the Directive. Secondly, where an authority is competent under national law to either

- open insolvency proceedings or
- establish that the employer's undertaking or business has been definitively closed down and that the viable assets are insufficient to warrant the opening of the proceedings.

Member States are given a wide amount of discretion to apply national definitions to concepts such as "employer", "employee", "pay", "right conferring immediate entitlement" and "right conferring prospective entitlement". Article 1 of the Directive provides a sweeping statement that the Directive

".... shall apply to employee's claims arising from contracts of employment or employment relationships and existing against employers who are in a state of insolvency within the meaning of Article 2(1)".

Article 1(2) immediately goes on to limit the scope of the Directive by allowing the Member States to exclude certain employees

"... by virtue of the special nature of the employee's contract of employment or employment relationship or of the existence of other forms of guarantee offering the employee protection equivalent to that resulting from this Directive."

The categories of employees whose claims may be lawfully excluded from the scope of the Directive are listed in an Annex to the Directive. The issue of the scope of these exclusions was examined in *Commission v Hellenic Republic*.[74] The Commission alleged that Greece had failed to provide guarantees for two categories of employees. Under Point I "Employees having a contract of employment, or an employment relationship, of a special nature" and under Point II "the master and members of the crew of a fishing vessel if, and to the

---

[74]  Case C-53/88 [1990] ECR I-3917.

extent that they are, remunerated by a share in the profits or gross earnings of the vessel... and the crews of sea-going vessels."

The ECJ would not uphold the Commission's complaint as regards the first category of employee. The ECJ also found that at the time of the Commission's complaint the Greek government had failed to comply with other parts of the Insolvency Directive, namely Articles 2, 4, 7 and 8. Although by the time of the hearing the Greek government had rectified the situation the ECJ was willing to issue a decalaration to the effect that the Greek government was in breach of its obligations under Community law. In *Miret*[75] the Court held that higher management staff may not be excluded from the scope of Directive 80/987/EEC, where they are classified under national law as employees and are not listed in section I of the Annex to the Directive.

In the second *Francovich* case[76] the ECJ held that the Directive is to be interpreted as applying to all employees, other than those in the categories listed in the Annex thereto, whose employers may, under the applicable national law, be made subject to proceedings involving their assets in order to satisfy collectively the claims of creditors.

The fact that the Directive thus protects only employees faced with a situation in which their employer is insolvent in accordance with that definition is not such as to call into question its validity in the light of the principle of equal treatment.

In the first place, in the exercise of the powers conferred on them by Article 100 EC, the Community institutions must be recognized as having a discretion in particular with regard to the possibility of proceeding towards harmonization only in stages, given the specific nature of the field in which coordination is sought and the difficulties involved in any harmonization.

In addition, it undoubtedly constitutes a further step towards providing improved working conditions and an improved standard of living for workers throughout the Community and towards the gradual harmonization of laws in the field for a system of guarantees previously available, in differing forms, in some Member States to be extended to all the Member States.

Finally, in the light of the difficulties inherent in the very concept of insolvency which the harmonization was intended to overcome, the objective criterion used to define the persons entitled to protection under that system is justified.

---

[75] Case C-334/92 *Teodoro Wagner Miret* v *Fondo de Garantia Salarial* [1993] ECR I-6911.

[76] Case C-479/93 *Andrea Francovich* v *Italian Republic* [1995] ECR I-3843

### 6.3.2. Provisions Concerning Guarantee Institutions

Article 3 obliges the Member States to take the necessary measures to ensure that guarantee institutions guarantee the payment of employee's outstanding claims resulting from contracts of employment or employment relationships relating to pay for the period prior to a given date over which the Member States have various options in choosing. The given date may be:

- either that of the onset of the employer's insolvency;
- or that of the notice of dismissal issued to the employee concerned on account of the employer's insolvency or
- that of the onset of the employer's insolvency or that on which the contract of employment or the employment relationship with the employee concerned was discontinued on account of the employer's insolvency.

The obligation of Article 3 is circumscribed by giving the Member States the option of limiting the liability of guarantee institutions in Article 4. Where an option is taken up Article 4(2) provides certain safeguards.

In the situation where the given date in Article 3(2) relates to the onset of the employer's insolvency the Member State must ensure the payment of outstanding claims relating to pay for the last three months of the contract of employment or employment relationship occurring within a period of six months preceding the date of the onset of the employer's insolvency. Where the given date is that of the notice of dismissal issued to the employee on account of the employer's insolvency the Member State must ensure the payment of outstanding claims relating to pay for the last 3 months of the contract of employment or employment relationship preceding the date of the notice of dismissal issued to the employee. Finally, where the given date is that of the onset of the employer's insolvency (or that on which the contract of employment/employment relationship was discontinued) the Member State must ensure the payment of outstanding claims relating to pay for the last 18 months of the contract of employment or employment relationship. However, Member States may limit the liability to make payment to pay corresponding to a period of 8 weeks or to several shorter periods totalling 8 weeks. Member States may also set a ceiling to the liability of employee's outstanding claims, justified by showing that higher payments go beyond the social objective of Council Directive 80/987/EEC. A Member State exercising this option must inform the Commission of the methods utilised to set the ceiling.

Article 5 stipulates that the Member States must establish detailed rules for the organisation, financing and operation of the guarantee institutions. These rules must comply with 3 principles:

(a)   the assets of the institutions shall be independent of the employers' operating capital and be inaccessible to proceedings for insolvency;

(b)   employers shall contribute to financing, unless it is fully covered by the public authorities;

(c)   the institutions' liabilities shall not depend on whether or not obligations to contribute to financing have been fulfilled.

The Commission took an infringement action against Italy for failure to implement Articles 3 and 5 of the Directive relating to the failure to guarantee outstanding claims of employees.[77] The Italian government had argued that the various provisions in force gave equivalent, if not greater protection, than Council Directive 80/987/EEC. The Commission successfully argued that the Italian system of paying a severance grant on the termination of employment from the Italian Guarantee Fund altered the guarantees specifically authorised by Council Directive 80/987/EEC. The guarantees from the Fund did not extend to the payment of outstanding claims for salaries of employees who had not been regularly paid while in employment because of the employer's insolvency. The ECJ pointed out that Articles 3 and 5 were intended to ensure the payment of such claims. Furthermore, the severance grant system did not apply to all classes of employee and all kinds of undertakings. For example, Directors, apprentices and homeworkers were excluded. These exclusions could not be justified under Italian law and were contrary to the Directive. Another failure of the operation of the Italian system was the fact that the guarantees were not automatically available but depended upon various conditions which were individually considered by the Inter-Ministerial Committee for Industrial Policy.

Italy failed to comply with the ECJ ruling and in a later case, *Francovich and Bonifaci v Italy*[78] the ECJ held that it was possible for an individual who has suffered loss as a result of a Member State's failure to implement the provisions of a Directive to sue the Member State for damages in the national courts (see Chapter One).

### 6.3.3. Relationship with Statutory Social Security

Articles 6-8 deal with the interaction of insolvency claims and statutory social security systems. Article 6 allows the Member States to exclude the obligations contained in Articles 3, 4 and 5 (described above) from applying to contribu-

---

[77]   Case 22/87 *EC Commission* v *Italy* [1989] ECR 143.

[78]   Joined Cases C-6/90 and C-9/90 [1991] ECR I-5357. See Szyszczak (1992b).

tions due under national social security schemes or under supplementary company or inter-company pension schemes outside the national statutory social security schemes. However, Article 7 obliges the Member States to take the necessary measures to ensure that non-payment of compulsory contributions due from the employer before the insolvency to insurance institutions under national statutory social security schemes does not adversely affect employee's benefit entitlement in respect of these insurance institutions inasmuch as the employees' contributions were deducted at source from the remuneration paid. The seriousness of the guarantees was discussed in *Commission* v *Italy*.[79]The ECJ held that Article 7 makes the guarantee of employees' entitlement to benefits subject to only one condition, namely that the employees' contributions of social security have been deducted from the remuneration paid to the employee.[80]The Italian government unsuccessfully argued that it was possible to deal with specific cases where social security contributions made it necessary for the employees to receive a pension.[81]The ECJ rejected this contention since the provision of the pension would be dependent upon the employer having made payments to a special adjustment fund. If the employer was insolvent, the provision of the pension would then depend upon employee contributions. Thus, the provision of automatic benefits, demanded by Article 7 was not met.[82]In addition, Article 8 imposes an obligation upon the Member States to ensure the protection of the interests of employees who have left the employment at the onset of the insolvency. These rights include immediate or prospective entitlement to old age benefits (including survivors' benefits) under supplementary company or inter-company pension schemes outside national statutory social security schemes.

The Member States are not precluded from applying or introducing measures which are more favourable to employees (Article 9) and Member States also have the option to take measures to avoid abuses and to refuse or reduce the liability in Article 3 (relating to guarantee institutions) or the guarantee obligation of Article 7 if it appears that fulfilment of the obligation is unjustifiable because of the existence of special links between the employee and the employer and of common interests resulting in collusion between them.

---

[79] Case 22/87 [1989] ECR 143.

[80] Para 28.

[81] This was possible under Article 13 of Law No 1338 12 August 1962 (Guri No 229, 11.9.1962).

[82] Para 30.

## 6.4. DUTY TO INFORM THE EMPLOYEE OF THE CONDITIONS APPLICABLE TO THE EMPLOYMENT CONTRACT

The development, in the Member States, of new forms of work has led to an increase in the number of types of employment relationships.[83] Faced with this development, certain Member States have considered it necessary to subject employment relationships to formal requirements.[84] These provisions are designed to provide employees with improved protection against possible infringements of their rights and to create greater transparency on the labour market. The relevant legislation of the Member States differs considerably on such fundamental points as the requirement to inform employees in writing of the main terms of the contract or employment relationship. Formal requirements in employment contracts may also serve different purposes such as warning the employee or serving as a proof of the contract or a means to support substantive employment protection rules, for example bans on discrimination.

It follows from Article 9 of the Rome Convention on the Law Applicable to Contractual Obligations that a contract of employment, is valid as regards form if it fulfills either the law of the *lex loci contractus* or of the *lex causa*. It will therefore often be somewhat difficult to assess whether an employment contract with connections to different Member States does or does not fulfill the formal requirements it should. Harmonization of formal requirements will consequently add to the legal certainty surrounding employment contracts.

In the continental European countries legislation plays a predominant role as a source of law in employment matters. Some 30 years ago the normal open-ended fulltime contract was more or less mandatory. During recent times these countries have allowed various forms of non-standard employment contracts (part-time, fixed-term, temporary, etc) in many instances on the condition that certain formal requirements are met.

In the Anglo-Saxon and Nordic states legislation has been used to a much lesser extent. All types of employment contracts have traditionally been lawful without formal requirements laid down by legislation. To a certain extent they are regulated by collective agreement. It must, however, be mentioned that United Kingdom and Irish legislation requires the employer to provide the employee with written particulars which constitute prima facie proof of the terms of the contract.

---

[83]  See further Kravaritou-Manitakis (1988).

[84]  Cf Nielsen (1990b).

Introduction of general rules at European level on form and proof of all contracts of employment irrespective of whether they are open-ended full-time contracts or non-standard types of contracts (fixed-term, part-time, etc) thus combines the continental European tradition of surrounding non-standard-employment contracts by formalities with the Anglo-Saxon tradition of requiring the employer to provide written particulars of the terms of the employment contract.

### 6.4.1. Purpose of Directive 91/533/EEC

Point 9 of the Social Charter 1989 states:

"The conditions of employment of every worker of the European Community shall be stipulated in laws, a collective agreement or a contract of employment, according to arrangements applying in each country."

Council Directive 91/533/EEC[85] on an employer's obligation to inform employees of the conditions applicable to the contract or employment relationship was adopted on 14 October 1991.[86] The Directive is based upon Article 100 EEC.[87]

According to the Preamble, it is the purpose of Directive 91/533/EEC to ensure that the conditions of employment of every worker of the Community shall be stipulated in laws, a collective agreement or a contract of employment, according to arrangements applying in each country. The Directive establishes at Community level the general requirement that every employee must be provided with a document containing information on the essential elements of his/her contract or employment relationship. In order to maintain a certain degree of flexibility in employment relationships, Member States are allowed to exclude certain limited cases of employment relationship from the Directive's scope of application.

---

[85]  OJ 1991 L 288/32.

[86]  Cf Clark and Hall (1992)

[87]  See the proposal from the EC Commission OJ C 24/1991; the Opinion of the European Parliament OJ C 240/1991; and the Opinion of the Economic and Social Committee OJ C 159/1991.

In 1996, a German Court (Landesarbeitsgericht Hamm) referred questions concerning the interpretation of the purpose of the Directive to the ECJ for a preliminary ruling.[88] The referring court asked:

1. In view of the objective, stated in the preamble to Council Directive 91/533/EEC ..., of 'providing employees with improved protection against possible infringements of their rights and to create greater transparency on the labour market', is it the purpose of Article 2 of the said Directive to modify (in the employee's favour) the burden of proof in that the list of minimum requirements in Article 2 (2) of Directive 91/533/EEC is intended to ensure that the employee does not encounter difficulties of proof regarding the listed points when enforcing his contractual rights in employment-law disputes?

2. If the answer to Question 1 is in the affirmative: has Article 2 (2) (c) (ii) of Directive 91/533/EEC been directly applicable since 1 July 1993 against the State acting as an employer in private law because:
- the Federal Republic of Germany did not (completely) implement Directive 91/533/EEC by 30 June 1993, the expiry date of the period for implementation,
- the abovementioned provision of the Directive is unconditional and can therefore be incorporated in national law without any further implementing act, the Directive confers upon the individual employee rights against the State acting as employer?

### 6.4.2. Scope

The Directive applies to every paid employee having a contract or employment relationship defined by the law in force in a Member State and/or governed by the law in force in a Member State. In view of the need to maintain a certain degree of flexibility in employment relationships, Member States are able to exclude certain limited cases of employment relationship from the Directive's scope of application. Member States may provide that the Directive shall not apply to employees having a contract or employment relationship:

(a)    -    with a total duration not exceeding one month, and/or
(b)    -    with a working week not exceeding eight hours; or
(c)    -    of a casual and/or specific nature provided, in these cases, that its non-application is justified by objective considerations.

As regards the concept of an employment contract there is an important difference between civil law and Nordic law on the one hand and Anglo-Irish

---

[88] C-253/96 *Helmut Kampelmann* v *Landschaftsverband Westfalen-Lippe*, C-254/96 *Wilfried Tilsch* v *Landschaftsverband Westfalen-Lippe*, C-255/96 *Dieter Klingelhöfer* v *Landschaftsverband Westfalen-Lippe*), C-256/96 *Heinrich Schmidt* v *Landschaftsverband Westfalen-Lippe*, C-257/96 *Stadtwerke Witten GmbH* v *Andreas Schade* and C-258/96 *Klaus Haseley* v *Stadtwerke Altena GmbH* pending

law on the other hand. The legal concept of a contract of employment in continental and Nordic Member States is broader than in Ireland and the United Kingdom and therefore various categories of workers who have statutory employment rights on the Continent are excluded therefrom in Ireland and the United Kingdom.

The continental European countries and the Nordic countries apply a broad concept of an employment contract resulting in nearly all persons being in employment also being covered by a contract of employment, whereas the United Kingdom applies a much narrower concept of contract of employment. The significance of the United Kingdom definition of a contract of employment is that nearly all statutory employment rights are limited to "employees" under a "contract of employment". The effect is to exclude about one-third of those in employment from protection. If a United Kingdom employer wants to circumvent employment rights the easy way to do so is not to enter into an employment contract but "only" an employment relationship.

It is partly because of the narrow British definition of an employment contract that employment directives use the words "contract of employment or employment relationship." The narrow English concept "employment contract" also influences the legal discussion in the Community on the implementation of Directives, see for example the following extract from a report on the Directives on equality:[89]

> "... the present author[90] believes that the contract of employment is a particularly unsuitable mechanism for drawing the boundaries of the Equality Directives."

Traditional elements in the definition of contracts of employment are: an agreement on performance of work, a certain element of time, remuneration, and above all the dependency or subordination of one party to another party. These criteria still seem to be the key concepts used to determine whether there is a contract of employment, or not.

### 6.4.3. Obligation to provide information

Under Article 2 an employer shall be obliged to notify an employee of the essential aspects of the contract or employment relationship. The information shall cover at least the following:

---

[89] Network of Experts on the implementation of the equality directives, Final Consolidated Report 1988 10.

[90] Ie the (then) co-ordinator for the network: Ferdinand von Prondzynski.

(a) the identities of the parties;

(b) the place of work; where there is no fixed or main place of work, the principle that the employee is employed at various places and the registered place of business or, where appropriate, the domicile of the employer;

(c) (i) the title, grade, nature or category of the work for which the employee is employed; or
(ii) a brief specification or description of the work;

(d) the date of commencement of the contract or employment relationship;

(e) in the case of a temporary contract or employment relationship, the expected duration thereof;

(f) the amount of paid leave to which the employee is entitled or, where this cannot be indicated when the information is given, the procedures for allocating and determining such leave;

(g) the length of the periods of notice to be observed by the employer and the employee should their contract or employment relationship be terminated or, where this cannot be indicated when the information is given, the method for determining such periods of notice;

(h) the initial basic amount, the other component elements and the frequency of payment of the remuneration to which the employee is entitled;

(i) the length of the employee's normal working day or week;

(j) where appropriate:
(i) the collective agreements governing the employee's conditions of work; or
(ii) in the case of collective agreements concluded outside the business by special joint bodies or institutions, the name of the competent body or joint institution within which the agreements were concluded.

3. The information referred to in paragraph 2 (f), (g), (h) and (i) may, where appropriate, be given in the form of a reference to the laws, regulations and administrative or statutory provisions or collective agreements governing those particular points.

In the abovementioned reference for a preliminary ruling[91] the German court also asked the following questions concerning what information the employer should provide:

3. If the answer to Question 2 is in the affirmative: must the information which the employer is required to give under Article 2 (2) (c) (ii) of Directive 91/533/EEC concerning the 'nature or category of the work' be understood as meaning the classification of a job in the sense that, if the employee's grading according to the salary scheme under a collective agreement requires fulfilment of the work specifications of a particular case of a salary grade, he must be able to see, from the

---

[91] C-253/96 *Helmut Kampelmann* v *Landschaftsverband Westfalen-Lippe*, C-254/96 *Wilfried Tilsch* v *Landschaftsverband Westfalen-Lippe*, C-255/96 *Dieter Klingelhöfer* v *Landschaftsverband Westfalen-Lippe*), C-256/96 *Heinrich Schmidt* v *Landschaftsverband Westfalen-Lippe*, C-257/96 *Stadtwerke Witten GmbH* v *Andreas Schade* and C-258/96 *Klaus Haseley* v *Stadtwerke Altena GmbH* pending

notification of his grading in a particular salary grade and case, whether he is entitled to

- advancement on the basis of a continuous period of satisfactory service or advancement by case in salary grades (C-253/96),
- advancement on the basis of a continuous period of satisfactory service (C-254/96, C-255/96, C-256/96),
- advancement on the basis of a continuous period of satisfactory service and/or advancement by case (C-257/96, C-258/96)?

4. If the answer to Question 3 is in the affirmative: does the notification pursuant to Article 2 (2) (c) (ii) of Directive 91/533/EEC bind the employer in the sense that he is bound by the classification of the job notified to the employee until such time as he (the employer) proves that the grading was incorrect, or at least until he shows conclusively (perhaps in the form of a job assessment) that he graded the employee mistakenly or that the classification of the work has been lowered in the course of time or by amendment to the collective agreement?

5. If the answer to Question 4 is in the affirmative: is the implementation in German law of Article 9 (2) of Directive 91/533/EEC by the Information Act of 20 July 1995 (Bundesgesetzblatt I, p. 946), to the effect that the employer has no obligation to give the employee written notification in the case of an employment relationship in existence when the Act comes into force, 'if and so far as an earlier document or a written contract of employment gives the particulars required' (paragraph 4, sentence 2, of the Information Act), to be regarded as in conformity with Community law, with the consequence that such earlier notifications which satisfy the requirements of Directive 91/533/EEC, whether it has been implemented or whether, in the absence of implementation, it is directly applicable, continue to be valid, with the consequence that, if the employer gives a more recent written notification (in the present case, in the course of proceedings) which conflicts with the earlier one, he must prove that the later notification is correct?

## 6.4.4. Means of information

Article 3 provides that the obligation to provide information may be met by means of a written contract, a letter of appointment or one or more other documents or, if they are lacking, a written statement signed by the employer.

## 6.4.5. Expatriate employees

In the case of expatriate employees, the latter must, in addition to the main terms of his or her contract or employment relationship, be supplied with relevant information connected with his or her secondment. According to Article 4 where an employee is required to work in a country or countries other than the Member State whose law and/or practice governs the contract or employment relationship, the document(s) referred to in Article 3 must be in his/her possession before his/her departure and must include at least the following additional information:

(a) the duration of the employment abroad;
(b) the currency to be used for the payment of remuneration;
(c) where appropriate, the benefits in cash or kind attendant on the employment abroad;
(d) where appropriate, the conditions governing the employee's repatriation.

The information referred to in paragraph 1(b) and (c) may, where appropriate, be given in the form of a reference to the laws, regulations and administrative or statutory provisions or collective agreements governing those particular points. Paragraphs 1 and 2 do not apply if the duration of the employment outside the country lasts for one month or less.

### 6.4.6. Change in the Terms

In order to protect the interests of employees in relation to obtaining a document, any change in the main terms of the contract or employment relationship must be communicated to them in writing.

Article 5 provides that any change in the details referred to in Articles 2(2) and 4(1) must be the subject of a written document to be given by the employer to the employee at the earliest opportunity and not later than one month after the date of entry into effect of the change in question. The written document referred to in paragraph 1 shall not be compulsory in the event of a change in the laws, regulations and administrative or statutory provisions or collective agreements cited in the documents referred to above.

### 6.4.7. More Favourable Provisions and Defence of Rights

The Directive does not affect the Member States' prerogative to apply or to introduce laws, regulations or administrative provisions which are more favourable to employees or to encourage or permit the application of agreements which are more favourable to employees. It is necessary for Member States to guarantee that employees can claim the rights conferred on them by the Directive. Member States shall introduce into their national legal systems such measures as are necessary to enable all employees who consider themselves wronged by failure to comply with the obligations arising from the Directive to pursue their claims by judicial process after possible recourse to other competent authorities.

# CHAPTER SEVEN

# INFORMATION, CONSULTATION AND WORKER PARTICIPATION

Collective labour law, which varies fundamentally from Member State to Member State, is the most difficult part of labour law to integrate into EU law. The issues dealt with in this Chapter are therefore highly controversial; many proposals have been put forward but have ended up being withdrawn without finding approval.[1] Most collective labour law issues are considered to be better suited for national action in accordance with the subsidiarity principle (discussed in Chapter One). The only major existing piece of EU legislation in this area is Directive 94/45/EC on European Works Councils in Community scale undertakings or groups of undertakings. In addition measures relating to information, consultation and participation rights in relation to collective redundancies and transfer of undertakings (discussed in Chapter Six) and with respect to the working environment (discussed under 7.2) have been adopted while proposals for board level worker representation in national and European companies are still being discussed (see under 7.4 and 7.5).

## 7.1. EU LAW AND COLLECTIVE LABOUR LAW

### 7.1.1. Collective Agreements

In Chapter One we discuss the limited role collective bargaining has hitherto played as a source of Community law or as a national source of implementing Community law and the prospects for the future of the "Social Dialogue" provided for in Article 118B EC. The TEU aimed to develop the role of collective bargaining at the European level.[2]

Collective bargaining at the European level exists in two major forms. The first being European wide framework agreements laying down basic principles which are then to be incorporated into national collective agreements. Only a

---

[1]   See Westermann (1984); Däubler (1977); Welch (1983); Pipkorn (1990).

[2]   Cf Guéry (1992) and Wedderburn (1992). See also Colaianni (1996).

very few of these collective agreements exist,[3] probably because of the low degree of internationalization of the trade union organizations. The few existing framework agreements at European level are very vague.[4]

The second type of European collective agreement is enterprise level cross-border collective agreements in multinational firms. A growing number of these agreements exist.[5] The current proposals for a European Works Council and for the European Company will (if adopted) develop this kind of European collective agreement. The existing voluntary schemes do not usually require more than divulgence of information while the draft Directive for a European Works Council goes beyond the information-only approach of the existing European level bodies and prescribes consultation and to some extent even negotiation (see below under 5.4).

At the national level there are major variations[6] between the Member States as regards the legal regulation of collective agreements in respect of negotiating rights and duties, levels of collective bargaining, the binding effect of the collective agreements, the right of workers to strike when a collective agreement is in force, extension of the normative effect of the agreement and its duration and coverage.

The 15 Member States can be divided into 3 labour law families:[7]

- 10 countries (Germany, France, Belgium, Holland, Luxembourg, Austria, Spain, Portugal, Italy and Greece) belong to the Roman-Germanic system
- 2 countries (England and Ireland) belong to the Anglo-Saxon system,
- 3 countries (Denmark, Finland and Sweden) belong to the Nordic system of labour regulation.

---

[3]  Cf Blanpain (1992b).

[4]  See as one example the Agreement between ETUC (European Trade Union Confederation) and CEEP (European Centre for Public Enterprises) concluded in September 1990, reprinted in *European Industrial Relations Review* (1991) p 30.

[5]  A survey of 31 multinational groups of undertakings operating in the Nordic countries and their cross border collective agreement arrangements has been carried out at the request of the Nordic Foundation for Industrial Development, see further Myrvang (1991). See also Gold and Hall (1990); Hall (1992) and the overview article in *European Industrial Relations Review* 228 and 229 (1993).

[6]  Cf Commission (1989).

[7]  Cf Commission "Comparative Study on Rules Governing Working Conditions in the Member States", Part 1, General Aspects, Bruxelles (1989).

The Nordic system[8] is based more on collective agreements and collective labour law than are the other systems.

### 7.1.2. Harmonization of National Collective Labour Law

There are many provisions in international labour law and Community labour law relating to individual employment law but rather few provisions on collective agreements.[9] This is an expression of the fact that it is easier to harmonize individual employment law than collective labour law.

In his article "On Uses and Misuses of Comparative Law" Otto Kahn-Freund argued that the the link between law and the political power-structure to-day constitutes the main impediment to legal "transplantations".[10] Applied to labour law this shows that collective labour law, which can hardly be altered without upsetting the balance of power between the "social partners" (trade unions and employers' organisations), is more difficult to transfer from country to country than individual employment law; and that rules on institutions and procedures are bound closer to the national context than are the substantive rules. In cases where the Constitution[11] codifies the political history of a country it is likewise "tough" law, which is relatively untransferable.

Germany[12] is the Member State which, at the national level, has the most elaborate institutional structures for worker participation. Much of the early Community discussion centred on the possibility and desirability of transferring the German model to the rest of Europe. These early proposals have failed and in the current proposals a much more pluralist approach has been adopted allowing for major national diversities (see under 5.5).

### 7.1.3. Multinational Enterprises

The trade unions have very few means of influencing the decisions of multinational enterprises on plant location within the European area.[13] One way of

---

[8]  Cf Bruun *et al* (1992).

[9]  See for example ILO-Convention No 87 and 98.

[10]  Cf Kahn-Freund (1978); Nielsen (1982).

[11]  Cf Ziskind (1984).

[12]  Cf Birk (1990); Adomeit (1989), Zachert (1989) and Däubler (1990).

[13]  On trade unions and multinationals, see Riddle (1976); ICFTU (1976).

obtaining such influence would be for the trade unions to internationalize to match the internationalization of multinational management. It has, however, proved very difficult for the trade unions to gain strength at the international level.[14]

Another way could be to use international law and Community law to provide for common minimum standards in multinational corporations irrespective of which European country they operate in and to guarantee effective rights of information, consultation and worker participation in multinationals. In 1977 the European Parliament called for the adoption of binding international measures on multinational groups.[15]

In the General Resolution of the ETUC Congress in Milan 1985 the ETUC stated:[16]

"Workers and their trade unions must be informed in full on all issues, whether economic, social or technical in nature, and irrespective of the size of the undertaking or department concerned. This information is absolutely essential if workers' representatives are to be in a position to be consulted and to exert real influence on any decisions. Binding international instruments must require employers to accept this, particularly in multinational companies."

At the ETUC Congress in Stockholm 1988 the ETUC called for:

- the right for workers' representatives to be fully informed, to be consulted and to negotiate on all important issues in the undertaking before decisions are taken;
- equal rights for the participation of worker representatives in all decision-making processes in the undertaking which are of concern to workers;
- extension of representation rights to all decision-making levels, according to how the undertakings, which are becoming more and more oriented towards the large Internal Market, are organised. Workers' representatives in all plants, irrespective of the structure of the undertakings operating on the Internal Market, must thus have the right to be informed and consulted on a firm's European plans and to negotiate on those plans and defend their interests jointly at the European level. The cost of this joint European representation of interests and of the information and consultation on the firm's European planning must be borne by the employer;
- the right for workers' representatives to be involved in the solving of problems concerning workers' interests, in particular so as to be able to influence the quality of decisions and to obstruct any decisions which are taken without prior negotiation, with arbitration being a possibility;

---

[14] Cf Wedderburn (1972).

[15] OJ C 1977 118/.

[16] ETUC (1991) p 4.

- the guaranteeing of these rights at European level through the establishment of a basic legal framework which can be extended by collective agreements. If certain provisions of this legal framework are implemented through collective agreements, a framework must be elaborated to have those agreements recognised, including any which concern the European planning of the company.

At the international level there are the Recommendations contained in the ILO-tripartite declaration on multinationals and the OECD Guidelines on Multinational Enterprise. They contribute to the development of a code of good practice requiring multinationals to respect national practices, to abstain from misuse of their power to transfer jobs and money from country to country and to provide workers with information and give them access to consultations with real decision-makers. The United Nations is preparing a Code of Conduct on Transnational Corporations.[17] These provisions are not binding and their legal effect is uncertain.[18]

A major reason for Community involvement in collective labour law issues is the growing importance of multinational enterprises which presumably will be increased by the development of the Internal Market. The Commission acknowledges the role of multinationals and has based its proposal[19] on the establishment of a European Works Council *inter alia* on the development of European-level information and consultation bodies in a number of large transnational undertakings or groups of undertakings and in drawing up its proposal has sought the views of management and employee representatives party to certain of these arrangements.

### 7.1.4. Information, Consultation and Worker Participation

The single collective labour law issue which has been most intensely dealt with at international and European level is information, consultation and worker participation. The question whether or not, and if so how, to establish cross-frontier rights of information and consultation[20] in relation to multinational em-

---

[17] The United Nations Code of Conduct on Transnational Corporations, London, Dordrecht, Boston 1988.

[18] Cf Horn (1980), Muchlinski (199 )

[19] COM(90) 581.

[20] Cf Nielsen (1990a).

ployers has during the last 20 years or so been the subject of discussion and proposals at the Community level.[21]

- In the Social Action Programme 1974 worker participation was a priority item.[22] The Programme called for the progressive involvement of workers or their representatives in the life of undertakings in the Community and the promotion of the involvement of management and labour in the economic and social decisions of the Community.
- At the national level the Member States use one or more of the following 4 methods of worker participation: shop stewards, safety representatives, works councils and board level workers' representation.
- At the Community level different models of increasing the workers' involvement in the life of the undertaking have been attempted. One model is worker participation in management bodies of the undertaking. This model underlies the draft Regulation for a European Company Statute[23] and the draft fifth Directive on Company Law.[24]

Another model is information and consultation of workers and/or workers' representatives in advance of important decisions leaving the institutional structure of the workers' representation to national practice. This model has been applied in the following adopted and proposed Directives:

- the Directive on collective redundancies[25]
- the Directive on the safeguarding of employees' rights in the event of transfers of undertakings[26]

---

[21]  Cf Docksey (1985) and (1986), Gold and Hall (1990) and Hall (1992).

[22]  Cf Shanks (1977).

[23]  *Bulletin of the EC* Supplement 4/75, COM(88) 320, OJ C 1989 263/, COM(91)174, OJ C 1991 138/, see below 5.5.

[24]  Amended Proposal for a Fifth Directive concerning the structure of public limited companies and the powers and obligations of their organs, O J C 1983 240/, *Bulletin of the EC* Supplement 6/83.

[25]  75/129/EEC. Discussed in Chapter Four.

[26]  77/187/EEC. Discussed in Chapter Four.

- the third company law Directive on mergers,[27] the sixth company law Directive on divisions[28] and the draft tenth Directive on cross-border mergers[29] refer to the information and consultation provisions in the transfer of undertakings Directive
- the framework Directive on the working environment[30]
- the draft Directive on voluntary part-time work[31]
- the draft Directive on temporary work[32]
- the draft Directive on atypical work[33]
- the draft Directive on information and consultation of the employees of undertakings with complex structures, in particular transnational undertakings (the so-called Vredeling-Directive).[34]

The Council Directive on the establishment of a European Works Council in Community-scale undertakings or groups of undertakings for the purposes of informing and consulting employees[35] provide for the establishment of a new transnational institution a European Works Council without interfering with national provisions on workers' representation at national level, including national group level as for example the French provisions on group works councils (comité de groupe) in Code du Travail Article L 439-1 to 5.[36]

---

[27]  78/855/EEC Article 12.

[28]  82/891/EEC Article 11.

[29]  O J C 1985 23/ Article 1(4), *Bulletin of the EC* Supplement 3/85.

[30]  89/391/EEC.

[31]  Amended Proposal O J C 1983 18/. This proposal has been withdrawn in conjunction with the presentation of new proposals on atypical work.

[32]  Amended Proposal O J C 1984 133/. This proposal has been withdrawn in connection with the presentation on proposals on atypical work.

[33]  COM(90) 228 SYN-280, Article 2(3) of the proposed Directive under Article 100 EEC.

[34]  Original proposal O J C 1980 297/, *Bulletin of the EC* Supplement 3/80, amended proposal O J C 1983 217/, *Bulletin of the EC* Supplement 2/83. This proposal has now been replaced by the proposal on the European Works Council.

[35]  94/45/EC. Proposal put forward in January 1991 in COM(90) 581, amended proposal of 16. September 1991 in COM(91) 345.

[36]  See Rodière (1990).

## 7.2. HEALTH AND SAFETY[37]

The most important Community provisions on information, consultation and worker participation are those found in the Framework Directive on the working environment[38] adopted under Article 118A EEC. The substantive law of this Directive is discussed in greater detail in Chapter 6. Only the worker participation aspect is dealt with here.

As the Directive is adopted under Article 118A ECit could have been adopted by qualified majority but is was approved unanimously. In view of the strong reservations some countries, in particular the UK, have had against other proposals on worker participation, it is perhaps surprising how easily worker participation rights in the field of the working environment were passed, but this is perhaps explained by the acceptance of employee involvement in health and safety matters in the UK.

### 7.2.1. Objective of Information, Consultation and Worker Participation

According to Article 1 of the Framework Directive 89/391/EEC on the Working Environment the object of the Directive is to introduce measures to encourage improvements in the safety and health of workers at work.

To that end it contains general principles concerning *inter alia* the informing, consultation, balanced participation in accordance with national laws and/or practices and training of workers and their representatives, as well as general guidelines for the implementation of the said principles.

In the Preamble to the Framework Directive 89/391/EEC information and balanced participation of the workers are called for in the following recitals:

> Whereas, in order to ensure an improved degree of protection, workers and/or their representives must be informed of the risks to their safety and health and of the measures required to reduce or eliminate these risks; whereas they must also be in a position to contribute, by means of balanced participation in accordance with national laws and/or practices, to seeing that the necessary protective measures are taken;
> Whereas information, dialogue and balanced participation on safety and health at work must be developed between employers and workers and/or their representatives by means of appropriate procedures and instruments, in accordance with national laws and/or practices;

---

[37]  See Walters (1990).

[38]  89/391/EEC.

In general terms the Directive's approach aims at establishing a policy for the industrial relations of the working environment based on participation rather than a conflictual view on the relations between workers and management.[39]

### 7.2.2. Workers, Employers and Workers' Representatives

Article 3 of the Framework Directive 89/391/EEC defines the persons involved in worker participation.

### 7.2.2.(i) Workers

For the purposes of the Directive a worker is any person employed by an employer, including trainees and apprentices but excluding domestic servants. Compared to the concept of a worker in Article 48 EC (discussed in Chapter 2) the concept in the Framework Directive is narrow. It only embraces those actually in employment, not job applicants or retired workers or students.

### 7.2.2.(ii) Employers: Community Law and Corporate Enterprise[40]

An employer is defined as any natural or legal person who has an employment relationship with the worker and has responsibility for the undertaking and/or establishment. Worker participation is often a controversial issue because of the complex structure of the employer, where important management decisions are made by central management in a parent company, while the employment contracts are entered into by local management in a subsidiary company. It is therefore an increasingly important question as to who is the employer. Does the Framework Directive provide for direct access of workers to the central management of their parent company, which may be located in another country, in working environment matters or does it only provide for consultation rights *viz à viz* local management? The answer depends on how the concept of an employer is interpreted by the ECJ.

In our view, an employer within the meaning of the Directive, must be the *real* decision maker. In some groups of companies the parent company makes the policy decisions concerning the working environment. If that is the case, the participation rights of the workers both of the parent company and of subsidiaries must be rights against the parent company.

---

[39] Cf Biagi (1990).

[40] Cf Bruun *et al* (1993) and Pipkorn (1990).

It could also be argued that the employer within the meaning of the Directive must be an entity which can act as an adequate counterpart to the workers' representatives which are defined by reference to national law and practice (see below). In some countries, for example Germany, a works council at group of undertakings level (Konzernbetriebsraat) exists which has competence in working environment matters. In order for it to have a counterpart on the employer side, the employer must also be able to be the central management of the group of undertakings.

Directive 94/45/EC contains a definition of a controlling undertaking, a definition which in the Nordic debate (notably in Norway) has been suggested as an appropriate basis for a statutory definition of the concept of an employer.

### 7.2.2.(iii) Workers' Representatives

A workers' representative with specific responsibility for the safety and health of workers is, according to the Directive, any person elected, chosen or designated in accordance with national laws and/or practices to represent workers where problems arise relating to the health and safety protection of workers at work.

By referring to national laws and practices as regards the designation of workers' representatives the Directive avoids the difficulties of harmonizing national institutional structures in this field. In some countries, for example Denmark, there are special safety representatives. In other countries, for example Germany, these matters are dealt with by the works councils.[41] The requirement that there must be balanced participation (see below) may, however, make it necessary to change some national provisions relating to the institutional set up.

### 7.2.3. Information

Article 10 of the Framework Directive provides that the employer shall take appropriate measures so that workers and/or their representatives in the undertaking and/or establishment receive, in accordance with national laws and/or practices which may take into account *inter alia* the size of the undertaking and/or establishment, all necessary information concerning:

(a)    the safety and health risks and protective and preventive measures and activities in respect of both the undertaking and/or establishment in general and each type of workstation and/or job;

---

[41]  Cf Weiss (1990b).

(b)   the measures taken pursuant to Article 8(2).

(c)   such information shall also be provided in a suitable form to temporary workers and hired workers present in the establishment or enterprise.

The employer shall take appropriate measures so that workers with specific functions in protecting the safety and health of workers, or workers' representatives with specific responsibility for the safety and health of workers shall have access, in order to perform their duties and in accordance with national laws and/or practices, to:

(a)   the risk assessment and protective measures referred to in Article 9(1)(a) and (b);

(b)   the list and reports referred to in Article 9(1)(c) and (d);

(c)   the information yielded by protective and preventive measures, inspection agencies and bodies responsible for safety and health.

### 7.2.4. Consultation and Participation

According to Article 11 of the Framework Directive employers shall consult workers and/or their representatives and allow them to take part in discussions on all questions relating to safety and health at work. This pre-supposes the consultation of workers, the right of workers and/or their representatives to make proposals, and balanced participation in accordance with national laws and/or practices.

### 7.2.4.(i) Balanced Participation in Advance and in Due Time

Workers with specific functions in protecting the safety and health of workers or workers' representatives with specific responsibility for the safety and health or workers shall participate in a balanced way, in accordance with national laws and/or practices, or be consulted in advance and in due time by the employer with regard to:

(a)   any measure which may substantially affect safety and health;

(b)   the designation of workers referred to in Article 8(2) and the activities referred to in Article 7(1);

(c)   the information referred to in Article 9(1) and Article 10;

(d)   the planning and organization of the training referred to in Article 12.

Workers with specific functions for the protection of the safety and health of workers at work, and workers' representatives, may call on the employer to take appropriate measures and submit to him/her relevant proposals by means of which all risks to workers may be reduced and/or sources of danger eliminated. The expression "balanced participation" is not very clear and is likely to give rise to referrals to the ECJ.[42]

In Denmark, workers are in principle only eligible as safety representatives if they fulfill the eligibility requirements for shop stewards, one of which is that they must be a member of a trade union. This fits uneasily with the right guaranteed in the Social Charter 1989 (see under 5.3) both to be and not to be a trade union member. It is doubtful whether such an exclusion of non-unionised workers is "balanced participation" within the meaning of the Directive.

### 7.2.4.(ii) Protection of Workers

The workers and workers' representatives may not be placed at any disadvantage because of their specific responsibility for the safety and health of workers. Employers must allow workers' representatives with specific responsibility for the safety and health of workers adequate time off work, without loss of pay, and provide them with the necessary means to enable such representatives to exercise their rights and functions derived from this Directive.

Workers and/or their representatives are entitled to appeal, in accordance with national law and/or practice, to the authority responsible for safety and health protection at work if they consider that the measures taken and the means employed by the employer are inadequate for the purposes of ensuring safety and health at work. Workers' representatives must be invited to - and be able to submit their observations at - inspection visits by the competent authorities.

### 7.2.5. Training

Article 12 of the Framework Directive on the working environment provides that employers shall ensure that each worker receives adequate safety and health training, in particular in the form of information and instructions specific to his/her workstation or job on recruitment, in the event of a transfer or a change of job, in the event of the introduction of new working equipment or a change in equipment, and in the event of the introduction of any new technology.

---

[42] Cf Biagi (1990).

## 7.3. THE SOCIAL CHARTER

### 7.3.1. Freedom of Association and Collective Bargaining

### 7.3.1.(i) Declaration of General Principles

The Social Charter 1989 contains some general principles concerning freedom of association and collective bargaining. Every employer and every worker in the EU shall have the right to belong freely to any professional or trade union organisation of his/her choice. This right shall entail recognition of the right to belong to a union, the freedom to negotiate and conclude collective agreements, the right to resort to collective action in the event of a conflict of interests including the right to strike and the freedom to join any association of a democratic nature or to renounce this right without any personal or occupational damage being thereby suffered by the individual concerned. The establishment and utilisation of procedures of conciliation, mediation and arbitration for the settlement of industrial disputes should also be encouraged. This right shall imply that relations based on agreements may be established between the two sides of industry at European level if they consider it desirable. The contractual agreements thus entered into may cover employment and working conditions, including measures of social protection for the workers concerned. To this end, the dialogue between the two sides of industry at European level must be developed, in particular at inter-occupational and sectoral level.

### 7.3.1.(ii) Implementing Measures at Community Level

Implementaion of the above principles is left mainly to the Member States in accordance with the subsidiarity principle. In the Action Programme on the implementation of the Social Charter 1989 the Commission reiterates the principles of the Social Charter but it does not propose any specific measures to implement these principles. The Commission will, in accordance with Article 118B EEC, endeavour to develop the dialogue between management and labour at European level which could, if the two sides consider it desirable, lead to relations based on agreement. Accordingly, the Commission has developed an ongoing dialogue procedure with the two sides of industry bringing together the leaders of the employers' organisations and the trade unions in the Community.

### 7.3.2. Right of Information, Consultation and Participation of Workers

The Social Charter 1989 provides that information, consultation and participation of workers must be developed along appropriate lines and in such a way as to take account of the laws, contractual agreements and practices in force in the Member States. This shall apply especially in companies or groups of companies having establishments or companies in several Member States.

In particular, these provisions shall be implemented in the following cases:

- when technological changes that have major implications for the workforce as far as working conditions and work organisation are concerned, are introduced into firms;
- in connection with restructuring operations in firms or mergers having an impact on the employment of workers;
- when transfrontier workers are affected by employment policies pursued by the firm where they are employed.

The completion of the Internal Market in which national economies will be closely associated will accelerate mutations and restructuring of a large number of European industries. While taking into account the existing diversity between Member States in this area, the Commission considers it necessary to propose appropriate instruments with the view to ensuring the generalisation of the principles of worker participation at Community level. There are a number of problems in using Community legislation in this area. The main questions on which there is disagreement are:

- the degree of employee participation, i.e. whether it should be restricted to information only as is usual in existing voluntary agreements or whether it should include consultation and negotiation rights;
- whether or not employees in European scale undertakings or groups of undertakings should have direct access to information from and consultation with central management;
- the role (if any) of trade unions and external experts;
- the desirability of adopting a legal instrument of a binding or a non-binding nature;
- the protection of the employer's secrets;
- the role of the principle of subsidiarity, i.e. the relationship between national and supra-national regulation, including the question whether Community legislation should be limited to problems of a cross-border nature;
- the corporate aspect, i.e. the problems relating to complex business structures on the part of the employer resulting in employment related decisions being taken at group level and not by the direct employer.

The European Parliament has adopted a Resolution on the Commission's Action Programme concerning the Social Charter 1989,[43] which goes further than any Commission proposals put forward so far. Point 45 stipulates that the Parliament:

»Calls on the Commission, with regard to information, consultation and participation of workers, to adopt the following measures:

(a)     a directive guaranteeing the right of workers and their representatives to information, prior consultation and participation in their undertakings, irrespective of their nature: transnational and others with a complex structure as well as national undertakings and the constitution of `European committees' of workers' representatives; information shall be provided and it shall be possible for the right to consultation and participation to be exercised before the decision is taken;

(b)     a directive incorporating in identical forms the rights to information and consultation, and in equivalent forms the right to participation, into the statutes of all companies, irrespective of their legal constitution - limited companies, European companies, cooperative, mutual benefit companies, self-management companies - and also into those of the European Economic Interest Grouping;

(c)     the right to information, prior consultation and participation shall cover company strategies and project, decisions relating to technological innovation, changes in the organisation of work, company statutes, production methods or economic planning and changes in the undertaking(s), in particular mergers at national or international level, take-over bids or share offers, closures or mass redundancies and the sale of companies or parts of companies; information shall be provided and it shall be possible for the right to consultation and participation to be exercised before the decision is given;

(d)     a directive on the social accounts of companies

(e)     a directive on the right of workers' representatives to consult experts of their choice from outside the company

(f)     a directive on procedures for the information, consultation and participation of workers at group level in groups of undertakings (irrespective of whether those undertakings have offices or plant in one or more Member States);

(g)     an action programme to underpin the information, consultation and participation of workers that provides, inter alia, for: recommendations, incentives for undertakings, publications, seminars and concessions for workers' representatives.«

Council Directive 92/56/EEC[44] amending Directive 75/129/EEC on the approximation of the laws of the Member States relating to collective redundancies (see Chapter 4) provides in Article 2(4) that the information and

---

[43]   A3- 0175/90 of 13.9.1990.

[44]   OJ L 1992 245/3.

consultation obligations laid down in Article 2, paragraphs 1, 2 and 3 apply irrespective of whether the decision regarding collective redundancies is being taken by the employer or by an undertaking controlling the employer.

In considering alleged breaches of the information, consultation and notification requirements laid down by the Directive, account shall not be taken of any defence on the part of the employer on the ground that the necessary information has not been provided to the employer by the undertaking which took the decision leading to collective redundancies.

This provision clarifies the legal position in case of redundancies in groups of companies and has been interpreted as the main change of the 1975 Directive.[45] Its aim is to ensure that the Directive's provisions apply in complex business structures.

## 7.4. DIRECTIVE 94/45/EC ON THE EUROPEAN WORKS COUNCIL

It has taken more than 20 years to reach agreement on this issue in the Council of Ministers. The original Commission proposals of 1970[46] and 1975[47] for a Regulation for a European Company Statute provided for the representation of the interests of workers in a European Works Council or Group Works Council. In 1980, the first Vrederling directive was proposed. It was revised in 1983.[48] In the Action Programme for the implementation of the Social Charter 1989, the Commission promised to present a proposal for a directive on the matter. The first proposal was presented in 1991.[49] It formed the basis for later proposals[50] leading to the current Directive 94/45/EC.

The Commission's proposal for a European Works Council has also taken into consideration various Resolutions of the European Parliament, particularly its Resolution of 16 March 1989[51] on the Commission's Memorandum on the

---

[45]  Cf *European Industrial Relations Review* 226, October 1992 p 24.

[46]  OJ 1970 C 124/1.

[47]  COM(75)150 final.

[48]  COM(80)423, OJ 1980 C 297/3, Bulletin of the EC, Supplement 3/80, and COM(83)292, OJ 1983 C 217/3, Bulletin of the EC, Supplement 2/83.

[49]  COM(90)58, OJ 1991 C 39/10, which was amended the same year by COM(91)345, OJ 1991 C 336/11. See Hall (1992) and Figge (1993).

[50]  OJ 1994 C 135/8, OJ 1994 C 199/10 and OJ 1994 C 277/3.

[51]  OJ 1989 C 96/163.

European Company Statute, in which the European Parliament called for the inclusion of provisions requiring the establishment of European Works Councils (as originally provided by the 1970 and 1975 proposals), and the Resolution of 15 February 1990 on the most important legislative proposals in the social field to be included in the Commission's work programme for 1990[52] which recommends, *inter alia*, "the setting up of European consultative committees in multinational undertakings".

On September 22, 1994, the Council of the European Union adopted the Directive on the establishment of a European Works Council or a procedure in Community-scale undertakings and Community-scale groups of undertakings for the purposes of informing and consulting employees.[53] The Directive should have been implemented in the Member States by September 22, 1996.

### 7.4.1. Background

All countries saw a rise in internationalization and structural changes in larger companies and groups of companies in the 1980's. Rights of information and consultation of employees built up in the 1970s partly lost significance as a result of this development where decisions were increasingly being taken by other legal entities than the formal employer and in many cases by a parent company situated abroad.

These problems, which exist in many multinational companies, received international attention and became the subject of international "soft law" provisions in the 1970's. The OECD countries approved "Guidelines for Multinational Enterprises" in 1976 and the ILO adopted in 1977 a tripartite declaration of principles concerning multinational enterprises and social policy. In the 1980s, the problem received renewed attention.

### 7.4.1.(i). The Draft Vredeling Directive [54]

A proposal for a Council Directive on procedures for informing and consulting the employees of undertakings with complex structures, in particular transnational undertakings[55] was submitted to the Council of Ministers in 1980

---

[52]  OJ 1990 C 68/68.

[53]  94/45/EC.

[54]  See Docksey (1985) and (1986).

[55]  OJ 1980 L 297/3. *Bulletin of the EC* Supplement 3/80.

and amended in 1983.[56] The proposal covered all undertakings or groups of undertakings having one or more establishments or subsidiaries in the Community and employing as a whole at least 1000 employees in the Community.

The draft Vredeling Directive contained two major obligations: a duty to provide periodic information and an obligation to give information in advance of important decisions. The proposal provided that Community or non-Community undertakings or parent undertakings, having establishments or subsidiaries in the Community, must regularly, inform and consult *via* the local management the employees' representatives provided by the law or practice of the Member States. No single body for employee representation was to be set up and the information and consultation procedures envisaged were channelled through the existing national representation structures. Adoption of the proposal required unanimity in the Council of Ministers. It met with heavy opposition in particular from the UK and was later replaced by the proposal leading to the adoption of Directive 94/45/EC on the establishment of a European Works Council discussed below.

### 7.4.1.(ii). Social Dialogue

Within the framework of the *Val Duchesse* social dialogue, the two sides of industry identified some common ground as to the desirability of information and consultation in connection with the introduction of new technology. The joint opinion adopted by ETUC, UNICE and CEEP states:[57]

> "The participants stress the need to motivate the staff at all levels of responsibility in firms and to develop their aptitude to change, amongst other ways by means of good information and consultation practices.
>
> They consider that such motivation will be all the higher if all the staff are in a position to understand the economic and social need for structural and technological change and the potential which such change offers to firms and to the workforce...
>
> Both sides take the view that, when technological changes which imply major consequences for the workforce are introduced in the firm, workers and/or their representatives should be informed and consulted in accordance with the laws, agreements and practices in force in the Community countries. This information and consultation must be timely".

---

[56] OJ C 1983 217/. *Bulletin of the EC* Supplement 2/83.

[57] COM(90) 581,7.

In 1989, the Opinion of the Economic and Social Committee on the social consequences of cross-frontier mergers[58] stated:

"Since, independently of [the European Company Statute], there is a need for information and participation rights for employees' representatives in connection with cross-frontier concentrations between undertakings, a Community framework should be devised for this. This framework ought to be based on national arrangements for employee representation, and provide for regular information and consultation of employees' representatives at European level".

The Economic and Social Committee's Opinion went on to propose that in cross-frontier undertakings and groups

"a European advisory committee of employee representatives [should] be set up alongside the group/undertaking management",

and that Community legislation should cover issues such as the composition of such a committee, the need for clearly defined information and consultation rights, the frequency of meetings, and the responsibility of the undertaking or group for meeting the operating costs of the committee."

On this occasion the Economic and Social Committee criticised the fact that the merger Regulation[59] is not accompanied by social policy law provisions and the Committee suggested that the Commission's approval of mergers under the Regulation be made conditional upon the establishment of a European Works Council in the undertaking. So far this suggestion has not been followed by the Commission but it has power under the Regulation to introduce such a requirement as a condition of approving cross-border mergers.

### 7.4.2 The Goal of the Directive

According to Article 1, the purpose of the Directive is to improve employees' rights to information and consultation within Community-scale undertakings and Community-scale groups of undertakings. In order to achieve this objective, a European Works Council or a similar procedure, shall according to Article 5.1, be established in all Community-scale undertakings and groups of undertakings. The intention is to guarantee information and consultation of employees in accordance with the Directive. The Directive applies only to undertakings or groups of undertakings having operations in two or more

---

[58]  OJ 1989 C 329/35.

[59]  89/4064/EEC.

Member States and having more than 1,000 employees within the EU. In addition, at least two of the company's entities must employ at least 150 persons.

### 7.4.3. Subsidiary Minimum Standard

The legal base of the Directive is Article 2.2 in the Agreement on Social Policy annexed to the EC Treaty. This means that the Directive only affects fourteen Member States, with the UK remaining outside the scope of its application.

The SPA introduced decisions by qualified majority in a number of areas, including information and consultation of workers. According to Article 2.2 of the Agreement the Council may adopt, by means of Directives, minimum requirements. The Directive on works councils includes a list of Subsidiary Requirements[60] in its annex which apply in some, but far from all, cases. In situations where the Subsidiary Requirements apply there is a minimum standard. Member States are not allowed to fall below this standard when implementing the Directive at national level.[61] No Member State can therefore introduce legislation below the level prescribed by EC law. On the other hand, a Member State can, if it so wishes, adopt legislation that exceeds the minimum EC level in operations based within the national borders. It is, for example, possible to lower the Directive's threshold concerning the number of employees or to require more far reaching rights to "co-determination" than the Directive in different situations.

The Directive's Subsidiary Requirements are subsidiary both in relation to agreements and in relation to passivity. The Subsidiary Requirements are, according to article 7, only applicable in the following three situations:

---

[60] The official Swedish text of the Directive uses the word "Tillägsföreskrifter" which directly translated into English would be "Complementary Requirements" and not, as in the English version, "Subsidiary Requirements". The Danish text (Subsidiære forskrifter) is in line with the English.

[61] The Commission's revised proposal for the Directive (COM (94) 228 final 3.6.1994) included a provision (article 12.3) that reads as follows: "This Directive shall not affect Member States' rights to apply or introduce laws, regulations or administrative provisions which are more favourable to employees or to allow or give priority to the application of collective agreements which are more favourable to employees." This provision was removed by the Council. However, despite this, there is no doubt that the Directive is setting a minimum standard, since it was adopted with the support of article 2.2 in the Social Agreement, which specifically refers to "minimum requirements."

1) The concerned parties (central management and the relevant negotiation body) agree to apply them.
2) Central management refuses to initiate negotiations to introduce a European works council or a similar procedure within six months of the employees' request for such measures.
3) Negotiations to introduce a European works council or a similar procedure have been initiated but the parties could not reach agreement within three years from the date of request for such negotiations.

The Subsidiary Requirements do not apply, ie there is no minimum standard, in the following four situations:

1) Employees do not, according to Article 5.1, request the initiation of negotiations and do not nominate a negotiating body.
2) A negotiating body has been nominated, but it decides with at least a two thirds majority not to initiate negotiations to establish a European works council or a procedure on information and consultation with employees, or decides to terminate the negotiations, according to Article 5.5.
3) An agreement is reached, in accordance with Article 6.2 or 3, between central management and the negotiating body to establish a European works council or procedure, which can be of any content including measures not meeting the EU subsidiary minimum requirements applicable in the absence of agreement.
4) An agreement exists between the parties prior to the national implementation of the Directive. Such agreements continue to be valid despite the Directive.

If an agreement entered into prior to the implementation of the Directive is to retain its validity it must be "an agreement covering the entire workforce, providing for the transnational information and consultation of employees." (Article 13.1) This means that all employees regardless of whether they work at sites with fewer than 150 employees are affected by the agreement.[62] In other words, the agreement should be applied to all. However, the parties on the employees' side do not have to represent all employees. One or more union representing a portion of the employees may conclude an agreement according to Article 13.1. The undertaking's management must ensure that the agreement is applied in a manner that encompasses all employees.

---

[62]  McGlynn (1995).

### 7.4.4. The Directive's Requirement of Information, Consultation and Negotiation

### 7.4.4.(i). Two Stages

The Directive deals with consultation, etc in two contexts. First, there must be negotiations regarding establishing a European works council or a procedure for information and consultation. Second, after the establishment of a works council or procedure, information and consultation must be undertaken within that framework and according to the requirements of the Directive.

### 7.4.4.(ii). Duty to Negotiate on the Establishment of a Works Council or a Procedure for Information and Consultation

In order to achieve the objective of the Directive, the central management shall initiate negotiations for the establishment of a EuropeanWorks Council or an information and consultation procedure on its own initiative or at the written request of at least 100 employees or their representatives in at least two undertakings or establishments in at least two different member states. For this purpose, a special negotiating body shall be established in accordance with the guidelines contained in the Directive.

The central management and the special negotiating body must according to Article 6 negotiate in a spirit of cooperation with a view to reaching an agreement on the detailed arrangements for implementing the information and consultation of employees. Without prejudice to the autonomy of the parties, the agreement referred to above between the central management and the special negotiating body shall determine a number of specific issues concerning the undertakings covered by the agreement, the composition of the European Works Council, etc. The central management and the special negotiating body may decide, in writing, to establish one or more information and consultation procedures instead of a European Works Council.

The obligation to negotiate is worded in a manner that is at least equivalent to the obligations prescribed by the directives on collective redundancies[63] and transfer of undertakings.[64] The content of the obligation to negotiate according to the transfer of undertakings directive has recently been interpreted by the ECJ in an infringement action against the UK which had failed to comply with

---

[63] Council Directive 75/129/EEC as amended by 92/56/EEC.

[64] Council Directive 77/187/EEC. This Directive has created a vivid debate in Sweden, see further SOU 1994:83.

the Directive by not requiring negotiations with a view to reaching an agreement.[65]

The obligation under Article 6 includes the duty to negotiate the establishment of a cross-boarder works council or alternative procedure. A similar obligation hardly exists in Nordic labour law and the Directive therefore raises a new issue for the Nordic countries. In Swedish literature[66] it has been argued that the duty to negotiate according to Article 6 goes further than the corresponding duty in the Swedish Act on co-determination contained in section 15. In our view this opinion is correct.

### 7.4.4.(iii). Information and Consultation Based on an Agreement Regarding a Works Council or an Alternative Procedure

Where negotiations according to Article 6 result in an agreement on information and consultation, such information and consultation shall take place in 0accordance with the agreement. The Directive's Subsidiary Requirements are not applicable, unless provision is made otherwise in the agreement.

The concept of consultation is defined in the Directive (Article 12.1, paragraph f) as "the exchange of views and establishment of dialogue between employees' representatives and the central management or any more appropriate level of management."

The Directive does not explicitly state when consultation should take place. It is not clear whether consultation should occur before a decision is taken or if it could take place after the decision is made and be more a follow-up discussion regarding consequences of the decision. The consultation concept does not require that employees be able to engage external experts at the cost of the employer, a right that employees enjoy under the Subsidiary Requirements.

The main rule is that the agreement can lay down a lower level of employee rights than the Subsidiary Requirements. It is for example possible to agree that meetings be held less frequently than once a year. The Directive's requirement of consultation and its definition thereof do, however, constitute a certain minimum requirement. In cases where an agreement does not include anything that can be considered consultation within the meaning of the Directive, there is no agreement under Articles 6.2 or 3 and the Subsidiary Requirements consequently apply. It is thus not possible to agree that the

---

[65] Case C-382/92 *Commission* v *UK* [1994] ECR I 2435.

[66] Fahlbeck (1995b).

employer shall provide one-way information only with no exchange of views and dialogue.

### 7.4.4.(iv). Consultation with European Works Councils According to the Subsidiary Requirements

The Subsidiary Requirements apply when negotiations on the establishment of a European works council or procedure for information and consultation do not lead to an agreement. It also applies if the central management refuses to negotiate or where the parties agree to use the Subsidiary Requirements. The Subsidiary Requirements provide for the establishment of a European works council (paragraph 1). The European works council shall in most cases form a committee with no more than three members (paragraph 1c). The committee shall be a sort of select committee for the council. Where exceptional circumstances arise that affect labour's interest to a considerable extent, the select committee or the works council have the right to be informed.

The European works council and the select committee may be assisted by external experts of their own choice, in so far as this is necessary for it to carry out its tasks (paragraph 6.). Central management is responsible for the cost of operating the works council (paragraph 7). Member States can lay down budgetary rules regarding the operation of the works councils, and therein limit funding to cover one external expert only.

The statutory right to management-funded experts that will result from the Directive is new in Nordic law. To date, similar rights have only existed on the basis of collective agreements.

### 7.4.4.(v). The Legal Nature of an Agreement on a European Works Council

The agreement to establish a European Works Council is entered into, "between the central management and the special negotiating body" (Article 6.1-2). The Directive does not prohibit the establishment of more than one works councils. Many councils can be established locally as long as there is a superior works council that has the right to negotiate with the central management in the group of undertakings.[67]

The principle of freedom of contract is a basic principle in Nordic labour law. This does not preclude certain duties to negotiate. The Directive on European Works Councils appears to be consistent with the principle of freedom of contract as understood in the Nordic countries but it introduces a new type of contract or an agreement *sui generis* which does not have the same

---

[67] Blanpain and Windey (1995) 76.

characteristics as a traditional Nordic collective agreement. In Finland and Sweden collective agreements are, in contrast to Denmark, defined by legislation as formal, written agreements which do not qualify as collective agreements unless certain formal or structural requirements are met. Legislation in Sweden and Finland stipulates that the parties to the agreement are, on the one hand, an employer or employers' organization, and on the other hand an employees' union (collective representation is required only on the side of the employees) and that the agreement, from a broad viewpoint, regulates the relationship between the employer and employee. Denmark and Norway lack a statutory definition of a collective agreement, but under normal circumstances the Finnish and Swedish conditions apply in Denmark and Norway as well.

A basic condition for an agreement to qualify as a collective agreement is that it is entered into by a trade union or in Denmark by another collectivity on the employee side. An agreement to establish a European Works Council in accordance with the Directive's Subsidiary Requirements will often not fulfill this prerequisite, at least not regarding Swedish and Finnish legislation. Even in Denmark, it is questionable whether or not such an agreement is binding for external employees, at least to the extent that it would infringe upon the right of those external workers to engage in industrial actions.

If an agreement on a European Works Council is to stipulate rights and obligations for parties not having concluded the agreement (the special negotiating body and the undertaking's central management) legislative changes are required in the Nordic countries.

### 7.4.5. National Level

Rules on works councils vary considerably from Member State to Member State. There are no proposals for harmonization of national provisions. Current Community proposals are confined to cross-border aspects leaving Member States to decide information and consultation matters as they find fit.

## 7.5. PARTICIPATION IN STRATEGIC MANAGEMENT DECISIONS

### 7.5.1. Employee Participation in Profits and Enterprise Results

The Capital Directive on the formation of public limited liability companies and the maintenance and alteration of their capital with a view to making such safeguards equivalent[68] provides in Article 41:

---

[68]  77/91/EEC, OJ 1977 L 26/1.

1. Member States may derogate from Article 9(1), Article 19(1)(a), first sentence, and (b) and from Articles 25, 26 and 29 to the extent that such derogations are necessary for the adoption or application of provisions designed to encourage the participation of employees, or other groups of persons defined by national law, in the capital of undertakings.

2. Member States may decide not to apply Article 19(1)(a), first sentence, and Articles 30, 31, 36, 37, 38 and 39 to companies incorporated under a special law which issue both capital shares and workers' shares, the latter being issued to the company's employees as a body, who are represented at general meetings of shareholders by delegates having the right to vote.

As an outcome of the Social Charter 1989 and the accompanying Action Programme the Council of Ministers adopted a Recommendation[69] on 27 July 1992 concerning the promotion of participation by employed persons in profits and enterprise results (including equity participation).

### 7.5.2. The European Economic Interest Grouping (EEIG)

In 1985 the Council adopted Regulation 85/2137/EEC on the European Economic Interest Grouping (EEIG).[70] The Regulation does not contain any worker participation provisions. In the Preamble it is stated that in matters not covered by the Regulation the laws of the Member States and Community law are applicable, for example, with regard to social and labour law, competition law, and intellectual property law.

This means that worker participation is governed by the law of the Member State in which the grouping is registered. According to Article 3(2)(c) a grouping may not employ more than 500 employees. This threshold which corresponds to the threshold in the German Betriebsverfassungsgesetz 1952 was inserted at the demand of Germany to avoid circumvention of the German employee participation provisions by German companies forming or joining an EEIG registered in another Member State with more lax worker participation rules.[71]

---

[69]  Council Recommendation 92/443/EEC, OJ 1992 L 245/53.

[70]  OJ 1985 L 199/1.

[71]  See further Hartard (1991).

### 7.5.3. The Draft Fifth Company Law Directive

The draft fifth Company Law Directive[72] has caused a great deal of controversy.[73] In the original proposal the structure of companies would be changed so that there would be two boards of directors, an executive board and a supervisory board. That proposal has now been modified so that there can be a single board provided that it is divided into executive and supervisory members. Further controversy has been caused by the employee participation provisions. Originally employee participation by appointment to the board was the only model in the proposed Directive. The current proposal provides for a choice between 3 models of worker participation:

- workers elect no less than one third and no more than half of the members of the supervisory board (German system)
- worker participation through a body representing the employees separate from the company organs
- worker participation through collectively agreed systems, to be agreed upon within the company.

Nevertheless there is considerable opposition to this measure, not least from the United Kingdom. The objection of the United Kingdom is that these types of provisions are irrelevant to company law. The draft Directive has also been criticised for the degree of detail it contains and the complicated and rigid procedures for informing and consulting employees. UNICE (the international employers organisation) fear that the enactment of the fifth Directive would increase the burden of regulation on companies.

### 7.5.4. The Draft Tenth Company Law Directive

In the proposal for a Tenth Council Directive based on Article 54(3)(g) EC concerning cross-border mergers of public limited companies[74] it is stipulated in Article 1(4) that protection of the rights of the employees of each of the companies involved in a cross-border merger shall be regulated in accordance

---

[72] Amended Proposal for a Fifth Directive concerning the structure of public limited companies and the powers and obligations of their organs, O J 1983 C 240/2, *Bulletin of the EC* Supplement 6/83.

[73] Cf Däubler (1977); Welch (1983).

[74] COM(84) 727 final, OJ C 1985 23/11.

with Directive 77/187/EEC on the transfer of undertakings (discussed in Chapter Six).[75]

### 7.5.5. The Draft Thirteenth Company Law Directive

On 19 January 1989 the Commission presented to the Council of Ministers a proposal for a thirteenth Directive[76] on company law concerning takeover and other general bids. In 1990 an amended proposal was presented.[77] These proposals were necessary since Council Directive 77/187/EEC on the transfer of undertakings does not cover takeovers. In relation to employees there may be problems both regarding the involvement of the employees of the offeror company and of the offeree company. The 1990 draft Directive adressed the problems of involving the employees of the offeree company and provided for a duty for the employer to inform representatives of employees. Article 19 of the draft Directive read:

> Information for representatives of employees of the offeree company
> 1. The board of the offeree company shall communicate to its employees' representatives, as designated by national legislation or customary practice in the Member States, the offer document and, where appropriate, the document refered to in Article 10(3) and (4), the opinion required by Article 14(1) and all documents or information made public in accordance with Article 11(1) concerning the revision, withdrawal and result of the bid.
> 2. Such documents or information shall be communicated immediately after they are made public in accordance with Article 11(1).

Negotiations on this proposal were suspended in June 1991 due to serious opposition from certain Member States. In its declaration to the European Council in Edinburgh in December 1992 on the subject of subsidiarity, the Commission indicated its intention to revise its proposal and reconfirmed this at the European Council in Essen in December 1994. In 1996 a new proposal[78] for a "framework" Directive was presented which is less detailed than the

---

[75] See further Däubler (1988).

[76] COM(88)823, OJ 1989 C 64/8.

[77] COM(90) 416 final, OJ 1990 C 240/7.

[78] COM(95)341, OJ 1996 C 162/5.

earlier drafts and contains no specific rules on information of employees. It is stated[79] in the Preamble (emphasis added):

> "10. The proposed Directive requires Member States to ensure a basic level of disclosure and information which will guarantee transparency during the takeover bid. It is left to Member States to determine how such transparency will be ensured. The process of informing the *employees of the offeree company* is not subject to a specific provision, which leaves Member States free to deal with this issue according to their usual practices."

## 7.5.6. The Draft European Company Statute: the SE[80]

### 7.5.6.(i) Historical Development

Procedures for informing and consulting employees of European-scale undertakings have been the subject of various Community proposals. The original Commission proposals of 1970[81] and 1975[82] for a European Company Statute provided for both worker participation in a Supervisory Board and the representation of the interests of workers in a European Works Council or Group Works Council.

The Commission's White Paper *Completing the Internal Market*,[83] provided for the preparation of a new European Company Statute, discussion of the amended 1975 proposal having been suspended by the Council of Ministers in 1982. Accordingly, proposals for a Council Regulation on the Statute for a European Company[84] and for a Council Directive complementing the Statute with regard to the involvement of employees in the European Company[85] were presented by the Commission to the Council of Ministers on 25 August 1989.

---

[79] In recital 10 in the Preamble.

[80] See Wedderburn (1990).

[81] OJ 1970 C 124/1.

[82] COM(75) 150 final.

[83] COM(85) 310.

[84] COM(89)268, OJ 1989 C 263/41.

[85] COM(89)268, OJ 1989 C 263/69.

Amended proposals were presented on 29 May 1991.[86] The Commision has also proposed Council Regulations on Statutes for European Associations, cooperative societies and mutual societies and accompanying Directives on employee involvement.[87]

### 7.5.6.(ii) Main Provisions of the Draft Directive

The draft Directive sets out measures to enable employees "to participate in the supervision and strategic development" of companies which are voluntarily formed throughout the Community in the form of a European public limited company (Societas Europeae, "SE"). Undertakings operating in more than one Member State, other than companies formed as European Companies, are not affected by its provisions, European Company status being optional for the undertakings concerned. A SE can be formed in four ways: by two companies in different Member States merging or forming a joint holding or subsidiary company or by a SE forming a subsidiary. The proposal offers a choice of various structures resembling the German, the French and the Scandinavian tradition:[88]

> *Model 1* ("the German model"): Employees' representatives appointed to the supervisory board or the one-tier board (between 1/3 and 1/2). A variant allows for co-option of such representatives, which is similar to the Dutch practice (Article 4).
> *Model 2* ("the French model"): A "separate body", with specified rights to consultation, to represent the employees (Article 5).
> *Model 3* ("the Scandinavian model"): Other models which may be "established by agreement", i.e. by collective agreement (Article 6).

Under Article 7 the representatives of the employees of the SE shall be elected in accordance with systems which take into account, in an appropriate manner, the number of staff they represent. All employees must be able to participate in the vote. The election shall be conducted in accordance with the laws or practices of the Member States.

The first members of the supervisory board or the administrative board to be appointed by the employees and the first members of the separate body representing the employees shall be appointed by the representatives of the employees of the founder companies in proportion to the number of employees

---

[86] COM(91) 174 final, OJ 1991 C 138/8. See also Hopt(1996).

[87] OJ 1992 C 99/17 and 37, amended OJ 1993 C 236/2 and 36.

[88] Cf Nagel (1990).

they represent and in accordance with the laws or practices of the Member States. Those first members shall remain in office until such time as the requirements for electing the representatives of the employees of the SE are satisfied.

The management board or the administrative board of the SE shall provide the representatives of the employees with such financial and material resources as enable them to meet and perform their duties in an appropriate manner. The practical arrangements for making available such financial and material resources shall be settled in consultation with the representatives of the employees of the SE.

Save as otherwise provided in the draft Directive, the status and duties of the representatives of the employees or of the body which represents them, for which provision is made in the establishments of the SE, shall be determined by the laws or practices of the Member States.

### 7.5.6.(iii) Alternative to National Law: Deregulation?

As regards the issues covered by the draft European Company Statute and the draft Directive on worker participation in SE Companies Community law replaces national law in that it provides an alternative option for companies.

A basic disagreement today is between those who favour European provisions which primarily facilitate business and those who favour a considerable amount of regulation in order to protect workers' interests. Daübler[89] argues with regard to the proposal for a European Company Statute that it is a gigantic attempt at deregulation:

"Der Vorschlag des Statuts einer SE erweist sich bei näheren Zusehen als gigantischer Versuch der Deregulierung. Ohne dass der Bestand nationaler Normen unmittelbar angetastet würde, wären die Unternehmen in der Lage, sich wesentlichen Teilen der nationalen Arbeitsrechts zu entziehen."

Compared to the drafts from the 1970's the Commission has lowered its expectations considerably. Most problems relating to the complex structures following from the fact that a SE will normally be part of a group of undertakings are passed by in silence.

---

[89] Daübler (1990). The quotation reads: On closer examination the proposal for a SE Statute is a gigantic attempt at deregulation. Companies can choose to opt out of important parts of national labour law without the core of national norms being directly set aside by Community law. [Translated by the authors.]

# CHAPTER EIGHT

# THE WORKING ENVIRONMENT

## 8.1. THE INTERNAL MARKET AND THE WORKING ENVIRONMENT

Working environment provisions make up an important part of the social dimension accompanying the development of the Internal Market. The period from 1 April 1992 to 1 April 1993 was designated the European Year for Health and Safety at Work.

The Community social and labour market policy under Article 118A EC aims at improving standards of living and working conditions, while the industrial policy pursued under Article 100A EC aims at abolishing trade barriers in order to enable *inter alia* machinery, technical equipment, chemical substances, etc to be marketed all over the Community. This double context makes the working environment an area of potential and actual conflict between a trend towards raising standards of protection for workers and a trend towards deregulation.

Even the working environment measures adopted under Article 100A EC are intended to respect a high level of protection. Article 100A(3) EC thus provides that proposals from the Commission concerning health, safety and environmental protection will take as a base a high level of protection.

So far, the Member States have not experienced situations where they have had to lower their level of protection concerning machinery and other technical equipment. But there are problems relating to the combination of the free trade in chemical substances and preparations and the protection of workers against the dangers of being exposed to hazardous agents, for example, carcinogens. In 1988, Denmark voted against Directive 88/379/EEC[1] on classification, labelling and packaging of dangerous preparations because of the gap between the traditional Nordic view on what is dangerous and the Community standard on this issue. Denmark has also disagreed with the Commission on Commission Directive of 5 March 1991[2] defining and laying down the detailed

---

[1]   OJ 1988 L 187/14.

[2]   91/155/EEC, OJ 1991 L 76/35, amended by 93/112/EC, OJ 1993 L 314/38.

arrangements for the system of specific information relating to dangerous preparations in the implementation of Article 10 of Directive 88/379/EEC (see below).

Different technical standards varying from country to country may affect Community policies in two ways. First, a national technical standard may operate as an import restriction hindering, or at least hampering, the free movement of goods within the Community. This may be a violation of Article 30 EC. Secondly, it is generally cheaper for the manufacturer to fulfil lower rather than higher technical requirements. Technical standards are therefore an important cost factor and differences from country to country may distort competition. For these reasons it is a high priority goal for the Community to remove technical barriers by way of harmonisation under Article 100A EC.

As the main rule, the Article 100A EC measures are directed towards those who operate on or govern the market in goods, in particular manufacturers and public authorities. These Directives do not provide for obligations to be placed on employers, whereas this is the case with the Directives based on Article 118A EC. The fact that it is lawful for a manufacturer to produce and market a product and unlawful for public authorities to hinder its presence on the market does not suffice to conclude that it is lawful for an employer to use it in the working environment. It may follow from the provisions of Article 118A EC (or from national provisions) that an employer is prohibited from using a lawfully marketed machine or substance in the working environment, for example, because it is possible to replace it with a less dangerous product (see below under 8.5 and 8.6).

## 8.2. THE CONCEPT OF THE WORKING ENVIRONMENT

According to Article 118A EC:

> "Member States shall pay particular attention to encouraging improvements, especially in the working environment, as regards the health and safety of workers and shall set as their objective the harmonisation of conditions in this area, while maintaining the improvements made.
>
> In order to help achieve the objective laid down in the first paragraph, the Council, acting by a qualified majority on a proposal from the Commission, in co-operation with the European Parliament and after consulting the Economic and Social Committee, shall adopt, by means of directives, minimum requirements for gradual implementation, having regard to the conditions and technical rules obtaining in each of the Member States."

In the Nordic countries, the concept of the working environment is well established. It has been used in the Nordic working environment legislation since the mid 1970's. In a Community context and in most Member States apart from Denmark, Sweden and Finland, it is a new concept introduced by the Single European Act 1986 in Article 118A EC and in Article 100A(4) EC (discussed in Chapter One).

In a Nordic context the working environment is a broad concept relating in particular to

- the arrangement of the work-place,
- the physical and socio-psychological conditions under which work is performed,
- the use of work equipment by workers at work, and
- the exposure of workers to toxic and other dangerous substances at work.

The Nordic concept of the working environment covers both physical aspects of the working conditions and psychological and social aspects thereof, such as monotony, lack of social contacts at work or a rapid work pace. In Norway the Working Environment Act 1977 also covers some contractual aspects of the employment relationship such as unfair dismissal, but this is not the general pattern in the Nordic countries. In contrast, at the European level, there is practically no case law and only few other sources of law to clarify the concept of the working environment in a EU context. The European Parliament has argued that a very wide interpretation embracing nearly all labour and employment law matters should be given to Article 118A EC.[3] The reason for this broad view is probably that Directives adopted under Article 118A EC require the cooperation procedure between the Council of Ministers and the Parliament under Article 149(2) EC. The Directives adopted so far cover mainly basic health and safety aspects of the (physical) working environment. The words "working environment" are rarely used in case law but are used fairly often in Directives adopted after the Single European Act, whereas the words "health and safety" are widely used.

In the judgments delivered by the ECJ the words "working environment" are rarely used whilst there is reference to "health and safety" much more often.[4] In *Criminal Proceedings Against Hansen & Søn*[5] the concept working environment is used in the ECJ's description of strict criminal liability in the system generally applicable in Denmark for the protection of the working

---

[3] Document A2-0226/1988. See also Hepple (1987).

[4] Tested by using the CD-ROM version of CELEX

[5] C-326/88 [1990] ECR 2911.

environment. In the *Lebon* case[6] on the interpretation of Regulation 1612/68/EEC and Article 7(2) EC the ECJ stated that the equality of treatment as regards social and tax advantages required by that provision contributes to the integration of migrant workers in the working environment of the host country in accordance with the objectives of the principle of free movement of workers as set out in Article 48 EC. In this case the working environment is not used as a concept relating to working conditions in particular workplaces but to the labour market and society at large.

The ECJ discussed the concept of working environment at length in *UK* v *Council*[7] where the UK sought annulment of the Directive on the organization of working time.[8] The Directive is adopted on the basis of Article 118A EC. In support of its action, UK relied on four pleas, alleging, respectively, that the legal base of the Directive was defective, breach of the principle of proportionality, misuse of powers, and infringement of essential procedural requirements. The UK contended that the Directive should have been adopted on the basis of Article 100 EC or Article 235 EC which require unanimity within the Council.

Article 118A(2) EC, read in conjunction with Article 118A(1) EC, empowers the Council to adopt, by means of directives, minimum requirements for gradual implementation, having regard to the conditions and technical rules obtaining in each of the Member States, with a view to 'encouraging improvements, especially in the working environment, as regards the health and safety of workers' by harmonizing conditions in this area, while maintaining the improvements made.

The ECJ held that there is nothing in the wording of Article 118A EC to indicate that the concepts of 'working environment', 'safety' and 'health' as used in Article 118A EC should be interpreted restrictively, and not as embracing all factors, physical or otherwise, capable of affecting the health and safety of the worker in his working environment, including in particular certain aspects of the organization of working time. On the contrary, the Court found that the words 'especially in the working environment' militate in favour of a broad interpretation of the powers which Article 118A EC confers upon the Council for the protection of the health and safety of workers. Moreover, such an interpretation of the words 'safety' and 'health' derives support in particular

---

[6]   Case 316/85 *Centre Public d'Aide Sociale de Courcelles* v *Marie-Christine Lebon* [1987] ECR 2811.

[7]   Case C-84/94, *United Kingdom* v *The Council of the European Union*, judgment of 12.11.1996, nyr.

[8]   93/104/EC, OJ 1993 L 307/18.

from the preamble to the Constitution of the World Health Organization to which all the Member States of the EU belong. Health is there defined as a state of complete physical, mental and social well-being that does not consist only in the absence of illness or infirmity.

It follows that, where the principal aim of the measure in question is the protection of the health and safety of workers, Article 118A EC must be used, albeit such a measure may have ancillary effects on the establishment and functioning of the Internal Market.

Furthermore, the organization of working time is not necessarily conceived as an instrument of employment policy. The approach taken by the working time directive, viewing the organization of working time essentially in terms of the favourable impact it may have on the health and safety of workers, is apparent from several recitals in its preamble. While it cannot be excluded that the Directive may affect employment, that is - in the view of the ECJ - clearly not its essential objective.

The literature on the subject is growing. Oliver[9] is of the opinion that the term "working environment" is wider than "the health and safety of workers". Ehlermann[10] in a discussion of Article 100A(4) EC states:

"The term "working environment" becomes really understable when one reads the new Article 118A, where improvements in the working envionment are clearly meant to promote health and safety of workers."

Barnard sees the Working Time Directive as a clear demonstration of the emerging grey area between traditional health and safety measures and the rights of employed persons.[11]

In this book we use the concept in accordance with the broad Nordic tradition outlined above and which has now been adopted by the ECJ in *UK* v *Council*.[12]

---

[9]   Oliver (1996) 356.

[10]   Ehlermann (1987) 392.

[11]   Barnard (1996) 321.

[12]   Case C-84/94, *United Kingdom* v *The Council of the European Union*, judgment of 12.11.1996, nyr.

## 8.3.  OVERVIEW  OF  THE  WORKING  ENVIRONMENT PROVISIONS[13]

### 8.3.1. Health and Safety Measures before the Single European Act 1986[14]

There has been some Community activity in this area since the early 1960's including the adoption in 1967 of the basic Directive on classification, labelling and packaging of dangerous substances[15] (see Chapter One).

In 1974 an Advisory Committee on Health and Safety was established and during the period before the adoption of the Single European Act 1986, the Council adopted two Action Programmes on Health and Safety. A Resolution on the First Action Programme on Health and Safety was adopted in 1978.[16] In 1984 it was replaced by the Second Action Programme.[17]

During this period a number of Directives specifically aimed at protecting health and safety were passed, namely:

- Council Directive for the provision of safety signs at places of work[18]
- Directive on the protection of workers from the risks related to exposure to vinyl chloride monomer,[19]
- the general hazardous agents Directive 80/1107/EEC on the protection of workers from the risks related to exposure to chemical, physical and biological agents at work,[20]

and three individual Directives concerning specific agents (lead, asbestos and noise):

---

[13]  See generally Neal and Wright (1992).

[14]  See for a general account Eberlie (1990) 81.

[15]  67/548/EEC, OJ 1967 L 196/1 with later amendments.

[16]  OJ 1978 C 165/1.

[17]  OJ 1984 C 67/2.

[18]  77/576/EEC, OJ 1977 L 229/12.

[19]  78/610/EEC, OJ 1978 L 197/12.

[20]  OJ 1980 L 327/8.

- Directive on the protection of workers from the risks of exposure at work to metallic lead and its ionic compounds,[21]
- Directive on the protection of workers from the risks related to exposure to asbestos at work[22]
- Directive on the protection of workers from risks related to exposure to noise at work.[23]

Other Directives were relevant to the working environment but protection of workers was incidental to their main aim. This applies, for example, to the Directive on major accident hazards connected with industrial activities.[24]

Generally, exposure of workers to dangerous substances was the main concern of the Community provisions relating to health and safety before the Single European Act 1986.

### 8.3.2. The Third Action Programme for Health and Safety 1987[25]

In 1987, the Commission issued its Third Action Programme on Health and Safety outlining its ideas on how the new Article 118A EC should be complemented by Directives and other measures. In the Programme, the concept of the working environment is seen in a broad perspective. It is stressed that it is important that working environment considerations be integrated into the organisation of work in order to prevent health and safety problems.

The Commission declared its intention of proposing a number of new health and safety Directives, Recommendations and other measures. The Programme was approved by the Council in December 1987.[26] It indicated that Directives would be proposed on:

- The organisation of safety
- Selection and use of plant and machinery
- Selection and use of personal protective equipment

---

[21]   82/605/EEC, OJ 1982 L 247/12.

[22]   83/477/EEC, OJ 1983 L 263/25.

[23]   86/188/EEC, OJ 1986 L 137/28.

[24]   82/501/EEC, OJ 1982 L 230/1.

[25]   COM (87)520 final Brussels.

[26]   Council Resolution on Safety, Hygiene and Health at Work of 21 December 1987, OJ 1988 C 28/1.

- Revision of the safety signs Directive
- Proscription Directive
- Medical assistance on ships
- Protection of agricultural workers using pesticides
- Safety in construction
- Carcinogenic agents
- Biological agents
- Cadmium compounds
- Amendment to the asbestos Directive
- Amendment to the lead Directive
- Amendment to the noise Directive
- Amendment to the Directive on the exposure of workers to hazardous agents
- Amendment to the exposure limit values Directive.

In addition, the Commission proposed to issue Recommendations on, *inter alia*:

- Ergonomic factors in process control systems
- Prevention of back injuries
- Safety in agricultural buildings and electricity
- Safety in sea-fishing
- A list of occupational diseases
- Assessment of exposure to dangerous agents
- Provision and organisation of occupational health services.

Most of these ideas have been realised and are discussed below. The Commission gave notice at the December 1988 Council of Ministers meeting of its decision to recommend additional Directives to cover temporary and mobile work sites, for example, in the construction industry, health and safety for fishing vessels, agriculture, modes of transport, extractive industries (open-cast mining, quarries, etc) and nuclear plants (see below under 8.9).

### 8.3.3. The 1989 Framework Directive

In June 1989, the Framework Directive 89/391/EEC[27] for the Introduction of Measures to Encourage Improvements in Safety and Health of Workers was approved by the Council of Ministers for implementation by Member States by 1 January 1993. Article 16 provides that a series of individual Directives shall be made to cover specific risks. Seven of these Directives have been adopted and are known as the "daughter Directives". The adoption of this Directive marks a change in method on the part of the Community from adopting Directives concerning specific risks or specific sectors to adopting an overall Directive which is to apply alongside a number of individual Directives

---

[27]  OJ 1989 L 183/1.

giving more details about the health and safety requirements concerning specific risks or sectors of employment.

### 8.3.3.(i) Outline of the Directive's Principal Provisions

The overall object of the framework Directive is, according to Article 1 (1), to introduce measures to encourage improvements in the safety and health of workers at work. To that end it contains general principles concerning the prevention of occupational risks, the protection of safety and health, the elimination of risk and accident factors, the information, consultation, balanced participation in accordance with national laws and/or practices and training of workers and their representatives, as well as general guidelines for the implementation of the said principles.[28]

The Directive is without prejudice to existing or future national and Community provisions which are more favourable to the protection of the safety and health of workers at work. The general objective is to be found in the Preamble, placed in the context of Article 118A EC. The means adopted to achieve the overall objective is to lay down general principles and general guidelines for the implementation of those principles. The general principles may be divided into two categories:[29] those directly concerned with the promotion of health and safety at work, and those concerned with the institutional structures and procedures which are considered a necessary part of that promotion. The worker participation aspect of the Directive has already been dealt with in Chapter Seven. The first category includes general principles concerning the prevention of occupational risks, the protection of safety and health, and the elimination of risk and accident factors. The scope of the Directive is intended to be extremely broad. Article 2(1) provides:

> The Directive applies to all sectors of activity, both public and private (industrial, agricultural, commercial, administrative, service, educational, cultural, leisure, etc.).

The Preamble also makes it clear that the Directive covers "all risks", and, in particular, those arising from the use at work of items covered by the "old" Framework Directive of 1980[30] on the Protection of Workers from the Risks related to Exposure to Chemical, Physical and Biological Agents at Work. The

---

[28]  On the Framework Directive see Baldwin and Daintith (1992).

[29]  Cf Neal (1990).

[30]  80/1107/EEC, OJ 1980 L 327/8.

parties covered by the Directive are the employers and the workers. These concepts have already been discussed in Chapter Five.

### 8.3.3.(ii) Obligations Provided for in the Directive

In order to achieve its ends, the Directive establishes a number of obligations for employers, coupled with a variety of obligations for workers. This approach is supplemented with a requirement for the introduction of appropriate health surveillance for workers and protection of particularly sensitive risk groups against the dangers which specifically affect them.

There is not the same detail in the description of workers' obligations as is the case for the employers' obligations. There are extensive requirements put on employers under Articles 5-12 (see below) but the general counterpart relating to workers in Article 13 only stipulates:

> It shall be the responsibility of each worker to take care as far as possible of his own safety and health and that of other persons affected by his acts or omissions at work.

The employer has a duty to ensure the safety and health of workers in every aspect related to the work (Article 5). Within the context of his/her responsibilities, the employer shall take the measures necessary for the safety and health protection of workers, including prevention of occupational risks and provision of information and training, as well as provision of the necessary organization and means. The employer shall be alert to the need to adjust these measures to take account of changing circumstances and the aim to improve existing situations.

The employer shall, according to Article 6, implement the measures referred to in the first subparagraph of paragraph 1 on the basis of the following general principles of prevention:

(a)    avoiding risks;
(b)    evaluating the risks which cannot be avoided;
(c)    combating the risks at source;
(d)    adapting the work to the individual, especially as regards the design of workplaces, the choice of work equipment and the choice of working and production methods, with a view, in particular, to alleviating monotonous work at a predetermined work-rate, thus reducing the effects on health;
(e)    adapting to technical progress;
(f)    replacing the dangerous by the non-dangerous or the less dangerous;
(g)    developing a coherent overall prevention policy which covers technology, organization of work, working conditions, social relationships and the influence of factors related to the working environment;

(h) giving collective protective measures priority over individual protective measures;

(i) giving appropriate instructions to the workers.

Without prejudice to the other provisions of the Directive, the employer shall, taking into account the nature of the activities of the enterprise and/or establishment:

(a) evaluate the risks to the safety and health of workers, *inter alia* in the choice of work equipment, the chemical substances or preparations used, and the fitting out of workplaces.

Subsequent to this evaluation and as necessary, the preventive measures and the working and production methods implemented by the employer must:
- assure an improvement in the level of protection afforded to workers with regard to safety and health,
- be integrated into all the activities of the undertaking and/or establishment and at all hierarchical levels;

(b) where he or she entrusts tasks to a worker, take into account the capabilities and, where appropriate, the handicaps of the worker concerned as regards health and safety;

(c) ensure that the planning and introduction of new technologies are the subject of consultation with the workers and/or their representatives, as regards the consequences of the choice of equipment, the working conditions and the working environment for the safety and health of workers.

The employer thus has several duties which may be enunciated as follows:[31]

**1. Duties of Awareness:** These are threefold, consisting, first, in a broad duty - which follows from the Preamble to the Directive - for the employer to keep informed of the latest advances in technology and scientific findings concerning workplace design; second, in a duty to identify and to evaluate risks to the safety and health of workers in the undertaking or establishment; and, third, a duty - closely linked to duties of instruction and training below - to be aware of the capabilities of workers at the undertaking or establishment as regards health and safety.

**2. Duties to Take Action to Ensure Safety and Health:** These twin duties constitute the "heart" of the Directive. They comprise:

(a) duty to eliminate avoidable risks;

(b) a duty to reduce the dangers posed by unavoidable risks.

**3. Duties of Strategic Planning to Avoid Risks to Safety and Health:** These duties reflect the need for both a general overview of safety and health needs and the implementation of a specific programme at the undertaking or establishment. The former is covered by the duty, in Article 6(2)(g), to develop a "coherent overall prevention policy". The latter is detailed in the Article 7 duties to develop and implement a system for the protection and prevention of occupational risks.

---

[31] Cf Neal (1990) 84.

**4. Duties to Train and Direct the Workforce:** The general duties of training for the workforce in matters of safety and health are set out in Article 12. In addition, there is a broad requirement in Article 6(2)(i) that employers, as part of their normal activity in managing and directing the work, should provide appropriate instructions to their workers, while Article 6(3)(d) makes it clear that employers must take appropriate steps to ensure that only "workers who have received adequate instructions" are to have access to areas where there is "serious and specific danger".
**5. Duties To Inform, Consult and Involve the Workforce:** These duties are extremely widely cast by the Directive. The details of what information is to be given by employers to workers and/or their representatives are set out in Article 10, while broad duties to provide for consultation and participation of workers are set out in Article 6(3)(c) and most importantly, in Article 11.
**6. Recording and Notification Duties:** A variety of obligations on the parts of employers and undertakings are set out in Article 9(1)(c) - listing of certain accidents and occupational illnesses at the undertaking or establishment - and Article 9(1)(d) - reports, for the benefit of relevant national authorities, on occupational accidents and occupational illness suffered by the workforce.

### 8.3.3.(iii) The Substitution Principle

It is a general principle in the Framework Directive 89/391/EEC (see above Article 6 (f)) that the employer has an overall duty to replace the dangerous by the non-dangerous or the less dangerous. This is called the *substitution principle* in the Nordic working environment legislation. This principle applies to technical equipment and to chemical substances and preparations as well as to everything else that might be dangerous in the working environment.

The substitution principle makes product safety an overrriding consideration in exercising the employer's choice of work equipment, chemical substances, etc (see below). Some employers might prefer to choose by economic criteria, for example, the choice of a cheap, dangerous product rather than a more expensive, less dangerous one. The Preamble to the Framework Directive states:

> ... the improvement of workers' safety and health at work is an objective which should not be subordinated to purely economic considerations;

The Preamble to the Directive must be taken into account when interpreting the substitution principle. Arguably this means that it will be unlawful for an employer to justify the choice of a more dangerous product for purely economic reasons. The substitution principle must, like all other Community law, be interpreted in accordance with the principle of proportionality.

340

## 8.3.3.(iv) Impact on National Law

The social policy Directives under Article 118A EC and especially the Framework Directive have generally been acknowledged by national labour lawyers as an improvement on national standards.[32] The above interpretation of the substitution principle means that Community law puts stricter requirements on the employer in this respect than national law has hitherto done.

In the proposal for the Framework Directive the Commission declared that the level of protection required by the Directive is higher than that already in existence in the Member States.[33] If any Member State might think otherwise it is free to uphold a higher standard provided that that standard is in conformity with the EC Treaty, especially Articles 30-36 EC (see below under 8.4). According to Article 118A(3) EC provisions adopted under Article 118A EC shall not prevent any Member State from maintaining or introducing more stringent measures for the protection of working conditions that are compatible with the Treaty.

In Chapter One we discuss the indirect effect of Directives. In *Kolpinghuis*[34] the ECJ ruled that there is a duty on the national courts to interpret national law in accordance with Directives both before and after the date of implementation. The national courts thus have a Community law duty to use the Framework Directive, for example, the substitution principle (see below under 8.5 and 8.6) as an interpretive tool when applying national law and to arrive at an interpretation in accordance with Community law if that is possible. They have had this duty since the adoption of the Directive on 12 June 1989 and were not at liberty to wait until the end of the transitional period (31 December 1992).

## 8.3.4. The Individual Directives

The Framework Directive 89/391/EEC provides in Article 16 that a series of individual Directives shall be made to cover specific risks. Thirteen of these Directives have been adopted so far:

---

[32] Cf Neal (1990); Weis (1990a); Mialon (1990); Montuschi (1990); Martinez (1990); Baldwin and Daintith (1992).

[33] COM(88)73, 3.

[34] Case 80/86 [1987] ECR 3982.

The first Directive lays down minimum health and safety requirements for the workplace.[35]

The second Directive prescribes minimum health and safety requirements for the use by workers of machines and equipment.[36]

The third Directive prescribes minimum health and safety requirements for the use by workers of personal protective equipment at the workplace,[37] with guidelines on selection and use in annexes.

The fourth Directive[38] makes minimum health and safety requirements for handling heavy loads where there is a risk of back injury for workers.

The fifth Directive[39] provides for minimum safety and health requirements for work with visual display screen units.

The sixth Directive[40] requires protection of workers against the risk of exposure to carcinogens at work.

The seventh Directive[41] requires protection of workers against the risk of exposure to biological agents at work.

The eighth Directive[42] provides for the implementation of minimum safety and health requirements at temporary or mobile constructions sites.

The ninth Directive[43] provides for minimum requirements for the provision of safety and/or health signs at work.

The tenth Directive[44] provides for the introduction of measures to encourage improvements in the safety and health at work of pregnant workers and workers who have recently given birth or are breastfeeding.

The eleventh Directive[45] concerns minimum requirements for improving the health and safety protection of workers in the mineral-extracting industries.

---

[35] 89/654/EEC, OJ 1989 L 393/1.

[36] 89/655/EEC, OJ 1989 L 393/13 amended by 95/63/EC, OJ 1995 L 335/28.

[37] 89/656/EEC, OJ 1989 L 393/18.

[38] 90/269/EEC, OJ 1990 L 156/9.

[39] 90/270/EEC, OJ 1990 L 156/14.

[40] 90/394/EEC, OJ 1990 L 196/1. A proposal for amending this Directive has been presented in COM(95)425, OJ 1995 C 317/16.

[41] 90/679/EEC, OJ 1990 L 374/1, amended by 93/88/EEC, OJ 1993 L 268/71.

[42] 92/57/EEC, OJ 1992 L 245/6.

[43] 92/58/EEC, OJ 1992 L 245/23.

[44] 92/85/EEC, OJ 1992 L 348/1.

[45] 92/91/EEC, OJ 1992 L 348/9.

The twelfth Directive concerns the minimum requirements for improving the safety and health protection of workers in surface and underground mineral-extracting industries.[46]

The thirteenth individual Directive concerns the minimum safety and health requirements for work on board fishing vessels.[47]

In addition to the above Directives two important Directives on the protection of young people at work[48] and on the organization of working time [49] have been adopted.

There has been an infringement proceeding against Spain[50] for failure to transpose the Framework Directive[51] and the first 6 individual Directives [52] correctly.

In *Crimal Proceedings against X* [53] the ECJ gave a preliminary ruling on the interpretation of the fifth Directive on work with display screens. The Court held that Article 9(1) of Council Directive 90/270/EEC must be interpreted as meaning that the regular eye tests for which it provides are to be carried out on all workers to whom the Directive applies and Article 9(2) is to be interpreted as meaning that workers are entitled to an ophthalmological examination in all cases where the eye and eyesight test carried out pursuant to Article 9(1) shows that this is necessary. Articles 4 and 5 of Directive 90/270/EEC apply to all workstations as defined in Article 2(b), even if they are not used by workers as defined in Article 2(c), and workstations must be adapted to comply with all the minimum requirements laid down in the Annex to the Directive.

The tenth individual Directive on pregnancy protection is discussed below on protection of women.

The second and third individual Directives are especially relevant to the problems relating to technical harmonization (see below under 8.5) and the

---

[46]  92/104/EEC, OJ 1992 L 404/10.

[47]  93/103/EC, OJ 1993 L 307/1.

[48]  94/33/EEC, OJ 1994 L 216/12.

[49]  93/104/EC, OJ 1993 L 307/18.

[50]  Case C-79/95 *Commission* v *Spain* nyr.

[51]  89/391/EEC.

[52]  89/654/EEC, 89/655/EEC, 89/656/EEC, 90/269/EEC, 90/270/EEC and 90/394/EEC.

[53]  Joined Cases C-74/95 and C-129/95 nyr.

sixth and seventh Directives are particularly important in relation to the free movement of chemical and other dangerous substances (see below under 8.6).

### 8.3.5. The Fourth Action Programme on Health and Safety

In 1995[54] the Commission adopted the Fourth Community Programme Concerning Safety, Hygiene and Health at Work. In the Fourth programme it is observed that in the past the main focus of EU action on health and safety at work has been legislative. This was particularly the case under the Third Action Programme, initiated in 1988, which coincided with the introduction of the SEA 1986. It gave the Commission a new competence under Article 118A EC to promote improved health and safety levels. In particular, it facilitated the establishment of minimum standards in health and safety which were important for the completion of the Internal Market and the freedom of movement of workers. It also assured workers that increased European integration would have a social as well as an economic dimension. In the Fourth Programme a new focus on information is proposed for the future. This is to ensure that the substantial body of EU health and safety legislation now in place is correctly and effectively communicated. A new initiative is launched aimed specifically at SME's. This programme, SAFE, (Safety Actions for Europe) will use best practices as a standard for the development of a work environment that is safe, productive and competitive. The key features of the Fourth Programme are threefold :

- Development of non-legislative measures, notably those promoting information, education and training. Particular emphasis will be given to practical measures which improve safety and health arrangements in firms under a new programme for safety actions for Europe (SAFE).
- Consolidation and implementation of existing laws. Attention will be focused on how existing legislation is being implemented, involving full use of all the legal powers at the disposal of the Commission. However, further necessary legislation on minimum standards at the European level will continue to play a key role in health and safety policy.
- More effective evaluation of the impact on safety and health of the Community's other policies. A number of policies, such as those for the environment, agriculture and chemicals, have an impact on safty and health at work.

The first part of the programme covers four types of action:

- Developing guidance notes and information material;
- Improving information, education and training;

---

[54] OJ 1995 C 203/2.

- Investigating key problem areas such as violence to employees, stress, specific measures for women, young people, etc...
- The SAFE Programme.

The second part of the programme deals with:

- Ensuring correct implementation by Member States of the Community legislation already adopted;
- Progress on Commission proposals already tabled;
- Review of existing Community legislation;
- New proposals for high risk activities or for certain categories of workers.

The third part focuses on safety and health in other policies:

- Establishing a more coherent approach for all Commission activity;
- Building links with third countries that have Association Agreements with the European Community;
- Improving cooperation inside the European Union, both with countries outside the Union and with international organisations.

## 8.4. TECHNICAL BARRIERS, STANDARDIZATION AND THE WORKING ENVIRONMENT

### 8.4.1. The Internal Market: Article 100A EC Measures

Until the mid 1980's the Community attempted to harmonize technical requirements by means of Directives which laid down binding provisions of a very detailed nature. This method of regulation resulted in very few Directives being adopted. To speed up the process of technical harmonization a new method of regulation was introduced in 1985 (see below 8.5.2.(i)). In 1983, the Council of Ministers adopted Directive 83/189/EEC[55] laying down a procedure for the provision of information in the field of technical standards and regulations. The Directive which was amended in 1988[56] and 1994[57] provided a standstill procedure for the adoption of new technical standards. Under this procedure, each Member State was obliged to notify the Commission of new proposals for national standards. The Commission would oppose

---

[55]  OJ 1983 L 109/8.

[56]  88/182/EEC, OJ 1988 L 81/75.

[57]  94/10/EC, OJ 1994 L 100/30.

them if they did not meet "essential requirements and have an objective in the public interest of which they constitute the main guarantee". The initial proposal for this Directive was published in October 1980 shortly after the decision of the ECJ in *Cassis de Dijon*.[58]

As discussed in Chapter One, the Commission has power under Article 118 EC to issue binding Decisions. By Decision 88/383/EEC[59] a procedure was established to monitor the working of national provisions and provisions adopted to implement the Article 100A EC and 118A EC Directives in the field of the working environment.

### 8.4.1.(i) The New Approach[60]

In 1985 the Community agreed a New Approach to Technical Harmonisation which was outlined in the Commission's White Paper.[61] According to the Commission, this new approach takes into consideration the principles elaborated by the ECJ in its interpretation of Articles 30 - 36 EC (see Chapter Five). In the Council Resolution of 7 May 1985[62] on the "new approach" to technical harmonization and standardization reference to voluntary standards was accepted as the appropriate method of giving technical expression to the essential requirements of Community Directives.

Under the new approach, technical requirements are divided into two groups: essential requirements and more detailed specifications. Only essential requirements are governed by binding Community legislation while the technical specifications are left to voluntary regulation by means, *inter alia,* of European standards. Directives lay down the essential requirements to which products must comply in order to ensure the protection of public health or safety, of the environment or the consumer. European standards are to be developed in respect of each Directive in order to provide manufacturers with a set of technical specifications recognized in the Directive as giving a presumption of conformity to the essential requirements. The European standards concerned, the so-called "harmonized standards", remain voluntary. Manufacturers are allowed to put on the Community market products which

---

[58]  Case 120/78 [1979] ECR 649.

[59]  OJ 1988 L 183/34.

[60]  Cf Burrows (1990) and Farr (1992).

[61]  COM(85)310 final, Brussels.

[62]  OJ 1985 C 136/1.

either meet other standards or no standards at all, subject to fulfilling the procedures for assessment of conformity laid down by the Directive.

The essential requirements laid down in Community Directives contain the only legal requirements which can be applied to the marketing of the kind of product covered within the Community. No additional legal requirements can be applied to the marketing of a product in a Member State. National rules which do not relate to essential requirements will not be harmonised at the Community level, but will be subject to mutual recognition. Although some harmonising activity may still take place in order to rationalise differing national standards.

The Council has adopted several Directives based on the new approach (toys, simple pressure vessels, construction products, electro-magnetic compatibility, machinery, personal protective equipment, gas appliances, medical devices and telecommunications terminal equipment). A large amount of work has been given to the European standardization bodies by means of individual "standardization mandates" from the Commission, which, after consultation of the standardization body concerned, establish the scope of the work, lay down any supplementary guidelines and fix the timetable by which the standards should be adopted.

### 8.4.1.(ii) European Standards

The optional European Standards, which are drawn up by CEN and CENELEC (see below) must respect the essential requirements in the relevant Directives. The Commission has a contract with CEN and CENELEC and is in practice in a position to ensure that a standard will conform with the relevant requirements. Problems which arise after the adoption of a standard can be referred to a Committee set up under Directive 83/189 EC[63] on an information procedure relating to technical standards for appropriate action to be taken.

All European standards are optional in their entirety. They are therefore different from essential requirements and technical Regulations which have the force of law. The making of standards has always been a function which has points of contact with public regulation in that it often, although not always, takes place within a regulatory framework. Being concerned with the facilitation of manufacturers' processes on a completely optional and voluntary basis, however, the process of establishing European standards is essentially a private sector task. This was so even before the introduction of the Community's New Approach to technical harmonisation in 1985.

---

[63]  OJ 1983 L 109/8.

Manufacturers may follow different methods of manufacture and obtain certification of conformity with any relevant essential requirement in order to be able to market their products produced by another method, or according to other criteria, as long as any relevant essential requirements are met.

Standards adopted *via* CEN and CENELEC must be incorporated into any national standard and national standards institutes become responsible for affixing a CE mark following an examination. No additional national requirements may prevent goods with the CE mark from circulating freely within the Community. The corollary to this is that in order to gain the benefit of the free movement of goods rules, a manufacturer must obtain the CE mark. If a manufacturer wishes to export, then the voluntary and optional procedures must be followed.

### 8.4.1.(iii) Standardization Organizations

The European standardization organization (CEN) was set up to ensure more effective implementation of international standards by national standardization bodies in Europe, the harmonization of divergent national standards or the preparation of standards where none existed.

An association of European national standard-bodies from the Member States of the EEC and EFTA, the Comité Européen de Normalisation - CEN, was established in 1961, to be followed in 1962 by a similar organization for the electrotechnical area (CENELCOM, which became CENELEC in 1973).

In the first twenty years the output of these European organizations was low.[64] CEN adopted 96 European standards between 1961 and 1982; CENELEC adopted in the same period 37 European standards and 303 harmonized documents (texts which, while containing common elements, allow for national deviations on a permanent or temporary basis). An important distinguishing feature of both organizations, however, was that their decisions on common European standards, once adopted, became binding on those members which had voted for them. Outside the limited area covered by common standardization work, national standardization bodies continued to develop their own standards independently.

A stronger regional orientation was given to European standardization after 1983, as a result of initiatives taken by the Community in order to eliminate technical barriers to intra-Community trade. The first of these was the adoption of Council Directive 83/189/EEC laying down an information procedure for standards and technical regulations. This Directive established the procedures

---

[64] Cf Commission *Green Paper on the Development of European Standardization: Action for Faster Technological Integration in Europe*, COM (90) 456 final.

for cooperation between the members of CEN/CENELEC and the Commission which still apply today.

In 1984 the Commission defined its relationship with CEN/CENELEC in General Guidelines for Cooperation. The Commission committed itself to following the New Approach as widely as possible, and to giving financial support to CEN/CENELEC. CEN/CENELEC agreed to coordinate their activity, to increase their resources, to align as far as possible with international standards, to ensure that all interested parties were associated with their work, and to maintain an effective information service. The financial aspects of Commission-CEN/CENELEC cooperation were laid down in a Framework Contract, first agreed in 1985 and renewed in 1989.

Following ratification of the European Single Act in 1987, the internal regulations of CEN/CENELEC were revised at the request of the Commission to permit the adoption and obligatory transposition of European standards by weighted majority vote. Under CEN/CENELEC rules, a draft European standard which receives a favourable vote from a qualified majority of member bodies is deemed to be adopted and is implemented by all.

The structure of CEN and CENELEC is that of associations of national standards bodies or electrotechnical committees, which have the last word on all questions relating to standardization activity at the European level. The budget of each European organization is voted on by the national members, as are its internal rules, work programmes, and decisions on the allocation of resources. In contrast to the situation at national level, the governing bodies of CEN contain no direct representation of other interests than of professional standardizers (such as public authorities, manufacturers, or other users of standards), although CENELEC is closely associated with the electrotechnical industry and appoints some of its office-holders from industry.

A comparison of the annual output of the organizations in 1989 with that of 1982 revealed: CEN adopted almost seven times as many standards in 1989 as in 1982 (130 instead of 19) and CENELEC six times as many standards and Harmonized Documents (126 compared to 20). But the distance between what has been achieved and the goal is still great. There are today about 1250 adopted European standardization documents of which about 800 in the electrotechnical area. The number of national standards in Germany, France and the United Kingdom is about 20,000, 13,000 and 10,000 respectively (a significant proportion of these is identical to or related to international or European standards).[65]

---

[65] Cf Commission *Green Paper on the Development of European Standardization: Action for Faster Technological Integration in Europe*, COM (90) 456 final, Brussels.

### 8.4.1.(iv) The Two Levels of European Standardization

European-level standardization work aims at the harmonization of separate national standards. The standards agreed within CEN and CENELEC have no formal status until the national standardization bodies transpose their content into national standards and withdraw any conflicting provisions.

This "two-stage" standardization in Europe has disadvantages. The first is delay; at least six months, and sometimes longer, is allowed under CEN/CENELEC rules for national transposition, and the rules are not always observed. Transposition can also lead to lack of clarity about which standards are harmonized at the European level and which are not, although CEN and CENELEC have laid down rules on the matter. Some national standards bodies do not apply fully the rules for identification of harmonized European Standards. If European industry cannot know at the end of the European standardization process which standards are identical across Europe, an essential point has been lost. The Commission in its Green Paper on European Standardization argues further:

> "More fundamentally, one may question whether national transposition is in the interests of the customers for European standards in every respect. By pursuing harmonization through the alignment of national standards national standardization bodies maintain copyright of the harmonized standards (the thereby exclusive rights to sales revenue) and reinforce the image of the national mark of conformity in the market place. The situation can arise therefore that the manufacturer of a product conforming to a European standard sold in all parts of the Community may have to obtain several different national marks of conformity in order to show the customer what he is buying; this is not what the 1992 programme is about.
>
> The Commission considers that all future European standards should exist in their own right and should not have to be transposed at national level before they can be used."[66]

### 8.4.1.(v) Testing and Certification

A major problem is how to assess conformity with the essential requirements. On 24 July 1989, the Commission sent a proposal to the Council of Ministers for a Council Decision on procedures for testing and certification and a Communication[67] on the Global Approach to testing and certification in which it confirmed the need for the creation of an autonomous body.

---

[66] *Ibid* p 42.

[67] COM(89) 209 final Brussels, OJ 1989 C 267/3.

The Council agreed on 21 December 1989[68] to the establishment of the European Organization for Testing and Certification (EOTC), which led to the formal signature of the Memorandum of Understanding between CEN, CENELEC, EFTA and the Commission on 25 April 1990. This new organization, which will operate alongside CEN and CENELEC, has now been set up by the four signatories for an experimental period which should end on 31 December 1992 with the constitution of a legally autonomous organization. In the meantime CEN and CENELEC accept, on a contractual basis, to provide the necessary administrative support.

On 13 December 1990 the Council adopted Decision 90/683/EEC on procedures for testing and certification.[69]

### 8.4.1.(vi) The Machinery Directive

With regard to the working environment, the most important of the Article 100A EC Directives on technical harmonization are the Machinery Directive[70] and the Directive on marketing of personal protective equipment.[71] These Directives are adopted in accordance with the New Approach described above.

The Machinery Directive lays down the essential health and safety requirements machinery must satisfy in order to be lawfully put on the market. When machinery satisfies these requirements Member States have a duty to admit the machinery access to their market. The provisions of the Directive do not affect Member States' entitlement to lay down, in due observance of the Treaty, such requirements as they may deem necessary to ensure that persons and in particular workers are protected when using the machines in question, provided that this does not mean that the machinery is modified in a way not specified in the Directive. Member States are not allowed to prohibit, restrict or impede the placing on the market and putting into service in their territory of machinery which complies with the provisions of the Directive. Machinery bearing an EC mark and accompanied by the EC declaration of conformity referred to in Article 3 of the Directive shall be regarded as conforming to the essential health and safety requirements of the Directive.

Where a national standard transposing a harmonized standard covers one or more of the essential safety requirements, machinery constructed in accordance

---

[68]  OJ 1990 C 10/1.

[69]  OJ 1990 L 380/13. See Corrigendum to this decision OJ 1991 L 115/68.

[70]  89/392/EEC, OJ 1989 L 183/9.

[71]  89/686/EEC, OJ 1989 L 399/18.

with this standard shall be presumed to comply with the relevant essential requirements. In the absence of harmonized standards, Member States shall take any steps they deem necessary to bring to the attention of the parties concerned the existing national technical standards and specifications which are regarded as important or relevant to the proper implementation of the essential safety and health requirements. Where a Member State or the Commission considers that the harmonized standards do not entirely satisfy the essential requirements, the Commission or the Member State concerned shall bring the matter before the Committee set up under Directive 83/189/EEC, giving the reasons for the complaint.

The Directive contains a safeguard clause. Where a Member State ascertains that machinery bearing the EC mark and used in accordance with its intended purpose is liable to endanger the safety of persons, it can take all appropriate measures to withdraw such machinery from the market, to prohibit the placing on the market, putting into service or use thereof, or to restrict free movement thereof. The manufacturer shall, in order to certify the conformity of machinery with the provisions of the Directive, draw up an EC declaration of conformity and shall affix an EC mark to the machinery.

### 8.4.2. The Social Dimension: Article 118A EC Directives

### 8.4.2.(i) The Second and Third Individual Directives Within the 1989 Framework Directive

The second and third individual Directives within the 1989 Framework Directive on Health and Safety are Article 118A EC corollaries to the Machinery Directive[72] and the Directive on marketing of personal protective equipment[73] adopted under Article 100A EC.

Under the second individual Directive within the 1989 Framework Directive, the employer shall take the measures necessary to ensure that the work equipment made available to workers in the undertaking and/or establishment is suitable for the work to be carried out or properly adapted for that purpose and may be used by workers without impairment to their safety or health. In selecting the work equipment which he/she proposes to use, the employer shall pay attention to the specific working conditions and character-istics and to the hazards which exist in the undertaking and/or establishment, in particular at the workplace, for the safety and health of the workers, and/or

---

[72]  89/392/EEC, OJ 1989 L 183/9.

[73]  89/686/EEC, OJ 1989 L 399/18.

any additional hazards posed by the use of work equipment in question. Where it is not possible fully to ensure that work equipment can be used by workers without risk to their safety or health, the employer shall take appropriate measures to minimize the risks. The employer must obtain and/or use work equipment which complies with the provisions of any relevant Community Directive which is applicable and the minimum requirements laid down in the Annex to the Directive, to the extent that no other Community Directive is applicable or is so only partially.

### 8.4.2.(ii) The Framework Directive 89/391/EEC

An employer is prevented from choosing work equipment that cannot lawfully be marketed under the Machinery Directive or other relevant Article 100A EC Directives (see above) but he/she does not have free choice between all lawfully marketed products which are capable of serving as work equipment. In choosing work equipment the employer must respect the general principles of prevention laid down in Article 6 of the Framework Directive (see under 3.3). This means that the more dangerous must be replaced by the non-dangerous or less dangerous (the substitution principle).

Article 6(d) provides for the principle of adapting the work to the individual, especially as regards *inter alia* the choice of work equipment. In view of the strong prohibition against direct and indirect sex discrimination in Community law (see in Chapter Four) there is no doubt that this means that work equipment must be chosen in a way that ensures a working environment adapted equally to men and women. It is unlawful, for example, for an employer to choose machinery which requires physical strength if it is technically possible to choose machinery that does not. As discussed in Chapter Four, the ECJ held in *Rummler*[74] that it is lawful to take physical strength into consideration in pay schemes if physical strength is necessary for the job, but it follows from the Framework Directive on the working environment that it is prohibited to make physical strength job-relevant if it is not necessary.

---

[74]  Case 237/85 [1986] ECR 2101.

## 8.5. DANGEROUS SUBSTANCES AND THE WORKING ENVIRON-MENT

### 8.5.1. The Internal Market: Article 100A EC Directives

### 8.5.1.(i) Classification, Packaging and Labelling of Dangerous Substances and Preparations

Directive 67/548/EEC[75] is the basic Directive on classification, packaging and labelling of dangerous substances whereas the same subject matter in relation to dangerous preparations is governed by Directive 88/379/EEC. For the purpose of those Directives "substances" means chemical elements and their compounds as they occur in the natural state or as produced by industry. "Preparations" means mixtures or solutions composed of two or more substances.

The purpose of Directive 67/548/EEC with later amendments[76] is to approximate the laws, regulations and administrative provisions of the Member States on classification, packaging, and labelling of dangerous substances which are placed on the market in the Member States of the Community.

The Directive contains a list of dangerous substances, together with particulars on the classification and labelling procedures in respect of each substance. The basic principle is that substances shall be classified, packaged and labelled in the country of origin (the country where they are produced or for the first time imported into the Community) according to a common set of rules. The Directive (as amended) provides for classification criteria and for a number of danger symbols, for example, a skull and crossbones. In an Annex to the Directive a number of Risk-phrases (R - 1, R - 2, R - 3, etc.) concerning the nature of the special risks attaching to dangerous substances are defined. This results in the Risk-phrases meaning the same in all Member States. R - 1 for example means "Explosive when dry" in all countries and in all languages. R-45 "May cause cancer" is used to define the scope of the sixth working environment Directive on carcinogens (see below). Similarly a number of Safety-sentences concerning recommended safety precautions are defined.

---

[75]  OJ 1967 L 196/1.

[76]  Last amendment by Commission Directive 96/56/EC adapting to technical progress Council Directive 67/548/EEC on the approximation of the laws, regulations and administrative provisions relating to the classification, packaging and labelling of dangerous, OJ 1996 L 236/35.

354

All packagings must, according to Article 6 of the Directive, be labelled with danger symbols and R-phrases in accordance with the Directive. If the packaging is accompanied by advice on safety precautions they must be expressed by means of S-phrases in accordance with the Directive.

Member States are precluded from making entry into their territory of substances classified, labelled and packaged in conformity with the Directive dependant upon notifications, examinations or relabelling of the substances.

In *Commission* v *Denmark*[77] the ECJ found that Denmark had infringed Directive 79/831/EEC on the seventh amendment to Directive 67/548/EEC by not according correctly labelled packagings with dangerous substances free access to the Danish market. The reason behind the Danish reluctance to fulfil its obligations under Directive 67/548/EEC with later amendments was the widespread view in Denmark that Danish criteria for classifying substances as dangerous were stricter than the Community provisions so that full implementation would lower the Danish standard of consumer and worker protection. After the ECJ's judgment Denmark gave up its resistance on this point and amended the Danish legislation.

Directive 88/379/EEC deals with the classification, packaging and labelling of dangerous preparations.[78] It was amended by Directive 96/665/EC[79] and Commission Directive of 5 March 1991[80] defining and laying down the detailed arrangements for the system of specific information relating to dangerous preparations in implementation of Article 10 of Directive 88/379/EEC. Directive 88/379/EEC was adopted in 1988 by eleven Member states with Denmark voting against it. The Directive contains particulars on the classification and labelling procedures in respect of dangerous preparations. Under Article 13 of the Directive Member States are precluded from prohibiting, limiting or hindering marketing of preparations which satisfy the provisions of the Directive.

### 8.5.1.(ii) Article 100A(4) EC

The general problem whether or not Denmark should adopt less stringent criteria for assessing risks and danger in order to adapt to Community standards is still a matter of debate in connection with the implementation of

---

[77] Case 278/85 [1987] ECR 4069.

[78] OJ 1988 L 187/14.

[79] OJ 1996 L 265/15.

[80] 91/155/EEC, OJ 1991 L 76/35, amended by 93/112/EC, OJ 1993 L 314/38.

the Commission Directive on technical data sheets defining and laying down the detailed arrangements for the system of specific information relating to dangerous preparations in implementation of Article 10 of Directive 88/379/EEC. In Denmark there has been strong criticism that acceptance of Directive 88/379/EEC and the ensuing Commission Directive on technical data sheets, which Denmark voted against, will mean shortening the Danish lists of preparations that have traditionally been looked upon as dangerous or involving risks. This includes shortening the Danish cancer list so that a number of preparations, which up until now, have had to be treated as involving risk of cancer can no longer be required to be labelled in that way.

It is therefore a matter of debate, involving political considerations, whether Denmark should invoke Article 100A(4) EC to uphold the traditional Danish views on what is dangerous. The legal scope of Article 100A(4) EC has been the subject of conjecture, two of the controversies being whether a Member State which voted for a Directive can invoke Article 100A(4) EC and whether new measures can be introduced applying this provision.[81] It seems likely that a Member State which voted against the Directive and which is upholding provisions in existence at the date of adoption of the Directive would stand a good chance of being succesful in a case before the ECJ.

### 8.5.2. The Social Dimension: Article 118A EC Directives

As described above (under 8.3) the hazardous agents Directive 80/1107/EEC and three specific Directives on lead, asbestos and noise were adopted before the SEA 1986. After the adoption of the SEA further Directives amending or complementing the hazardous agents Directive have been proposed and in some cases adopted under Article 118A EC.

### 8.5.2.(i) The Proscription Directive and the Asbestos Directive

The Proscription Directive 88/364/EEC[82] was adopted in 1988 as the fourth individual Directive within the hazardous agents Directive 80/1107/EEC. It prohibits four carcinogens listed in an Annex to the Directive.

---

[81]  See Oliver (1996); Ehlermann (1987); Gulmann (1987).

[82]  OJ 1988 L 179/44.

The Asbestos Directive[83] was amended in 1991 by Council Directive 91/382/EEC[84] on the protection of workers from the risks related to exposure to asbestos at work.

### 8.5.2.(ii) Occupational exposure value limits

Occupational exposure value limits are governed by the hazardous agents Directive 80/1107/EEC which was amended in 1988 by Directive 88/642/EEC[85] to develop Community provisions on exposure value limits. The proposal originally introduced binding exposure limit values but the adopted Directive only provides for the development of limit values that are *advisory* and not mandatory for Member States. In May 1991 the Commission issued a Directive[86] on establishing *indicative limit values* by implementing Council Directive 80/1107/EEC on the protection of workers from the risks related to exposure to chemical, physical and biological agents at work.

### 8.5.2.(iii) The Proposed Benzene Directive

In 1987, the Commission presented a proposal to reduce and control exposure to benzene at work.[87] The proposed Directive on benzene was intended to become the fifth individual Directive within the hazardous agents Directive 88/1107/EEC. In June 1988 the Council of Ministers reached a common position on the proposal. The European Parliament rejected the Council's common position which under Article 149(2) EC, means that the Council only will be able to adopt the Directive with unanimity. The proposal has not been adopted.

It was the first time the European Parliament used the powers given to it in Article 149(2) EC by the SEA 1986. The difference of opinion between the Council and the European Parliament reflects the underlying conflict in this area between the goal of promoting a free market for dangerous substances and the concern for worker protection. The European Parliament is generally more strongly committed to working environment protection than the Council of

---

[83]   83/477/EEC, OJ 1983 L 263/25.

[84]   OJ 1991 L 206/6.

[85]   OJ 1988 L 356/74.

[86]   91/322/EEC, OJ 1991 L 177/22.

[87]   COM(85) 669.

Ministers whose majority is strongly in favour of facilitating the free movement of dangerous substances.

### 8.5.2.(iv) The Sixth and Seventh Individual Directives within the 1989 Framework Directive

The sixth individual Directive[88] within the 1989 Framework Directive requires protection of workers against the risk of exposure to carcinogens at work and the seventh individual Directive[89] requires protection of workers against the risk of exposure to biological agents at work. These two Directives may be seen as Article 118A EC corollaries to Directive 67/548/EEC with later amendments and Directive 88/379/EEC as amended. They provide for protection of workers in situations which, under Directive 67/548/EEC and Directive 88/379/EEC, are to be assessed as dangerous or involving risks. The scope of the Carcinogens Directive is defined by reference to Directive 67/548/EEC and Directive 88/379/EEC as substances or preparation labelled R 45 "May cause cancer" or as a substance or preparations covered by an Annex to the Directive. The reference to Directive 67/548/EEC and Directive 88/379/EEC in the Carcinogens Directive and the Biological Agents Directive means that the lax risk and danger assesment criteria in the Article 100A EC Directives directly affect the level of working environment protection.

### 8.5.2.(v) The Framework Directive 89/391/EEC

As is the case with technical equipment the employer is precluded from choosing dangerous substances and preparations that are not lawfully on the market. Within the supply on the market the employer must choose in compliance with the general obligations in the Framework Directive. The substitution principle means that wherever it is possible there is a duty on the employer to substitute the non dangerous or less dangerous for the dangerous. The question of what is dangerous in relation to the Framework Directive 89/391/EEC must be answered in the light of the purpose of that Directive (improvement of working conditions) which is quite different from the purpose of Directive 67/548 and Directive 88/379 (establishment of a free movement for dangerous substances and preparations).

---

[88]  90/394/EEC, OJ L 196/1.

[89]  90/679/EEC, OJ L 374/1.

## 8.6. IMPLEMENTATION OF THE SOCIAL CHARTER

The adoption of Directive 89/391/EEC has brought the working environment into a general framework. Alongside this development the Community continues to show particular interest to special groups and special situations. A number of working environment Directives and measures were promised in the Commission's Action Programme relating to the implementation of the Social Charter.[90]

### 8.6.1. Special Risk Groups and Particularly Dangerous Work Situations

As noted above the eighth Directive[91] within the Framework Directive provides for the implementation of minimum safety and health requirements at temporary or mobile constructions sites, the ninth Directive[92] for minimum requirements for the provision of safety and/or health signs at work, the tenth Directive[93] provides for the introduction of measures to encourage improvements in the safety and health at work of pregnant workers and workers who have recently given birth or are breastfeeding, the eleventh Directive[94] concerns minimum requirements for improving the health and safety protection of workers in the mineral-extracting industries and the twelfth Directive concerns minimum requirements for improving the health and safety protection of workers in the extractive industries for the exploitation of minerals in mines and quarries. All these provisions are directed towards special groups and/or special situations. As another example of this policy the Council Directive[95] on the minimum safety and health requirements for improved medical treatment on board vessels may be mentioned. In addition the Commission has proposed Directives on temporary or mobile work sites,[96] on health and safety for fishing

---

[90]  COM(89) 568 final Brussels 1989.

[91]  92/57/EEC, OJ L 245/6.

[92]  92/58/EEC, OJ L 245/23.

[93]  92/85/EEC, OJ L 348/1.

[94]  92/91/EEC, OJ L 348/9.

[95]  93/103/EC, OJ L 307/1.

[96]  COM(90) 275 final, Brussels 1990.

vessels,[97] on safe transport to work of workers with reduced mobility[98] and on nuclear plants. Directive 90/641/EURATOM on protection of workers against exposure to ioning radiation at work was adopted on 4 December 1990.[99]

### 8.6.2. Occupational Diseases

Occupational disease is a field where the Community has adopted mainly soft law. As early as the 1960's, the Commission issued Recommendations on occupational diseases (see Chapter One) and in *Grimaldi*[100] the ECJ ruled that Recommendations, although not binding, must be taken into account when interpreting national law. In 1990 the Commission, using its powers under Article 155 EC, issued a new Recommendation 90/326 on the adoption of a European list of occupational diseases.[101]

### 8.6.3. Arrangement of Working Time[102]

In 1990, the Commission proposed a Directive on adaptation of working time containing provisions on daily, weekly and yearly rest periods and on nightwork and shiftwork.[103] This has proved to be a very controversial issue where agreement was only reached after the adoption of the Maastricht Treaty when the directive on the organization of working time[104] was adopted. The United Kingdom contested the validity of the directive.[105] In its judgment on this issue, the ECJ held that a distinction must be drawn between the second sentence of Article 5 of the working time Directive and its other provisions. As

---

[97]  COM(90) 272 final, Brussels 1990.

[98]  COM(90) 588 final Brussels 1991, OJ C 68/91.

[99]  OJ 1990 L 349/21.

[100]  Case C-322/88 [1989] ECR 4407.

[101]  OJ 1990 L 160/39.

[102]  See on working time provisions in the Community generally Blanpain and Köhler (1988).

[103]  COM(90) 317 final Brussels, OJ C 224/90.

[104]  93/104/EC, OJ 1993 L 307/18.

[105]  Case C-84/94, *United Kingdom* v *The Council of the European Union*, judgment of 12.11.1996, nyr. Discussed in Chapter One.

to the second sentence of Article 5, which provides for Sunday normally to be included in the weekly rest period, the Court found that the Council has failed to explain why Sunday, as a weekly rest day, is more closely connected with the health and safety of workers than any other day of the week. The second sentence of Article 5, which is severable from the other provisions of the directive, was therefore annulled.

The other measures laid down by the Directive, which refer to minimum rest periods, length of work, night work, shift work and the pattern of work, relate to the 'working environment' and reflect concern for the protection of 'the health and safety of workers'. Since, in terms of its aim and content, the Directive has, as its principal objective, the protection of the health and safety of workers by the imposition of minimum requirements for gradual implementation, neither Article 100 EC nor Article 100a EC could have constituted the appropriate legal basis for its adoption. The ECJ therefore held that the Directive was properly adopted on the basis of Article 118A EC, save for the second sentence of Article 5, which was annulled.

### 8.6.4. Protection of Women at Work

### 8.6.4.(i). Special Protection, Night Work, etc

Application of special protective legislation for women, for example prohibition against night work for women, work underground, etc, has historically been widespread in many Member States, but is now in the process of being abolished. In *Stoeckel*[106] the ECJ ruled that the prohibition against night work for women in the French Code du Travail Article 213-1 is a violation of the Equal Treatment Directive.[107] The provisions in the French Code du Travail were adopted in order to implement ILO Convention 89 of 9 July 1948 concerning Nightwork of Women Employed in Industry. France ratified that convention in 1953 (ie before the establishment of the EC).

In the *Levy* case[108] the ECJ was asked whether Articles 1 to 5 of Directive 76/207/EEC are to be interpreted as meaning that national legislation prohibiting night work solely for women amounts to discrimination, having regard *inter alia* to Article 3 of ILO Convention No 89. Article 234 EC provides that the rights and obligations arising from agreements concluded

---

[106] Case C-345/89 *Criminal Proceedings against Alfred Stoeckel* [1991] ECR I-4047.

[107] Council Directive 76/207/EEC, OJ 1976 L 39/40.

[108] Case C-158/91 [1993] ECR I-4287.

before the entry into force of the EC Treaty are not affected by it. The ECJ held that while it is true that equal treatment of men and women constitutes a fundamental right recognized by the Community legal order, its implementation, even at Community level, has been gradual, requiring the Council to take action by means of Directives. Those Directives allow, temporarily, certain derogations from the principle of equal treatment. In those circumstances, it is not sufficient to rely on the principle of equal treatment in order to evade performance of the obligations which are incumbent on a Member State in that field under an earlier international agreement and observance of which is safeguarded by the first paragraph of Article 234 EC. In proceedings for a preliminary ruling, it is not for the ECJ but for the national court to determine which obligations are imposed by an earlier international agreement on the Member State concerned and to ascertain their ambit so as to be able to determine the extent to which they constitute an obstacle to the application of Article 5 of Directive 76/207/EEC.

Following the judgment in *Stoeckel*, the French Government denounced ILO Convention No 89 on 26 February 1992, with effect from 26 February 1993. The *Levy* judgment is therefore without practical effect as regards France. In *Minne*[109] similar questions were asked in relation to Belgian law. The ECJ ruled that national provisions prohibiting night-work for both men and women but providing for systems of derogations which differ on grounds of sex are not permissible unless justified on grounds of necessary protection of women. It also addressed the position of national courts with regard to obligations towards non-member countries arising under agreements concluded prior to the EEC Treaty and irreconcilable with those arising under Article 5 of Directive 76/207/EEC and the application of the rule of precedence set out in Article 234 EC. The Court held that national courts are under a duty to ensure that Article 5 of the directive is fully complied with by leaving unapplied any contrary provision of national legislation, unless the application of such a provision is necessary in order to ensure the performance by the Member State concerned, pursuant to the first paragraph of Article 234 EC, of obligations arising from agreements concluded with non-member countries before the entry into force of that Treaty. It falls to the national court, and not to the ECJ, to ascertain, with a view to determining the extent to which those obligations constitute an obstacle to the application of Article 5 of Directive 76/207/EEC, what are the obligations thus imposed on the Member State concerned by an earlier international agreement and whether the national provisions in question are designed to implement those obligations.

---

[109] Case C-13/93 *Office National de L'Emploi* v *Madeleine Minne* [1994] ECR I-371.

In view of the judgment in *Stoeckel* and the French Republic's denunciation of ILO Convention 89, the Commission took the view that the French legislation was incompatible with Article 5 of Directive 76/207/EEC and that the France was therefore bound to remedy that incompatibility. Since France failed to comply with this view, the Commission brought an infringement action against France.[110] In its defence the French Government submitted that there was no longer any discrimination in law or in fact in France between nightwork by men or women. Since ILO Convention No 89 was denounced, Article L 213-1 of the Code du Travail was no longer applicable in France because Article 5 of Directive 76/207/EEC had direct effect and consequently individuals were entitled to rely on it before national courts in order to have the contested provision set aside. The ECJ held that because Article L 213-1 of the Code du Travail had been retained, individuals were in a position of uncertainty as to their legal situation and exposed to unwarranted criminal proceedings. It therefore declared that by maintaining in force Article L 213-1 of the Code du Travail prohibiting nightwork by women in industry whereas no such prohibition exists in relation to men, the French Republic had failed to fulfil its obligations under Article 5(1) of Council Directive 76/207/EEC.

### 8.6.4.(ii). Pregnancy

In Chapter Four we discussed Article 2(3) of Directive 76/207/EEC, which allows for special protection to be afforded to women in relation to pregnancy and maternity. In 1990, the Commission presented a proposal[111] for a Directive concerning measures to encourage improvements in the safety and health of pregnant workers, women workers who have recently given birth and women who are breastfeeding. The proposal was presented as an individual Directive within the Framework Directive on the working environment 89/391/EEC and was adopted in October 1992 as the tenth individual Directive within the Framework Directive. In order to be accepted by the Member States the Commission's proposal has been watered down considerably.

The pregnancy Directive provides for maternity leave of at least 14 weeks with pay or an allowance equivalent to what the woman would receive in case of illness (Article 8). This will mean a raised standard of protection in most Member States. Article 9 provides for time off work to attend antenatal examinations if these have to take place during working hours. Articles 3, 4, 5 and 6 focus upon the hazards capable of affecting pregnant women and those

---

[110] Case C-197/96 *Commission* v *French Republic* judgment of 13.3.1997, nyr.

[111] COM(90) 406 and COM(90). Adopted Directive 92/85/EEC, OJ 1992 L 348/1.

women who have recently given birth. The Directive provides for restrictions on night work (Article 7) and exposure to a number of dangerous agents or work processes listed in an Annex to the Directive. Dangerous chemical substances are identified by reference to the Risk phrases established by Directive 67/548/EEC. The comparatively lax Community standard concerning labelling of chemical substances thus affects this Directive.

Article 10 codifies the ECJ decisions on pregnancy discrimination (discussed in Chapter Four) by prohibiting the dismissal of pregnant women or women who have recently given birth during the period of their pregnancy to the end of the fourteen week period of maternity leave. Only in exceptional circumstances, not connected with their condition may women be dismissed on grounds permitted under national legislation or practice and the competent authority must give its consent where applicable to any such dismissal. The employer must cite the substantiated grounds for the dismissal in writing and Member States must take the necessary measures to protect female workers from any unlawful dismissal.

The Member States had two years in which to implement the provisions of the Directive and the Member States must report to the Commission four years after the Directive's adoption on the practical implementation of the Directive. The Council of Ministers will re-examine the Directive on the basis of these reports within at least five years of the adoption of the Directive.

A Danish court has made a reference to the ECJ for a preliminary ruling[112] where questions were asked concerning Article 119 EC and Directives 75/117/EEC, 76/207/EEC and 92/85/EEC, ie the tenth of the abovementioned individual Directives on pregnancy protection. The case is mainly concerned with a number of pregnancy related questions, namely the following:

> Does Community law, including Article 119 and Directives 75/117/EEC, 76/207/EEC and 92/85/EEC preclude national legislation from exempting employers from the obligation to pay normal wages to pregnant employees who are absent from work in cases where:
> 1. the absence is attributable to the fact that the pregnancy substantially aggravates an illness that is otherwise unconnected to the pregnancy;
> 2. the absence is attributable to an illness caused by the pregnancy;
> 3. the absence is attributable to the fact that the pregnancy shows a morbid development and that continued work would create a risk for the health of the woman or her unborn child;
> 4. the absence is attributable to general pregnancy-related inconveniences that occur in any normal pregnancy and, moreover, do not result in incapacity for work;

---

[112] Case C-66/96 *Handels- og Kontorfunktionærernes Forbund i Danmark (HK) and others* v *Fællesforening for Danmarks Brugsforeninger (FDB) and others* pending.

5. the absence results from a medical opinion intended to protect the unborn child but which is not based on an actual morbid condition or special risks for the unborn child;
6. the absence is attributable to the fact that the employer, on the basis of the pregnancy alone, takes the view that he cannot provide work for the pregnant employee, despite the fact that the latter is not unfit for work,
and in situations 1 to 3 and 6 the State guarantees that the pregnant employee will receive the same rate of benefit as she would receive if on sick leave, whereas in situations 4 and 5 no State benefit is received, and the employer, moreover, is required under national legislation to provide full pay during illness?

The ECJ also made some remarks on pregnancy protection in *Gillespie*.[113] The pregnancy Directive did not apply *ratione temporis* to the facts of that case. The main questions in *Gillespie* therefore concerned Article 119 EC and the Equal Pay Directive, see above in chapter Four. The ECJ stated, however, that the amount payable could not be so low as to undermine the purpose of maternity leave, namely the protection of women before and after giving birth.

Advocate general Tesauro found Directive 92/85/EEC important in *Habermann-Beltermann*[114] concerning the interpretation of the Equal Treatment Directive (76/207/EEC), see above in chapter Four. The facts of that case took place at a time when the pregnancy Directive was adopted but had not yet come into force. The pregnancy Directive provides that pregnant women carrying out night-time work are to be given the right to be transferred to daytime work or allowed a period of leave (Article 7), without the loss of employment in any circumstances (Article 10). The Advocate General used these provisions to support the interpretation he gave to Article 5(1) of the Equal Treatment Directive, which is that a contract of employment may not be terminated on account of pregnancy, even where there is a statutory prohibition on night-time work.

In *Webb*,[115] the ECJ also referred to the pregnancy Directive as a relevant context in which to interpret the Equal Treatment Directive. The Court stated

21 In view of the harmful effects which the risk of dismissal may have on the physical and mental state of women who are pregnant, have recently given birth or are breastfeeding, including the particularly serious risk that pregnant women may be prompted voluntarily to terminate their pregnancy, the Community legislature

---

[113] Case C-342/93 *Joan Gillespie and others* v *Northern Health and Social Services Boards, Department of Health and Social Services, Eastern Health and Social Services Board and Southern Health and Social Services Board* [1996] ECR I-0475.

[114] Case C-421/92 *Gabriele Habermann-Beltermann* v *Arbeiterwohlfahrt, Bezirks-verbank NDB/OPF EV* [1994] ECR I-1657.

[115] Case C-32/93 *Carole Louise Webb* v *Emo Air Cargo (Uk) Ltd* [1994] ECR I-3567.

subsequently provided, pursuant to Article 10 of Council Directive 92/85/EEC of 19 October 1992 on the introduction of measures to encourage improvements in the safety and health at work of pregnant workers and workers who have recently given birth or are breastfeeding (OJ 1992 348, p. 1), for special protection to be given to women, by prohibiting dismissal during the period from the beginning of their pregnancy to the end of their maternity leave.

## 8.6.5. Atypical Work Contracts[116]

There has been a growth in many different forms of atypical employment since the late 1970's, a phenomenon which has been quite widely discussed in the labour law literature.[117] Cordóva[118] makes a comprehensive classification of atypical employment relationships and related matters covering the following:

.   self-employment
.   atypical employment contracts
    -   triangular employment relationships (temporary work contracts, sub-contracting and secondments, labour pools etc)
    -   home-based work
    -   part-time employment
    -   solidarity and relay contracts
    -   fixed-term contracts
    -   training/employment contracts

.   clandestine work
    -   undeclared work
    -   family work
    -   work performed by foreigners without valid work permits
    -   work in "micro-enterprises"

The Commission's proposals for Directives on atypical work contracts only address problems relating to part-time and temporary work. The proposals have been separated into three: one under Article 100 EEC on part-time and temporary work, one under Article 100A EC on part-time and temporary work and a third one under Article 118A EC on temporary work.

---

[116] See Kravaritou-Manitakis (1988); Nielsen (1990b); Carley (1990) and Mückenberger (1991).

[117] See for example Birk (1987), Cordóva (1986), Kravaritou-Manitakis (1988), Lyon-Caen (1980), Mückenberger (1989), Mückenberger (1991), Dickens (1992), Smith (1985), Veneziani (1992).

[118] Cordóva (1986) 641.

- Proposal for a Council Directive on the approximation of the laws of the Member States relating to certain employment relationships with regard to working conditions[119]
- Proposal for a Council Directive on the approximation of the laws of the Member States relating to certain employment relationships with regard to distortions of competition[120]
- Proposal for a Council Directive supplementing the introduction of measures to encourage improvements in the safety and health at work of temporary workers.[121]

The Directive based on Article 118A EC was adopted 25 June 1991[122] while the other two atypical work draft Directives have lain dormant in the Council of Ministers from December 1990 until the adoption of the Maastricht Treaty after which the issue has been referred to the social partners for negotiations under the Social Policy Agreement, so far without result. The Article 118A EC Directive aims to complete the provisions in the framework Directive 89/391/EEC in respect of temporary workers. It covers temporary work both when the contract is made directly between and employer and a worker and when the temporary worker is employed through a temporary work agency. The Directive aims to ensure that temporary workers receive the same conditions of health and safety at work as other workers. A contract between a user company and a temporary work agency which assigns a temporary worker to a job must specify: the nature of the task to be performed; the occupational qualifications required; the place of work; the hours of work; particular features of the position to be filled; and particularly, whether or not the job falls within the category of major health and safety risks as defined by national legislation. The temporary worker must be informed of these facts and of any risks he/she might face, and receive appropriate training if necessary (Article 3). Without prejudice to the liability of the temporary employment agency, Member States must ensure that user undertakings and/or establishments are responsible for the duration of a temporary work assignment, for the health, safety and hygiene conditions governing the work involved (Article 4).

Before temporary workers take up any activity requiring special occupational qualifications or skills or special medical supervision, they must be informed by the user company of the risks involved, and, where necessary, receive appropriate training (Article 5). Temporary workers must not be used

---

[119] COM(90) 228 final.

[120] COM(90) 228; amended proposal in COM(90) 533 final.

[121] COM(90) 228 final; amended proposal in COM(90) 533 final.

[122] 91/383/EEC.

for work requiring special medical supervision over a long period, except in exceptional cases. In such case, Member States must take the necessary measures to ensure that the workers concerned receive medical supervision beyond the expiry of the temporary employment contract (Article 6).

### 8.6.6. Young Persons at Work

Council Directive 94/33/EC of 22 June 1994 on the protection of young people at work provides that Member States shall take the necessary measures to prohibit work by children. They shall ensure, under the conditions laid down by the Directive, that the minimum working or employment age is not lower than the minimum age at which compulsory full-time schooling as imposed by national law ends or 15 years in any event.

Member States shall ensure that work by adolescents is strictly regulated and protected under the conditions laid down in the Directive and in general that employers guarantee that young people have working conditions which suit their age. They must also ensure that young people are protected against economic exploitation and against any work likely to harm their safety, health or physical, mental, moral or social development or to jeopardize their education.

The Directive shall apply to any person under 18 years of age having an employment contract or an employment relationship defined by the law in force in a Member State and/or governed by the law in force in a Member State.

### 8.7. ILO TREATIES

Neither the EU nor the EC is a member of ILO but the EC has status as an observer. There are some ILO conventions on working environment issues, notably ILO Convention 153 on working time and rest periods in road transport, ILO Convention 162 on asbestos and ILO Convention 170 on the use of chemical substances at the work place. These conventions have given rise to conflicting views among the Commission, the Council of Ministers and the Member States as to the competence of the Community to enter into ILO treaties. The ECJ delivered an opinion on this question at the basis of Article 228 EC on 19 March 1993 where it held that the Community and the Member States share the competence to accede to ILO Convention No 170.[123]

---

[123] Opinion 2/91 [1993] ECR I-1061. See further Nielsen and Szyszczak (1994).

# Bibliography

Addison, J. and Siebert, S. *Labour Markets in Europe Issues of Harmonisation and Regulation* (London, The Dryden Press, 1997).

Adinolfi, A. "The Implementation of Social Policy Directives Through Collective Agreements" (1988) 25 *Common Market Law Review* 291.

Arnull, A. *The General Principles of EEC Law and the Individual* (London, Frances Pinter/Leicester University Press, 1990).

Arrowsmith, S. »Public Procurement as an Instrument of Policy and the Impact of Market Liberalisation« (1995) 111 *Law Quarterly Review* 235.

Atkins, S. and Luckhaus, L. "The Social Security Directive and UK Law" in McCrudden, C. (ed) *Women, Employment and European Equality Law* (London, Eclipse, 1987).

Baldwin, R. and Daintith T. (eds) *Harmonization and Hazard. Regulating Workplace Health and Safety in the European Community* (London, Graham & Trotman, 1992).

Banks, K. "L'Article 118A, élément dynamique de la politique sociale communautaire" (1993) No 5-6 *Cahiers de Droit Européen* 537.

Barents, R. "The Internal Market Unlimited: Some Observations on the Legal Base of Community Legislation" (1993) 30 *Common Market Law Review* 85.

Barnard, C. "A Social Policy for Europe: Politicians 1 Lawyers 0" (1992) 8 *International Journal of Comparative Labour Law and Industrial Relations* 3.

⎯⎯⎯ "The External Dimension of Community Social Policy: The Ugly Duckling of External Relations" in Emilou, N. and O'Keeffe, D. (eds) *The European Union and World Trade Law: After the GATT Uruguay Round* (Chichester, Wiley, 1996a).

⎯⎯⎯ "The Economic Objectives of Article 119" in Hervey, T. and O'Keeffe, D. (eds) *Sex Equality Law in the European Union* (Chichester, Wiley, 1996b).

⎯⎯⎯ *EC Employment Law* (Chichester, Wiley, 1996c).

Bell, M. and Waddington, L. "The 1996 Intergovernmental Conference and the Prospects of a Non-Discrimination Treaty Article" (1996) 25 *Industrial Law Journal* 320.

Bercusson, B. "Fundamental Social and Economic Rights in the European Community" Cassese, A., Clapham, A. and Weiler, J. (eds) *Human Rights and the European Community: Methods of Protection, Vol II* (Baden-Baden, Nomos, 1991).

⎯⎯⎯ "The European Community's Charter of Fundamental Rights for Workers" (1990) 53 *Modern Law Review* 624.

⎯⎯⎯ *European Labour Law* (London, Butterworths, 1996).

Betten, L. (ed) *The Future of European Social Policy* (Kluwer, Deventer, 1989).

Betten, L. (ed) *The Employment Contract in Transforming Labour Relations* (Deventer, Kluwer, 1995).

Bieback, K-J. *Indirect Sex Discrimination within the Meaning of Directive (CE) 79/7 in the Social Security Law of the EC Member States* (Commission Brussels, V/1333/96-EN. February 1996).

Bieber, R. and Monar, J. (eds) *Justice and Home Affairs in the European Union. The Development of the Third Pillar* (Brussels, European Interuniversity Press, 1995).

Biagi, M. »From Conflict to Participation in Safety: Industrial Relations and the Working Environment in Europe 1992« (1990) 6 *The International Journal of Comparative Labour Law and Industrial Relations* 67.

Birk, R. »Flexibilisierung des Arbeitsrechts - eine europäische Herausforderung - Einführung« (1987) *Zeitschrift für ausländisches und internationales Arbeits- und Sozialrecht* 222.

Blanpain, R. "1992 and Beyond: The Impact of the European Community on the Labour Law Systems of the Member Countries" (1990) 11 *Comparative Labour Law Journal* 403.

Blanpain, R., Hepple, B., Sciarra, S. and Weiss, F. *Fundamental Social Rights: Proposals for the Union* (Peeters, 1996).

Blanpain, R and Engels C. *European Labour Law* (Kluwer, Deventer, 1995 3rd and revised edition).

Burrows, N. "The Promotion of Women's Rights by the European Economic Community" (1980) 17 *Common Market Law Review* 191.


Chalmers, D. "The Single Market: From Prima Donna to Journeyman" in Shaw, J. and More, G. (eds) *New Legal Dynamics of the European Union* (Oxford, Clarendon, 1995).

Collins, D. "Social Policy" in Lodge, J. (ed) *Institutions and Policies of the European Community* (London, Frances Pinter, 1983).

Coppel, J. and O'Neill, A "The Court of Justice: Taking Rights Seriously?" (1992) 29 *Common Market Law Review* 669; (1992) 12 *Legal Studies* 227.

Coussins, M. "Equal Treatment and Social Security" (1994) 19 *European Law Review* 123.

Cremona, M. "Citizens of Third Countries: Movement and Employment of Migrant Workers Within the European Union" (1995/2) *Legal Issues of European Integration* 87.

Crosby, S. "The Single Market and the Rule of Law" (1991) 16 *European Law Review* 451.

Cullen, H. "From Migrants to Citizens? European Community Policy on Intercultural Education" (1996) 45 *International and Comparative Law Quarterly* 109.

Cullen, H. and Campbell, E. "The Future of Social Policy-Making in the European Union" paper presented at the W.G. Hart Legal Workshop, July 1996, London.

Curtin, D. *Irish Employment Equality Law* (Dublin, Round Hall Press, 1989).

_____ "The Constitutional Structure of the Union: A Europe of Bits and Pieces" (1993) 30 *Common Market Law Review* 17.

_____ "Annotation Case C-271/91 *Marshall v Southampton and South West Hampshire Area Health Authority* (1994) 31 *Common Market Law Review* 631.

Davies, P. "The Emergence of a European Labour Law" in McCarthy, W. (ed) *Legal Interventions in Industrial Relations: Gains and Losses* (Oxford, Blackwell, 1992).

Deakin, S. and Wilkinson, F. *The Economics of Employment Rights* (London, Institute for Employment Rights, 1991).

De Búrca, G. "The Principle of Proportionality and Its Application in EC Law" (1993) *Yearbook of European Law* 105.

Dehousse, R. "Community Competences: Are There Limits To Growth?" in Dehouse, R. (ed) *Maastricht: An Ever Closer Union?* (Munich, Law Books in Europe, 1994).

De Witte, B. (ed) *European Law of Education* (Nomos, Baden-Baden, 1989).

Docksey, C. "The Principle of Equality Between Women and Men as a Fundamental Right Under Community Law" (1991) 20 *Industrial Law Journal* 258.

d'Oliveira, J. "Fortress Europe and (Extra-Communitarian) Refugees: Co-operation in Sealing off the External Borders" in Schermers, H. *et al* (eds) *Free Movement of Persons in Europe* (Dordrecht, Martinus Nijhoff, 1995).

Däubler, W. »The Employee Participation Directive - A Realistic Utopia?« (1977) 14 *Common Market Law Review* 457.

_____ »Grenzüberschreitende Fusion und Arbeitsrecht - Zum Entwurf der Zehnten gesellschaftsrechtlichen Richtlinie« (1988) *Der Betrieb* 1850.

_____ *Sozialstaat EG? Die andere Dimension des Binnenmarktes* (Gütersloh 1989).

_____ »Mitbestimmung - ein Thema für Europa?« (1990) 24 *Kritische Justiz* 14.

_____ *Trends in German Labour Law* in Wedderburn, Lord et al. *Labour Law in the Post-industrial Era* (Dartmouth, Aldershot, 1994).

Eeckhout, P. *The European Internal Market and International Trade* (Oxford, Clarendon, 1994).

Ellis, E. "The Definition of Discrimination in European Community Sex Equality Law" (1994) 19 *European Law Review* 563.

Elman, R. (Ed) *Sexual Politics and the European Union: The New Feminist Challenge* (Providence, Berghahn Books, 1996).

Emerson, M. *Re-drawing the Map of Europe* (Centre for Economic Performance, London School of Economics, 1996).

Emiliou, N. "Opening Pandora's Box: The Legal Basis of Community Measures Before the Court of Justice" (1994) 19 *European Law Review* 488.

Evans, A. "Development of European Community Law Regarding the Trade Union Rights and Related Rights Migrant Workers" (1979) 26 *International and Comparative Law Quarterly* 354.

_____ "Third Country Nationals and the Treaty on European Union" (1994) 5 *European Journal of International Law* 199.

Everling, U. *The Right of Establishment in the Common Market* (Chicago, Commerce Clearing House, 1964).

Everson, M. "Women and Citizenship of the European Union" in Hervey, T. and O'Keeffe, D. (eds) *Sex Equality in the European Union* (Chichester, Wiley, 1996).

Falkner, G. "The Maastricht Protocol on Social Policy: Theory and Practice" (1996) 6 *Journal of European Social Policy* 1.

Farmer, P. "Article 48EC and the Taxation of Frontier Workers" (1995) 20 *European Law Review* 310.

Fenwick, H. and Hervey, T. "Sex Equality in the Single Market: New Directions for the European Court of Justice" (1995) 32 *Common Market Law Review* 433.

Fitzpatrick, B. and Szyszczak, E. "Remedies and Effective Judicial Protection in Community Law" (1994) 57 *Modern Law Review* 434.

Flynn, J. "How Well Will Article 100A(4) Work? A Comparison With Article 93" (1987) 24 *Common Market Law Review* 689.

_____ "Vocational Training in Community Law and Practice" (1988) 8 *Yearbook of European Law* 59.

Forman, J. "The Equal Pay Principle Under Community Law: A Commentary on Article 119 EEC" (1982) 1 *Legal Issues of European Integration* 17.

Frazer, T. "The New Structural Funds, State Aids and Interventions on the Single Market" (1995) 20 *European Law Review* 7.

Fredman S. 'European Community Discrimination Law: A Critique' (1992) 21 *Industrial Law Journal* 119.

_____ "The Poverty of Equality: Pensions and the ECJ" (1996) 25 *Industrial Law Journal* 91.

Freedland, M. "Vocational Training in EC Law and Policy - Education, Employment or Welfare" (1996) 25 *Industrial Law Journal* 110.

Green, N., Hartley, T. and Usher, J. *The Legal Foundations of the Single European Market* (Oxford, Oxford University Press, 1991).

Greenwood, C. "Nationality and the Limits of the Free Movement of Persons in Community Law" (1988) *Yearbook of European Law* 185.

Guild, E. *The Emerging Immigration and Asylum Policies of the European Union* (Deventer, Kluwer, 1996).

Habermas, J. "Citizenship and National Identity: Some Reflections on the Future of Europe" (1992) 12 *Praxis International* 1.

Hailbronner, K. "Visa Regulations and Third Country-Nationals in EC Law" (1994) 31 *Common Market Law Review* 969.

Hall, M. "Industrial Relations and The Social Dimension of European Integration" in Hyman, R. and Ferner (eds) *New Frontiers in Industrial Relations* (Oxford, Blackwell, 1994).

Hall, S. *Nationality, Migration Rights and Citizenship of the Union*, (Dordrecht, Martinus Nijhoff, (1995).

_____ "Loss of Union Citizenship in Breach of Fundamental Rights" (1996) 21 *European Law Review* 129.

Handoll, J. "Article 48(4) EEC and Non-National Access To Public Employment" (1988) 13 *European Law Review* 223.

Hargreaves, S. "Social Europe After Maastricht: is the United Kingdom really opted out?" (1997) *The Journal of Social Welfare and Family Law* 2.

Harmsen, R. "A European Union of Variable Geometry: Problems and Perspectives" (1994) 45 *Northern Ireland Law Quarterly* 109.

Hedemann-Robinson, M. "Indirect Discrimination Law in the EC: Appearance Rather Than Reality?" (1996) 2 *International Journal of Discrimination and the Law* 85.

Hendriks, A. "The Right to Freedom of Movement and the (Un)lawfulness of AIDS/HIV Specific Travel Restrictions from A European Perspective" (1990) *Nordic Journal of International Law* 186.

Henley, A. and Tsalotus, E. "Corporatism and the European Labour Market after 1992" (1992) 30 *British Journal of Industrial Relations* 567.

Hennis, W. "Access to Education in the European Communities" (1990) 3 *Leiden Journal of International Law* 35.

Hepple, B. "The Crisis in EEC Labour Law" (1987) 18 *Industrial Law Journal* 129.

_____ *European Social Dialogue - Alibi or Opportunity?* (London, Institute of Employment Rights, 1993).

Herbert, F. "Social Security and Indirect Discrimination " in McCrudden, C. (ed) *Equality of Treatment Between Women and Men in Social Security* (London, Butterworths, 1994).

Hervey, T. "The Future for Sex Equality Law in the European Union" in Hervey, T. and O'Keeffe, D. (eds) *Sex Equality Law in the European Union* (Chichester, Wiley, 1996).

Hervey, T. and Rostant, P. "After *Francovich*: State Liability and British Employment Law" 1996) 4 *Industrial Law Journal* 259.

Hoogenboom, T. "Integration Into Society and Free Movement of non-EEC Nationals!" (1992) 3 *European Journal of International Law* 36.

Hoskins, M, "Tilting the Balance: Supremacy and National Procedural Rules" (1996) 21 *European Law Review* 365.

Hoskyns, C. *Integrating Gender* (London, Verso, 1996).

Hoskyns, C. and Luckhaus, L. "European Community Directive on Equal Treatment in Social Security" (1989) 17 *Policy and Politics* 321.


Johnson, E. and O'Keeffe, D "From Discrimination to Obstacles to Free Movement: Recent Developments Concerning the Free Movement of Workers 1989-1994" (1994) 31 *Common Market Law Review* 1313.


Keeling, E. and Shipwright, A. "Some Taxing Problems concerning Non-Discrimination and the EC Treaty" (1995) 20 *European Law Review* 580.

Kenner, J. "Economics and Social Cohesion: The Rocky Road Ahead" (1994/1) *Legal Issues of European Integration* 1.

Kessler, F. and Meer, F. "La dynamique de l'Article 118A du Traité de Rome" (1992) No 2 *Revue Internationale de Droit Économique* 129.

Kilpatrick, C. "Production and Circulation of EC Night Work Jurisprudence" (1996) 25 *Industrial Law Journal* 169.

Klabbers, J. "Informal Instruments Before the European Court of Justice" (1994) 31 *Common Market Law Review* 997.

Korella, G. and Twomey, P. (eds) *Towards a European Immigration Policy* (Brussels, European Interuniversity Press, 1993).

Kravaritou-Manitakis, Y. *New Forms of Work. Labour Law and Social Security Aspects in the European Community* (Luxembourg: Office for Official Publications of the European Communities, European Foundation for the Improvement of Living and Working Conditions, Dublin, 1988).

Krugman, P. and Venables, A. "Integration, Specialisation and Adjustment" (1996) *European Economics Review* 959.

Kuper, B.O. "The Green and White Papers of the European Union: The Apparent Goal of Reduced Social Benefits" (1994) 4 *Journal of European Social Policy* 129.


Laenerts, K. "Education in European Community Law After 'Maastricht'" (1994) 31 *Common Market Law Review* 7.

Lane, R. "New Community Competences Under The Maastricht Treaty" (1993) 30 *Common Market Law Review* 939.

Laske, C. "The Impact of the Single European Market on Social Protection for Migrant Workers" (1993) 30 *Common Market Law Review* 515.

Laslett, J. "The Mutual Recognition of Diplomas, Certificates and Other Evidence of Formal Qualifications in the European Community" (1990/1) *Legal Issues of European Integration* 1.

Lasok, P. "Employed and Self-Employed Persons in EEC Social Security Law" (1982) 4 *Journal of Social Welfare Law* 323.

Lodge, J. "Towards A Human Union: EEC Social Policy and European Integration" (1978) 4 *British Review of International Studies* 120.

Lonbay, J. "Education and the Law: The Community Context" (1989) 14 European Law Review 363.

Luckhaus, L. "The Role of the 'Economic' and the 'Social' in Social Security and Community Law" in *National and European Law on the Threshold to the Single Market* (Peter Lang, 1993).

_____ "Payment for Caring: a European Solution?" (1986) *Public Law* 526.

Lyon-Caen, G. "Collective Bargaining and Community Legal Instruments" Paper Presented to a Conference on the Legal Formulation and Implementation of the Social Dimension of the Internal Market, Florence, 4-6 December 1989.


Mac Dougall, Sir D. *Report of a Study Group on the Role of Public Finance in European Integration*, Brussels, Commission, 1977.

Majone, M. "The European Community Between Social Policy and Social Regulation" 31 *Journal of Common Market Studies* 153.

Marenco, G. "The Notion of Restriction on the Freedom of Establishment and Provision of Services in the Case-Law of the Court" (1991) 1 *Yearbook of European Law* 111.

Martín, J.M.F. *The EC Public Procurement Rules. A Critical Analysis* (Clarendon Press, Oxford, 1996).

McCrudden, C. "Comparable Worth: A Common Dilemma" (1986) 11 *Yale Journal of International Law* 396.

_____ "The Effectiveness of European Equality Law" (1993) 13 *Oxford Journal of Legal Studies* 320.

_____ (ed) *Equality of Treatment Between Women and Men in Social Security* (London, Butterworths, 1994).

McGlynn, C. "European Works Councils: Towards Industrial Democracy" (1995) *Industrial Law Journal* 78.

_____ "EC Sex Equality Law: Towards a Human Rights Foundation" in Hervey, T. and O'Keeffe, D. (eds) *Sex Equality Law in the European Union*, (Chichester, Wiley, 1996).

McMahon, J. *Education and Culture in European Community Law* (London, The Althone Press, 1995).

More, G. "Equal Treatment of the Sexes in European Community Law: What Does Equal Mean?" (1993) 1 *Feminist Legal Studies* 45.


Neunreither, K. "Subsidiarity as a Guiding Principle for European Community Activities" (1993) 28 *Government and Opposition* 206.

Nicolaides, P. "Economic Aspects of Services: Implications For A GATT Agreement" (1989) 23 *Journal of World Trade Law* 125.

Nielsen, H. K. »Public Procurement and International Labour Standards« (1995) *Public Procurement Law Review* 94.

_____ »The Concept of Discrimination in ILO Convention No 111« (1994) *The International and Comparative Law Quarterly* 827.

Nielsen, R. "Annotation of Case C-177/88 *Dekker* and Case C-179/88 *Aldi* (1992)" 29 *Common Market Law Review* 160.

_____ *Equality in Law between Men and Women in the European Community. Denmark* (Martinus Nijhoff, The Hague, 1995).

_____ *Employers Prerogatives - in a European Nordic Perspective* (Copenhagen Business School Press, 1996)

Nielsen, R. and Szyszczak, E. "Case Note on *Sloman Neptun* " (1994a) *Journal of Social Welfare Law* p 121.

Nielsen, R. and Szyszczak, E. "Case Note on *ILO Convention* 170 (1994b) *Journal of Social Welfare Law* p 401.


O'Keeffe, D. "Equal Rights for Migrants: the Concept of Social Advantages in Article 7(2), Regulation 1612/68" (1985) 5 *Yearbook of European Law* 93.

_____ "The Schengen Conventions: a suitable model for European Integration?" (1991)11 *Yearbook of European Law* 185.

_____ "The Free Movement of Persons and the Single Market" (1992a) 17 *European Law Review* 3.

_____ "Judicial Interpretation of the Public Service Exception to the Free Movement of Workers" in Curtin, D. and O'Keeffe, D. (eds) *Constitutional Adjudication in European Community and National Law* (Ireland, Butterworths, 1992b).

_____ "Judicial Interpretation of the Public Service Exception to the Free Movement of Workers" in Curtin D, and O'Keeffe, D. (eds) *Constitutional Adjudication in European Community and National Law* (Ireland, Butterworths, 1992).

_____ "Union Citizenship" in O'Keeffe, D. and Twomey. P. (eds) *Legal Issues of the Maastricht Treaty* (London, Chancery, 1994).

_____ "The Emergence of a European Immigration Policy" (1995) 20 *European Law Review* 20.

O'Leary, S. "The Court of Justice as a Reluctant Constitutional Adjudicator: An Examination of the Abortion Case" (1992) 16 *European Law Review* 138.

_____ "The Relationship Between Community Citizenship and the Protection of Fundamental Human Rights" (1995) 32 *Common Market Law Review* 519.

_____ *The Evolving Concept of Community Citizenship From The Free Movement of Persons to Union Citizenship* (Kluwer, 1996a).

_____ "Resolution by the Court of Justice of Disputes Affecting Family Life" in Hervey, T. and O'Keeffe, D. (eds) *Sex Equality Law in the European Union* (Chicester, Wiley, 1996b).

Oliver, P. "General Principles of Community Law and Horizontal Effect" *EU ZW* 13/1993, 393.


Pais Macedo van Overbeek, J. "Aids/HIV Infection and The Free Movement of Workers Within the European Economic Community" (1990) 27 *Common Market Law Review* 791.

Peers, S. "Towards Equality: Actual and Potential Rights of Third-Country Nationals in the European Union" (1996a) 33 *Common Market Law Review* 7.

_____ "The Visa Regulation: Free Movement Blocked Indefinitely" (1996) 21 *European Law Review* 150.

_____ "Border in Channel: Continent Cut Off" (1997a) *The Journal of Social Welfare and Family Law.*

_____ "Undercutting Integration: Developments in EU Policy on Third Country Nationals" (1997b) 22 *European Law Review.*

_____ "'Social Advantages' and Discrimination in Employment: Case Law Confirmed and Clarified" (1997c) 22 *European Law Review* 157.

Pennings, F. (ed.) *Introduction to European Social Security Law* (Deventer, Kluwer, 1994).

Pertek, J. "Free Movement of Professionals and Recognition of Higher Education Diplomas" (1992) *Yearbook of European Law* 293.

Phelan, D. "Right to Life of the Unborn v Promotion of Trade in Services: the European Court of Justice and the Normative Shaping of the European Union" (1992) 55 *Modern Law Review* 670.

Pickup, D. "Reverse Discrimination and Freedom of Movement for Workers" (1986) 23 *Common Market Law Review* 135.

Pieters, D. "Will `1992' lead to the Co-ordination and Harmonisation of Social Security?" in Pieters, D (ed) *Social Security in Europe* (1991).

Prechal, S. Case C-450/93 *Kalanke v Freie Hansestadt Bremen* [1995] ECR I-3051 (1996) 33 *Common Market Law Review* 1245.

Scharpf, F. "Community and Autonomy: Multi-level Policy-making in the European Union" (1994) 1 *Journal of European Public Policy* 219.

Schiek, D. "Positive Action in Community Law" (1996) 25 *Industrial Law Journal* 239.

Schutte, J. "Schengen: Its Meaning for the Free Movement of Persons in Europe" (1991) 28 *Common Market Law Review* 549.

Sciarra, S. "Dynamic Integration of National and Community Sources: The Case of Night Work For Women" in Hervey, T. and O'Keeffe, D. (eds) *Sex Equality Law in the European Union* (Chichester, Wiley, 1996).

Serdjenian, *Inventory of Positive Action in Europe* (Brussels, EC Commission, 1994).

Shanks, M. *European Social Policy Today and Tomorrow* (Oxford, Pergamon Press, 1977).

Shaw, J. "Social Policy After The Treaty of Maastricht" (1992) 3 *The Journal of Social Welfare and Family Law* 255.

Simitis, S. "Dismantling or Strengthening Labour Law: The Case of the European Court of Justice" (1996) 2 *European Law Journal* 156.

Simmonds, K. "The Concertation of Community Migration Policy" (1988) 25 *Common Market Law Review* 177.

Snyder, F. "The Effectiveness of European Community Law: Institutions, Processes, Tools and Techniques" (1993) 56 *Modern Law Review* 19.

Sohrab, J. "Women and Social Security" (1994) *Journal of Social Welfare Law* 5
_____ *Sexing The Benefit* (Brookfield, Dartmouth, 1996).

Spicker, P. `Concepts of Subsidiarity in the European Community' (1996) 5 *Current Politics and Economics in Europe* 163.
_____ `Exclusion' (1997) 35 *Journal of Common Market Studies* 133.

Streeck, W. "European Social Policy After Maastricht: The `Social Dialogue' and `Subsidiarity'" (1994) 15 *Economic and Industrial Democracy* 151.
_____ `Neo-Voluntarism: A New European Social Policy Regime?' (1995) 1 *European Law Journal* 1.

Sundberg-Weitmann, B. *Discrimination on Grounds of Nationality. Free Movement of Workers and Freedom of Establishment under the EEC-Treaty* (Amsterdam, North-Holland, 1977).

Szyszczak, E. "Pay Inequalities and Equal Value Claims" (1985) 48 *Modern Law Review* 139.

_____ `Race Discrimination: The Limits of Market Equality?' in Hepple, B. and Szyszczak, E.(eds) *Discrimination: The Limits of Law* (Mansell, London, 1992a).

_____ "First Report on the Application of the Community Charter of the Fundamental Social Rights of Workers" (1992b) 21 *Industrial Law Journal* 149.

_____ "Social Policy: A Happy Ending Or A ReWorking of the Fairy Tale?" in O'Keeffe, D. and Twomey, P, (eds) *Legal Issues of the Maastricht Treaty* (Chichester, Wiley, 1993).

_____ "Social Rights As General Principles of Community Law" in Neuwahl, N. and Rosas, A. (Eds) *The European Union and Human Rights* (The Hague, Nijhoff, 1995).

_____ "Making Europe More Relevant To Its Citizens" (1996a) 21 *European Law Review* 351.

_____ "Fourth Medium-Term Community Action Programme on Equal Opportunities for Women and Men (1996 - 2000) (1996b) 25 *Industrial Law Journal* 225.

_____ "Remedies in Sex Discrimination Cases" in Lonbay, J. and Biondi, A. (Eds) *Remedies For Breach of EC Law* (Chichester, Wiley, 1997).

Szyszczak, E. and Delicostopolous, J. "Intrusions into National Procedural Autonomy: The French Paradigm" (1997) 22 *European Law Review* 141.

Tatchell, P. *Europe in the Pink - Lesbian and Gay Equality in the New Europe* (London, GMP Publishers, 1992).

Teague, P. "Constitution or Regime? The Social Dimension to the 1992 Project" (1989) 27 *British Journal of Industrial Relations* 310.

Temple Lang, J. "The Sphere in Which Member States Are Obliged To Comply With The General Principles of Law and Community Fundamental Rights Principles" (1991/92) *Legal Issues of European Integration* 23.

Uçarer, E. and Puchala, D. (eds) *Immigration into Western Societies Problems and Policies* (London, Pinter, 1997).

Vanistendael, F. "The Consequences of Schumacker and Wielockx: Two Steps Forward in the Tax Procession of Echternach" (1996) 33 *Common Market Law Review* 255.

Van Langendomck, "Social Security Legislation in the EEC" (1973) 2 *Industrial Law Journal* 17.

Vinals, J. and Jimeno, J `Monetary Union and European Unemployment' (Centre for Economic Performance, London School of Economics, 1996).

Vogel-Polsky, E. "What Future Is There For A Social Europe Following The Strasbourg Summit?" (1990) 19 *Industrial Law Journal* 65.

Waaldijk, E. and Clapham, A. *Homosexuality: A European Community Issue* (1993).
Waddington, L. *Disability, Employment and the European Community* (London, Blackstone, 1995).
Ward, A. "Effective Legal Sanctions in EC Law: A Moving Boundary in the Division of Competence" (1995) 1 *European Law Journal* 205.
Ward, I. "Beyond Sex Equality: the limits of sex equality law in the new Europe" in Hervey, T. and O'Keeffe, D. (eds) *Sex Equality Law in the European Union* (Chichester, Wiley, 1996).
_____ "Law and Other Europeans" (1997) 35 *Journal of Common Market Studies* 79.
Warner, J.P. "EC Social Policy in Practice: Community Action on Behalf of Women and Its Impact in the Member State" (1984) 23 *Journal of Common Market Studies* 141.
Watson, P. *Social Security Law in the European Communities* (Mansell, London 1980).
Wattel, P. "The EC Court's Attempts to Reconcile the Treaty Freedoms with International Tax Law" (1996) 33 *Common Market Law Review* 223.
Weatherill, S. Annotation on Case 186/87 *Cowan v. Le Trésor Public* [1989] ECR 195 (1989) 26 *Common Market Law Review* 563.
_____ Annotation on Case C-415/93 *Union Royal Belge des Sociétés de Football Association ASBL v Bosman* [1995] ECR I-4921 (1996) 33 *Common Market Law Review* 991.
Weiler, J. "The Transformation of Europe" (1991) 100 *Yale Law Journal* 2403.
Wellens, K., and Borchardt, G. "Soft Law in European Community Law" (1989) 14 *European Law Review* 267.
White, R. "Free Movement of Workers and Social Security" (1992) 17 *European Law Review* 522.
Whiteford, E. *Adapting to Change: Occupational Pension Schemes, Women and Migrant Workers* (The Hague, Kluwer, 1997).
Worre, T. "First No, Then Yes: The Danish Referendums on the Maastricht Treaty 1992 and 1993" (1995) 33 *Journal of Common Market Studies* 235.
Wouters, J. "The Case Law of the Court of Justice in Direct Taxes: Variation Upon a Theme" (1994a) 1 *Maastricht Journal of European and Comparative Law* 179.
_____ "Fiscal Barriers to Companies' Cross-Border Establishment in the Case-Law of the Court of Justice" (1994b) 14 *Yearbook of European Law* 73.
Wulf-Mathies, M. "The Structural Funds After 1999" *Regional Policy and Cohesion Newsletter*, No. 31 August 1996.
Wyatt, D."The Direct Effect of Community Social Law - Not Forgetting Directives" (1983) 8 *European Law Review* 241.

Wyatt, D. and Dashwood, A. "The Social Security of Migrant Workers and Their Families" (1977) 14 *Common Market Law Review* 411.

_____ *European Community Law* (3rd ed, 1993, Sweet and Maxwell, London).

Wikely, N. "Migrant Workers and Unemployment Benefit in the European Community" (1988) 10 *Journal of Social Welfare Law* 300.

Zilioli, C. "The Recognition of Diplomas and Its Impact on Education Policies" in De Witte, P. (ed) *European Community Law of Education* (Baden-Baden, Nomos, 1989).

# Cases

Case 75/63 *Unger* v *Bestuur* [1964] ECR 1977; 69

Case 15/69 *Württembergische Milchverwertung-Südmilch-AG* v *Salvatore Ugliola* [1969] ECR 363; 80

Case 92/63 *Nonnenmacher* v *Social Verzekeringsbank* [1964] ECR 281; 131

Case 80/70 *Defrenne* v *Belgian State* (No. 1) [1971] ECR 445; 151

Case 20/71 *Sabbatini* v *European Parliament* [1972] ECR 345; 151

Case 32/71 *Chollet* v *European Commission* [1972] ECR 363; 151

Case 129/70 *Macarthys Ltd.* v *Smith* [1979] ECR 1275; 166

Case 152/73 *Sotgiu* v *Deutsche Bundespost* [1974] ECR 153; 79, 80

Case 167/73 *Commission* v *France* [1974] ECR 359; 68

Case 2/74 *Reyners* v *Belgian State* [1974] ECR 631; 91, 94, 97

Case 6/74 *Bonsignore* v *Oberstadtdirektor of the City of Cologne* [1975] ECR 297; 111

Case 8/74 *Procureur du Roi* v *Benoît and Gustave Dassonville* [1974] ECR; 222, 226

Case 9/74 *Casagrande* v *Landeshauptstadt Munich* [1974] ECR 773

Case 21/74 *Airola* v *Commission* [1975] ECR 221; 67

Case 33/74 *van Binsbergen* [1974] ECR 1299; 91

Case 36/74 *Walrave* v *Union Cycliste Internationale* [1974] ECR 1405; 68

Case 41/74 *van Duyn* v *Home Office* [1974] ECR 1337; 110, 111

Case 32/75 *Christini* v *S.N.C.F.* [1975] ECR 1085; 80, 81, 85

Case 36/75 *Rutili* v *Minister of the Interior* [1975] ECR 1219; 56, 110, 111, 113

Case 43/75 *Defrenne* v *Sabena (No 2)* [1976] ECR 455; 19, 25, 26, 152, 162

Case 48/75 *Procureur du Roi* v *Royer* [1976] ECR 497; 66, 77, 86

Case 118/75 *Watson* v *Belmann* [1976] ECR 1185; 78, 95

Case 13/76 *Gaetano Donà* v *Mario Mantero* [1976] ECR 1333; 221

Case 33/76 *Rewe-Centralfinanze eG and Rewe Zentral Ag* v *Landwirtschaftskammer fur das Saarland* [1976] ECR 1989; 58

Case 35/76 *Amministrazione delle Finanze dello Stato* v *Simmenthal SpA* [1976] ECR 1871; 224

Case 71/76 *Thieffry* v *Conseil de l'ordre des Avocats à la Cour de Paris* [1977] ECR 765; 102

Case 78/76 *Firma Steinike und Weinlig* v *Federal Republic of Germany* [1977] ECR 595; 236

Case 79/76 *Fossi* v *Bundesknappschaft* [1977] ECR 667; 132

Case 11/77 *Patrick* v *Ministre des Affaires Culturelles* [1977] ECR 1199; 102

Case 30/77 *Regina* v *Bouchereau* [1977] ECR 1999; 109-112

Case 149/77 *Defrenne* v *Sabena* (No 3) [1978] ECR 1365; 55, 154

Case 16/78 *Choquet* [1978] ECR 2293; 79

Case 106/78 *Simmenthal* v *Amministrazione delle Finanze* [1978] ECR 629; 165

Case 115/78 *J Knoors* v *Ministry of Economy* [1979] ECR 399; 107

Case 120/78 *Rewe-Zentral* v *Bundesmonopolverwaltung für Brantwein* [1979] ECR 649; 87, 223, 225, 344

Case 136/78 *Ministre Public* v *Auer* [1979] ECR 437; 108

Case 175/78 *R* v *Saunders* [1979] ECR 1129; 107

Case 207/78 *Ministère Public* v *Even* [1979] ECR 2019; 81, 83

Case 237/78 *CRAM* v *Toia* [1979] ECR 2645; 130

Case 98/79 *Pecastaing* v *Belgian State* [1980] ECR 691; 114

Case 129/79, *Macarthys Ltd* v *Wendy Smith* [1980] ECR 1275; 168

Case 131/79 *R* v *Secretary of State for Home Affairs ex parte Santillo* [1980] ECR 1585; 114

Case 157/79 *Regina* v *Pieck* [1980] ECR 2171; 77

Case 69/80 *Worringham* v *Lloyds Bank Ltd* [1981] ECR 767; 153, 157

Case 96/80 *Jenkins* v *Kingsgate (Clothing Productions) Ltd* [1981] ECR 911; 153, 155, 168

Case 155/80 Summary Proceedings against *Sergius Oebel* [1981] ECR 1993; 224

Case 279/80 *Criminal Proceedings Against Webb* [1981] ECR 3305; 93

Case 12/81 *Garland* v *British Rail Engineering* [1982] ECR 359; 156, 164, 210

Case 19/81 *Burton* v *British Railways Board* [1982] ECR 555; 161, 173

Case 53/81 *D M Levin* v *Secretary of State for Justice* [1982] ECR 1035; 69

Case 58/81 *Commission* v *Luxembourg* [1982] ECR 2175; 157

Case 61/81 *EC Commission* v *United Kingdom* [1982] ECR 2601; 155, 166, 168

Joined Cases 62 and 63/81 *Seco SA* v *Establissement d'Assurance contre la Vieillesse et l' Invalidite* [1982] ECR 223; 240

Case 65/81 *Reina* v *Landeskredit Bank Baden Würtemberg* [1982] ECR 33; 81

Case 91/81 *EC Commission* v *Italy* [1982] ECR 2133; 262

Joined Cases 115 and 116/81 *Adoui* v *Belgian State and City of Liège* [1982] ECR 1665; 111, 115

Case 283/81 *Srl CILFIT and Lanificio di Gavardo SpA* v *Ministry of Health* [1982] ECR 3415; 264

Case 35-36/82 *Morson and Jhanjan* v *State of Netherlands* [1983] ECR 3723; 107

Joined Cases 75 and 117/82 *Razzouk and Beydoun* v *Commission* [1984] ECR 1509; 158

Case 139/82 *Piscitello* v *INPS* [1983] ECR 1427; 132

Case 152/82 *Sandro Forcheri and Marisa Marino, married Forcheri,* v *Belgium and ASBL Institut supérieur de sciences humaines appliquées - Ecole ouvrière supérieure* [1983] ECR 2323; 75

Case 163/82 *Commission* v *Italy* [1983] ECR 3273; 180

Case 165/82 *EC Commission* v *United Kingdom* [1983] ECR 3431; 173, 178

Joined Cases 286/82 and 26/83 *Luisi and Carbone* v *Ministero del Tesoro* [1984] ECR 377; 95

Case 14/83 *Von Colson and Kamann* v *Land Nordrhein-Westfalen* [1984] ECR 1891; 57, 185

Case 19/83 *Knud Wendelboe m fl* v *L J Music* [1985] ECR 457; 264, 267, 278

Case 23/83 *Liefting* v *Directie van het Academish Zienkenthuis* [1984] ECR 3225; 158

Case 107/83 *Ordre des Avocats au Barreau de Paris* v *Klopp* [1984] ECR 2971; 98, 99

Case 135/83 *H B M Abels* v *The Administrative board of the Bedrijfsvereniging voor de Metaalindustrie en de Electrotechnische Industrie* [1985] 469; 264, 269

Case 143/83 *EC Commission* v *Denmark* [1985] ECR 427; 155, 156

Case 179/83 *FNV* v *The Netherlands* [1985] ECR 511; 269

Case 180/83 *Moser* v *Land Baden-Württenberg* [1984] ECR 2539; 107

Case 184/83 *Hofmann* v *Barmer Ersatzkasse* [1984] ECR 3047; 175, 180

Case 186/83 *Arie Botzen et al* v *Rotterdamsche Droogdok Maatschappij BV* [1985] ECR 519; 269, 271, 272, 275

Case 215/83 *EC Commission* v *Belgium* [1985] ECR 1039; 256, 263

Case 237/83 *Prodest* v *Caisse Primaire d'Assurance Maladie de Paris* [1984] ECR 3153; 68

Case 248/83 *EC Commission* v *Germany* [1985] ECR 1459; 178

Case 249/83 *Hoeckx* v *Centre Public d'Aide Sociale de Kalmthout* [1985] ECR 973; 80

Case 384/85 *Borrie-Clarke* v *The Chief Adjudication Officer* [1987] ECR 2865; 193

Case 12/86 *Demirel* v *Stadt Schwabisch Gmund* [1987] ECR 3719; 118, 119

Case 24/86 *Vincent Blaizot* v *University of Liège* [1988] ECR 379; 55, 146

Case 39/86 *Sylvie Lair* v *University of Hannover* [1988] ECR 3161; 82, 85, 139

Case 45/86 *Commission v Council* [1987] ECR 1493; 146

Case 63/86 *Commission v Italy* [1988] ECR 129; 97

Case 126/86 *Zaera* v *National Institute of Social Security* [1987] ECR 3697; 19

Case 157/86 *Murphy* v *An Bord Telecom Eireann* [1988] ECR 673; 167

Case 196/86 *Conradi, Hereth et soc. Metro* v *Direction de la Concurrence et des Prix* [1987] ECR 4469; 101

Case 197/86 *Brown* v *Secretary of State for Scotland* [1988] ECR 61; 81, 139

Case 222/86 *Heylens* v *UNECTEF* [1987] 4097; 102

Case 249/86 *EC Commission v Germany* [1989] ECR 1263; 74

Case 263/86 *Belgium* v *René Humbel and Marie-Thérèse Edel* [1988] ECR 5365; 89, 138, 147

Case 287/86 *Landsorganisationen i Danmark for Tjenerforbundet i Danmark* v *Ny Mølle Kro* [1987] ECR 5465; 270, 272-274, 278, 279

Case 292/86 *Gullung v Conseil de l'ordre des Avocats* [1988] ECR 111; 101

Case 302/86 *Commission v Denmark* [1988] ECR 4607; 223

Case 312/86 *Commission v France* [1988] ECR 6315; 175, 183

Case 318/86 *Commission v France* [1988] ECR 3559; 175, 179

Case 324/86 *Foreningen af Arbejdsledere i Danmark* v *Daddy's Dance Hall A/S* [1988] ECR 739; 265, 270, 272

Case 22/87 *Commission v Italy* [1989] ECR 143; 287, 288

Case 31/87 *Gebroeders Beentjes BV* v *The Netherlands* [1988] ECR 4635; 242

Case 42/87 *Commission v Belgium* [1988] ECR 5445; 146

Case 80/87 *Dik and others* v *College van Burgemeester en Wethouders der Gemeente Arnheim/College van Burgemeester en Wethouders der Gemeente Winterswijk* [1988] ECR 1601; 193

Case 101/87 *P Bork International A/S under konkurs* v *Foreningen af arbejdsledere i Danmark* and *Jens E Olsen, Karl Hansen et al and HK* v *Junckers Industrier A/S* [1988] 3057; 272, 273, 278

Case 143/87 *Stanton* v *INASTI* [1988] ECR 3877; 99

Case 144 and 145/87 *Harry Berg and Johannes Theodourus Maria Busschers* v *Ivo Martin Besselsen* [1988] ECR 2559; 270, 278

Case 186/87 *Ian William Cowan* v *Trésor Public* [1989] ECR 195; 95

Case 196/87 *Steymann* v *Staatssecretaris van Justititie* 1988] ECR 6159; 221

Case 235/87 *Matteucci* v *Communauté Francaise de Belgique* [1989] ECR 5589; 138

Case 242/87 *Commission v Council* [1989] ECR 1425; 146

Case 305/87 *Commission v Greece* [1989] ECR 1461; 97

Case 321/87 *Commission v Belgium* [1989] 997; 78

Case 344/87 *I Bettray* v *Ministry of Justice* [1989] ECR 1621; 69

Case 379/87 *Anita Groener* v *The Minister for Education and the City of Dublin Vocational Educational Committee* [1989] ECR 3967; 80

Joined Cases 389 and 390/87 *G B C Echternach and A Moritz* v *The Dutch Ministry for Education and Science* [1989] ECR 723; 138

Case C-3/88 *Commission v Italy* [1989] ECR 4035; 98

Case 9/88 *Lopes da Veiga* v *Staatssecretaris van Financien* [1989] ECR I-2989; 68, 119

Case 33/88 *Pilar Allué & Mary Carmel Coonan* v *Universita degli Studi di Venezia* [1989] ECR 1591; 72, 79

Joined Cases 48/88 *Achterberg te Riele* v *Sociale Verzekeringsbank,* Case 106/88 *Bersen-Gustin* v *Sociale Verzekeringsbank,* Case 107/88 *Egbers-Reuvers* v *Sociale Verzekeringsbank* [1989] ECR 1963; 188

Case C-53/88 *Commission* v *Greece* [1990] ECR I-3931; 285

Joined Cases C-54/88, C-91/88 and C-14/89 Criminal Proceedings Against Nino, Prandina, Goti and Pierinin [1990] ECR I-3537; 109

Case C-102/88 *Ruzius-Wilbrink* v *Bestuur van de Bedrijsvereniging voor Overheidsdiensten* [1989] ECR 4311; 195

Case C-109/88 *Handels-og-Kontorfunktionærernes Forbund i Danmark* v *Dansk Arbejdsgiverforening (acting for Danfoss)* [1989] ECR 3199; 169

Case 128/88 *De Felice* [1989] ECR 923; 131

Case 130/88 *Van de Bijl* v *Staatssecretaris van economische zaken* [1989] ECR 3089; 103, 144

Case C-145/88 *Torfaen Burrough Council* v *B&Q PLC* [1989] ECR 3851; 224

Case C-171/88 *Rinner-Kühn* v *FWW Spezial-Gebäudereiningung GmbH & Co Kg* [1989] ECR 2743; 154, 156, 158, 169, 196

Case C-177/88 *Dekker* v *Stichting Vormingscentrum voor Jong Volwassenen* [1990] ECR I-3941; 59, 181, 186

Case C-179/88 *Handels-og Kontorfunktionærernes Forbund i Danmark (acting for Birthe Hertz)* v *Dansk Arbejdsgiverforening (acting for Aldi Marked A/S)* [1990] ECR I-3979; 181

Case C-262/88 *Barber* v *Guardian Royal Exchange Assurance Group* [1990] ECR I-1889; 53, 156, 159, 163

Case C-265/88 *Criminal Proceedings Against Lothar Messner* [1989] ECR 4209; 78

Joined Cases C-297/88 and C-197/89 *Dzodzi* v *Belgium* [1990] ECR I-3783; 118

Case C-306/88 *Rochdale Burrough Council* v *Stewart John Anders* [1992] ECR I-6457; 225

Case C-322/88 *Salvatore Grimaldi* v *Fonds des maladies professionnelles* [1989] ECR 4407; 56, 358

Case C-2/89 *Kits Van Heyningen* [1990] ECR I-1795; 126

Case C-33/89 *Kowalska* v *Freie und Hansestadt Hamburg* [1990] ECR I-2591

Joined Cases C-51/89, C-90/89, and C-94/89 *United Kingdom* v *Council* [1991] ECR I-2757; 164

Case C-49/89 *Corsica Ferries, France* v *Direction generale des douanes français* [1989] ECR 4441; 89

Case C-61/89 *Criminal Proceedings Against Bouchoucha* [1990] ECR I-3551; 108

Case C-68/89 *Commission* v *Netherlands* [1991] ECR I-2637; 78

Case C-106/89 *Marleasing SA* v *La Commercial Internacional de Alimentacion SA* [1990] ECR I-4135; 57

Case C-113/89 *Rush Portuguesa Limitada d'Immigration* [1990] ECR I-1417; 89, 125 240

Case C-184/89 *Nimz* v *Freie und Hansestadt Hamburg* [1991] ECR I-297; 157, 164, 165, 169

Case C-192/89 *Sevince* v *Staatssecretaris van Justitie* [1990] ECR I-3161; 119

Case C-213/89 *R v Secretary of State for Transport ex parte Factortame* [1990] ECR I-2433; 96

Case C-221/89 *R v Secretary of State for Transport ex parte Factortame* [1991] ECR I-3905

Case C-229/89 *Commission* v *Belgium* [1991] ECR I-2205; 195, 196, 249

Case C-288/89 *Gouda* v *Commissariat voor de Media* [1991] ECR I-4007; 92

Case C-292/89 *G D Antonissen* v *Secretary of State for Home Affairs* [1991] ECR I-745; 70, 77, 120

Case C-300/89 *Commission* v *Council* [1991] ECR I-2867; 34

Case C-306/89 *Commission v Greece* [1991] ECR I-5863; 94

Case C-308/89 *Di Leo v Land Berlin* [1990] ECR I-4185; 138

Case C-312/89 *Union departmentale des syndicats CGT de l'Aisne v Conforama et al* [1991] ECR I-997; 225

Case C-332/89 *Criminal Proceedings against André Marchandise et al* [1991] ECR I-1027; 225

Case C-340/89 *Vlassopoulou v Ministerium für Justiz, Bundes-und Europaangelegenheiten Baden-Würtemberg* [1991] ECR I-235; 102, 142

Case C-345/89 *Ministere Public v Stoeckel* [1991] ECR I-4047; 175, 359

Case C-356/89 *Newton* v *Chief Adjudication Officer* [1991] ECR I-3107; 132

Case C-357/89 *Raulin v Netherlands Ministry of Education and Science* [1992] ECR I-1027; 70, 82, 140, 141, 147

Case C-362/89 *Giuseppe d' Urso and Adriana Ventadori and Others* v *Ercole Marelli Elettromeccanica Generale spa and Others* [1991] ECR I-4105; 265, 269

Case C-363/89 *Roux v Belgium State* [1991] ECR I-273; 66, 86

Case C-373/89 *Caisse d'assurance Sociale pour Travailleurs Independants "Integrity" v Rouvray* [1990] ECR 1243; 194

Case C-3/90 *Bernini v Minister of Education and Science* [1992] ECR I-1071; 70, 82, 139

Joined Cases C-6/90 and C-9/90 *Francovich and Bonifaci v Italy* [1991] ECR I-5357; 56, 263, 288

Case C-18/90 *Office National de l'emploi v Kziber* [1991] ECR I-199; 120

Case C-31/90 *Johnson* v *Chief Adjudication Officer* [1991] ECR I-3723; 188

Case C-41/90 *Klaus Höfner and Fritz Elser* v *Macrotron Gmbh* [1991] ECR I-1979; 228

Case C-58/90 *Commission v Italy* [1991] ECR I-4193; 86

Case C-159/90 *SPUC v Grogan* [1991] ECR I-4685; 52, 88

Case C-179/90 *Merci Convenzionali Porto di Genova spa* v *Siderurgica Gabrielli spa* [1991] ECR I-5889; 228

Case C-204/90 *Hans-Martin Bachmann* v *Belgian State* [1992] ECR I-249; 104

Case 208/90 *Emmott v Minister for Social Welfare* [1991] ECR I-4269; 59, 192, 199

Case C-213/90 *Association de Soutien aux Travailleurs Immigrés v Chambre des Employés Privés* [1991] ECR I-74; 32, 84

Case 243/90 *R v Secretary of State For Social Security ex parte Florence Smithson* [1992] ECR I-467; 189

Case C-295/90 *European Parliament v Council* [1992] ECR I-4193; 34, 146

Case C-304/90 *Reading Borough Council* v *Payless Diy Limited, Wickes Building Supplies Limited, Great Mills (South) Limited, Homebase Limited, B & Q Plc* [1992] ECR I-6493; 225

Case C-326/90 *Commission v Belgium* [1992] ECR I-5517; 130

Case C-330-331/90 *Ministerio Fiscal v Lopez Brea* [1992] ECR I-323; 109

Case C-332/90 *Volker Steen v Deutsche Bundespost (1)* [1992] ECR I-341

Case C-351/90 *Commission v Luxembourg* [1992] ECR I-3945; 98

Case C-360/90 *Arbeiterwohlfart der Stadt Berlin e V v Monika Bötel* [1992] ECR I-3589; 165

Case C-369/90 *Micheletti and others v Delegacion del Gobierno en Cantabria* [1992] ECR I-4239; 67

Case C-338/91 *H Steenhorst-Neerings* v *Bestuur van de Bedrijfsvereniging voor Detailhandel* [1993] ECR I-5475; 59, 199

Case C-19/92 *Dieter Kraus* v *Land Baden-Württemberg* [1993] ECR I-1663; 66, 103, 108, 143

Case C-42/92 *Thijssen* v *Controledienst voor de Verzekerigen* [1993] ECR I-4047; 94

Case C-91/92 *Faccini Dori* v *Recreb* [1994] ECR 3325; 57

Case T-96/92 *Comité Central D' Entreprise de la Societé Génerale des Grandes Sources and Others* v *Commission* [1995] ECR II-1213; 231

Case T-96/92 R *Comité Central D' Entreprise de la Societé Génerale des Grandes Sources and Others* v *Commission* [1992] ECR II-2579; 232

Case C-109/92 *Wirth* v *Landeshauptstadt Hannover* [1993] ECR I-6447; 89, 147

Case C-118/92 *Commission* v *Luxemburg* [1994] ECR I-1891; 84

Case C-127/92 *Enderby* v *Frenchay Health Authority and the Secretary of State for Health* [1993] ECR I-5535; 59, 170

Case C-132/92 *Birds Eye Walls Ltd.* v *Roberts* [1993] ECR I- 5579; 166

Case C-154/92 *Remi Van Cant* v *Rijksdienst voor pensioenen* [1993] ECR I-3811; 198

Case C-275/92 *Her Majesty's Custom and Excise* v *Schindler* [1994] ECR I-1039; 93

Case C-319/92 *Haim* v *Kassenzahnarztliche Vereinigung Nordrhein* [1994] ECR I-425; 144

Case C-334/92 *Teodoro Wagner Miret* v *Fondo de Garantia Salarial* [1993] ECR I-6911; 286

Case C-343/92 *Roks* [1994] ECR I-571; 196

Case C-379/92 *Criminal proceedings against Matteo Peralta* [1994] ECR I-3453; 233

Case C-382/92 *Commission* v *United Kingdom* [1994] ECR I-2435; 220, 266, 281, 283

Case C-383/92 *Commission* v *United Kingdom* [1994] ECR I-2479; 258

Case C-392/92 *Christel Schmidt* v *Spar- und Leihkasse der Früheren Ämter Bordesholm, Kiel und Cronshagen* [1994] ECR I-1311; 272, 274

Case C-399/92 *Stadt Lengerich* v *Angelika Helmig et al* [1994] ECR I-5727; 165

Case C-404/92 P *X* v *Commission* [1994] ECR I-4737; 210

Case C-410/92 *Johnson* v *Chief Adjudication Officer* [1994] ECR I-5483

Case C-419/92 *Ingetraut Scholz* v *Opera Universitaria di Cagliari and Cinzia Porcedda* [1994] ECR I-505; 72

Case C-421/92 *Gabriele Habermann-Beltermann* v *Arbeiterwohlfahrt, Bezirksverbank Ndb/Opf EV* [1994] ECR I-1657; 182, 363

Case C-1/93 *Halliburton Services BV* v *Staatssecretaris van Financien* [1994] ECR I-1137; 98

Case C-7/93 *Bestuur van het Algemeen Burgerlijk Pensioenfonds* v *G. A. Beune* [1994] ECR I-4471; 157

Case T-12/93 *Comité Central d'Entreprise de la Société Anonyme Vittel and Comité d'Etablissement de Pierval and Féderation Génerale Agroalimentaire* v *Commission* [1995] ECR II-1247; 231

Case C-13/93 *Office National de L'Emploi* v *Madeleine Minne* [1994] ECR I-371; 176, 360

Case C-28/93 *Maria Nelleke Gerda van den Akker and Others* v *Stichting Shell Pensioenfonds* [1994] ECR I-4527

Case C-32/93 *Carole Louise Webb* v *EMO Air Cargo* [1994] ECR I-3567; 182, 363

Case C-18/93 *Corsica Ferries, Italia* v *Corpo dei piloti del porto di Genova* [1994] ECR I-1783; 89

Case C-37/93 *Commission* v *Belgium* [1993] ECR I-6295

Case C-43/ 93 *Raymond vander Elst* v *Office des Migrations Internationales* [1994] ECR I-3803; 90, 125, 240

Joined Cases C-46/93 and C-48/93 [1996] *Brasserie du Pecheur SA v Federal Republic of Germany and R v Secretary of State For Transport ex parte Factortame* ECR I-1029; 58

 Case C-57/93 *Anna Adriaantje Vroege* v *NCIV Instituut voor Volkshuisvesting BV and Stichting Pensioenfonds NCIV* [1994] ECR I-4541

Case C-58/93 *Yousfi v Belgian State* [1994] ECR I-1353; 121

Case C-128/93 *Geertruida Catharina Fisscher* v *Voorhuis Hengelo BV and Stichting Bedrijfspensioenfonds voor de Detailhandel* [1994] ECR I-4583; 161

Case C-132/93 *Volker Steen* v *Deutsche Bundespost (2)* [1994] ECR I-2715

Case C-154/93 *Tawil-Albertini v Ministre des Affairs Sociales* [1994] ECR I-451; 144

Case C-279/93 *Finanzamt Köln-Altstadt* v *Roland Schumacker* [1995] ECR I-225; 105

Case C-297/93 *Rita Grau-Hupka* v *Stadtgemeinde Bremen* [1994] ECR I-5535

Case C-308/93 *Cabanis-Issarte* [1996] ECR I-2097; 81, 121, 129

Case C-316/93 *Vaneetveld v SA Le Foyer* [1994] ECR I-763; 57

Case C-317/93 *Nolte v Landesverischerungsansalt Hannover* [1995] ECR I-4625; 170, 188, 249

Case C-342/93 *Joan Gillespie and others* v *Northern Health and Social Services Boards, Department of Health and Social Services, Eastern Health and Social Services Board and Southern Health and Social Services Board* [1996] ECR I-0475; 157, 166, 362

Case C-355/93 *Eroglu v Land Baden-Württemburg* [1994] ECR I-5113; 120

Case C-392/93 *R v HM Treasury ex parte British Telecommunications plc* [1996] ECR I-1631; 58

Case C-400/93 *Specialarbejderforbundet i Danmark* v *Dansk Industri for Royal Copenhagen A/S* [1995] ECR I-1275; 170

Case C-412/93 *Société d'Importation Edouard Leclerc-Siplec* v *TF1 Publicité Sa and M6 Publicité Sa* [1995] ECR I-179; 226

Case C-415/93 *Union Royale belge des sociétés de football association ASBL* v *Jean-Marc Bosman* [1995] ECR I-4921; 68, 73, 99

Joined Cases C-430/93 and C-431/93 *Jeroen Van Schijndel and Johannes Nicolaas Cornelis Van Veen* v *Stichting Pensioenfonds Voor Fysiotherapeuten* [1995] ECR I-4705; 58

Case C-434/93 *Bozkurt v Staatssecretaris van Justitie* [1995] ECR I-1475; 119

Case C-443/93 *Vougioukas* v *IRA* [1995] ECR I-4033; 132

Case C-444/93 *Megner and Scheffel* [1995] ECR I-474; 170, 188, 196

Case C-449/93 *Rockfon A/S* v *Specialarbejderforbundet i Danmark* [1995] ECR I-4291; 260

Case C-450/93 *Eckhard Kalanke* v *Freie Hansestadt Bremen* [1995] ECR I-3051; 170, 183

Case C- 457/93 *Lewark* [1996] ECR I-243; 165

Case C-472/93 *Spano* [1995] ECR I-4321; 269

Case C-473/93 *Commission v Luxembourg* nyr; 72

Case C-479/93 *Andrea Francovich (2)* v *Italy* [1995] ECR I-3843; 286

Case C-2/94 *Denkavit Internatuional BV v Kramer van Koophandel en Fabrieken voor Midden-Gelderland and others* nyr; 59

Case C-5/94 *R v Ministry of Agriculture, Fisheries and Food, ex parte Hedley Lomas (Ireland) Ltd* [1996] ECR I-2553; 58

Case C-7/94 *Landesamt für Ausbildungsforung Nordrhein-Westfalen v Gaal* [1995] ECR I-1031; 75, 138

C-8/94 *Laperre v Bestuurscommissie Beroeps zaken in de Provincie Zuid-Holland* [1996] ECR I-273; 197

Case C-13/94 *P v S and Cornwall CC* [1996] ECR I-2143; 177

Case C-48/94 *Rygaard v Strø Mølle Akustik* [1995] ECR I-2745; 272, 275

Case C-55/94 *Reinhard Gebhard* v *Consiglio dell'Ordine degli Avvocati e Procuratori di Milano* [1995] ECR I-4165; 66, 87, 97, 103

Case C-80/94 *G. H. E. J. Wielockx* v *Inspecteur der Directe Belastingen* [1995] ECR I-2493; 105

Case C-84/94, *United Kingdom* v *The Council of the European Union*, judgment of 12.11.1996, nyr.; 31, 330, 331, 358

Case C-103/94 *Krid v CNVATS* [1995] ECR I-719; 121

Case C-107/94 *Asscher v Staatssecretaris van Financien* [1996] ECR I-3089; 106

Case C-116/94 *Meyers v Adjudication Officer* [1995] ECR I-2131; 177, 190

Case C-137/94 *R v Secretary of State* for *Health ex parte Richardson* [1995] ECR I-3407; 198

Case C-151/94 *Commission v Luxembourg* [1995] ECR I-3685; 106

Case C-164/94 *Arantis v Land Berlin* [1996] ECR I-135; 103, 143

Joined Cases C-171/94 and C-172/94 *Merckx and Neuhuys* v *Ford Motors Company Belgium* [1996] ECR I-1253; 271, 272

Case C-173/94 *Commission v Belgium* nyr; 72

Case C-175/94 *R v Secretary of State For the Home Department ex parte John Gallagher* [1995] ECR 4253; 115

Case C-177/94 *Criminal Proceedings Against Perfili* [1996] ECR I-161; 93

Case C-193/94 *Criminal Proceedings Against Skanavi and Chryssanthakopoulos* [1996] ECR I-929; 79

Case C-214/94 *Boukhalfa v Bundesrepupublik Deutschland* [1996] ECR I-2253; 68

Case C-228/94 *Atkins v Wrekin DC and Department of Transport* [1996] ECR I-3633; 199

Case C-237/94 *O'Flynn v Adjudication Officer* [1996] ECR I-2617; 83

Case C-272/94 *Criminal Proceedings Against Guiot and Climatec SA* [1996] ECR I-1905; 90, 240

Case C-277/94 *Z Taflan Met* judgment of 10 September 1996, nyr; 129

Case C-278/94 *Commission v Belgium* judgment of 12 September 1996, nyr; 83

Case C-280/94 *Van Damme* [1996] ECR I-179; 188, 196

Case C-290/94 *Commission v Greece* nyr; 72

Case C-315/94 *Peter de Vos v Stadt Bielefeld* [1996] ECR I-1417; 82

Case C-13/95 *Ayse Süzen* v *Zehnacker Gebäudereinigung GmbH Krankenhausservice* judgment of 11.3.1997, nyr.; 272, 275

Case C-66/95 *R v Secretary of State For Social Security ex parte Eunice Sutton* Judgment of 22 April 1997, nyr.; 59, 186, 199

Joined Cases C-74/95 and C-129/95 *Crimal Proceedings against X* nyr.; 341

Case C-79/95 *Commission v Spain* nyr.; 341

Case C-126/95 *A. Hallouzi-Choho v Bestuur van de Sociale Verzekeringsbank* Judgment of 3 October 1996, nyr; 121, 129

Case C-171/95 *Tetik v Land Berlin* Judgment of 23 January 1997, nyr; 121

Case C-180/95 *Nils Draempaehl* v *Urania Immobilienservice OHG* judgment of 22 April 1997, nyr; 59, 186

Case C-243/95 *Hill* pending; 169

Case C-285/95 *Kol v Land of Berlin*, pending; 119

Case C-305/95 *Plapied and Gallez* pending; 157

Case C-344/95 *Commission v Belgium* judgment of 20 February 1997, nyr; 70

Case C-336/95 *Pedro Burdalo Trevejo ea* v *Fondo de Garantía Salarial* nyr

Case C-351/95 *Kadiman* judgment of 17 April 1997; 119

Case C-386/95 *Eker v Land Baden-Württemberg,* pending; 119

Case C-409/95 *Hellmut Marschall v Land Nordrhein-Westfalen* pending; 185
Case C-66/96 *Handels- og Kontorfunktionærernes Forbund i Danmark (HK) and others* v *Fællesforening for Danmarks Brugsforeninger (FDB) and others* pending; 362
Case C-197/96 *Commission* v *French Republic* judgment of 13.3.1997, nyr; 360
Case C-249/96 *Grant v S.W. Trains* pending; 164, 210
Joined Cases C-253/96 to C-258/96 *Helmut Kampelmann* v *Landschaftsverband Westfalen-Lippe, Wilfried Tilsch* v *Landschaftsverband Westfalen-Lippe, Dieter Klingelhöfer* v *Landschaftsverband Westfalen-Lippe, Heinrich Schmidt* v *Landschaftsverband Westfalen-Lippe, Stadtwerke Witten GmbH* v *Andreas Schade* and *Klaus Haseley* v *Stadtwerke Altena GmbH*, pending; 294

Opinion 2/91 *Re ILO Convention No 170* [1993] ECR I-1061; 32, 56

# Index